THEY DARE TO SPEAK OUT
THIRD EDITION

PEOPLE AND INSTITUTIONS CONFRONT ISRAEL'S LOBBY

PAUL FINDLEY

Lawrence Hill Books

Library of Congress Cataloging-in-Publication Data
Findley, Paul, 1921–
    They dare to speak out : people and institutions confront Israel's lobby/ Paul
Findley.— 3rd ed.
        p. ; cm.
    Includes bibliographical references and index.
    ISBN 1-55652-482-X
    1. United States—Foreign relations—Israel. 2. Israel—Foreign relations—
United States. 3. American Israel Public Affairs Committee. 4. Jews—United
States—Politics and government. 5. Zionists—United States—Political
activity. 6. Arab-Israeli conflict. I. Title.
E183.8.I7F56 2003
327.7305694—dc21   2002155505

Cover and interior design by Rattray Design

©1985, 1989, 2003 by Paul Findley
All rights reserved
Third edition
Published by Lawrence Hill Books
An imprint of Chicago Review Press, Incorporated
814 North Franklin Street
Chicago, Illinois 60610
ISBN 978-1-55652-482-0
Printed in the United States of America

To our grandchildren
Andrew, Cameron, Henry, and Elizabeth.
May they always be able
to speak without fear.

Contents

Preface

SHORTLY AFTER World War II, a small band of United States partisans for Israel marshaled self-discipline and commitment so effectively that they succeeded in ending free and open debate in America whenever Middle East issues are considered.

Their primary goal was to assure broad, substantial, unconditional, and ultimately blind support for Israel by the U.S. government. In seeking that goal, these partisans forced a severe anti–Arab and anti-Muslim bias into U.S. Middle East policy that has since raised costly economic, political, and military barriers to the American national interest. The most harmful part of this process was the disappearance of unfettered discussion of the United States' relationship to the Arab–Israeli conflict. These biases and restrictions, though unwritten, are as effective as if they had been carved in stone. Even in the legislative chambers on Capitol Hill, the nation's highest and most hallowed halls of debate, discussion on the Middle East is virtually nonexistent.

In a 1983 interview for the first edition of this book, the late I. F. "Izzy" Stone, a widely respected author, commentator, and self-styled radical, told me why many of his fellow Jews work so aggressively to stifle free speech. He explained that, because Jews in Israel seem constantly at war with Arabs, Jews in America feel that they are in the same war. To them, free speech is a luxury that can be sacrificed where debate might weaken U.S. support for an Israel at war. Stone summed it up, "When people are at war, it is normal for civil liberties to suffer." As long as Israel is at war, most U.S. Jews "feel they have to fight and keep fighting." Nowhere has this been more obvious than in Israel's post–September 11 incursions into the occupied territories.

This reaction is almost instinctive, prompted by deeply felt anxieties, fears, and outrage that arise mainly from the common bond of religion and the knowledge of unspeakable Jewish death and suffering in the Nazi Germany Holocaust during World War II. It is not confined to people of the Jewish faith. To Muslims and many non-Muslims worldwide, the present suffering of Palestinians—to them, a latter-day holocaust—evokes a similar reaction in which free speech and other basic rights are sometimes casualties.

April 2002 provided evidence that strong passions persist on both sides. Deputy Secretary of Defense Paul Wolfowitz, well known for his bias in favor of Israel, received a lesson in anti-Palestinian fervor when addressing a large crowd of people gathered for a pro-Israel rally at the U.S. Capitol. He tried to tell the crowd, "Innocent Palestinians are suffering and dying as well, and it is critical that we recognize and acknowledge that fact." His words were drowned out by boos and the shouted slogan "No more Arafat."[1]

A third of the way around the world, U.S. Ambassador Donald Neumann was booed for making a similar plea to a crowd of Bahraini citizens gathered to protest Israel's latest invasion of Palestine. After standing with the protesters for a minute of silence for the victims of the Israeli onslaught, Neumann remained standing and asked for a moment of silence for innocent Israeli victims of Palestinian terrorism. The crowd turned hostile and shouted back its refusal.[2]

Six weeks later, the scene in Bahrain remained hostile. Neumann issued an advisory, suggesting that U.S. citizens avoid crowds and vary their travel routes when away from home. He reported several beatings of U.S. military personnel, American vehicles being pelted with eggs, and local vehicles swerving near U.S. cyclists and pedestrians.[3]

Open Season on Palestinians

The Patriot Act brought about many changes in America, but it did not alter Israel's total domination of Capitol Hill. In 2001 Israel quickly endorsed President Bush's war on terrorism and Congress applauded Israel's war on Palestinians, accepting Israeli Prime Minister Sharon's duplicitous argument that eradicating "terrorists" from the occupied territories was an essential part of Bush's worldwide military campaign.

Supporting Israeli wars was normal procedure on Capitol Hill. Thanks to the effectiveness of the pro-Israel lobby, the United States had long been the key, indispensable ally in all of Israel's military victories over Arabs. Despite frequent claims over the years that it sought only policies that were fair to both sides—the "honest broker" role—the U.S. government provided critical support to Israel's expansionist campaigns without interruption since President Lyndon B. Johnson gave clandestine aid to Israel's June 1967 war against the Arabs. The American people remain largely unaware of U.S. complicity in these wars, although it is widely recognized in all countries outside the United States. To this day, Americans are poorly informed about the level of U.S. military and economic aid to Israel, not to mention our government's record of near-perfect support of Israel in critical votes in the United Nations Security Council.[4]

In April 2002 Sharon ordered the invasion of the territories on the pretext of rooting out the leaders who organized suicide bombings carried out inside Israel by individual Palestinians. The bombings spread fear throughout Israel, not just in areas adjacent to the occupied territories. Even armed Israeli soldiers and police officers did not feel safe. The bombers could rarely be identified in advance, as they were of both sexes and varied ages.

Sharon's counterattack was brutal and massive, utilizing tanks, helicopter gunships, and other arms—all donated to Israel through the U.S. government's military assistance program. It left major cities in the occupied territories heavily damaged and the Palestinian authority headquarters in shambles and isolated. Accurate casualty statistics may never emerge, but the UN Report on Jenin put the Palestinian death toll in Jenin alone at 52. It reported that 497 people had been killed and 1,477 were wounded during the entire military sweep. These figures were compiled from a distance, because the Israeli government, supported by Washington, refused to permit the UN inspection team to visit Jenin.

The invasion did not halt suicide bombings, but it left the Palestinian population more tightly repressed than ever before. It also left Palestinians and their sympathizers outraged at the crucial support provided to the invaders by the U.S. government.

For twelve days following the assault, Israeli forces barred a UN relief mission headed by special envoy Terje Roed-Larsen, from entering the Jenin refugee camp. During this period ambulances were routinely turned away, and scores of injured Palestinians bled to death. After finally being allowed to enter and tour the camp, Roed-Larsen said, "We have expert people here who have been in war zones and earthquakes, and they say they have never seen anything like it. It is horrifying beyond belief." He told reporters that 300 buildings had been destroyed and 2,000 people were left homeless.[5]

The Israelis did everything they could to prevent reports of the immense destruction from reaching American eyes and ears. Riad Abdelkarim, a Los Angeles physician who writes commentaries on the Middle East for U.S. newspapers and who served as a relief worker during the assault on Jenin, was arrested and held for several weeks by Israeli authorities after sending an eyewitness report on the devastation in the camp to U.S. newspapers.

Outraged by U.S. complicity in the assault, Palestinian officials in Jenin rejected a U.S. Agency for International Development shipment of tents, food, and children's toys. Their reason: the camp had been destroyed by U.S.-donated weapons.[6]

"A Special Relationship with Israel"

During Israel's month-long invasion, President Bush publicly demanded that Sharon order the immediate withdrawal of Israeli forces. Given Bush's position as chief executive of the United States, Israel's chief benefactor, one would have expected Sharon to offer at least a touch of conciliation. Instead, with supreme arrogance, he announced simply that his war measures were not finished, and that withdrawal would not occur until they were. Faced with this defiance, Bush unaccountably praised Sharon as a "man of peace" and reminded reporters of the obvious: the United States has "a special relationship with Israel." He failed to explain what this relationship entails: letting Israeli prime ministers defy the demands of U.S. presidents, control Palestinians and their land by force of arms, and violate with impunity international laws and conventions on human rights.

Sharon's 2002 war on Palestinians was in several ways reminiscent of the bloody 1982 massacres he waged on the Palestinian refugee camps at Sabra and Shatila. Sharon called both of them assaults on terrorism. In both wars, the U.S. president—in 1982, Ronald Reagan—demanded that Israel stop the war. In both, the prime minister of Israel—in 1982, Menachem Begin—defied the presidential demand. In the greatest irony of all, when both assaults came to an end, Congress promptly appropriated funds to resupply Israel's war machine—$150 million in 1982, $200 million in 2002. To free up funds for the bonus to Israel, the House Appropriations Committee, in a curious reordering of priorities, cut $75 million from a project to reinforce cockpit doors to guard against intrusions by hijackers.[7]

Sharon's war prompted huge anti-Israel and anti-American protests worldwide. One in Rabat, Morocco, drew an estimated 1.5 million people—fully 6 percent of the nation's population. Surprisingly large protests also took place in Washington, D.C., New York, and other major U.S. cities. They received little media attention.

"Laughingstock of the World"

A Time-CNN poll showed that 60 percent of Americans favored reducing or completely eliminating aid to Israel if Sharon failed to withdraw his troops from Palestinian areas. The same poll showed 75 percent favoring Bush's diplomatic initiatives for Middle East peace.[8]

That sentiment was not represented on Capitol Hill in Washington, where both the House of Representatives and the Senate acted as if they were committees of the Israeli Knesset. During deliberations on Sharon's war, almost all speeches were sympathetic to Israel, echoing Sharon's "war of survival" theme.

On May 2, 2002, both the Senate and the House of Representatives adopted resolutions that praised Sharon's war and pledged full support of Israel. Although the House resolution was slightly more hostile to the Palestinian cause than the Senate version, the *Atlanta Constitution* columnist Martha Ezzard wrote that "Republican leaders in the House and Democratic leaders in the Senate entered into a schoolyard-like contest to see who could be the best pro-Israel cheerleader, approving resolutions that made Sharon appear as blameless for the loss of any innocent lives as Mother Teresa."[9]

In the House, Representative Peter DeFazio (D-OR), one of twenty-one who voted "no" on the resolution, declared that it put the House of Representatives on record "to the right of Ariel Sharon and the Likud Party." Representative Nick J. Rahall (D-WV), who also voted against it, predicted that the resolution would make the House "the laughingstock of the world." Earlier, DeFazio had found only thirteen colleagues willing to sign a balanced resolution.

In the end, 352 of the 435 members voted yes. Twenty-one voted no. Twenty-eight others heeded the advice of Representative Marcy Kaptur (D-OH), by voting "present." During the House debate, Kaptur warned of a "corrosive" effect: "This one-sided resolution will only fan the killing frenzy. . . . I fear it represents crass domestic politics in this election year. . . . Let us be a true partner for peace, not just with Israel but as well with the Arab states in the region."[10]

In the Senate, only Democrats Ernest Hollings (D-SC) and Robert Byrd (D-WV) voted against the resolution. Hollings told his colleagues that Sharon "is making more terrorists than he is getting rid of."[11]

Nihad Awad, executive director of the Council on American Islamic Relations (CAIR), responded, "It is truly disturbing to see American elected officials falling over themselves in an unseemly attempt to 'pledge allegiance' to a foreign government and its domestic lobby."[12]

Unprecedented War-Making Authority

What a difference a year can make. Within twelve months, America became, for the first time, the target of a massive, lethal assault by foreign terrorists on its own soil. Congress subsequently granted the president unprecedented authority to make war and police the world. Bush used that authority to launch a costly war in Afghanistan, with a larger one expected to follow against Iraq. Meanwhile, at home, Congress curbed precious civil liberties. All the while, several fundamental questions begged for attention:

- Why America? What, if anything, did the United States do to provoke 9/11?
- Do grievances against America remain? If so, what should America do to redress them?
- Why did almost every other nation reject or ignore President Bush's call for a multinational assault on Iraq?

These are urgent questions. They reach into the heart of the frantic, wrenching ordeal in which America finds itself, and yet, incredibly they are left unanswered—or worse, are largely unasked.

Welcome to my quest for the answers, a search that began unwittingly midway through my congressional career. It continues to this day.

1

Rescue and Involvement

"How DID A congressman from the corn-hog heartland of America get entangled in Middle East politics?" people ask. Like most rural congressmen, I had no ethnic constituencies who lobbied me on their foreign interests. As expected, I joined the Agriculture Committee and worked mainly on issues such as farming, budget, and welfare reform.

Newly appointed in 1972 to the subcommittee on Europe and the Middle East, I had represented the Springfield, Illinois, area for twelve years without attracting much attention at home or abroad.

Eight short years later, my involvement in Middle East politics would bring me infamy among many U.S. Jews, notoriety in Israel, and applause throughout the Arab world. By 1980, in urban centers of pro-Israel activism—far from the local Jews in central Illinois who knew and trusted me—I found myself in the most expensive congressional campaign in state history. Thanks to a flow of hostile dollars from both coasts and nearby Chicago, I became "the number one enemy of Israel" and my re-election campaign the principal target of Israel's lobby.

Prodded by a professor at Illinois College when I first joined the subcommittee, I had already begun to doubt the wisdom of U.S. policy

1

in the Middle East. In the early years, I kept these doubts private, but not because I feared the political consequences. In fact, I naively assumed I could question our policy anywhere without getting into trouble. I did not realize how deeply the roots of Israeli interests penetrated U.S. institutions.

In matters pertaining to Middle East policy, members of Congress generally paid attention only to what Israel wanted. Arab American lobbies, fledgling forces even today, were nonexistent. Muslim organizations were in their infancy. Arab embassies showed little interest in lobbying. Even if a congressman wanted to hear the Arab viewpoint, he would have had difficulty finding a spokesman to explain it.

My personal involvement with Middle East politics started with a situation that had no direct connection to the Arab–Israeli conflict. It began in the spring of 1973 when a letter arrived from Mrs. Evans Franklin, a constituent who wrote neighborhood news for a weekly newspaper I had once edited. In this letter, she pleaded for my help in securing the release of her son, Ed, from a faraway prison. He had been convicted of espionage and sentenced to five years' solitary imprisonment in Aden, the capital of the Marxist People's Democratic Republic of [South] Yemen. After reading her plea, I had to consult a map. I knew only that Aden had once been a major British base.

Had it not been for a series of canceled airline flights, his mother told me, Franklin would never have set foot in Aden. Returning from Ethiopia to his teaching post in Kuwait, he was rerouted through Aden and then delayed there by the cancelation of his departing flight. His luck worsened. Unaware of local restrictions, he photographed a prohibited area. The Adenese were still nervous about blonde-haired visitors, remembering the commando raid the British had conducted shortly after they left Aden six years earlier. When Franklin snapped the pictures, he was immediately arrested. After being kept in an interrogation center for months, he was finally brought to trial, where he was convicted and sentenced. My efforts to secure his release proceeded for the most part without aid from the State Department. Our government had had no relations, diplomatic or otherwise, with Aden since a 1969 coup moved the country's regime dramatically to the left. This meant that the State Department could do nothing directly. I asked a friend in the Egyptian embassy in Washington, D.C., to help. Franklin's parents, people of modest means living in a rural crossroads village, sent a request to Salim Rubyai Ali, South Yemen's president, seeking executive clemency. I sent a similar request. Our government asked Britain to intervene through its embassy in Aden. There was no response to any of these initiatives.

In December 1973 I visited Abdallah Ashtal, Aden's ambassador to the United Nations in New York, to ask if I could go personally to Aden and make a plea for Franklin's release. Ashtal, a short, handsome, youthful diplomat who was taking evening graduate courses at New York University, promised a prompt answer. A message came back two weeks later that I would be welcome.

If I decided to go, I would have to travel alone. I would be the first congressman—in either the House or the Senate—to visit Aden since the republic was established in 1967, and the first U.S. official to visit there since diplomatic relations were severed in the wake of the coup two years later. Although this was an exciting prospect, it caused me some foreboding. Moreover, I had no authority as an envoy. South Yemen, sometimes called "the Cuba of the Arab world," was regarded by our State Department as the most radical of the Arab states. A State Department friend did nothing to relieve my concern when he told me that Aden's foreign minister got his job "because he killed more opponents than any other candidate."

Troubling questions came to mind. How would I be received? I discussed the trip with Alfred L. Atherton, Jr., assistant secretary of state for Near East and South Asia affairs. I asked him, "If they lock me up, what will you do first?" He smiled and said, "Look for another congressman to come get you out!"

Still, I was probably the only person able to help. Franklin's mother told me, "I doubt if Ed can survive five years in a Yemen jail." My wife, Lucille, expressed deep concern over the prospects of the trip but agreed that I had little choice but to go.

I also thought the trip might be an opportunity to open the door to better relations with a vital but little-known part of the world. With the imminent reopening of the Suez Canal, better relations with Aden could be important to U.S. interests in the Indian Ocean. After all, Aden, along with French-held Djibouti, was a guardian of a world-famous and vitally important strait, the gateway to the Suez Canal. If the Soviets, already present with aid missions and military advisers, succeeded in dominating the Aden government, they could effectively control the canal from the south. It was obvious that, Franklin's potential release aside, the United States needed good relations with Aden.

I decided that I must go. The trip was set for late March 1974.

From Middle East scholars, I learned that Secretary of State Henry Kissinger, who was soon to begin shuttle negotiations between Israel and Egypt, was held in high esteem in Aden. I asked him for a letter that I could take with me which would be as explicit as possible about United States–Aden relations. A personal letter arrived three days before I left. In it, Kissinger said he welcomed my "humanitarian mission" to Aden and added, "Should the occasion arise, you may wish to inform those officials whom you meet of our continuing commitment to work for an equitable and lasting Middle East peace and of our desire to strengthen our ties with the Arab world."

The letter was addressed to me, not to the Aden government. It was a diplomatic "feeler." I hoped it would convince any officials I met that the United States wanted to establish normal relations with Aden.

A good traveler always brings gifts. At the suggestion of an Egyptian friend, I secured scholarships from three colleges in Illinois to present to South Yemeni students. I also located and had specially bound two Arabic language translations of *The Prairie Years*, Carl Sandburg's biography of Abraham Lincoln. In addition, I carried two small busts of Lincoln—my state's most celebrated leader—hoping he would be known even in Aden.

I left Washington, D.C., early enough to visit Syria before heading south to Aden. Syria had not had normal diplomatic relations with the United States since the 1967 war with Israel, and despite its growing importance, no member of the House of Representatives had visited there for five years. To my surprise, President Hafez Assad of Syria agreed to receive me without advance appointment. Perhaps he was intrigued by the presence of a U.S. congressman who said he had an open mind about Middle East issues.

Assad received me in the spacious second-floor reception room of his offices. A tall, thickset man with a prominent forehead and a warm, quiet manner, Assad made his points forcefully but without a hint of hostility. While sipping small cups of rich Syrian coffee, he voiced his pain over the United States' support of Israel's actions: "We are bitter about the guns and ammunition you provide to Israel, and why not? But bitterness is not hostility. In fact, we have very warm feelings about the American people. Despite the war, the Syrian people like Americans and have for years."

While sympathizing, I took the initiative, urging him to restore full diplomatic relations and to take a page from the public relations book of the Israelis. I suggested that he come to the United States and take his case directly to the American people via television.

Assad responded, "Perhaps we have made some mistakes. We should have better public relations. I agree with what you say and recommend, but I don't know when I can come to the United States."

As I rose to leave, Assad said, "You have my mandate to invite members of your Congress to visit Syria as soon as possible. They will be most welcome. We want those who are critical as well as those who are friends to come."

While I later personally extended Assad's invitation to many of my colleagues and then, in a detailed official report, to all of them, few accepted. The first congressional group did not arrive until 1978, four years later.

After my interview with Assad, I was driven late at night from Damascus to Beirut for the flight to Aden. As our car approached the Syria–Lebanon border, I could hear the sound of Israel's shelling of Lebanon's Mt. Hermon. It was a sobering reminder that, seven years after the 1967 war, the fighting still continued.

In 1974 Beirut was still the "Paris of the Middle East," a western-like city with a lively nightlife and bustling commerce. A new Holiday Inn had just opened near the harbor. Every street seemed to boast two international banks, at least three bookstores, and a dozen restaurants. A year later the Holiday Inn became a battleground between Phalangist militia, backed by Israel, and the Lebanese left coalition, including Palestinians, which were helped by various Arab governments and by Moscow. Its walls were ripped open by shells, its rooftop pavilion littered with the bodies of fallen snipers. The vicious civil war, which began in 1975, had turned Beirut into a city of rubble.

But even in 1974, the Palestinians in the refugee camps did not share the prosperity of the city. I passed the hovels of Sabra and Shatila, where, nine years later, the massacre of hundreds of Palestinian civilians would shock the world. My embassy escort said, "These miserable camps haven't improved in twenty years."

I also passed the Tel Zaatar refugee camp, whose wretched inhabitants would soon suffer a fate even more cruel. A year later, it was under seige for forty-five days by rightist "Christian" militias, armed and advised by Israel's Labor government. Fifteen thousand Palestinians were killed, many of them after the camp surrendered. Virtually every adult male survivor was executed. That slaughter was barely noted by the world press. Today hardly anyone, save the Palestinians, remembers it.

At that time, the spring of 1974, however, I had no premonition of the tragedies to come. I boarded the Aden-bound plane at Beirut with just one person's tragedy on my mind—that of Ed Franklin.

Mission in Aden

In Aden, to my surprise and pleasure, I was met by a delegation of five youthful officials, three of them cabinet ministers. Mine was the only gray hair in sight that night. The group had stayed up until 2:00 A.M. to meet the plane. "Welcome. We have your quarters ready," said the government's chief of protocol. Good news! This meant, I felt, that I would not be stuck off in a hotel room. My quarters turned out to be a rambling old building which, in imperial days, was the residence of the British air commander. A tree-shaded terrace—a rarity in Aden—looked over the great harbor, a strategic prize ever since white men first rounded the Cape of Good Hope in the sixteenth century. Blackbirds chattered overhead.

I received permission to visit Franklin at 7:15 that first night. I found him under guard in an apartment on the second floor of a small modern building. When I entered, he was standing by a couch in the living room. We had never seen each other before.

"I presume you are Congressman Findley," he said.

Despite the emotion of the occasion, I smiled, sensing how Dr. Livingston must have felt years before in Africa.

After sixteen months of confinement, Franklin was thin, almost gaunt. His trousers were several sizes too big, but his blonde hair was neatly combed, his face was cleanly shaved, and he was surprisingly well tanned. He looked much older than his thirty-four years.

We were able to talk alone. I said, "You're thin, but you look well." He answered, "I'm very glad you came, and I feel pretty well. Much better now that you're here. A few days ago when I used a mirror for the first time in months, I was shocked at how I look." He said he developed the tan from daily exercise in the prison yard, adding that he had been transferred to the flat two days before, obviously because authorities did not want me to see the prison.

"Here is a box of food items your family asked me to deliver." When I said that, his face, which until then had displayed no emotion, fell. "I guess this means I am not going home with you."

I said, "I don't know."

Franklin changed the subject. "I had to leave my Bible at the prison. I hated to, because I like to read it every day."

I said, "Many people have been praying for you."

He responded, "Yes, I knew at once, even before I got word in letters from home. I could feel it."

Franklin told me he had not been physically abused but said the food was terrible and some of the rules bothered him. "I am not allowed to have a pen and paper. I like to write. I once wrote poetry on a sack, but then my pencil was discovered and taken from me. Still, I like the Arab world. Maybe someday when the American embassy is reopened, I could even get a job here."

I assured him: "I'll do my very best to secure your release, or at least shorten your term. That's why I'm here, and I'll try to see you again before I leave. I'll also try to get approval for you to have a pencil and paper."

On the way back to my quarters, I passed on Franklin's request for writing materials to my escort officer, who answered simply, "I will report your request." I spent Friday, a Muslim day of worship, touring the nearby desolate countryside. The main tourist attraction was an ancient, massive stone that was used to store the area's scarce rainfall. That evening the British consul, a compassionate man who had occasionally delivered reading material to Franklin, joined me for dinner. The British had long ago understood the importance of maintaining diplomatic relations even with hostile regimes and, shortly after their stormy departure from Aden, they established an embassy there.

On Saturday morning Foreign Minister M. J. Motie came to my quarters for a long discussion of United States–Yemen relations. The plight of the Palestinians under Israeli occupation was at the top of his agenda, Franklin at the top of mine. He complained, "The United States is helping Saudi Arabia foment subversion along Yemen's borders." I told him I was troubled by this charge, was unaware of such activity, and hoped to help improve relations. Motie responded, "While the past is not good, the present looks better, but we need a substantial sign of friendship. For example, we need aid in buying wheat."

After the discussion, I spent a long and fruitless afternoon trying to fill a shopping list my family had sent with me. The bazaar had little but cheap Japanese radios and a few trinkets. It had even fewer shoppers. I returned to the guest house empty-handed, only to find an assortment of gifts, each neatly wrapped. Among them was a *jambia*, the traditional curved Yemeni dagger, and a large ceremonial pipe. The gifts were accompanied by a card bearing the words: "With the compliments of the president."

Were these gifts merely sweeteners to take the place of Franklin on my homeward journey? Or were they a harbinger of success? I dared not believe the latter. I had received no hint that the government would even shorten Franklin's sentence. At least it had acceded to his request for paper and pencil.

My second visit with Franklin was more relaxed than the first. He accepted the pencils and paper I brought him with the comment, "I hope I won't need them except for tonight." I responded that I had no reason to hope he would be able to leave with me, but that, strictly on my own hunch, I felt that he would be released soon.

I met with President Ali the night before my scheduled departure inside the heavily guarded compound where the president both lived and had his offices. I was ushered into a long reception hall adorned with blue flowered carpeting and gold drapes that covered three walls. The fourth side opened into a large courtyard. Two rows of ceiling fans whirred overhead. In the center of this large hall was a lonely group of gold upholstered sofas and chairs.

By the time I reached the circle of furniture, President Ali, the foreign minister of Aden, and an interpreter were walking through the same door I had entered. The president needed no introduction. I had seen Ali's picture in many places around Aden, but frankly it did him little justice. He was a tall, well-built man of forty. His black hair had a touch of gray. His skin was dark, his bearing dignified. He was soft-spoken, and two gold teeth glistened when he smiled. After we exchanged greetings, I thanked him for his hospitality and for the gifts. Then I launched into my own presentation of gifts: first the book and bust, then the scholarships.

What he was waiting for, of course, was the letter from Kissinger, which would indicate the weight the United States gave my mission. When I handed it to him, I tried to broaden its importance.

"Perhaps Your Excellency will permit me to explain," I said. This letter formally presents the desire of the United States to reestablish diplomatic relations. This is important. Our government needs these relations in order to understand Aden's policies and problems. The president of the United States and the secretary of state are limited in foreign policy. They can do only whatever the Congress will support, so it is also important for congressmen to gain a better understanding of Aden's situation and of the Arab world in general."

Ali responded: "Aden is the shining example of the republic. Other areas of our country are quite different. The people are much poorer." I gulped. I had seen only Aden, Ali's "shining example," which struck me as very poor, so I could only guess at conditions elsewhere.

While I took notes, Ali told me that the antipoverty efforts of his government were handicapped by "subversion" from neighboring states. He said, bluntly, "The belief is held by the people of our country that all suffering, all damage caused by subversives, is really the work of the United States government. All military equipment we capture is United States equipment." Some of it, he said, was outside this building, placed there for me to examine.

I interjected that this information was not known in the United States, and I underscored the need for diplomatic relations so this sort of injury would stop. He nodded. "I favor relations with the United States, but they must relate to grievances now seen by my people." He added, "Aden does not wish to be isolated from the United States."

Ali thanked me for the gifts, indicating the interview was over. I sensed this was my long-awaited opportunity, my chance to launch into an appeal for Franklin.

It was not needed. Ali interrupted by saying simply, "Regarding the prisoner, as soon as I heard of your interest in him, I saw to it that he received preferential treatment. I have carefully considered your request and your desire that he be released. I have decided to grant your request. When you want him, you may have him."

I could scarcely believe what I had heard. "When you want him, you may have him." I was so overcome with joy I half-stumbled leaving the room. Franklin was free. In fact, he was waiting at my quarters when I returned. We were on the plane at 6:00 the next morning, headed for Beirut, and then to New York and finally St. Louis, where a joyous family welcomed Franklin home.

I am convinced that the main reason for Franklin's release was the decision by our government to probe ever so cautiously for better relations with Yemen. Caution was necessary, because there were those in both nations who did not wish to see relations improved. Ali was the least Marxist of a three-man ruling junta. In the State Department, even some "Arabists," still resentful over Yemen's expulsion of the United States presence years before, rejected Aden as nothing but a "training ground for PLO terrorists." Others, such as Kissinger, felt differently. Ed Franklin had provided the opportunity to begin the probing.

But the U.S. government fiddled, hedged, and stalled for three years. Jimmy Carter replaced Gerald Ford in the White House, and Cyrus Vance became secretary of state. Our government turned down Aden's request to buy wheat on credit, then refused to consider a bid to buy three used airliners. The United States kept putting off even preliminary talks. At a second meeting with me in September 1977—this time in New York, where he addressed the United Nations—Ali restated his desire for renewed relations with the United States and suggested that I report our discussion to Secretary of State Vance. I did so, and after my report, Vance and Foreign Minister Motie of South Yemen agreed to exploratory talks. To me, this appeared like a momentous breakthrough. The talks were to begin in Aden in just a few weeks, shortly after New Year's Day. Sadly, procrastination took over.

No precise date for the meetings had been set when I returned to the Middle East with a number of other congressmen in January 1978. I altered my own itinerary to include a side trip to Aden. Before I left the group, we met with Secretary of State Vance, whose travels happened to cross ours, and with Saudi Arabia's Crown Prince Fahd, a large, impressive man who spoke eloquent English and who would soon become the

Saudi monarch. Fahd spoke approvingly of my efforts in Aden and asked me to tell officials there that Saudi Arabia was ready to resume sending them economic aid.

"It's a Good Omen"

As I saw when I arrived, the scene in Aden had improved. South Yemen had already exchanged ambassadors with former enemy Saudi Arabia, even though the two nations still had disputes over territory. Aden had also just agreed to diplomatic relations with Jordan. The local radio station no longer harangued American and Saudi "imperialists." This time my wife, Lucille, accompanied me. We were assigned to the same guest house I had used before, where the principal change was the presence of a well-stocked refrigerator.

President Ali received us, this time with an honor guard, in the same spacious hall we had used before. Although he avoided comment on Saudi Arabia's offer of aid, Ali spoke of Crown Prince Fahd with great warmth.

Then he added, "We are looking forward to the expected arrival of the diplomatic delegation from the United States before the end of the month." I am sure my face fell. I knew the delegation was not coming that month. In fact, the mission had been delayed indefinitely. A few days before, Vance had told me the bad news but had not explained why. When I expressed the hope that Ali had been notified of the delay, Vance had replied, "We will take care of it." Unfortunately, no one had.

Ali was left waiting, day by day, for a group that would not arrive. I did not feel free to tell him of the change, so I listened and tried to look hopeful. I knew the delay would strengthen his local critics, who opposed reconciliation with the United States.

I changed the subject. "Some of our strategists say you have let the Soviets establish a naval base here. Do you have a comment?"

He strongly protested. "That is not true. We do not allow the Soviets, or any foreign nation, to have a military base in our territory. But we do cooperate with the Soviets because they help us." Ali concluded our discussion by giving me a message to Washington:

> Please extend my warm greetings to President Carter. Kindly inform him that we are eager to maintain smooth and friendly relations between Dem-

ocratic Yemen and the United States. We recognize that President Carter is concerned about maintaining friendly relations with all countries. We feel that is a positive policy. We believe our relations should be further strengthened.

As we parted, I gave Ali a pottery vase our daughter Diane had made for him. He said, "That's very nice. Please thank your daughter. I admire it." Then he stepped to the door to admire something else—rain, which is a rarity in Aden.

"It's a good omen," he said.

I left Aden more convinced than ever that diplomatic relations would help the United States and our friends in the region. The United States and Saudi Arabia had a common interest in minimizing the Soviet presence in South Yemen. We needed a diplomatic mission there. Back in Washington, I missed no opportunity to press this recommendation on Secretary Vance and the White House staff.

At the White House a month later, I was able to make a personal appeal to President Jimmy Carter. Carter said he was "surprised and pleased" by Ali's message: "His words are surprisingly warm. We've been hoping to improve our situation there." I urged that there be no further delays. "Another cancellation would be baffling to President Ali, to say the least," I cautioned. Carter thanked me and assured me that he would "take care of the matter."

Carter was true to his word. Five months after my last meeting with Ali, a team of State Department officials arranged to visit Aden on June 26, 1978, for "exploratory talks" to discuss, "in a noncommittal way," the resumption of diplomatic negotiations. Ali was to meet them on the day of their arrival.

It was too late. Aden's Marxist hard-liners had decided to act. Concerned by Ali's initiatives for improved relations with the United States and Saudi Arabia, radicals seized fighter planes, strafed the presidential quarters, took control of the government, and, on the day the U.S. delegation was scheduled to arrive, arrested Ali. He was executed by a firing squad. Ambassador Ashtal called from New York to tell me the delegation would still be welcome, but that the U.S. mission was scrubbed. After traveling as far as Sana'a, the capital of North Yemen, the State Department officials returned to Washington.

Distressed over the execution of Ali, I asked Ashtal for an explanation. He replied, "It's an internal matter of no concern to the outside world." Still, Ali's fate troubled me. It still does. I have often wondered whether my goodwill visit and Ali's decision to release Franklin contributed to the president's downfall and death.

My journeys to Aden had broad personal implications. After years on Capitol Hill, I heard for the first time the Arab perspective, particularly the plight of the Palestinians. I began to read about the Middle East, talk with experts, and try to understand the region. Arabs emerged as human beings.

Reports of my experiences made the rounds, and soon my office became a stopping place for people going to and from the Middle East—scholars, business people, clerics, government officials. It was unusual for anyone in Congress to visit Arab countries and take an interest in their problems. I began to speak out in Congress. I argued from what I considered to be a U.S. viewpoint—neither pro-Israel nor pro-Arab. I declared that our unwillingness to talk directly to the political leaders of the Palestinians, like our reluctance to talk to President Ali in Yemen, handicapped our search for peace. Diplomatic communication with other parties, however alien, however small, is a convenience to our government. It does not need to be viewed as an endorsement. Thus, I asked, why not talk directly to PLO Chairman Yasser Arafat, the acknowledged political voice of the Palestinians? One reason, I discovered, was that Henry Kissinger, who had provided help on my road to Aden, had agreed to an Israeli request, under which the U.S. government would not communicate formally with the PLO until the organization recognized the right of Israel to exist. It was a tough demand, especially in light of Israel's flat refusal to accept a Palestinian state as its neighbor, but Kissinger had agreed to it.

To help break the ice, I decided to communicate with Arafat myself, not to negotiate anything but to serve, as best I could, as a bridge of information between the U.S. government and an important Arab community. I met the PLO leader for the first time in January 1978 in Damascus, just before meeting with Ali in Aden for what would be the last time. Before the meeting with Arafat, I had the same misgivings that I felt before going to Aden four years earlier. Meeting Arafat crossed the line that Kissinger, at Israel's demand, had drawn.

"I Stand Behind the Words"

To my surprise I discovered that Arafat, who received us in a heavily guarded second-floor apartment, was not a wild-eyed, gun-waving fanatic. Welcoming our small group, which included Mrs Findley and several other members of Congress, he spoke softly and listened attentively. He was bareheaded and nearly bald. This took us by surprise, because in public he was always attired in the Palestinian headdress or military cap. To questions about PLO terrorism, he repeated his usual litany, but coming directly from his lips the words had added force: "I am a freedom fighter. We are fighting for justice for our people, the four million Palestinians dispossessed and scattered by three decades of war."

Later that year, I had a second and more productive meeting with the PLO leader, again in Damascus. This time I was alone. With Arafat were Abu Hassan, his security leader who was soon to die in a car bombing in Beirut, and Mahmoud Labadi, his public affairs officer, who later deserted Arafat and joined Syrian-supported hard-liners. Such was the ferment in the Palestinian community. I wanted Arafat to clarify the terms under which the PLO would live at peace with Israel. Was he ready to recognize Israel? In a four-hour discussion that stretched late into the night, he provided the answer. Working carefully word by word, and phrase by phrase, he fashioned a statement and authorized me to report it to Carter—and to the public.

> The PLO will accept an independent Palestinian state consisting of the West Bank and Gaza, with a connecting corridor, and in that circumstance will renounce any and all violent means to enlarge the territory of that state. I would reserve the right of course to use non-violent, that is to say diplomatic and democratic means, to bring about the eventual unification of all of Palestine. We will give de facto recognition to the State of Israel. We would live at peace with all our neighbors. —Damascus, November 30, 1978.

I wrote the words on a legal sheet and read them back several times so he could ponder their full meaning. I asked Arafat if he would sign his name on the paper bearing the words. He answered, "No, I prefer not to sign my name, but I stand behind the words. You may quote me."

I was elated, perhaps too much so. Arafat's pledge contrasted sharply with the harsh rhetoric of earlier Palestinian public statements which called, in effect, for the elimination of the State of Israel. It was not, of course, everything Israel or the United States would want, but it was an encouraging start, and it belied the image of the fanatic who believed only in violence. During the long interview we covered many points, and, determined to protect my credibility, I asked Arafat to identify statements he did not wish to make public. The carefully drafted pledge was not one of these. He wanted the world to know what he pledged, and, clearly, he expected a positive response from President Carter. To use one of the PLO leader's favorite expressions, he had "played a card" in authorizing me to transmit this statement. It was a step beyond anything his organization had officially proclaimed before.

Tragically, it brought no reaction from the U.S. government. I later learned that Secretary of State Vance privately recommended that the administration "take note" of it, but his suggestion was rejected. In a subsequent interview on NBC's *Meet the Press*, Arafat—always a nimble actor—sidestepped questions about the pledge. Carter's newly appointed special ambassador to the Middle East, Robert Strauss, a prominent Democrat who had previously served as chairman of the Democratic National Committee, was intrigued by my communication with Arafat and became a frequent visitor to my office.

I often thought that bringing Arafat and Strauss together would be important to the peace process. The fact that Strauss is Jewish would have helped thousands of Jews in Israel put aside their government's hard line. But Strauss, despite his unique intimate relationship with Carter and his demonstrated ability to negotiate complicated problems on both the international and domestic scene, never received full presidential backing on the Middle East. Late in his diplomatic mission, just before he was shifted to the chairmanship of Carter's ill-fated campaign for re-election, Strauss told me, "If I had had my way, I would have been talking directly to Arafat months ago."

I found myself being drawn deeper into Middle East politics. Early one Sunday, Assistant Secretary of State Harold Saunders called for help. At Arafat's behest, Kuwait was demanding consideration of a United Nations resolution that was sympathetic to the Palestinians. The United States, because of Israel's objections, would not support it, but did not want to go on record against it. The vote was scheduled for the following Tuesday. Saunders hoped that, given more time, he could find a formula that would satisfy both the Arab states and the United States. Mindful of Carter's rule against even informal talks with the PLO, Saunders carefully avoided directly asking that I call Arafat. Nevertheless, I knew Saunders well enough to grasp the real purpose of his call to me. I told him I would try to persuade Arafat to postpone the scheduled vote.

My call to Arafat's office went through instantly, which was unusual for the chaotic Beirut exchange. I urged Arafat to postpone the UN vote, arguing that the delay would cost him nothing and would earn him U.S. gratitude. Two hours later Kuwait postponed the vote. That same weekend, Carter's ambassador to the UN, Andrew Young, had acted less cautiously than Saunders. He'd met to discuss the same issue with Zuhdi Labib Terzi, the PLO observer at the UN. So firm was Carter's edict against talking with the PLO that this incident led to Young's resignation.

I was soon on the phone again with the State Department. This time my help, through Arafat, was needed in getting the U.S. hostages out of our embassy in Tehran. In our 1978 meeting, Arafat had told me of his close relationship with the revolutionaries in Iran. I saw this crisis as an opportunity for Arafat to help in a humanitarian cause and, perhaps, to open the door for peaceful discussions on a broader scale. This time Arafat was away from headquarters, but I had a long talk with his deputy, Mahmoud Labadi, whom I had met during my second interview with Arafat.

Labadi reminded me that Arafat had taken my advice on the UN confrontation but, in Labadi's words, "got nothing in return." He was right. Labadi told me he disagreed with me regarding the situation in Iran but would carefully report my recommendation to his leader. Once more, Arafat cooperated. He sent an envoy to Khomeini, and, according to Saunders, that envoy successfully arranged the release of the first eleven hostages.

For this, the Carter administration thanked Arafat privately—very privately. Publicly, the Carter spokesmen did nothing to discourage the unfounded speculation that the PLO had actually conspired with Iran to seize the hostages. The reverse was true. Just before he left office, Vance told me that he was in "almost daily" communication with Arafat and his staff, enlisting PLO help during the protracted Iranian hostage ordeal, but he never said so publicly.

On several occasions during off-the-record meetings at the White House, I urged Carter to publicly acknowledge Arafat's moderate cooperative course. I was warned that failure to do so would strengthen more radical forces. I later learned that Vice President Walter Mondale, more than any other personality in the administration, had argued persuasively against making any public statements that acknowledged PLO cooperation.

Labadi never forgave Arafat for this cooperation. He later deserted the PLO leader and joined the rebels who were laying siege to Arafat at Tripoli.

Turmoil in the Middle West

While I was organizing my one-man peace initiative, my critics were organizing to throw me out of office. Partisans back home, who had watched my re-election margins grow to 70 percent in 1978, correctly surmised that my unusual activities in foreign policy would provide them the money to attack me in the upcoming elections. In the spring of 1979, an aggressive former state legislator, David Robinson, strongly encouraged by pro-Israel activists, began campaigning full-time for the Democratic nomination for the congressional seat I had held for nineteen years. Three months before the March 1980 primary, David Nuessen, the popular Republican mayor of Quincy, Illinois, challenged my renomination in a professionally managed campaign that was supported mainly by pro-Israel political action committees and individuals. Their contributions financed a relentless pummeling that bruised me more than I realized. I squeaked through the primary with only 55 percent of the vote.

It was a year of surprises, the greatest being the reaction to my candidacy of Dr. Arthur Burns, former chairman of the Federal Reserve Board and, in 1980, the U.S. ambassador to the Federal Republic of Germany. Just after the primary election, I explained my campaign challenge in a telephone conversation with him. Burns responded generously, "We simply cannot afford to lose you. Your re-election is very important to the entire nation." Gratified, I made a modest request: "If you will put those sentiments in a letter I can use in the campaign, that would be a great help."

His endorsement was not a high priority objective. In fact, I did not even think to ask for it until he praised my record, but I expected Burns to agree without hesitation, as we had been friends throughout my career. Our views on fiscal and economic policies were identical.

His answer was the deepest wound in a traumatic year: "Oh, I couldn't do that. It's your views on the PLO. I'm sorry." I was stupefied. I am used to surprises—and disappointments—but his refusal left me speechless. No event, before or since, disclosed to me so forcefully the leverage of the pro-Israel lobby on the U.S. political scene. This great, kind, generous Jewish elder statesman, a personal friend, could not ignore the lobby and say a public good word for my candidacy. I report this episode for this reason: If an otherwise stalwart man like Burns felt intimidated, lesser men and women who do speak out are truly courageous.

Meanwhile, Democrat Robinson solicited campaign contributions by advertising in Jewish newspapers throughout the country, where he called me a "practicing anti-Semite, who is one of the worst enemies that Jews and Israel have ever faced in the history of the U.S. Congress." He drew funds from each of the fifty states. Robinson and I raised about $600,000 each. It was the most expensive congressional campaign in Illinois history. College students from both coasts and in between came to central Illinois on Robinson's behalf, manning phone banks and canvassing door-to-door.

Midway through my speech to the Chicago Council on Foreign Relations, a man burst into the hall and shouted, "We've received a call. There's a bomb in the room." The crowd of five hundred made a fast exit. The police later found a pipe loaded with bubble gum in the grand piano on the stage. Later, Robinson activists converged on Detroit, Michigan, where I was a delegate to the Republican convention, to picket and amuse onlookers with the chant, "Paul, Paul, he must go. He supports the PLO."

Trapped on a Bus with Percy

At first, my plight escaped the attention of the Ronald Reagan presidential campaign. In fact, when Reagan's scheduling office learned that I was having a fundraising luncheon in Springfield, his manager asked if Reagan could stop by, as he would be nearby that day. That unsolicited warmth quickly chilled. New York City organizers warned Reagan's managers: "Appear friendly with Findley and you lose New York." This led them to take unusual measures to keep their candidate a safe distance from me.

Springfield, located in the heart of my district, posed a problem, because it was the home of the first Republican president, Abraham Lincoln, and therefore a "must visit" for the party's presidential candidates. During a day in Illinois, a candidate simply could not pass by Springfield. The Reagan team was concerned about how to make the expected pilgrimage and still keep me out of camera range.

Greg Newell, chief of scheduling, first planned to finesse the problem by having Reagan deliver a major address from the steps of the Lincoln home at the very moment he knew I would be attending my major fundraiser of the year halfway across town. Just for insurance, Newell moved Reagan's Springfield appearance to the Lincoln Tomb, all the way across town. He also scrubbed Reagan's speech, a move designed to minimize press interest in the Springfield stop.

I realized, however, that most of my supporters would also want to see Reagan when he came to town. To accommodate them (and to assure good attendance at my own function), I rescheduled my fundraiser early enough so those attending—myself included—could also attend the Reagan appearance at the tomb.

Reagan's manager passed on an order quietly, or so they thought, that read: "Under no circumstance is Findley to get near Reagan," even though elsewhere in Illinois, congressional candidates were to appear on speaking platforms with him. Learning of the order, Don Norton, my campaign manager, vented his outrage to Reagan's headquarters. The Reagan team shifted gears again. This time they declared that all congressmen were to be treated alike during the day in Illinois: none was to share a platform with Reagan. Representative Ed Madigan, who later became Reagan's secretary of agriculture, was irritated to learn that he would have to either speak before Reagan's arrival in Bloomington that day or wait until Reagan had left the platform. Madigan opted to make no speech at all.

At Springfield, Reagan campaign staffer Paul Russo had only one assignment, but it was an important one. He was to keep me out of camera range when Reagan was nearby. Unaware at the time of the panic of

Reagan's crew, I was literally corralled behind a rope fifty feet away while Reagan was photographed in the ceremonial "rubbing Lincoln's nose" on a statue at the tomb entrance.

At the next stop, a coal mine near Springfield, Russo's team tried to keep me on a bus and in the process trapped my friend, Senator Charles H. Percy, too. Their goal was to keep only me away from Reagan during his remarks to the crowd. But Percy had the misfortune to be on the bus with me, so he too was detained. Together we managed to force the door open, but only after Reagan had concluded his remarks and left the area.

Bob Hope Backs Out

The Reagan team's panic even spread to Hollywood. Bob Hope, who never wavered under enemy fire on war fronts in World War II and who withstood heavy criticism for his support of President Nixon's Vietnam policies, encountered a new and more devastating line of fire when he agreed to appear at a fundraising event for me in Springfield.

Two years earlier I had organized a seventy-fifth birthday party for Hope in the House of Representatives in Washington. It was the most fun-filled moment in the chamber that I can remember. Hope and his wife sat in the gallery as one congressman after another voiced praise of the great entertainer. The tributes filled fourteen pages of the Congressional Record. Gratefully recalling the unique party, Hope agreed to help with my 1980 campaign. His manager, Ward Grant, knowing from the start I was being opposed by pro-Israel activists because of my work on Middle East policy, declared, "We need men in Congress who speak their mind." Coast-to-coast pressure quickly brought a change. Don Norton recalled receiving an urgent telephone message from Hope's manager:

> Grant told me that Hope was getting tremendous pressure from Jews and non-Jews all over the country. He said it's gotten to the point where Hope's lawyer of thirty-five years, who is Jewish, has threatened to quit. The pressure was beyond belief, like nothing they had ever experienced before, and Hope just couldn't come.

Stunned, Norton pleaded that the event was widely publicized, all arrangements were made, tickets were sold, and enthusiasm was high. His plea was to no avail. When Norton told me of the crisis, I tried to get a call through to Hope himself, hoping to persuade him to reconsider. Failing to get a call through, I wrote a confidential letter, giving Hope details of my unpublicized endeavors the year before to promote understanding between PLO leader Arafat and Robert Strauss, President Carter's special emissary to the Middle East. I sent him copies of messages I had transmitted at the request of the two leaders. I asked Hope to keep the information confidential, because the U.S. government was maintaining a public posture of refusing to communicate with the PLO. My letter brought no response, nor were my phone calls returned.

Happily, Strauss—a prominent Democrat and a Jew—agreed to help. Encountering him one afternoon on the steps of the House of Representatives, I explained my problem and asked him to talk to Hope. By then Strauss had left his diplomatic post and was chairman of Carter's campaign for re-election. In a remarkable gesture of magnanimity to a Republican in the midst of a hotly contested election, Strauss agreed, adding, "Maybe I can help him understand the 'crazy' pressure he is getting." He gave me phone numbers where Hope could reach him. In a wire to Hope I said: "[Strauss] will be glad to talk with you or anyone about the value of my work and what he described as the 'crazy pressure' you have been receiving."

By then, however, the "crazy pressure" had taken its toll, and Hope never made the call. I still have a souvenir of my chat with Strauss. It bears the phone number he gave me and my record of his parting words: "I wish you the best. I hope we both make it November 4, because we need to work together on the problems that remain."

A few days later, I finally got a call through to Hope. He was not his usual bubbly self. I assured him it had never occurred to me that he would have such an avalanche of protest calls, but now that the event had been scheduled, it would hurt if he failed to come.

Hope interjected: "I read those letters you sent me. You should go public on this. Defend yourself with the facts." I responded, "I just can't do that. It is highly secret information, and releasing it might hurt the peace process Carter is trying to advance." He paused, then said, "I just don't need this problem. I've been getting all these calls. It's too much pressure. I don't want to get involved."

Hope did not come. Happily, only one ticket holder asked for a refund. The sellout crowd heard a stirring address by my friend and colleague, Representative Guy Vander Jagt of Michigan, who agreed to fill in at the last minute.

Lobby pressure also intervened when former President Gerald R. Ford agreed to appear in my behalf, this time in Alton, Illinois. The first sign of trouble was a call from Palm Springs, in which Ford's secretary reported that the former president had to cancel his date because his staff had mistakenly booked him to speak at a meeting of the Michigan Bar Association the same day. There was no other time that Ford could speak for me, the caller said, before election day. To determine if some accommodation could be arranged, Bob Wichser, my assistant, called the Michigan Bar Association, only to learn that there was no conflict— no event was scheduled on the day in question.

I was puzzled. I had worked closely with Ford during the sixteen years he was Republican leader of the House, noting with admiration that he had never let disagreement on a policy issue keep him from campaigning for Republican congressmen seeking re-election. When I finally reached Ford by phone, he said, "Paul, I've got to be up-front with you. I've got to be candid. If I come out and support you, at every press conference I will be badgered and dogged with the question of how I could campaign for Reagan and then go and support Findley with his views on the PLO."

Despite these setbacks and the nationwide campaign against me, I won in 1980 with 56 percent of the vote. I assumed the worst was over. What more could the pro-Israeli activists do? Accordingly, I continued my endeavors for Middle East peace and did not anticipate the severe new challenges related to the Arab–Israeli dispute that were yet to come. In late 1981 a federal court, responding to shifts in population, ordered boundary changes in my district that removed Jacksonville, my old hometown, and added, Decatur, the city with the nation's highest unemployment. Marginally Democratic before the border changes, the new district was now substantially so. In addition, local industry was in a deep depression and farmers were restless.

I was unopposed in the 1982 primary, but a strong Democratic opponent, Richard Durbin, emerged in the general election. Experienced and popular, he quickly picked up the resources that Robinson had amassed, including Robinson's list of nationwide contributors. The Associated Press reported: "Israel's American supporters again are pouring money into an emotional drive to unseat Central Illinois Representative Paul Findley." On the plus side, Reagan's lieutenants were helping me this time. Vice President George H. W. Bush, my former House colleague, brushed aside pro-Israeli complaints from Texas and appeared at an event on my behalf in Springfield.

This time, re-election was not to be. I lost by 1,407 votes, less than 1 percent of the total cast. In a vote that close, almost any negative development could account for the difference. The attack by pro-Israel activists was only one of several factors. Nevertheless, the American Israel Public Affairs Committee (AIPAC), Washington's principal pro-Israel lobby, claimed credit for my defeat. In a report to a Jewish gathering in Austin, Texas, a few days after election day, Thomas A. Dine, the organization's executive director, said his forces brought 150 students from the University of Illinois to my district to "pound the pavements and knock on doors." He concluded, "This is a case where the Jewish lobby made a difference. We beat the odds and defeated Findley." He later estimated that $685,000 of the $750,000 raised by Durbin came from Jews. With my supporters raising almost exactly the same sum, the contest once again set a new state recording for total campaign spending.

No Ready Answers

The campaign to remove me from Congress started early in 1979 and spanned most of the next four years. It attracted the attention and financial resources of pro-Israel people in every state in the Union. Reports from friends suggested its national scope. Senator Bob Dole of Kansas, my seatmate on the House Agriculture Committee for six years, told me he heard pro-Israel leaders in Kansas speak with great emotional intensity about my candidacy both before and after election day. Clarence Palmby, the former undersecretary of agriculture, learned that my defeat was the principal 1982 political objective of the partners in a large New York City law firm.

After twenty-two years in Congress, losing was, of course, a disappointment. But my main reaction was wonderment. I was puzzled by the behavior of the pro-Israel activists. Why did they go to such trouble to eliminate me from Congress? Why did people from all over the country, who did not know me personally and very likely knew little of my record, dig so deeply into their own pockets, many of them contributing $1,000 to my opponents? What sustained this commitment for a four-year period?

Israeli activists could find few flaws in my voting record. Over the years I voted consistently for aid to Israel. Sometimes I was critical of Egypt and other Arab states. Even when, in an effort to force Israel to halt its attacks on Lebanon, I tried to get President Carter to suspend aid, I voted for all measures that authorized future military and economic aid to Israel. Interestingly, many Israelis and U.S. Jews shared my views about the Arab–Israeli dispute. Beyond Middle East policy, I supported causes that most Jews applauded: civil rights, community action programs, equal rights for women, a freeze on nuclear weapons, and normalization of relations with China.

Moreover, I was but one of 435 members of the House of Representatives. While senior among Republicans, I was just one of nine on the Foreign Affairs Subcommittee dealing with the Middle East. When I criticized Israel, whether I spoke in committee or on the floor of the House of Representatives, I almost always stood alone. Surely the lobby for Israel realized that I posed no serious threat. Could Israel's supporters not tolerate even one lonely voice of dissent?

Or was the lobby's goal to make an example of me in the Elizabethan tradition? According to legend, Queen Elizabeth occasionally hanged an admiral just to keep others on their toes. Was I chosen for a trip to the political gallows to discourage other congressmen from speaking out?

I could not reconcile the harsh tactics I experienced with the traditional Jewish advocacy of civil liberties, a record I had admired all my life. In Congress, I worked closely with Jewish colleagues, including Allard Lowenstein and Ben Gilman. In my wonderment, I pressed Doug Bloomfield, a friend on the AIPAC staff, for an explanation. He shrugged. "You were the most visible critic of Israeli policy. That's the best answer I can give." It was hardly adequate.

The unanswered questions led to others.

Do other congressmen have similar experiences? To be sure, those who speak out are few in number, but it seemed implausible that the lobby would target me alone. I wanted the facts. What about the president and the vast array of "movers and shakers" employed in the executive branch? What pressures, if any, do they experience? A lobby formidable enough to intimidate two former presidents of the United States must have great leverage at the highest levels of government.

What of those in other occupations? The lobby had forced Bob Hope to back down. Did it have similar power over people in different professions? On campus, for example, does tenure and the tradition of academic freedom give immunity to teachers and administrators from the kind of pressure I received? Do members of the clergy escape it? How about people in business, large and small? And, vitally important in our free society, how about reporters, columnists, editorial writers, publishers, and the commentators on television and radio?

Deep questions. To me, crucial questions.

There were no ready answers, so I decided to seek them. I began my quest by calling the Capitol Hill offices of the American Israel Public Affairs Committee.

King of the Hill

WASHINGTON IS A city of acronyms, and today one of the best known in Congress is AIPAC. The mere mention of it brings a sober, perhaps furtive, look to the face of anyone on Capitol Hill who deals with Middle East policy. AIPAC—the American Israel Public Affairs Committee—is now the preeminent power in Washington lobbying.

In 1967, as a fourth-term congressman just named to the House Foreign Affairs Committee, I had never heard of it. One day, in private conversation in the committee room, I voiced a brief criticism of Israel's military attack on Syria. A senior Republican, William S. Broomfield of Michigan, responded with a smile, "Wait till Si Kenen over at AIPAC hears what you've said." He was referring to I. L. Kenen, then executive director of AIPAC, whose name was just as unfamiliar to me as the organization he headed. I learned later that Broomfield was not joking. AIPAC sometimes finds out what congressmen say about Middle East policy even in private conversations, and those who criticize Israel do so at their political peril.

AIPAC is only a part of the Israeli lobby, but in terms of having a direct effect on public policy it is clearly the most important. The organization has deepened and extended its influence in recent years. It is no overstatement to say that AIPAC has effectively gained control of virtually all of Capitol Hill's action on Middle East policy. Almost without exception, House and Senate members do its bidding, because most of them consider AIPAC to be the direct Capitol Hill representative of a political force that can make or break their chances at election time.

Whether based on fact or fancy, the perception is what counts: AIPAC means power—raw, intimidating power. Its promotional literature regularly cites a tribute published in the *New York Times*: "The most powerful, best-run and effective foreign policy interest group in Washington." A former congressman, Paul N. "Pete" McCloskey, puts it more directly: Congress is "terrorized" by AIPAC.[1] Other congressmen have not been so candid on public record, but many House and Senate members privately agree.

The Washington presence of AIPAC is only the most visible tip of this lobby. Its effectiveness rests heavily on the nationwide foundation built by U.S. Jews who function through more than 200 groups. A professional on the AIPAC staff says:

> I would say that at most two million Jews are interested politically or in a charity sense. The other four million are not. Of the two million, most will not be involved beyond giving some money.[2]

Actually, those who provide the political activism for all organizations in U.S. Jewry probably do not exceed 250,000. The lobby's most popular newsletter, AIPAC's *Near East Report,* goes to about 60,000 people, a distribution that the organization believes is read by most U.S. citizens who take a responsibility in pro-Israeli political action, whether their primary interest is AIPAC, B'nai B'rith, the American Jewish Committee, the Anti-Defamation League, the Jewish National Fund, the United Jewish Appeal, or any of the other main national groups. The newsletter is also sent, without charge, to news media, congressmen, key government officials, and other people prominent in foreign policy. AIPAC members get the newsletter as a part of their annual dues.

In practice, the lobby groups function as an informal extension of the Israeli government. This was illustrated when AIPAC helped draft the official statement defending Israel's 1981 bombing of the Iraqi nuclear reactor, then issued it at the same hour that Israel's embassy did.[3]

No major Jewish organization ever publicly takes issue with positions and policies adopted by Israel.[4] Thomas A. Dine, executive director of AIPAC from 1981 to 1993, spoke warmly of President Reagan's peace plan when it was announced in September 1982, but as soon as Israel rejected the plan, Dine fell silent. This close coordination sometimes inspires intragovernment humor. "At the State Department we used to predict that if Israel's prime minister should announce that the world is flat, within twenty-four hours Congress would pass a resolution congratulating him on the discovery," recalls Don Bergus, former ambassador to Sudan and a retired career diplomat.[5]

To Jewish organizations, however, lobbying Washington is serious business, and they look increasingly to AIPAC for leadership. Stephen S. Rosenfeld, deputy editor of the *Washington Post* editorial page, rates AIPAC as "clearly the leading Jewish political force in America today."[6]

AIPAC's charter defines its mission as legislative action, but it now also represents the interests of Israel whenever there is a perceived challenge to that country's interests in the news media, the religious community, on U.S. college campuses—anywhere. Because AIPAC's staff members are paid from contributions by American citizens, they need not register under the Foreign Agents Registration Act. In effect, however, they serve the same function as foreign agents.

Over the years the pro-Israel lobby has thoroughly penetrated this nation's governmental system, and the organization that has made the deepest impact is AIPAC, to whom even a president of the United States turned when he had a vexing political problem related to the Arab–Israeli dispute.

The Ascendancy of Thomas A. Dine

In October 1983 President Ronald Reagan, faced with rising public opposition to the presence of U.S. Marines in Lebanon, sought help from the American Israel Public Affairs Committee. The terrorist bombing that would kill more than 200 marines as they slept in their barracks at the Beirut airport was yet to come. Still, four marines had already died, three by sniper fire, and congressional concern was rising. Democratic

Congressman Sam Stratton of New York, a veteran known for his hawkish views, called the marines "sitting ducks" and predicted heavy casualties. He wanted them out of Lebanon.

Others cited the War Powers Resolution and questioned whether the president had the authority to keep forces in a hostile environment such as Beirut for more than ninety days without the express approval of Congress. Some congressmen began drawing parallels between the marine presence in Lebanon and the beginnings of the disastrous U.S. experience in Vietnam.

President Reagan objected, as had his predecessors, to the restrictions imposed by the War Powers legislation. If he accepted its terms, he would have to withdraw the forces within ninety days or get Congress to approve an extension. If he insisted that the law did not apply because the situation was not hostile, events might quickly prove him wrong. Regardless, he would have a rebellious Congress on his hands.

Reagan decided to finesse the problem. He asked Congress for legislation that would allow him to keep the existing force of marines in Lebanon for eighteen months. This would please the "strict constructionists" who felt that the chief executive must live with the War Powers Resolution. It would also suit his own needs, because he was confident that the orderly removal of the marines would occur within the eighteen-month period.

Thanks to extraordinary help from an unlikely quarter, Reagan's plan had relatively clear sailing in the House of Representatives. Speaker Thomas P. "Tip" O'Neill, the most prominent elected Democrat in the nation, gave the legislation his strong support. To O'Neill, it was a question of patriotism, and enough Democrats answered his call to assure passage of the legislation in the Democrat-controlled body.

But the Senate, although controlled by his fellow Republicans, posed a more difficult problem for the president. An informal "nose count" showed a close vote and probably defeat. The president decided he needed help, and he enlisted the cooperation of Thomas A. Dine, the slender, aggressive, dark-haired young Capitol Hill staff veteran who then headed AIPAC.

Reagan's appeal to Dine for support on the marine issue was without precedent. The pending bill contained no money for Israel, and AIPAC and other Israeli lobby groups had kept hands off the Lebanon controversy. Pro-Israeli forces did not want other Americans to blame Israel if the marines should encounter more trouble. Certainly Israel already bore enough responsibility for U.S. problems in Lebanon.[7] It had discreetly but effectively helped to engineer the original marine presence in Beirut by agreeing to withdraw its forces from Beirut in favor of a multinational force, provided the United States was included. (The multinational force would have been unnecessary had Israel not invaded Lebanon in the first place.) Although AIPAC privately wanted the marines to stay in Lebanon, under the circumstances its leadership preferred to stay in the background.

The White House call to Dine was exceptional for another reason: Reagan needed help with Senators who were normally his most stalwart supporters.[8] The president was unsure of the votes of twelve Republicans, among them John Warner of Virginia, Dan Quayle of Indiana, William Cohen of Maine, and James A. McClure of Idaho. All were generally regarded as hawkish on military matters and all except McClure were strong supporters of Israel. Learning of the presidential plea, one AIPAC staffer said, "If the White House is worried about those votes, the bill is going down."

Despite its reluctance to get publicly involved in the sensitive issue, AIPAC made the calls. Nine of the twelve senators, including the four mentioned above, voted with the president and helped him win a narrow 54–46 victory.[9]

AIPAC's role in the outcome was not noted in most media reports of the dramatic event, but an elated President Reagan called Dine personally to express his thanks. Michael Gale, then handling White House relations with the Jewish community, provided a transcript of the conversation with the suggestion that AIPAC publicize it. AIPAC declined, preferring to maintain its low profile on the issue, so Gale gave the text to CNN's Wolf Blitzer, who at the time wrote for the *Jerusalem Post* and had previously written for AIPAC's *Near East Report*. The *Post* quoted Reagan as saying to Dine, "I just wanted to thank you and all your staff for the great assistance you gave us on the War Powers Act resolution. . . . I know how you mobilized the grassroots organizations to generate support."[10]

"Well, we try to use the telephone," responded Dine. "That's part of our job. And we wanted to do it and will continue to do it. . . . We want to work together, obviously."

Work together they did. The Reagan executive branch established a relationship with AIPAC of unprecedented intimacy. It was not the first time, however, that the White House or the State Department had turned to the lobbying group for help. Although these high level approaches are little known even on Capitol Hill, they actually occur every time foreign aid legislation is up for a vote. Whoever controls the White House finds that securing congressional approval of foreign aid is a challenge and, as the legislation includes economic and military aid to Israel, naturally looks to AIPAC for help. Except for a few humanitarian and church-related organizations, AIPAC serves foreign aid's only domestic constituency.

Without AIPAC, foreign aid legislation would not have been approved at the $15 billion-plus level in 2001, and might have difficulty surviving at all. A candid tribute to the lobby came from John K. Wilhelm, the executive director of the presidential commission that made recommendations in late 1983 on the future direction of foreign aid.[11] Briefing a world hunger board at the State Department in January 1984, Wilhelm, a career veteran in the Agency for International Development, said the active support of the pro-Israeli lobby was "vital" to congressional approval of foreign aid. (In the early 1960s, when aid to Israel was modest—less than $100 million a year—a foreign-aid bill squeaked through the House of Representatives by a scant five votes. But AIPAC was then in its infancy.)

AIPAC also crafted the strategy that produced a $510 million increase in 1983 aid for Israel—an astonishing increase, considering it came just after the indiscriminate bombing of Beirut and complicity of Israeli forces in the massacre of Palestinian refugees in the Sabra and Shatila refugee camps, events that aroused unprecedented public criticism of Israeli policy.

The administration opposed the 1983 increase but was outmaneuvered. By the time Judge William Clark, who at the time was National Security Adviser to President Reagan, sent an urgent appeal to Republican Senator Mark Hatfield to block the increase, the issue was already settled. AIPAC had locked in support by persuading a majority on the Appropriations Committee that the increase was a simple question of being for or against Israel. No one wanted to champion the negative side.

AIPAC had already confounded the administration on the House side, where the White House had argued against the increase for budgetary reasons, contending it would be at the expense of other needy countries. This argument was demolished when AIPAC lobbyists presented elaborate data showing how the extra aid to Israel could be accomplished without cutting support for other countries. An AIPAC lobbyist summed it up: "The administration lobbyists really didn't do their homework. They didn't have their act together." By 1984 the aid level had risen to over $2 billion a year—all of it in grants with no repayment required—and the approval margin was 112.

In February 1983 Secretary of State George Shultz named a "blue ribbon" panel of prominent citizens to recommend changes in the foreign aid program. Of the forty-two on the commission, twenty-seven were Senate or House members with primary responsibility for handling foreign aid legislation. The others had been prominent in administering foreign aid in years past.

Only one full-time lobbyist was named to the panel: AIPAC's executive director, Thomas A. Dine. To my knowledge, it was the first time that a lobbyist had been selected for such a prestigious government assignment, and Dine's selection was particularly surprising because it put him in a close working relationship with the handful of people who formulate and carry out policy on the very matter AIPAC was set up to influence—aid to Israel.

A more enviable position for a lobbyist could hardly be imagined. Former Senator James Abourezk, head of the American-Arab Anti-Discrimination Committee, commented:

> It would make as much sense to let the president of Lockheed Corporation serve on a Defense Department board which decides what planes our air force will buy.

In November Dine took an even bigger step up the ladder of Washington prestige and influence.[12] He was invited to the White House for a private meeting with National Security Adviser Robert C. McFarlane, President Reagan's closest advisor on day-to-day policy in the Middle East. On the agenda were two foreign policy topics of great sensitivity:

the Lebanese situation and the proposal to help Jordan establish a rapid deployment force. Both of these issues were, of course, of vital interest to Israel. Dine's invitation came just a week after he received the President's jubilant phone call thanking him for his help in getting the War Powers Resolution authority extended.

In January 1984 *Washingtonian* magazine listed Dine among the most influential people in the nation's capital.

Dine's reputation has even stirred Arab capitals. In 1984 King Hussein of Jordan publicly blamed AIPAC, in part, for the decline of U.S. influence and leadership for peace in the Middle East.[13] He also criticized the inordinate influence of the Israeli lobby on U.S. presidential candidates. He said the candidates had to "appeal for the favors of AIPAC, Zionism, and Israel."

One development especially provoked the king: For ten days beginning in mid-March 1984, Dine personally took part in direct foreign policy negotiations with Undersecretary of State Lawrence S. Eagleburger and National Security Adviser McFarlane.[14] During one session, Eagleburger offered to withdraw a widely publicized proposal to sell antiaircraft missiles to Jordan if AIPAC would drop its support of legislation requiring the removal of the U.S. embassy in Israel from Tel Aviv to Jerusalem.

By then, King Hussein's sharp criticism of the United States—and AIPAC—had appeared in U.S. newspapers, and Dine knew it had strengthened congressional opposition to the sale of the missiles. At the time Eagleburger made his proposition, AIPAC already had forty-eight senators committed in opposition, and he received pledges from six more the next day.[15] Thus, AIPAC was able to kill the sale without cutting a deal on other issues.

After he rejected Eagleburger's offer, Dine promised that AIPAC would cease active opposition to a proposal to help Jordan establish a rapid deployment force and would lobby to work out a compromise on the bill to transfer the U.S. embassy from Tel Aviv to Jerusalem if the administration would take two important steps: first, refuse to sell Stinger antiaircraft missiles to Saudi Arabia; second, issue a public letter announcing that it would engage in no further indirect communications with the Palestine Liberation Organization.[16] Although the public letter did not appear, the administration backed away from the Stinger sales to both Saudi Arabia and Jordan.

Dine emerged from these negotiations with his prestige greatly enhanced. Richard Murphy, assistant secretary of state for Near East and South Asia affairs and the official charged with the development and administration of U.S. policies relating to the Middle East, was not invited to the Eagleburger–McFarlane–Dine negotiations, nor was he notified of the administration's decision to cancel the proposed sale of Stinger missiles until twelve hours after AIPAC received the information.

The *Washington Post* concluded that the episode "raised questions about the propriety of the administration's making deals on foreign policy issues with a private, special-interest organization." Dine had a ready response: "We think it's better to be strong and criticized, than weak, ignored, and not respected."

In part, the unprecedented presidential consideration was a tribute to Dine's combination of ingratiating manner, tough, relentless spirit, and sheer dynamism. Under Dine, AIPAC's membership has risen from 11,000 to more than 50,000, and its annual budget had grown from $750,000 to more than $3 million.

Dine's influence was felt in power centers beyond the Oval Office. He received calls from presidential candidates as well as presidents, and he reported that former Vice President Walter Mondale "bounces ideas off us" before issuing statements on Middle East policy. And most congressional actions affecting Middle East policy were either approved or initiated by AIPAC.

Broadening the Network

To accomplish these feats for Israel—sometimes cooperating with the president of the United States, sometimes not—AIPAC's director utilized a team of hard-driving, able professionals and kept them working together smoothly. Policy lines were kept clear and the troops are well-disciplined. AIPAC's role is to support Israel's policies, not to help formulate them, so AIPAC maintained daily telephone communication with the Israeli embassy, and Dine's successor as executive director Howard Kohr met personally with embassy officials at least once a week.

Although AIPAC has a small staff in comparison to other major U.S. Jewish organizations, it taps the resources of a broad nationwide network of unpaid activists. Annual membership meetings in Washington are a major way to rally the troops. Those attending hear prominent U.S. and Israeli speakers, participate in workshops and seminars, and contribute financially to the cause. The conferences attract top political talent: the Israeli ambassador, senior White House and State Department officials, and prominent senators and House members. Recent conferences featured Senators Tom Daschle of South Dakota and John McCain of Arizona, Representative Tom DeLay of Texas, former and current Israeli Prime Ministers Ehud Barak and Ariel Sharon, and Texas Governor George W. Bush—the year he was elected president.

The White House is also well represented at such conferences. While serving as Reagan's vice president, former U.S. president George Herbert Walker Bush assured AIPAC delegates that the Reagan administration would keep fighting against anti-Semitism at the United Nations and criticized three Democratic presidential candidates—Walter Mondale, Gary Hart, and Jesse Jackson—for being "soft on anti-Semitism."

Ties to other interest groups are carefully cultivated. Christian outreach was announced as AIPAC's newest national program, and Merrie White, a "born-again Christian," was introduced as the director of relations with the Christian community. According to Art Chotin, Dine's deputy, the goal was nothing less than to "bring that community into AIPAC." He noted the presence of fifty Christians representing thirty-five states as evidence of progress already made toward this end. White helped organize the annual Religious Roundtable Prayer Breakfast for Israel the following February. Chris Gerstein, AIPAC's political director, came to the position after seven years as special assistant to the president of the International Union of Operating Engineers.

AIPAC's coast-to-coast outreach is enhanced by its speaking program. Its officers, staff members, and representatives filled more than 900 dates in 1982 alone. Receptions are held in scores of smaller cities. "Parlor briefings" in the homes of Jewish leaders across the country help raise money to supplement revenue from membership dues. Social events on Capitol Hill help spread the word to the thousands of high school and college students who work as interns in the offices of senators and congressmen or in committee offices.

Tours of Israel, which other Jewish groups arrange, help to establish a grassroots base for AIPAC's program. For example, in April 1982, the Young Leadership Mission, an activity of United Jewish Appeal, arranged for 1,500 U.S. Jews to take one-week tours. "The visitors were given a view of the magnificence you will find in any country," observed an AIPAC staff member. He said the tour had profound impact: "It built spirit for the cause, and it raised money. The pitch for funds was the final event. It came right after the folks walked out of the memorial to the Holocaust." The effect was awesome. "The tour directors have it down to a science," he reported. "They know how to hit all the buttons." The United Jewish Appeal and Israel share the proceeds. Larry Kraftowitz, a Washington journalist who attended a similar tour, calls the experience "profound." He adds, "I consider myself more sympathetic to the New Jewish Agenda goals [than current Israeli government policy], but I must say I was impressed."

Tours are not just for Jews. Governors, members of state legislatures, and community leaders, including news media personnel, are also given the opportunity for expense-paid tours of Israel. Trips are also arranged for our nation's leaders, especially those on Capitol Hill. While AIPAC does not itself conduct the tours, it facilitates the process. Over half the membership of Congress has traveled to Israel, about half on what is deemed official business at the expense of the U.S. government. With few exceptions, Jewish organizations or individuals paid the expenses of the rest.

Another group of potentially influential—but often overlooked—Washington functionaries that AIPAC tries to influence is made up of congressional staffers. AIPAC works with Israeli universities, who arrange expense-paid tours for staff members who occupy key positions. These annual trips are called the Hal Rosenthal Program, named for former Republican Senator Jacob Javits's staff aide, who was gunned down by a Palestinian terrorist on the first such trip.

AIPAC is as successful at keeping lawmakers from visiting Arab countries as it is in presenting only Israel's views. When the National Association of Arab Americans, working through the World Affairs Council of Amman, invited all congressmen and their spouses to an expense-paid tour of Jordan with a side trip to the West Bank in 1983, a notice in AIPAC's *Near East Report* quickly chilled prospects for participation. It questioned how Amman, without Israeli cooperation, could get the tourists across the Jordan River for events scheduled in the West Bank. It also quoted Don Sundquist, a Republican congressman from Tennessee, as expressing "fear" that if any of his colleagues accepted the trip they would be "used" by anti-Israeli propagandists. Only three congressmen made the trip. A 1984 tour was cancelled for lack of acceptances.

AIPAC's outreach program is buttressed by a steady stream of publications. In addition to "Action Alerts" and the weekly *Near East Report*, it issues position papers and monographs designed to answer, or often discredit, critics and to advance Israel's objectives.

The most controversial publication of all was an "enemies list" issued as a "first edition" in the spring of 1983. A handsomely printed 154-page paperback entitled *The Campaign to Discredit Israel*, it provided a "directory of the actors": 21 organizations and 39 individuals AIPAC identified as inimical to Israeli interests.

Included were such distinguished public servants as former Undersecretary of State George W. Ball, retired ambassadors Talcott Seelye, Andrew Killgore, John C. West, and James Akins, and former Senator James Abourezk. There were also five Jewish dissenters and several scholars on the list.

Seemingly unaware of the AIPAC project, the Anti-Defamation League of B'nai B'rith almost simultaneously issued its own "enemies list," titled *Pro-Arab Propaganda in America: Vehicles and Voices*. It too was identified as a "first edition," and lists thirty-one organizations and thirty-four individuals. These books were nothing more than blacklists, reminiscent of the worst tactics of the McCarthy era.

A similar "enemies list" was employed in AIPAC's extensive program at colleges and universities.

They Get the Word Out Fast

Through its "Action Alert" mailings, AIPAC keeps more than one thousand Jewish leaders throughout the United States informed on current issues. An "alert" usually demands action to meet a legislative challenge on Capitol Hill, requesting a telephone call, telegram, or, if need be, a personal visit to a reluctant congressman.

The network can have almost instantaneous effect. One day I whispered to a colleague in the Foreign Affairs Committee that I might offer an amendment to a pending bill cutting aid to Israel. Within thirty minutes, two other congressmen came to me with worried looks, reporting that they had just had calls from citizens in their home districts who were concerned about my amendment.

Paul Weyrich, who worked as a Senate aide before becoming a political analyst, details the effectiveness of AIPAC:

> It's a remarkable system they have. If you vote with them, or make a public statement they like, they get the word out fast through their own publications and through editors around the country who are sympathetic to their cause. Of course, it works in reverse as well. If you say something they don't like, you can be denounced or censured through the same network. That kind of pressure is bound to affect Senators' thinking, especially if they are wavering or need support.[17]

This activism is carried out by an elaborate system of officers, committees, and councils that give AIPAC a ready, intimate system for political activity from coast to coast. Officers meet once a month to confer with Executive Director Kohr on organization and management. Each of its five vice presidents can expect to eventually serve a term as president. A large executive committee is invited to Washington every three months for briefings. A recent national council listed more than 200 names. These subgroups include the leadership of most major U.S. Jewish organizations.

The AIPAC staff is not only highly professional and highly motivated but also thoroughly experienced. Prior to joining AIPAC, director Howard Kohr was a management fellow for the Department of Defense, deputy director of the National Jewish Coalition, and assistant Washington representative of the American Jewish Committee.

Lobbyists for AIPAC have almost instant access to House and Senate members and feel free to call them at their homes in the evening. Republican Congressman Douglas Bereuter of Nebraska, an exception, received no lobbyists, AIPAC or otherwise, but the doors were wide open to AIPAC lobbyists at the offices of almost all other congressmen. A congressional aide explained why:

Professionalism is one reason. They know what they are doing, get to the point, and leave. They are often a useful source of information. They are reliable and friendly. But most important of all, they are seen by congressmen as having direct and powerful ties to important constituents.

The result is a remarkable cooperation and rapport between lobbyist and legislator. Encountered in a Capitol corridor one day, an AIPAC lobbyist said, "Tomorrow I will try to see five members of the House. I called this morning and confirmed every appointment, and I have no doubt I will get in promptly." Two days later, even he seemed somewhat awed by AIPAC's clout. He reported, "I made all five. I went right in to see each of them. There was no waiting. Our access is amazing."

This experience contrasts sharply with the experience of most other lobbyists on Capitol Hill. One veteran lobbyist reflected with envy on the access that AIPAC enjoys: "If I can actually see two congressmen or senators in one long day, it's been a good one."

Despite its denials, AIPAC keeps close records on each House and Senate member. Unlike other lobbies, which keep track of only a few "key" issues voted on the House or Senate floor, AIPAC takes note of other activities, too—votes in committees, cosponsorship of bills, signing of letters, and even whether speeches are made. "That's depth!" exclaims an admiring Capitol Hill staff member.

An illustration of lobby power occurred October 3, 1984, when the House of Representatives approved a bill to remove all trade restrictions between the United States and Israel; 98.5 percent (416) voted in the affirmative, despite the strong opposition of the AFL-CIO and the American Farm Bureau Federation. The vote was 416–6 on legislation that normally would elicit heavy reaction because of its effect on markets for commodities produced in the United States.

As they voted, few were aware of a Commerce Department study that found that the duty-free imports proposed in the bill would cause "significant adverse effects" on U.S. producers of vegetables.[18] Because the White House wanted the bill passed, notwithstanding its effects on jobs and markets, the study was classified "confidential" and kept under wraps. One congressman finally pried loose a copy by complaining bitterly—and correctly—to the White House that AIPAC had secured a copy for its own use.

"I Cleared It with AIPAC"

Until his defeat in an upset on November 6, 1984, Congressman Clarence D. "Doc" Long, a seventy-four-year-old Democrat from Maryland, exemplified the strong ties between AIPAC and Capitol Hill. He delivered for Israel as chairman of the House Appropriations Subcommittee, which handles aid to Israel.

The tall, gray-haired, former economics professor at Johns Hopkins University trumpeted his support: "AIPAC made my district their number one interest." AIPAC supported Long for a good reason: he held the gavel when questions about funding Israeli aid came up. The lobby wanted him to keep it. Chairmanships are normally decided by seniority, and next in line after Long was David Obey of Wisconsin, who earned lobby disfavor in 1976 by offering an amendment to cut aid to Israel by $200 million.[19] "Doc" Long never had any misgivings about aid to Israel, and he helped his colleagues defeat Obey's amendment by a vote of 342–32.

Sitting at a table in the House of Representatives restaurant during a late House session in 1982, Long explained:

> Long ago I decided that I'd vote for anything AIPAC wants. I didn't want them on my back. My district is too difficult. I don't need the trouble [pro-Israeli lobbyists] can cause. I made up my mind I would get and keep their support.

The conversation turned to one of Obey's questions about the high levels of Israeli aid. Long said, "I can't imagine why Dave would say things like that." A colleague chided, "Maybe he's thinking about our own national interest."

In September 1983, Long led a battle to get U.S. marines out of Lebanon. He proposed an amendment that would have cut funding for the operation in sixty days. John Hall, a reporter who knew Long's close ties with the lobby, asked Long, "Are you sure this amendment won't get you in trouble?" Without hesitation, the congressman replied, "I cleared it with AIPAC." He was not joking. This was not the first congressional proposal to be cleared in advance with the Israeli lobby, but it was the first time the clearance had been specifically acknowledged in the public record. The proposal to cut aid to Lebanon provoked a lively debate but, opposed by such leaders as Speaker Tip O'Neill and Lee Hamilton of Indiana, chairman of the Subcommittee on Europe and the Middle East, the measure failed, 274–153.

Although heavily supported by pro-Israeli interests—eighteen pro-Israel political action committees chipped in $31,250 for Long's 1982 re-election campaign—Long denies a personal linkage:

> Nobody has to give me money to make me vote for aid to Israel. I've been doing that for twenty years, most of the time without contributions.

The money and votes that Israel's supporters provided to Long's candidacy were insufficient in 1984. Although pro-Israel PACs (political action committees) gave him $155,000—four times the amount that went to any other House candidate—Long lost by 5,727 votes, less than 3 percent of those cast. A factor in his defeat was advertising sponsored by people prominent in the National Association of Arab Americans, who attacked Long for his uncritical support of Israel's demands. Obey, Long's likely successor as chairman, was the only Democrat on the panel who did not accept money from pro-Israel political action committees.

"They Have Never Forgiven Me"

On one occasion, Israel's U.S. lobby had a hand in putting a vice president out of office. In a letter to me dated April 20, 1988, former Vice President Spiro T. Agnew credited AIPAC and other elements of Israel's U.S. lobby with keeping him from becoming president. Before resigning the vice presidency over corrupt payments dating from his career as governor of Maryland, Agnew was the idol of conservatives. They loved his caustic and sometimes entertaining attacks on liberals, whom he once called "nattering nabobs of negativism."

In the letter, Agnew said he was engaged in a second reading of my book, *They Dare to Speak Out*, and added:

> Although you do not speak of my experience in your book, I trace the advent of my difficulties to a confrontation with this same lobby. In 1971, President Nixon wished me to visit Kuwait and Saudi Arabia to provide a little balance to the teeming of congressmen who run to Israel on the slight-

est pretext. The White House staff suggested that I also go to Israel, but I declined on the basis that doing so would substantially diminish the signal that my visits were trying to send to the Arab countries. AIPAC raised hell, and I received a torrent of letters and calls from Jewish friends and acquaintances as well as numerous requests for appointments with Jewish pressure groups. I stuck to my guns and did not visit Israel, and they have never forgiven me. And they made sure that I would not become president.

In subsequent correspondence, Agnew asked me not to place the text of his letter on the public record during his lifetime. In a curious twist to the Agnew history, I was among those who did not want him to succeed Nixon, but my reasons differed from those he ascribed to AIPAC. I was uneasy with Agnew's brand of Republicanism in early 1973 and had a discussion with Senator Charles "Mac" Mathias (R-MD) and a few other Republicans over what, if anything, could be done to keep the vice president from becoming the party's presidential nominee in 1976. The question proved moot when, faced with corruption charges, Agnew resigned the vice presidency in October 1973. Richard Nixon resigned a year later. After serving a prison term, Agnew returned to private life as a business consultant. He died in 1996.

Outreach on an International Scale

AIPAC champions not only Israel's U.S. causes, but its international ambitions as well. The lobby recently began an international outreach program, serving Israel's interests by facilitating U.S. aid to other countries. In 1983 it tried to help Zaire, Israel's new African friend. Israel wanted Zaire to get $20 million in military assistance requested by President Reagan, but AIPAC decided against assigning the lobbying task to its regular staff. Instead, it secured the temporary services of a consultant, who buttonholed members of the House Committee on Foreign Affairs. The amendment failed, but the effort helped to pay the debt that Israel incurred when Zaire extended full diplomatic recognition to Israel the previous year.

Columnists Rowland Evans and Robert Novak viewed the initiative as the first step in an Israeli program "to broker aid favors for other pariahs on the congressional hit list to enhance its influence." They described this new effort by Israel as "an exercise of domestic political power by a foreign nation that raises troubling questions."

Beyond AIPAC to the PAC

AIPAC differs from most lobbies in that it avoids endorsing candidates publicly and does not raise or spend money directly in partisan campaigns. Campaign involvement is officially left to private individuals and pro-Israel political action committees (PACs). More than 3,000 PACs are registered under federal law, and most are clearly affiliated with special-interest lobbies. There are fifty-three PACs that focus on support for Israel, although none lists an affiliation with AIPAC or any other Jewish organization.

The first pro-Israel political action committees were organized in 1979. By 1982 they had mushroomed to a total of thirty-one. Pro-Israel PACs contributed more than $1.8 million to 268 different election campaigns during the 1981–82 Federal Election Commission reporting cycle, putting them in the highest political spending range.[20] By mid-August 1984, the list had increased to seventy-five PACs, and they had accumulated $4.25 million for the 1984 federal elections.

These numbers dropped significantly by the 1999–2000 election cycle, in which fifty-three pro-Israel PACs distributed approximately $2 million among 316 campaigns. The reason for this decline is that individual fund-raisers have largely supplanted PACs as the primary means of raising pro-Israel money for candidates. The decline in the number of pro-Israel PACs does not, therefore, indicate a decline in pro-Israel activism. According to former Democratic National Committee head Steve Grossman, who has raised hundreds of thousands of dollars for pro-Israel candidates, "The record will show there is far more money going to pro-Israel candidates than during the days when PACs were created." This isn't to say that pro-Israel PACs have completely ceased their activities: "Since a contribution of $10,000 can't really make a difference, what we try to do is thank our friends," says Morris Amitay, who heads the pro-Israel Washington PAC.[21]

Few of these PACs bear names or other information disclosing their pro-Israeli interest, nor do any list affiliations with AIPAC or other pro-Israeli or Jewish organizations. Most choose to obscure their pro-Israel character by using a bland title, such as the "Committee for 18," "Arizona Politically Interested Citizens," "Joint Action Committee for Political Affairs," or "Government Action Committee." Yet all are totally committed to one thing: Israel.

"No one is trying to hide anything," protests Mark Siegel, founder of the pro-Israeli National Bipartisan Political Action Committee and a former White House liaison with the Jewish community. He insists that the bland names were chosen because "there are those in the political process who would use the percentage of Jewish money [in a given race] as a negative." The PAC Siegel heads was originally formed to help in the late Senator Henry Jackson's 1978 presidential bid.

Norman Silverman, who helped to found the Denver-based Committee for 18, is more explicit, saying that the name selection became "an emotional issue." Some of the organizers, mainly younger people, wanted the committee's Jewish identity plainly set forth in its name. "Others," Silverman noted, "said they didn't want to be a member if we did that."

Richard Altman, former executive director of the highly influential—and exclusively pro-Israel—National Political Action Committee, spoke candidly about PAC contributions to the political process: "Money makes the political engine run. To elect a friend, you have to pay for it—and we're not the only ones who know that."[22]

As a matter of fact, AIPAC sometimes drops all pretenses of staying apart from fund-raising. For instance, a pro-Israel political action committee was organized in Virginia in 1983 during a workshop sponsored by AIPAC. In addition, financial help does not stop at United States borders. Jewish Americans living in Israel are solicited for political action in the United States. Newton Frolich, a former Washington lawyer who moved to Israel in 1977, founded the Jerusalem-based Americans in Israel Political Action Committee. Through the committee, Frolich says, Americans in Israel can "keep making their contribution" to the U.S. political process. The contribution comes back, of course, in the form of enormous U.S. grants to Israel—greater than to any other country.

A lobby veteran who is now engaged full-time in fund-raising worries about appearances. AIPAC's former executive director, Morris Amitay, feels that smaller local PACs are best and fears that large, well-publicized, national PACs may create the impression that Jews exercise too much political power. He founded the relatively small Washington Political Action Committee, which dispensed $193,722 in 106 races during the 1999–2000 elections.[23]

Too much or not, Jewish influence in fundraising is widely recognized. Given recent campaign finance reforms, the "middle-sized" contributions of individual donors have become especially valuable. Laws banning "soft money" prevent huge cash donations from corporations and extremely wealthy individuals to political parties. The focus is thus placed on individual donors, who by law may only contribute up to $2,000 directly to a candidate per election cycle, and up to $10,000 to a political action committee. Since PACs may contribute $10,000 per candidate, individuals often contribute the $2,000 limit directly to a candidate, and also the $5,000 limit to one or more PACs supporting the same candidate. In all, an individual donor can effectively contribute up to $57,000 to one candidate per election. Jewish donors are especially sought after. According to the Jewish weekly *Forward*, " . . . in the 1999–2000 election cycle, some twenty of the top fifty individual donors of soft money were Jewish."[24] That kind of generosity is not ignored by politicians.

In August 1983 the *Wall Street Journal* reported that "several ranking Congressmen—most of whom wouldn't comment on the record for this story—say they believe the political effect of Jewish PAC money is greater than that of other major lobbies because it is skillfully focused on one foreign policy issue."

Focused it is. The pro-Israel PACs concentrate exclusively on federal elections and focus heavily on Senate races and on House members who occupy key foreign policy assignments. PAC leader Mark Siegel says that the PACs concentrate on the Senate because it is the "real battleground" on questions of foreign policy. In 1999–2000, PACs invested $1,083,101 in Senate races, with $961,505 going to House contests.[25]

Guided by AIPAC, PACs choose their targets with care. In 1982 when Lynn Adelman, a Jewish state senator in Wisconsin, mounted the first primary election challenge that Democrat Clement J. Zablocki had experienced in thirty years, AIPAC recommended against an all-out effort. AIPAC was unhappy with Zablocki's record, but did not consider him a problem. Furthermore, it concluded that Adelman could not win. Adelman received only $9,350 from thirteen pro-Israel political action committees. The contest made national news, because Zablocki was chairman of the House Committee on Foreign Affairs, through which all Israeli aid measures must go. Despite AIPAC's low-key recommendation, a letter soliciting funds for Adelman cited two "gains" if Zablocki lost: "Adelman's election not only means a friend of Israel in Congress, but also that the House Committee on Foreign Affairs will have a friend of Israel as its new chairman," referring to Dante Fascell of Florida, the Democrat who was next in line to succeed Zablocki. Zablocki was re-elected by a two-to-one margin.

After the 1982 election—a year before he was elected chairman of the Foreign Affairs Committee after the sudden death of Zablocki, Fascell remarked:

> The whole trouble with campaign finances is the hue and cry that you've been bought. If you need the money, are you going to get it from your enemy? No, you're going to get it from your friend.[26]

"Our Own Foreign Policy Agenda"

Much of the American Israel Public Affairs Committee's work in 1982 centered on expanding grassroots support, enlarging outreach programs to the college and Christian communities, and helping pro-Israel political action committees sharpen their skills. These efforts were largely aimed at increasing the lobby's influence in the Senate. AIPAC wanted no repetition of its failure to block the 1981 AWACS sale to Saudi Arabia.

One way in which AIPAC increases the number of its Senate friends is illustrated by its interventions in a critical race in Missouri. AIPAC stood by a friend and won. Republican Senator John C. Danforth, an ordained Episcopal minister, was opposed for re-election by a Jewish Democrat, Harriett Woods. In the closely fought contest, the non-Jewish Danforth found that an unblemished record of cooperation brought him AIPAC support even against a Jewish challenger. The help was crucial, as Danforth won by less than 1 percent of the vote.

AIPAC also weighed in heavily in Maine, helping to pull off the upset victory of Democratic Senator George Mitchell over Republican Congressman David Emery. *The Almanac of American Politics* rated Mitchell "the Democratic Senator universally regarded as having the least chance for re-election." Defeated for governor by an independent candidate in 1974, he was appointed to fill the Senate vacancy caused when Senator Edmund Muskie resigned in 1980 to become President Carter's secretary of state. He had never won an election.

Encouraged by AIPAC, twenty-seven pro-Israel political action committees, all based outside Maine, contributed $77,400 to Mitchell's campaign. With this help, Mitchell fooled the professionals and won handily. In a post-election phone call to AIPAC director Thomas A. Dine, Mitchell promised: "I will remember you."

In another example, Republican Senator David Durenberger of Minnesota received for his 1982 re-election bid $57,000 from twenty pro-Israeli political action committees, with $10,000 of it coming from the Citizens Organized PAC in California. This PAC contributed $5,000 during a breakfast meeting four months after Durenberger voted against the sale of AWACS planes to Saudi Arabia, and added $5,000 more by election day. Directors of the PAC include Alan Rothenberg, the law partner of Democratic National Chairman Charles Manatt.

In close races, lobby interests sometimes play it safe by supporting both sides. In the 1980 Senate race in Idaho, for example, pro-Israeli activists contributed to their stalwart friend, Democrat Frank Church, chairman of the Senate Foreign Relations Committee, but also gave to his challenger, Republican Congressman Steven D. Symms. One reason for the dual support was the expected vote in the Senate the next year on the AWACS sale to Saudi Arabia—during the campaign both Symms and Church were listed as opposing it. With the race expected to be close, the lobby believed it had a friend in each candidate and helped both.

Symms defeated Church by a razor-thin margin, but the investment in Symms by pro-Israeli interests did not pay off. By the time the new senator faced the AWACS vote he had changed his mind. His vote approving the AWACS sale helped to give AIPAC one of its rare legislative setbacks.

In a post-election review in its newsletter, *Near East Report*, AIPAC concluded that the new Senate in the 98th Congress would be "marginally more pro-Israel." As evidence, it noted that two of the five new senators were Jewish: Frank Lautenberg, Democrat of New Jersey, and Chic Hecht, Republican of Nevada, each "with long records of support for Israel." It could also count as a gain the election of Democrat Jeffrey Bingaman of New Mexico, who defeated Republican Senator Harrison Schmitt. Voting for the AWACS sale to Saudi Arabia and opposing foreign aid had given Schmitt bad marks, and AIPAC gave its support to his challenger, Bingaman, in the campaign.

Because favored candidates need more money than PAC sources provide, AIPAC also helps by providing lists for direct mail fundraising. The appeal can be hard-hitting. An example is the literature mailed in early 1984 on behalf of Republican Senator Rudy Boschwitz of Minnesota. Fellow Republican Lowell Weicker wrote the introductory letter, citing him as a "friend of Israel in danger." He noted Boschwitz's key position as chairman of the subcommittee "that determines the level of aid our country gives to Israel," and praised his efforts to block military sales to Saudi Arabia. The appeal included tributes by Senator Bob Packwood and Wolf Blitzer, then the Washington correspondent for the *Jerusalem Post.*

AIPAC has convinced Congress that it represents practically all Jews who vote. Columnist Nat Hentoff reported this assessment in the *Village Voice* in June 1983 after a delegation of eighteen dissenting rabbis had scoured Capitol Hill trying to convince congressmen that some Jews oppose Israeli policies.[27] The rabbis reported that several congressmen said they shared their views but were afraid to act. Hentoff concluded: "The only Jewish constituency that's real to them [congressmen] is the one that AIPAC and other spokesmen for the Jewish establishment tell them about."

An Ohio congressman speaks of AIPAC with both awe and concern:

AIPAC is the most influential lobby on Capitol Hill. They are relentless. They know what they're doing. They have the people for financial resources. They've got a lot going for them. Their basic underlying cause *is* one that most Americans sympathize with.

But what distresses me is the inability of American policy makers, because of the influence of AIPAC, to distinguish between our national interest and Israel's national interest. When these converge—wonderful! But they don't always converge.

After the 1982 elections, Thomas A. Dine summed up the significance of AIPAC's achievements: "Because of that, American Jews are thus able to form our own foreign policy agenda."[28]

Later, when he reviewed the 1984 election results, Dine credited Jewish money, not votes: "Early money, middle money, late money."[29] He claimed credit for defeating Republican Senators Charles Percy of

Illinois and Roger Jepsen of Iowa and Democratic Senator Walter Huddleston of Kentucky, all of whom incurred AIPAC's wrath by voting for the sale of AWACS planes to Saudi Arabia. Dine said these successes "defined Jewish political power for the rest of this century."

Our allies are aware of America's tendency to place lobby interests over the interests of the United States. After AIPAC blocked a $1.6 billion arms sale to Jordan, King Hussein complained, "The United States is not free to move except within the limits of what AIPAC, the Zionists, and the State of Israel determine for it." A Democratic senator conversing with a visiting European diplomat put it bluntly: "All of us here are members of Likud now."[30]

3

Stilling the Still, Small Voices

THE YOUTHFUL congressman from California listened as his House colleagues expressed their views. His earnest manner and distinctive shock of hair roused memories of an earlier congressman, John F. Kennedy. For more than an hour, between comments of his own, Representative Paul N. "Pete" McCloskey yielded the floor to other congressmen, twenty-three in all. While they cooperated by requesting from Speaker Thomas P. "Tip" O'Neill allocations of time for the debate, most of them did so in order to avoid a sticky issue. They were ducking legislative combat, not engaging in it.

Real debate was almost unknown regarding the subject McCloskey had chosen—aid to Israel. Most congressmen, fearing lobby pressure, carefully avoid statements or votes that might be viewed as critical of Israel. Not McCloskey. Admired for his courage and independence, he began opposing the Vietnam war long before most Americans. He withstood the lobbying of Greek Americans to cut off military aid to Turkey, consistently supported controversial civil rights measures, and now challenged conventional wisdom on Middle East policy. He and I were members of

51

a tiny band of congressmen who were willing to criticize Israel publicly, and both of us would soon leave Capitol Hill involuntarily.

On that June afternoon in 1980, most of McCloskey's colleagues provided him debate time—and joined him in the discussion—because they saw this as the only way to keep him from forcing them to vote on an amendment to cut aid to Israel. Some of them privately agreed with McCloskey's position, but they did not want his amendment to come to a vote. If that happened, they would find themselves in the distressing circumstance of reacting to the pressure of Israel's lobby by voting against McCloskey's amendment—and their own consciences.

In offering his amendment, McCloskey called for an end to the building of Israeli settlements in the territory in the West Bank of the Jordan River, which Israel held by force of arms.[1] To put pressure on Israel to stop, he wanted the United States to cut aid by $150 million—the amount he estimated Israel was annually spending on these projects. In the end, tough realities led him to drop his plan to bring the amendment to a vote:

> Friend and foe alike asked me not to press the amendment. Some of my friends argued that if I did get a roll call, the amendment would have been badly defeated. If that happened, they argued, Israel would take heart—saying "Sure, somebody spoke out, but look how we smashed him." Every Jewish congressman on the floor of the House told me privately that I was right.[2]

Representative James Johnson, a Republican from Colorado and one of the few to support McCloskey, was aware of the pressure other congressmen were putting on him.[3] Johnson declared that many of his colleagues privately opposed Israel's expansion of settlements, but said that Congress was "incapable" of taking action contrary to Israeli policy: "I would just like to point out the real reason that this Congress will not deal with the gentleman's amendment is because [it] concerns the nation of Israel."

It was not the first time peer pressure had stopped amendments viewed as anti-Israeli, and McCloskey was not the first to back down to accommodate colleagues. Such pressure develops automatically when amendments restricting aid to Israel are discussed. Many congressmen are embarrassed by the high level of aid—Israel receives one-third of all U.S. foreign aid—and feel uncomfortable being recorded as favoring it.

But, intimidated by Israel's friends, they are even less comfortable being recorded in opposition. How much of the lobby's power is real, and how much is illusion, is beside the point. Because they perceive it as real, few congressmen wish to take a chance. Worrying endlessly about political survival, they say: "Taking on the Israeli lobby is something I can do without. Who needs that?" On several occasions, sensing I was about to force a troublesome vote on aid to Israel, a colleague would whisper to me, "Your position on this is well known. Why put the rest of us on the spot?"

Most committee action, like the work of the full House, is open to the public, and none occurs on Israeli aid without the presence of at least one representative of AIPAC. This ensures that any criticism of Israel will be quickly reported to key constituents. The offending congressman may have a rash of angry telephone messages to answer by the time he returns to his office from the hearing room.

Lobbyists for AIPAC are experts on the personalities and procedures of the House. If Israel is mentioned, even behind closed doors, they quickly get a full report of what transpired. The lobbyists know that a roll call vote on aid to Israel will receive overwhelming support. In fact, administration lobbyists count on this support to carry the day for foreign aid worldwide. Working together, the two groups of lobbyists pursue a common interest by keeping the waters smooth and by frustrating "boat rockers" like McCloskey.

Assaulting the Citadels

For McCloskey, compromise was an unusual experience. Throughout his public career he usually resisted pressures, even when his critics struck harshly.

This was true when he became nationally prominent as a critic of the Vietnam war—an effort that, in 1972, led him to a brief but dramatic campaign for the presidency.[4] His goal was a broad and unfettered discussion of public issues, particularly the war. The wrong decisions, he believed, generally "came about because the view of the minority was not heard or the view of thinking people was quiet."[5] He contended that the Nixon administration was withholding vital information on a variety of issues. He charged it with "preying on people's fear, hate, and anger."[6]

When McCloskey announced his bid for the presidency, his supporters sighed, "Political suicide." His opponents, particularly those in the party's right wing, chortled the very same words. Although the Californian recognized that his challenge might jeopardize his seat in Congress, he nevertheless denounced the continuation of the war: "Like other Americans, I trusted President Nixon when he said he had a plan to end the war."[7] McCloskey agonized over the fact that thousands of U.S. soldiers continued to die, and that U.S. airpower, using horrifying cluster bombs, rained violence on civilians in Vietnam, Laos, and Cambodia.[8]

McCloskey knew of war's effects firsthand.[9] As a marine in Korea, he was wounded while leading his platoon in one of several successful bayonet assaults on entrenched enemy positions. He emerged from the Korean war with a Navy Cross, a Silver Star, and two Purple Hearts. He later explained that this wartime experience gave him "a strong sense of being lucky to be alive."[10] It also toughened him for subsequent assaults on entrenched enemies of a different sort—endeavors that brought no medals for bravery.

For protesting the war, McCloskey was branded "an enemy of the political process," and even accused of communist leanings.[11] "At least fifty right-wing members of the House believe McCloskey to be the new Red menace," wrote one journalist.[12] The allegation was ridiculous, of course, but party stalwarts in California clearly were restive. So much so, according to the *California Journal,* that McCloskey "needed the personal intervention of then Vice President Gerald R. Ford to save him in the 1974 primary."

His maverick ways exacted a price. He was twice denied a place on the Ways and Means Committee.[13] Conservatives on the California delegation rebuffed the liberal Republican's bid for membership, even though he was entitled to the post on the basis of seniority.

By the time of his ill-fated 1980 amendment on aid to Israel, McCloskey had put himself in the midst of the Middle East controversy. After a trip to the Middle East in 1979, he concluded that new Israeli policies were not in America's best interests. He was alarmed over Washington's failure to halt Israel's construction of West Bank settlements—which the administration itself had labeled illegal—and to stop Israel's illegal use of U.S.-supplied weapons. The congressman asked, "Why?"

The answer was not hard to find. The issue, like most relating to the Middle East, was too hot for either Congress or the White House to handle. A call for debate provoked harsh press attacks and angry constituent mail. To McCloskey, the attacks were ironic. He viewed himself as supportive of both Jewish and Israeli interests. As a college student at Stanford University in 1948, he had helped lead a successful campaign to open Phi Delta Theta fraternity for the first time to Jewish students.[14] He reminded a critic, Earl Raab of San Francisco's *Jewish Bulletin,* that he had "voted for all the military and economic assistance we have given to Israel in the past."[15] McCloskey also vigorously defended Israel's right to lobby: "Lobbying is and should be an honorable and important part of the American political process."[16] He described the American Israel Public Affairs Committee as "the most powerful [lobby] in Washington," and insisted that there was "nothing sinister or devious" about it.

Still, McCloskey had raised a provocative question: "Does America's 'Israeli lobby' wield too much influence?"[17] In an article for the *Los Angeles Times* he provided his answer: "Yes, it is an obstacle to real Mideast peace." McCloskey cited the risk of nuclear confrontation in the Middle East and the fundamental differences between the interests of Israel and the United States. He observed that members of the Jewish community demand that Congress support Israel in spite of these differences. This demand, he argued, "coupled with the weakness of Congress in the face of any such force, can prevent the president, in his hour of both crisis and opportunity, from having the flexibility necessary to achieve a lasting Israeli–Palestinian peace."

He pleaded for full discussion:

> If the United States is to work effectively toward peace in the Mideast, the power of this lobby must be recognized and countered in open and fair debate. I had hoped that the American Jewish community had matured to the point where its lobbying efforts could be described and debated without raising the red flag of anti-Semitism. . . . To recognize the power of a lobby is not to criticize the lobby itself.

The article appeared shortly before McCloskey's bid for his party's nomination for the 1982 senatorial race in California. It was an unorthodox opening salvo, to say the least, and most of the reaction was critical. One of the exceptions was an analysis by California's *Redlands Daily Facts*, which called his campaign a "brave but risky business."[18] The newspaper described him as "the candidate for those who want a man with whom they will disagree on some issues, but who has the courage of his intelligent convictions."

On the other hand, Paul Greenberg, in a syndicated article in the *San Francisco Examiner*, wrote that McCloskey had accused the Israeli lobby of "busily subverting the national interest," and he linked him with notorious anti-Semite Gerald L. K. Smith.[19] This time, McCloskey did not need to fight back. A few days later, the same newspaper published an opposing view.[20] Columnist Guy Wright noted that Greenberg had accused McCloskey of McCarthy-era tactics without quoting "a single line from the offensive speech." Wright observed that this was itself a common tactic of McCarthyism. He cited with approval several of McCloskey's recommendations on foreign policy and concluded: "Now I ask you. Are those the ravings of an anti-Semite? Or fair comment on issues too long kept taboo?"

Such supportive voices were few. An article in the *B'nai B'rith Messenger* charged that McCloskey had proposed that all rabbis be required to register as foreign agents, declaring that he had made the proposal in a meeting with the editors of the *Los Angeles Times*.[21] The author assured his readers that the tidbit came from a "very reliable source," and the charge was published nationally. The charge was a complete fabrication, and *Times* editor Tony Day was quick to back up McCloskey's denial.[22]

The *Messenger* published a retraction a month later, but the accusation lingered on.[23] The Washington office of the Israeli lobby was apparently not even aware of the retraction. In an interview about McCloskey two years later, Douglas Bloomfield, legislative director for AIPAC, repeated the accusation as fact.[24] Such false information may have colored his view of McCloskey, whom he described as "bitter" with "an intense sense of hostility" toward Jews:

> I hesitate to use the term that he was anti-Semitic. Being anti-Israeli is a political decision. Being anti-Semitic is something totally different. I think he did not just creep over the boundary.

Despite the *Messenger's* retraction, there was no letup in criticism of McCloskey. The *Messenger* charged McCloskey with denigrating "the Constitutional exercise of petitioning Congress," with "obstreperous performances," and with marching on a "platform of controversy unmindful of the fact that the framework of his platform is dangerously undermined with distortion, inaccuracy, and maybe even malicious mischief."[25] Another Jewish publication published his picture with the caption, "Heir to Goebbels."[26] An article in the *Heritage Southwest Jewish Press* used such descriptive phrases as "No. 1 sonovabitch," "obscene position against the Jews of America," "crummy," and "sleazy" in denouncing him.[27]

Although used to rough and tumble partisanship, McCloskey was shocked by the harshness of the attacks. No rabbis or Jewish publications defended him. One of a small number of individual Jews who spoke up on his behalf was Merwyn Morris, a prominent businessman from Atherton, California. Morris argued that "McCloskey is no more anti-Semitic than I am"—but he still switched his support to McCloskey's opponent in the senatorial election.[28]

Josh Teitelbaum, who had served for a short time on McCloskey's staff and was the son of a Palo Alto rabbi, resigned from McCloskey's staff partly because he disagreed with the congressman's attitude toward Israel. But he also defended his former employer: "McCloskey is not anti-Semitic, but his words may give encouragement to those who are."[29]

McCloskey's views on Israel complicated—to put it mildly—campaign fund-raising.[30] Potential sources of Jewish financial support dried up. One former supporter, Jewish multimillionaire Louis E. Wolfson, wrote: "I now find that I must join with many other Americans to do everything possible to defeat your bid for the U.S. Senate and make certain that you will not hold any future office."[31]

Early in the race, when McCloskey was competing mainly with Senator S. I. Hayakawa for the nomination, he felt he had a chance. Both were from the northern part of the state, where McCloskey had his greatest strength. After Hayakawa dropped out and Pete Wilson, the popular mayor of San Diego, entered the contest, McCloskey's prospects decreased.

When the primary election votes were counted, McCloskey had won the North but lost the populous South. He finished 10 percentage points behind Wilson. Still, his showing surprised the experts. Polls and forecasters had listed him third or fourth among the four contenders right up to the last days. Congressman Barry Goldwater, Jr., the early favorite, emerged a poor third, and Robert Dornan, another congressional colleague, finished fourth.

The final tally on election day was close enough to cause a number of people to conclude that without the Jewish controversy McCloskey might have won. All three of McCloskey's opponents received Jewish financial support. Stephen S. Rosenfeld, deputy editorial page editor of the *Washington Post*, drew a definite conclusion: "Jewish political participation" had defeated McCloskey.

The lobby attack did not end when the polls closed, nor did McCloskey shun controversy. On September 22, 1982, a few days after the massacre of almost two thousand Palestinians in the Sabra and Shatila refugee camps near Beirut, McCloskey denounced a proposed new $50 million grant for Israel in a speech on the House floor.[32] He warned that the action "might be taken as a signal of our support for what Israel did last Thursday in entering West Beirut and creating the circumstances which led directly to the massacre." Despite his protest, the aid was approved.

In the closing hours of the Ninety-seventh Congress, after fifteen years as a member of "this treasured institution," McCloskey invoked George Washington's Farewell Address in his own farewell, citing the first president's warning that "a passionate attachment of one nation for another produces a variety of evils."[33] McCloskey found this advice "eminently sound" and said that Congress, in action completed the day before, had demonstrated a "passionate attachment" to Israel by voting more aid per capita to that country "than we allow to many of the poor and unemployed in our own country," despite evidence that "Israel is no longer behaving like a friend of the United States."

McCloskey's Academic Freedom

With his political career interrupted, if not ended, McCloskey planned to return to a partnership in the Palo Alto law firm he had helped to establish with John Wilson, a fellow graduate of Yale Law School, years before. "Many of my old clients are still clients," he said, "and I wanted to go back to them. I never thought of going anywhere else."[34]

But others had different thoughts about McCloskey's future. Ken Oshman, president of the Rolm Corporation, the firm's biggest client, warned that his company "might take their law business elsewhere" if McCloskey were to rejoin the firm.[35] The senior partners invited McCloskey to lunch. They told him that the episode would not cause them to withdraw their invitation, but that they wanted McCloskey to be "aware of the problem." McCloskey's response: "I don't want to come back and put you under that burden." In a letter to Oshman, McCloskey expressed his dismay. In reply, the industrialist said his company really wouldn't have taken its business elsewhere, but he reiterated his disagreement with McCloskey's views on Israel.

McCloskey accepted a partnership with the San Francisco law firm of Brobeck, Phleger & Harrison, but the pressures followed him there.[36] The firm received a telephone call from a man in Berkeley, California, who identified himself only as a major shareholder in the Wells Fargo bank, one of the law firm's major clients. He said that he intended to go to the next meeting of the shareholders and demand that the bank transfer its law business to another firm. The reason: the San Francisco firm was adding to its partnership a "known anti-Semite" who supported the Palestine Liberation Organization and its chairman, Yasser Arafat. McCloskey's partners ignored the threat, and the bank did not withdraw its business.

A tracking system initiated by the Anti-Defamation League of B'nai B'rith (ADL) assured that McCloskey would have no peace, even as a private citizen. The group distributed a memorandum containing details of his actions and speeches to its chapters around the country.[37] According to the memo, it was designed to "assist" local ADL groups with "counteraction guidance" whenever McCloskey appeared in public.

Trouble dogged him even on the campus. McCloskey accepted an invitation from the student governing council of Stanford University to teach a course on Congress at Stanford.[38] Howard Goldberg—a council member and also director of the Hillel Center, the campus Jewish club—told the group that inviting McCloskey was "a slap in the face of the Jewish community."[39] Student leader Seth Linfield held up preparation of class materials, then demanded the right to choose the guest lecturers.[40] McCloskey refused, asserting that the young director had earlier assured him he could choose these speakers himself.

Difficulties mounted as the semester went on. Guest speakers were not paid on time. McCloskey felt obliged to pay such expenses personally, then to seek reimbursement. His own remuneration was scaled downward as the controversy developed.[41] Instead of the $3,500 stipend originally promised, Linfield later reduced the amount to $2,000, and even that amount was in doubt. According to a report in the *San Jose Mercury News*, the $2,000 would be paid only if Linfield was satisfied with McCloskey's performance.[42] One student, Jeffrey Au, complained to school authorities that the controversy impaired academic quality.[43] Responding, Professor Hubert Marshall wrote that he viewed the student activities as "unprecedented and a violation of Mr. McCloskey's academic freedom."[44]

When the situation was finally resolved—by means of an apology from Provost Albert H. Hastorf—McCloskey told the *Peninsula Times Tribune*, "Stanford doesn't owe me an apology." He said his satisfaction came when all but one of the fifty students rated his class "in the high range of excellence," but he warned that other schools might face trouble. He noted that the American Israel Public Affairs Committee "has instructed college students all over the country to take [similar] actions."

McCloskey Goes to Court

AIPAC's endeavors did not stop McCloskey from seeking out justice in issues related to the Middle East. In 1993, the district attorney of San Francisco released 700 pages of documents implicating the Anti-Defamation League of B'nai B'rith, a major Jewish organization that calls itself "a defender of civil rights," in a vast spying operation. The targets of the ADL operation were American citizens who were opposed to Israel's repression of Palestinians and to the South African government's policy of apartheid. The ADL was also accused of passing on information to both governments. After experiencing "great political pressure," the district attorney dropped the charges, prompting victims to file a suit against the ADL for violation of their privacy rights. They chose Pete McCloskey as their attorney.

McCloskey and his clients, two of whom were Jews who had been subjected to spying after criticizing Israeli policy in the occupied territories, revealed an extensive operation headed by ADL undercover operative Roy Bullock, whose files contained the names of 10,000 individuals and 600 organizations, including thousands of Arab Americans and national civil rights groups such as the NAACP. Much of Bullock's information was gained illegally from confidential police records. In April 2002, after a nine-year legal battle, McCloskey won a landmark $150,000 court judgment against the ADL. His clients issued the following statement:

> Many questions must still be answered about the activities of the ADL and its nonprofit status as an "education organization." The settlement offered by the ADL is recognition on its part that it could not afford to go to a trial in front of a jury and face the likelihood that more of its dirty secrets would be revealed.

"It Didn't Cripple Us. . . ." But—

While McCloskey, a leader in the white Republican establishment, battled for universal human rights and against further U.S. involvement in the Vietnam War, a black Baptist preacher from the District of Columbia, known nationally as a street activist, pursued the same goals within Democratic ranks.

Good friends, both were members of the House of Representatives, and both undertook controversial journeys to Lebanon in behalf of peace. Both paid a price for their activism, but the preacher survived politically, while the ex-marine did not. Their work for justice in the Middle East—not their record of activism for civil rights at home or opposition to the Vietnam War—caused trouble for both of them.

In large measure, Reverend Walter Fauntroy's problems began over another black leader's endeavors for justice in the Middle East. Andrew Young resigned under fire as the U.S. ambassador to the United Nations in August 1979, after it was revealed that he had met with the PLO's UN observer, Zuhdi Labib Terzi. Many blacks were outraged by the resignation, blaming it on Israeli pressure and, like Young, found unreasonable the policy that prohibited our officials from talking even informally with PLO officials.[45]

Relations between American blacks and Jews—longtime allies in the civil rights movement—had already been strained by disagreements over affirmative action programs intended to give blacks employment quotas, and by Israel's close relations with the apartheid regime in South Africa. The resignation of Young, the most prominent black in the Carter administration, intensified the strain. "This is the most tense moment in black and Jewish relations in my memory," said the Reverend Jesse Jackson shortly after Young's resignation.

During the civil rights movement of the 1960s, Fauntroy, one of the blacks most disturbed by the resignation, had worked with Young in the Southern Christian Leadership Conference (SCLC) under Reverend Martin Luther King, Jr. They had acquired the nickname "The Brooks Brothers" because of their habit of wearing suits and neckties at civil rights marches, while most of the other participants were dressed more casually.

To show support for Young and disagreement with U.S. policy, Fauntroy and SCLC President Joseph Lowery traveled to New York in the fall of 1979 to meet with Terzi.[46] Fauntroy said he hoped to help establish communication between Arabs and Israelis and to promote a nonviolent solution to Middle East problems, adding, "Neither Andy Young nor I, nor other members of the SCLC, apologize for searching for the relevance of Martin Luther King, Jr.'s policies in the international political arena."[47]

While Terzi said he was "happy and gratified" at the meeting with the black leaders and that he hoped "much more will be learned by the American people," prominent members of Washington's Jewish community were upset.[48]

"I don't think a responsible congressman should have any truck with terrorists," complained Rabbi Stanley Rabinowitz.[49] Although many American Jews echoed this sentiment, a few stood by Fauntroy. Prominent businessman Joseph B. Danzansky said Fauntroy "has a right to do what he thinks his position entitles him to do."[50] Danzansky, a friend and political ally of Fauntroy, added, "I'd be very shocked if there were any trace of anti-Jewish feeling. I have confidence in him as a human being."

In an attempt to calm the critics and demonstrate their "fairness," Fauntroy, Lowery, and other SCLC leaders met with U.S. Jewish leaders and with Israel's UN ambassador, Yehuda Blum.[51] Afterward, Fauntroy told reporters that the black leaders were "asking both parties [in the Middle East dispute] to recognize each other's human rights and the right of self-determination." But pro-Israel interests saw the outcome differently. Howard Squadron, president of the American Jewish Committee, emerged from the meeting to say that SCLC's contact with Terzi was "a grave error, lending legitimacy to an organization committed to terrorism and violence."[52]

Against this tense background, black leaders from across the United States convened in New York to express their concern over Young's resignation and to affirm their right to speak out on matters of foreign policy.

Some said they were making "a declaration of independence" in matters of foreign policy.[53] Said Fauntroy:

> In every war since the founding of this nation, black citizens have borne arms and died for their country. Their blood was spilled from Bunker Hill to Vietnam. It is to be expected that should the United States become drawn into war in the Middle East, black Americans once more will be called upon to sacrifice their lives.[54]

His words were prophetic of the sacrifices blacks were soon to make in Lebanon. While blacks constitute only 10 percent of the total U.S. population, 20 percent of the marines killed in the terrorist truck bombing in Beirut—47 of 246—were black.

Fauntroy's views led to a loss of financial support from Jewish donors. "It didn't cripple us," says Fauntroy, "it just made us more resourceful and more sensitive to our need to put principle above politics on questions that bear on nonviolence and the quest for justice."[55] It hurt fund-raising for his personal campaign: "No question about that. Some of my former close supporters flatly stated to me that they were not going to contribute to my candidacy because I had taken the position that I did."

He demonstrated his persistence three weeks later when he joined Lowery on a controversial trip to the Middle East. As they departed, Lowery declared their determination to "preach the moral principles of peace, nonviolence, and human rights."[56]

In a meeting with Yasser Arafat, they appealed for an end to violence, asking the PLO leader to agree to a six-month moratorium on violence. Arafat promised to present the proposal to the PLO's executive council. Fauntroy recalls the dramatic moment, "We asked Dr. Harry Gibson of the United Methodist Church to pray. Then a Roman Catholic priest said a prayer in Arabic. We wept. At the end of the prayer, someone—I don't know who—started singing 'We Shall Overcome,' and Arafat immediately crossed his arms and linked hands."[57]

Some American Jews feared the emotional meeting symbolized a new "black alliance" with the PLO and a betrayal of their own support of civil rights for blacks. They rejected the black leaders' insistence that they were impartial advocates of peace.

At a news conference at his New Bethel Baptist Church, Fauntroy described his mission for peace and said he would persist: "I am first and foremost a minister of the gospel, called to preach every day that God is our father and all men are our brothers, right here from this pulpit."[58] He added: "I could not be true to my highest calling if, when an opportunity to do so arose, I refused." He challenged his critics: "So let anyone who wishes run against me. Let anyone who wishes withdraw his support. It doesn't matter to me."

Reflecting on the problems created by his quest for self-determination of people in the Middle East, as well as in the District of Columbia, Fauntroy calls it "a growing experience." He continued to grow through the 1980s as a leading civil rights activist. His act of civil disobedience on behalf of the black people of South Africa—he refused to leave the office of the ambassador of South Africa until nine South African labor leaders were released, and was escorted out in handcuffs—focused national attention on the issue. His endeavors helped prompt Congress to impose economic sanctions against South Africa, a step that would eventually lead to the freeing of Nelson Mandela and the end of the apartheid regime.

"Three Calls Within Thirteen Minutes"

Only a few members of the House of Representatives have criticized Israeli policy in recent years, reflecting mainly the vigilance and skill of Israel's U.S. lobby. It reacts swiftly to any sign of discontent with Israel, especially by those assigned to the House Foreign Affairs Committee.

A young man working in 1981 in the office of the late Democratic Congressman Benjamin S. Rosenthal of New York, who was then the leader of the House's "Jewish caucus," witnessed firsthand the efficiency of this monitoring. Michael Neiditch, a staff consultant, was with Rosenthal in his office one morning when, just before 9:00, the phone rang.[59] Morris Amitay, then executive director of AIPAC, had just read the Evans and Novak syndicated column that morning in the *Washington Post*, and he didn't like what he read.[60] The journalists reported that Rosenthal had recently told a group of Israeli visitors: "The Israeli occupation of the West Bank is like someone carrying a heavy pack on his back—the longer he carries it, the more he stoops over, but the less he is aware of the burden." Rosenthal had personally related the incident to Robert Novak. Although he used the descriptive image "ever so gently," according to Neiditch, it caused a stir.

Amitay chided Rosenthal for speaking "out of turn." About five minutes later, Ephraim "Eppie" Evron, the Israeli ambassador to the United States, called with the same message. Then, just a few minutes later, Yehuda Hellman of the Conference of Presidents of Major Jewish Organizations called. Again, the same message. Neiditch remembers that Rosenthal looked over and observed, "Young man, you've just seen the Jewish lobby's muscles flex." Neiditch recalls: "It was three calls within thirteen minutes."

Another senior committee member, an Ohio congressman who was more independent of Israel's interests than Rosenthal, nevertheless found his activities closely watched. Republican Charles Whalen felt the pressure of the lobby when he accepted a last-minute invitation to attend a February 1973 conference in London on the Middle East.[61] It was held under the auspices of the Ford Foundation. No Israeli representative was present, but to his surprise, on his return to Washington, Whalen was called on by an Israeli lobby official who demanded all of the meeting's details—the agenda, those present, why Whalen went, and why Ford had sponsored it.

Whalen recalled, "It was just amazing. They never let up." Whalen believed it was the last such conference Ford sponsored. "They got to Ford," Whalen speculated, adding that the experience was a turning point in his own attitude toward the lobby: "If I couldn't go to a conference to further my education, I began to wonder, 'What's this all about?'"

A Minnesota Democrat had reason for similar wonderment after he left Congress. Richard Nolan, a businessman in Minneapolis, discovered the reluctance of his former colleagues to identify themselves with a scholarly article on the Middle East.[62] He individually approached fifteen congressmen, asking each to insert in the *Congressional Record* an article that discussed the potential for the development of profitable U.S. trade with Arab states. Written by Ghanim Al-Mazrui, an official of the United Arab Emirates, it proposed broadened dialogue and rejec-tion of malicious stereotypes. Under House rules, when such items are entered in the *Record,* the name of the sponsoring member must be shown. Nolan reports, "Each of the fifteen said it was a terrific article that should be published but added, 'Please understand, putting it in under my name would simply cause too much trouble.' I didn't encounter a single one who questioned the excellence of the article, and what made it especially sad was that I picked out the fifteen people I thought most likely to cooperate." The sixteenth congressman he approached, Democrat David E. Bonior of Michigan, agreed to Nolan's request. The article appeared on page E 4791 of the October 5, 1983, *Record.* It was one of those unusual occasions when the *Congressional Record* contained a statement that might be viewed as critical of poli-cies or positions taken by Israel or, as in this case, promoting dialogue with the Arabs.

It was one of several brave steps by Bonior that made him a future target of Israel's lobby. Speaking before the Association of Arab Ameri-can University Graduates in Flint, Michigan, two months before the 1984 election, Bonior called for conditions on aid to Israel, declaring that the United States has been "rewarding the current government of Israel for undertaking policies that are contrary to our own," including Israel's disruption of "U.S. relations with long-standing allies such as Jor-dan and Saudi Arabia."

"An Incredible Burst of Candor"

Even those high in House leadership who represent politically safe districts are not immune from lobby intimidation. They encounter lobby pressure back home, and sometimes they vote against their own conscience.

In October 1981 President Reagan's controversial proposal to sell AWACS (intelligence-gathering airplanes) and modifying equipment for F-15 fighter aircraft to Saudi Arabia was under consideration in the House. Congressman Daniel Rostenkowski, chairman of the Ways and

Means Committee and one of the most influential legislators on Capitol Hill, got caught in the Israeli lobby's counterattack. It was the first test of strength between the lobby and the newly installed president. Under the law, the sale would go through unless both the House and the Senate rejected it. The lobby strategy was to have the initial test vote occur in the House, where its strength was greater. A rejection by the House, it was believed, might cause the Senate to follow suit.

Under heavy pressure from the lobby, Rostenkowski cooperated by voting no. Afterward, he told a reporter for Chicago radio station WMAQ that he actually favored the sale but voted as he did because he feared the "Jewish lobby."[63] He contended that the House majority against the sale was so overwhelming that his own favorable vote "would not have mattered." Overwhelming it was, 301 to 111. Still, the Israeli lobby's goal was to ensure the highest possible number of negative votes in order to influence the Senate vote. To the lobby, Rostenkowski's vote did matter very much.

Columnist Carl Rowan called Rostenkowski's admission "an incredible burst of candor."[64] While declaring "it is as American as apple pie for monied interests to use their dough to influence decisions" in Washington, Rowan added, "There are a lot of American Jews with lots of money who learned long ago that they can achieve influence far beyond their numbers by making strategic donations to candidates. . . . No Arab population here plays such a powerful role." Rostenkowski, however, was not a major recipient of contributions from pro-Israeli political action committees. In the following year, his campaign received only $1,000 from such groups.[65]

While the lobby is watchful over the full membership of the House, particularly leaders like Rostenkowski, it gives special emphasis to the members of the Foreign Affairs Committee, where the initial decisions are made on aid, both military and economic.

Allegiance to Israeli interests sometimes creates mystifying voting habits. Members who are "doves" on policy elsewhere in the world are unabashed "hawks" where Israel is concerned. As Stephen S. Rosenfeld of the *Washington Post* wrote in May 1983:

A Martian looking at the way Congress treats the administration's aid requests for Israel and El Salvador might conclude that our political system makes potentially life-or-death decisions about dependent countries in truly inscrutable ways.[66]

Rosenfeld was intrigued by the extraordinary performance of the Foreign Affairs Committee on one particular day, May 11, 1983. Scarcely taking time to catch its breath between acts, the panel required the vulnerable government of El Salvador to "jump a series of extremely high political hurdles" in order to get funding "barely adequate to keep its nose above water," while, a moment later, handed to Israel, which was clearly the dominant military power in the Middle East, "a third of a billion dollars more than the several billion dollars that the administration asked for it." One of Israel's leading partisans, Congressman Stephen J. Solarz, spoke with enthusiasm for the El Salvador "hurdles" and for the massive increase to Israel.

Outdoing the United Jewish Appeal

Stephen J. Solarz, a hardworking congressman who for eighteen years represented a heavily Jewish district in Brooklyn, prides himself on accomplishing many good things for Israel. Since his first election in 1974, Solarz established a reputation as an intelligent "eager beaver," widely traveled, aggressive, and totally committed to Israel's interests. In committee, he seemed always bursting with the next question before the witness could respond to his first.

In a December 1980 newsletter to his constituents, he provided an unprecedented insight into how Israel—despite the budgetary restraints under which the U.S. government labors—is able to get ever-increasing aid. Early that year he started his own quest for increased aid. He reported that he persuaded Secretary of State Cyrus Vance to come to his Capitol Hill office to talk it over. There he threatened Vance with a fight for the increase on the House floor if the administration opposed it in committee. Shortly thereafter, he said, Vance sent word that the administration would recommend an increase—$200 million extra in military aid—although it was not as much as Solarz desired.

His next goal was to convince the Foreign Affairs Committee to increase the administration's levels. Solarz felt an increase approved by the committee could be maintained on the House floor. The first step was a private talk with Lee H. Hamilton, chairman of the subcommittee on Europe and the Middle East, the panel that would first deal with the request. Tall, thoughtful, scholarly and cautious, Hamilton prided himself on staying on the same "wavelength" as the majority—whether in committee or on the floor. Never abrasive, he usually worked out differences ahead of time and avoided open wrangles. Representing a rural Indiana district with no significant Jewish population, he was troubled by Israel's military adventures but rarely voiced criticism in public. He guarded his role as a conciliator.

Solarz found Hamilton amenable: "He agreed to support our proposal to increase the amount of [military assistance] . . . by another $200 million." That would bring the total increase to $400 million. Even more important, Hamilton agreed to support a move to relieve Israel of its obligation to repay any of the $785 million it would receive in economic aid. The administration wanted Israel to pay back one-third of the amount.

"As we anticipated," Solarz reported, "with the support of Congressman Hamilton, our proposal sailed through both his subcommittee and the full committee and was never challenged on the floor when the foreign aid bill came up for consideration." Democrat Frank Church of Idaho, the chairman of the Senate Foreign Relations Committee, and Jacob Javits, senior Republican—both strongly pro-Israeli—guided proposals at the same level smoothly through their chamber.

Solarz summed it up: "Israel, as a result, will soon be receiving a grand total of $660 million more in military and economic aid than it received from the U.S. government last year." He reflected upon the magnitude of the achievement:

> Through a combination of persistence and persuasion, we were able to provide Israel with an increase in military–economic aid in one year alone which is the equivalent of almost three years of contributions by the national UJA [United Jewish Appeal].

In his newsletter Solarz said that he sought membership on the Foreign Affairs Committee "because I wanted to be in a position to be helpful to Israel." He explained that, while "most members of Congress, Republicans as well as Democrats" support Israel, "it is the members of the Foreign Affairs Committee in the House, and the Foreign Relations

Committee in the Senate, who are really in a position to make a difference where it counts—in the area of foreign aid, upon which Israel is now so dependent."

Solarz's zeal was unabated in September 1984 when, as a member of the House–Senate conference on Export Administration Act amendments, he demanded in a public meeting to know the legislation's implications for Israel.[67] He asked Congressman Howard Wolpe, "Is there anything that the Israelis want from us, or could conceivably want from us that they weren't able to get?"[68] Wolpe responded with a clear "no." Solarz pressed, "Have you spoken to the [Israeli] embassy?" Wolpe responded, "I personally have not," but he admitted, "my office has." Solarz tried again. "You are giving me an absolute assurance that they [the Israelis] have no reservation at all about this?" Finally convinced that Israel was content with the legislation, Solarz relaxed. "If they have no problem with it, then there is no reason for us to."

A veteran Ohio congressman observed:

> When Solarz and others press for more money for Israel, nobody wants to say "No." You don't need many examples of intimidation for politicians to realize what the potential is. The Jewish lobby is terrific. Anything it wants, it gets. Jews are educated, often have a lot of money, and vote on the basis of a single issue—Israel. They are unique in that respect. For example, antiabortion supporters are numerous but not that well educated, and don't have that much money. The Jewish lobbyists have it all, and they are political activists on top of it.[69]

He divided his colleagues into four groups:

> For the first group, it's rah, rah, give Israel anything it wants. The second group includes those with some misgivings, but they don't dare step out of line; they don't say anything. In the third group are congressmen who have deep misgivings but who won't do more than try quietly to slow down the aid to Israel. Lee Hamilton is an example. The fourth group consists of those who openly question U.S. policy in the Middle East and challenge what Israel is doing. Since Findley and McCloskey left, this group really doesn't exist anymore.

He put himself in the third group: "I may vote against the bill authorizing foreign aid this year for the first time. If I do, I will not state my reason."

Solarz never wavered in his commitment to Israel. A 1992 taped conversation with former AIPAC president David Steiner revealed that the organization was involved in "negotiations" with newly elected President Bill Clinton over who would become the new secretary of state— Solarz was AIPAC's leading preference.

Another congressman, although bringing much the same level of commitment when he first joined the committee, later underwent a change.[70]

"Bleeding a Little Inside"

Democratic Congressman Mervyn M. Dymally, former lieutenant governor of California, came to Washington in 1980 with perfect credentials as a supporter of Israel. He said, "When you look at black America, I rank myself second only to Bayard Rustin in supporting Israel over the past twenty years."[71] Short, handsome, and articulate, Dymally was the first black American to go to Israel after both the 1967 and 1973 wars.

In his successful campaign for lieutenant governor, he spoke up for Israel in all the statewide Democratic canvasses. He cofounded the Black Americans in Support of Israel Committee, organized pro-Israeli advertising in California newspapers, and helped to rally other black officials to the cause. In Congress, he became a dependable vote for Israeli interests as a member of the Foreign Affairs Committee.

Nevertheless, in 1982 the pro-Israeli community withdrew its financial support of Dymally. The following year, the AIPAC organization in California marked him for defeat, and began seeking a credible opponent to run against him in 1984. Explaining this sudden turn of events, Dymally cited two "black marks" against his pro-Israeli record in Congress. First, he "occasionally asked challenging questions about aid to Israel in committee"; although his questions were mild and not frequent, he stood out because no one else was even that daring. Second—far more damning in the eyes of AIPAC—he met twice with PLO leader Yasser Arafat. Both meetings were unplanned. The first encounter took place in 1981 during a visit to Abu Dhabi, where Dymally stopped to meet the local minister of planning while on his way back from a foreign policy conference in southern India.[72] The minister told him he had just met with Arafat and asked Dymally if he would like to see him. Dymally recalled, "I was too chicken to say 'no,' but I thought I was safe in doing it. I figured Arafat would not bother to see an obscure fresh-man congressman, especially on such short notice."

To his surprise, Arafat invited him for an immediate appointment. This caused near panic on the part of Dymally's escort, an employee of the U.S. embassy, who was taking Dymally on his round of appoint-ments in the ambassador's car, a vehicle bedecked with a U.S. flag on the front fender. Sensitive to the U.S. ban on contact between administra-tion personnel and PLO officials, the flustered escort removed the flag, excused himself, and then directed the driver to deliver Dymally to the Arafat appointment. "He was really in a sweat," Dymally recalled.

After a brief session with Arafat, he found a reporter for the Arab News Service waiting outside. Dymally told him Arafat expressed his desire for a dialogue with the United States. That night Peter Jennings reported from London to a nationwide American audience over ABC's evening news program that Dymally had become the first congressman to meet Arafat since Ronald Reagan was elected president. The news caused an uproar in the Jewish community, with many Jews doubting Dymally's statement that the meeting was unplanned. Stella Epstein, a Jewish member of Dymally's congressional staff, quit in protest.

Dymally met the controversial PLO leader again in 1982 in a simi-larly coincidental way.[73] He had gone to Lebanon with his colleagues, Democrats Mary Rose Oakar of Ohio, Nick Rahall of West Virginia, and David E. Bonior of Michigan, and Republican Pete McCloskey to meet with Lebanese leaders, visit refugee camps, and view the effects of the Israeli invasion. Dymally was shocked by what he saw. "There's no way you can visit those [Palestinian] refugee camps without bleeding a little inside," he said. After the group's arrival they accepted an invitation to meet with Arafat, who was then under siege in Beirut.

Dymally's trouble with the Jewish community grew even worse. Dymally was wrongly accused of voting in 1981 for the sale of AWACS to Saudi Arabia. He actually voted the way the Israeli lobby wanted him to vote, against the sale. Moreover, to make his position explicit, during the House debate he stated his opposition in two separate speeches.[74] He made the second speech, which was written for him by one of his sup-porters, Max Mont of the Jewish Labor Committee, "because Mont complained that the first was not strong enough," Dymally explained.

Still, the message either did not get through or was conveniently for-gotten. Carmen Warshaw, long prominent in Jewish affairs and Democratic Party politics in California—and a financial supporter of his campaigns—accosted Dymally at a public dinner and said, "I want my money back."[75] Dymally responded, "What did I do, Carmen?" She answered, "You voted for AWACS."

Dymally found membership on the Foreign Affairs subcommittee on the Middle East a "no win" situation. He has alienated people on both sides. While one staff member quit in protest when he met Arafat, another, Peg McCormick, quit in protest when he voted for a large aid package that included money to build warplanes in Israel.[76]

For a time, Dymally stopped complaining and raising questions about Israel in committee. Asked why by the *Wall Street Journal*, he cited the lobby's role in my own loss in 1982 to Democrat Richard J. Durbin. He told the *Journal* reporter, "There is no question the Findley–Durbin race was intimidating."[77] Dymally found intimidation elsewhere as well. Whenever he complained, he said, he received a prompt visit from an AIPAC lobbyist, who was usually accompanied by a Dymally constituent.[78] He met one day with a group of Jewish constituents, "all of them old friends," and told them that, despite his grumbling, in the end he always voted for aid to Israel. He said: "Not once, I told them, have I ever strayed from the course." One of his constituents spoke up and said, "That's not quite right. Once you abstained." "They are that good," marveled Dymally. "The man was right."

Fourteen Freshmen Save the Day

Under the watchful eye of Israel's lobby, congressmen will go to extreme measures to help move legislation to provide aid to Israel. Just before Congress adjourned in December 1983, a group of freshmen Democrats helped the cause by taking the extraordinary step of changing their votes in the printed record of proceedings, a step congressmen usually shun because it makes them look indecisive. This day, however, under heavy pressure from pro-Israel constituents, the first-term members buckled and agreed to switch in order to pass a piece of catchall legislation known as a Continuing Resolution. The resolution provided funds for programs that Congress had failed to authorize in the normal fashion, among them aid to Israel. Passage would prevent any interruption in this aid.[79]

For once, both the House Democratic leadership and AIPAC were caught napping. Usually in complete control of all legislative activities that relate to Israel, AIPAC failed to detect the brewing rebellion. Concern over the budget deficit and controversial provisions in the bill for Central America led these freshman Democrats to oppose their own leadership. Unable to offer amendments, they quietly agreed among themselves to oppose the whole package.

When the roll was called, the big electric board over the Speaker's desk showed defeat—the resolution was rejected, 206–203.[80] Twenty-four first-term Democrats had deserted the leadership and voted no. Voting no did not mean they opposed Israeli aid. Some of them, concerned over the federal deficit, viewed their vote as a demand to the leadership to schedule a bill raising taxes. For others, it was simply a protest. But for Israel it was serious.

"The Jewish community went crazy," a Capitol Hill veteran recalls. AIPAC's professionals went to work.[81] Placing calls from their offices just four blocks away, they activated key people in the districts of a selected list of the errant freshmen. They arranged for "quality calls" to individuals who had played a major role in the recent congressional election. Each person activated was to place an urgent call to his or her congressman, insist on getting through personally, and use this message:

> Approval of the Continuing Resolution is very important. Without it, Israel will suffer. I am not criticizing your vote against it the first time. I am sure you had reasons. However, I have learned that the same question will come up for vote again, probably tomorrow. I speak for many of your friends and supporters in asking that you change your vote when the question comes up again.

Each person was instructed to report to AIPAC after making the calls. The calls were accordingly made and reported. The House of Representatives took up the question at noon the next day. It was the same language, word for word, that the House had rejected two days before. Silvio Conte, senior Republican on the Appropriations Committee, knowing the pressure that had been applied, challenged the freshmen Democrats to "stick to their guns" as "men of courage."[82] Republican leader Bob Michel chided those unable to "take the heat from on high."[83]

Some of the heat came, of course, from the embarrassed Democratic leadership, but AIPAC was the institution that brought about changes in votes. On critical issues, congressmen responded to pressures from home, and, in such circumstances, House leaders had little leverage. To Republicans Conte and Michel, the main issue was the need for budgetary restraint.[84] They argued that the measure should be rejected for that reason. During the debate, no one mentioned that day—or any other day—the influence of the Israeli lobby.

The urgent telephone messages from home carried the day. When the roll was called, fourteen of the freshmen—a bit sheepishly—changed their votes.[85] They were: C. Robin Britt (NC), Jim Cooper (TN), Richard J. Durbin (IL), Edward J. Feighan (OH), Sander M. Levin (MI), Frank McCloskey (IN), Bruce A. Morrison (CT), James R. "Jim" Olin (VA), Timothy J. Penny (MN), Harry M. Reid (NV), Bill Richardson (NM), Norman Sisisky (VA), John M. Spratt, Jr. (SC), and Harley O. Staggers, Jr. (WV).

To give the freshmen an excuse they could use in explaining their embarrassing shift, the leadership promised to bring up a tax bill. Everyone knew it was just a ploy—the tax bill had no chance to become law. But the excuse was helpful, and the resolution was approved 224–189.[86] The flow of aid to Israel continued without interruption.

Subsidizing Foreign Competition

The final vote on the 1983 Continuing Resolution authorized a remarkable new form of aid to Israel. It included an amendment, crafted by AIPAC and sponsored by ardently pro-Israeli Congressmen Clarence Long of Maryland and Jack Kemp of New York, that permitted $250 million of the military grant aid to be spent in Israel on the development of a new Israeli fighter aircraft, the Lavi. The new fighter would compete for international sales with the Northrop F-20 and the General Dynamics R16—both specifically designed for export. The amendment authorized privileged treatment never before extended to a foreign competitor. It was extraordinary for another reason: it set aside a U.S. law that requires all foreign aid procurement funds to be spent in the United States.

During debate of the bill, Democrat Nick J. Rahall of West Virginia, was the only congressman who objected.[87] He saw the provision as threatening U.S. jobs at a time of high unemployment:

> Approximately 6,000 jobs would be lost as a direct result of taking the $250 million out of the U.S. economy and allowing Israel to spend it on defense articles and services which can just as easily be purchased here in the United

States. Americans are being stripped of their tax dollars to build up foreign industry. They should not have to sacrifice their jobs as well.

That day, Rahall was unable to offer an amendment to strike or change this provision because of restrictions the House had established before it began debate. All that he, or any other member, could do was to vote for or against the entire Long–Kemp amendment, which included controversial provisions for El Salvador and international banks, as well as aid to Israel. The amendment was approved 262–150. Unlike Rahall's, most of the 150 negative votes reflected opposition to other features of the amendment, not to the $250 million subsidy to Israel's aircraft industry.

The following May, during the consideration of the bill appropriating funds for foreign aid, Rahall offered an amendment to eliminate the $250 million, but it was defeated 379–40. Despite the amendment's obvious appeal to constituents connected with the U.S. aircraft industry, fewer than 10 percent of House members voted for it. It was the first roll call vote on an amendment dealing exclusively with aid to Israel in more than four years, and the margin of defeat provided a measure of AIPAC's power.

After the vote, AIPAC organized protests against the forty legislators who had supported the amendment. Rahall recalls that AIPAC carried out a campaign "berating those brave forty congressmen."[88] He adds, "Almost all of those who voted with me have told me they are still catching hell from their Jewish constituency. They are still moaning about the beating they are taking."

The "brave" congressmen got little thanks.[89] Two ethnic groups, the American-Arab Anti-Discrimination Committee and the National Association of Arab Americans, congratulated Rahall on his initiative and urged their members to send letters of congratulation to each of the congressmen who supported his amendment. The results were meager. As the author, Rahall could expect to receive more supportive mail than the rest. He received "less than ten letters" and speculates that the other thirty-nine got even fewer.[90]

"Don't Look to Congress to Act"

The reluctance of congressmen to speak critically of Israel was apparent in 1983 when the House gave President Reagan permission, under the War

Powers Act, to keep U.S. Marines in Lebanon for eighteen months. The vote took place a few days before the tragic truck bombing killed more than 240 marines in Beirut. At the time the House acted, however, several marines had already died. A number of congressmen warned of more trouble ahead, opposed Reagan's request, and strongly urged withdrawal of the U.S. military force. Five took the other side, mentioning the importance of the marine presence to the security of Israel's northern border.

In all, ninety-one congressmen spoke, but they were silent on the military actions Israel had carried out in Lebanon during the previous year—unrestricted bombing of Beirut, forced evacuation of PLO fighters, and aiding in the massacres at Sabra and Shatila by surrounding the camps, allowing Lebanese Christian Phalange fighters in and refusing to allow fleeing refugees out, sending them back to be slaughtered.[91] These events had altered the Lebanese scene so radically that President Reagan felt impelled to return the marines to Beirut. Israel's actions had necessitated the marines' presence, yet none of these critical events was mentioned among the thousands of words expressed during the lengthy discussion.

A veteran congressman, with the advantage of hindsight, explained it directly.[92] Just after the terrorist attack that killed U.S. Marines who were asleep in their Beirut compound, Congressman Lee Hamilton was asked if Congress might soon initiate action on its own to get the marines out of Lebanon. The query was posed by William Quandt, a Middle East specialist who had served in the Carter White House, at the close of a private discussion on Capitol Hill involving a small group of senior congressmen. Hamilton, a close student of both the Congress and the Middle East, responded, "Don't look to Congress to act. All we know is how to increase aid to Israel."

Hamilton's statement has proved true. Aid to Israel—despite our country's budget problems and Israel's defiant behavior toward the United States in its use of U.S.-supplied weapons and its construction of settlements on occupied territory—continues to increase, with no peak in sight.

Bonior and Secret Evidence

The voices of protest in the House of Representatives became less audible in 2001 with the announcement by Democrat David Bonior of Michigan that he would not seek re-election. Bonior, a member of the House since 1976 and Democratic Whip since 1992, was known for his strong positions on environmental, labor, and human rights issues, and has always fought for social and economic justice. He sponsored the Secret Evidence Repeal Act (H.R. 2121) in the 106th Congress, and a similar bill (H.R. 1266) in the 107th. Virtually every person against whom secret evidence has been used has been an Arab Muslim, and Bonior—who pro-Israel Washington PAC founder Morris Amitay called "the poster child for the pro-Arab cause in this country"—long opposed the discriminatory and unconstitutional use of secret evidence.[93] Severely crippled by newly instituted redistricting, Bonior lost his bid for the governorship of Michigan in the 2002 elections.

"Here We Go Again"

Another blow to honest debate in the House was the retirement of Congressman Thomas Campbell (R-CA), who cosponsored the Secret Evidence Repeal Act with Bonior. In November 2000, Campbell lost his bid to unseat Dianne Feinstein (D-CA) in the U.S. Senate race, and resumed a teaching post at Stanford Law School. Feinstein would go on to propose and pass Senate Resolution 247, which the American–Arab Anti-Discrimination Committee described as "a one-sided message to the American people and our friends and allies throughout the world that American elected officials are only concerned about Israel in the Middle East."

A similar resolution was introduced by Tom DeLay (R-TX) in May 2002 in the House of Representatives. It passed by a vote of 352–21, with twenty-nine abstentions. Thirty-three members did not vote, suggesting discontent with the legislation modified by fear of AIPAC. The resolution, which extensively condemned Palestinian suicide attacks and Palestinian President Yasser Arafat but offered no criticism whatsoever of Israel's aggressive policy of collective punishment, was called "unbalanced and . . . counterproductive" by Congressman Jim Moran (D-VA). John Dingell (D-MI), who called the resolution "one-sided" and "provocative," noted that its passage—at a time when President George W. Bush was expressing his sternest criticism yet of Israel—"will undermine the administration, diminish U.S. leverage with the Palestinians, and further damage U.S. credibility in the region." Nick Rahall (D-WV) put it more bluntly: "Here we go again. How many times has this body passed resolutions of this nature that are so unbalanced, so one-sided, that we become the laughingstock of the world?"[94]

Some members voted to open up debate on the resolution, with the intention of including new language that would offer more balance. As Congressman Mark Green (R-WI) noted the day of the vote, however, "in a House of 435 members, there were only eighty-two who voted with me on this, and only three of those were Republicans. I wish we had more, because I think we would have ended up with a better piece of legislation."[95]

Despite the eloquence of courageous members of Congress—whose ranks included Jesse L. Jackson, Jr. (D-IL), Lois Capps (D-CA), David Price (D-NC), Peter DeFazio (D-OR), Jay Inslee (D-WA), Amory Houghton (R-NY), Marcy Kaptur (D-OH), Cynthia McKinney (D-GA), and of course David Bonior—anti-Palestinian oratory became deafening on the Republican side of the House of Representatives. It was an especially depressing development to Republicans like myself.

The resolution was a factor in the defeat of a five-term Democrat, Earl Hilliard, in the Alabama runoff primary on June 25, 2002. Hilliard, a supporter of Palestinian statehood, was one of the twenty-one who voted against the resolution. Arab American and Muslim groups rallied financial support in his campaign, but Harvard-educated Artur Davis, according to Hilliard, was able to outspend him by a larger margin, thanks to strong support from New York City Jews. Davis focused on charges of ethics violations by Hilliard and accused him of links with terrorism. Both candidates are African American.

As evidence of the pro-Israel bias in the House, soon-to-retire majority leader Richard Armey (R-TX), proposed on May 1, 2002, that Palestinians simply vacate the West Bank. Prodded in an interview by MSNBC's Chris Matthews, Armey said, "I happen to believe that the Palestinians should leave." Faced with protests, Armey said, days later, that he meant to say that Palestinian terrorists should leave.

The week before, Tom DeLay, Armey's heir apparent as majority leader and future creator of the controversial "Israel First" resolution, told the annual AIPAC convention, "As long as I'm in Congress, I'll use every tool at my disposal to ensure that the Republican conference in the House of Representatives continues to preserve and strengthen America's alliance with the State of Israel."[96]

4

The Deliberative Body Fails to Deliberate

JUST OFF THE second-floor corridor connecting the central part of the U.S. Capitol building with the Senate wing is the restored old Senate chamber, where visitors can look around and imagine the room echoing with great debates of the past. Action there gave the Senate its reputation as the "world's greatest deliberative body," where no topic was too controversial for open debate.

In most respects, that reputation is deserved and honored. In fact, all five former senators—John C. Calhoun, Daniel Webster, Henry Clay, Robert LaFollette, and Robert Taft—who are pictured in the ornate reception room near the large chamber now used by the Senate were distinguished by their independence and courage, not by conformity.

Today, on Middle East issues at least, independence and courage are almost unknown, and the Senate deliberates not at all. This phenomenon was the topic of discussion during a breakfast meeting in 1982 between Crown Prince Hassan of Jordan and Senator Claiborne Pell of

Rhode Island, the senior Democrat on the Senate Foreign Relations Committee.[1] Pell explained with candor his own record of consistent support for Israel and his failure to recognize Arab interests when he told the Jordanian leader, "I can be honest with you, but I can't be fair." Pell's record is typical of his colleagues.

Since the establishment of modern Israel in 1948, only a handful of senators have said or done anything in opposition to the policies of the government of Israel. Those who break ranks find themselves in difficulty. The trouble can arise from a speech, an amendment, a vote, a published statement, or a combination of these. It may take the form of a challenge in the next primary or general election. Or the trouble may not surface until later—after service in the Senate has ended. Such was the destiny of a senator from Illinois.

"Adlai, You Are Right, But—"

The cover of the October 1982 edition of the monthly magazine *Jewish Chicago* featured a portrait of Adlai E. Stevenson III, Democratic candidate for governor of Illinois. In the background, over the right shoulder of a smiling Stevenson, an Arab, rifle slung over his shoulder, glared ominously through a kaffiyeh that covered his head and most of his face. The headline announcing the issue's feature article read, "Looking at Adlai Through Jewish Eyes."

The illustration and article were part of an anti-Stevenson campaign conducted by some of the quarter-million people in Chicago's Jewish community who wanted Stevenson to fail in his challenge to Governor James R. Thompson, Jr.

Thompson, a Republican, was attempting a feat sometimes tried but never before accomplished in Illinois history: election to a third term as governor.[2] Normally, a Republican in Illinois can expect only minimal Jewish support at the polls. A crucial part of the anti-Stevenson campaign was a caricature of his Middle East record while he was a member of the United States Senate.[3] Stevenson was presented as an enemy of Israel and an ally of the PLO.

Stevenson was attempting a political comeback after serving ten years in the Senate, where he had quickly established himself as an independent.[4] During the oil shortage of the mid-1970s he alarmed corporate interests by suggesting the establishment of a government corporation to handle the marketing of all crude oil. He warned of the "seeds of destruction" inherent in nuclear proliferation and called for international safeguards to restrain other nations from using nuclear technology to manufacture weapons. Concerned about the country's weakening position in the international marketplace, he called for government-directed national economic strategies to meet the challenge of foreign competition.

Stevenson lacked the flamboyant extroverted character of many politicians. *Time* magazine described him as "a reflective man who seems a bit out of place in the political arena."[5] Effective in committee, where most legislation is hammered out, he did not feel comfortable lining up votes.[6] "I'm not a backslapper or logroller," he said. "I don't feel effective running about buttonholing Senators."

Chicago Daily News columnist Mike Royko wrote of Stevenson's lack of charisma in a tone of affectionate teasing:

> The most dangerous element in politics is charisma. It makes people get glassy-eyed and jump and scream and clap without a thought in their heads. Adlai Stevenson never does that. He makes people drowsy. His hair is thinning. He has all the oratorical fire of an algebra teacher. His clothes look like something he bought from the coroner's office. When he feels good, he looks like he has a virus. We need more politicians who make our blood run tepid.[7]

Royko could have added that Stevenson also had none of the self-righteousness often found on Capitol Hill. Although a "blue blood," as close to aristocracy as an American can be, he displayed little interest in the cocktail circuit or the show business of politics.[8] On a congressional tour of China in 1975 he didn't seem to mind when the other three senators received lace-curtained limousines and he and his wife, Nancy, were assigned a less showy sedan.

During his second Senate term, he became disillusioned with the Carter administration.[9] He saw it as "embarrassingly weak" and more concerned with retaining its power than with exercising it effectively. In 1979 he announced he would not seek re-election to the Senate, but he mentioned a new interest: the presidency. He might run for the White House the next year. "I'm going to talk about ideas and see if an idea can

still triumph, or even make a dent," he said.[10] It didn't. Stevenson ultimately decided not to run. With Senator Edward Kennedy in the race,
he felt he would get little media attention.[11] By the time Kennedy pulled
out, Stevenson concluded it was too late to get organized.

After a year's breather, in 1981 he announced his interest in running
for the governorship of Illinois. This time he followed through.

The make-up of his campaign organization, the character of his campaign, and the support he had received in the past in Jewish neighbor-
hoods provided little hint of trouble ahead from pro-Israeli quarters.

Several of the most important members of his campaign team were
Jewish: Philip Klutznick, president emeritus of B'nai B'rith and an organizer of the Conference of Presidents of Major Jewish Organizations, who
agreed to organize Stevenson's main campaign dinner; Milton Fisher,
prominent attorney and chairman of his finance committee; Rick Jasculca, a public relations executive who became Stevenson's full-time press
secretary.[12]

Stevenson chose Grace Mary Stern as his running mate for the position of lieutenant governor. Her husband was prominent in Chicago Jewish affairs. Stevenson himself had received several honors from Jewish
groups in preceding years.[13] He had been selected by the Chicago Jewish community as its 1974 Israel Bond "Man of the Year," commended
by the American Jewish Committee for his legislative work against the
Arab boycott of Israel in 1977, and honored by the government of Israel,
which established the Adlai E. Stevenson III Chair at the Weizmann
Institute of Science in Rehovot. Stevenson had every reason to expect
that organized Illinois Jewry would overlook his occasional mildly critical position of Israeli policy.

But trouble developed. A segment of the Jewish community quietly
launched an attack that would cost him heavily. Stevenson's detractors
were determined to defeat him in the governor's race and thus discourage a future Stevenson bid for the presidency. Their basic tool was a document provided by the AIPAC in Washington.[14] It was presented as a
summary of Stevenson's Senate actions on Middle East issues—although
it made no mention of his almost unblemished record of support for
Israel and the tributes the Jewish community had presented to him in
testimony of this support. Like most AIPAC documents, it would win
no prizes for balance and objectivity.

For example, AIPAC pulled from a twenty-one-page report that Stevenson had prepared after a 1976 trip to the Middle East just this lonely phrase: "There is no organization other than the PLO with a broadly recognized claim to represent the Palestinians." This was a simple statement of fact. But the writer of the *Jewish Chicago* article, citing the AIPAC "summary," asserted that these words had helped to give Stevenson "a reputation as one of the harshest critics of both Israel policy and of U.S. support for the Jewish state." Stevenson's assessment of the PLO's standing in the Palestinian community was interpreted as an assault on Israel.

In fact, the full paragraph in the Stevenson report from which AIPAC took its brief excerpt is studied and reasonable:

> The Palestinians are by general agreement the nub of the problem. Although badly divided, they have steadily increased in numbers, economic and military strength, and seriousness of purpose. They cannot be left out of any Middle East settlement. Their lack of unity is reflected in the lack of unity within the top ranks of the PLO, but there is no organization other than the PLO with a broadly recognized claim to represent the Palestinians.[15]

The Stevenson report was critical of certain Israeli policies but hardly hostile to Israel. "The PLO," he wrote, "may be distrusted, disowned, and despised, but it is a reality, if for no other reason than that it has no rival organization among Palestinians."

Stevenson went on to issue a challenge to the political leaders of America:

> A new order of statesmanship is required from both the Executive and the Legislative Branches. For too long, Congress has muddled or gone along without any real understanding of Middle Eastern politics. Neither the United States, nor Israel, nor any of the Arab states will be served by continued ignorance or the expediencies of election year politics.

None of this positive comment found its way into the AIPAC report, the *Jewish Chicago* article, or any of the anti-Stevenson literature that was distributed within the Jewish community during the 1982 campaign.

The anti-Stevenson activists noted with alarm that in 1980 Stevenson had sponsored an amendment to reduce aid to Israel, and the year before had supported a similar amendment offered by Republican

Senator Mark O. Hatfield of Oregon.[16] The Hatfield amendment proposed to cut by 10 percent the amount of funds available to Israel for military credits.

Stevenson's amendment had focused on Israeli settlements in the occupied territories, which President Carter and earlier administrations characterized as both illegal and an obstacle to peace but did nothing to discourage beyond occasional expressions of regret. Stevenson proposed withholding $150 million in aid until Israel halted both the building and planning of additional settlements. The amendment did not cut funds; it simply withheld a fraction of the $2.18 billion in total aid authorized for Israel that year. In speaking for the amendment, Stevenson noted that the outlay for Israel amounted to 43 percent of all U.S. funds allocated for such purposes worldwide:

> This preference for Israel diverts funds from the support of human life and vital American interests elsewhere in an interdependent and unstable world. . . . If it could produce stability in the Middle East or enhance Israel's security, it could be justified. But it reflects continued U.S. acquiescence in an Israeli policy that threatens more Middle East instability, more Israeli insecurity, and a continued decline of U.S. authority in the world. Our support for Israel is not the issue here. Israel's support for the ideals of peace and justice which gave it birth is at issue. It is, I submit, for the Israeli government to recognize again that Israel's interests are in harmony with our own, and for that to happen, it is important that we do not undermine the voices for peace in Israel or justify those, like Mr. Begin, who claim U.S. assistance from the Congress can be taken for granted.[17]

The amendment, like Hatfield's, was overwhelmingly defeated.

After the vote on his amendment, Stevenson recalls, he received apologetic comments.[18] "Several Senators came up and said, 'Adlai, you are right, but you understand why I had to vote against you. Maybe next time.'" Stevenson did understand why: lobby intimidation produced the negative votes. He found intimidation at work on another front too: the news media. He offered the amendment, he explained, "because I thought the public was entitled to a debate on this critical issue," but news services gave it no attention. Stevenson added,

> That's another aspect of this problem. It's not only the intimidation of the American politicians, it's also the intimidation of some American journal-

ists. If it's not the journalists, then it's the editors and perhaps more so the publishers.

Anti-Stevenson campaigners also found it expedient to portray him as a supporter of Arab economic blackmail, despite his widely hailed legislative record to the contrary. Stevenson was actually the principal author of the 1977 legislation to prohibit American firms from cooperating with the Arab boycott of Israel.[19] But in the smear campaign conducted against him in his gubernatorial bid his legislative history was rewritten. He was actually accused of trying to undermine the anti-boycott effort.

In fact, Stevenson, in a lonely and frustrating effort, saved the legislation from disaster. For this achievement, he received a plaque and praise from the American Jewish Committee.[20] The chairman of the National Jewish Community Relations Council, Theodore R. Mann, wrote to Stevenson, expressing the organization's "deep appreciation for your invaluable contribution to the adoption of that landmark legislation."[21] He added that the legislation "not only reassures the American Jewish community as to the commitment of America to fairness and nondiscrimination in international trade but, more fundamentally, stands as a reaffirmation of our nation's profound regard for principle and morality."

Jewish Chicago, making no mention of Stevenson's success in the anti-boycott effort or the unstinting praise he received from Jewish leaders, reported that he encountered "major conflicts" with "the American Jewish leadership" over the boycott legislation.[22]

A flyer distributed by an unidentified "Informed Citizens Against Stevenson Committee," made the same charge.[23] Captioned, "The Truth About Adlai Stevenson," it used half-truths to brand Stevenson as anti-Israel during his Senate years and concluded: "It is vitally important that Jewish voters be fully informed about Stevenson's record. Still dazzled by the Stevenson name, many Jews are totally unaware of his antagonism to Jewish interests." The "committee" provided no names or addresses of sponsoring individuals. Shirley Friedman, a freelance writer in Chicago, later identified the flyer as her own. The message on the flyer concluded: "Don't forget: It is well known that Stevenson considers the governor's chair as a stepping stone to the presidency. Spread the word—let the truth be told!"

The word indeed spread in the Chicago Jewish community throughout the summer and fall of 1982.[24] The political editor of the *Chicago*

Sun-Times reported in June that some activists for Thompson had been "working quietly for months to assemble a group to mobilize Jewish voters" against Stevenson.[25]

The result of their efforts was the "Coalition for the Re-election of Jim Thompson," which included Jewish Democrats who had not backed Thompson previously. When Republican Senator Rudy Boschwitz of Minnesota, a strong supporter of Israel, came to Chicago in October to address a breakfast gathering sponsored by the Coalition, he declared that, as a senator, Stevenson was "a very steadfast foe of aid to Israel."[26]

"Smear and Innuendo"

A major problem was the unprinted but widely whispered charge of anti-Semitism against Stevenson—a man, who, like his father, had spent his life championing civil rights for all Americans. "I learned after election day there was that intimation throughout the campaign," recalls Stevenson.[27]

Phil Klutznick's daughter, Mrs. Bettylu Saltzman, who worked on Stevenson's campaign staff, remembered, "There was plenty of stuff going around about him being anti-Semitic.[28] It got worse and worse. It was a much more difficult problem than anyone imagined."

Stevenson's running mate, Grace Mary Stern, recalled: "There was a very vigorous [anti-Stevenson] telephone campaign in the Jewish community."[29] She said that leaflets charging Stevenson with being anti-Israel were distributed widely at local Jewish temples, and added that there was much discussion of the anti-Semitism accusation: "There was a very vigorous campaign, man to man, friend to friend, locker room to locker room. We never really came to grips with the problem."

Campaign fund-raising suffered accordingly. The Jewish community had supported Stevenson strongly in both of his campaigns for the Senate. After his remarks in the last years of his Senate career, some of the Jewish support dried up. "Many of my most generous Jewish contributors stayed with me, but the organization types, the professionals, did not," Stevenson recalled.[30] He believed the withdrawal of organized Jewish support also cut into funds from out-of-state that he otherwise would have received. In the end, Thompson was able to outspend Stevenson by better than two to one.[31]

Fed up by early September with unfounded charges of anti-Semitism, Stevenson finally responded, charging that a "subterranean campaign of smear and innuendo" was being waged by supporters of Thompson.[32] His press secretary, Rick Jasculca, complained that the material distributed by the Coalition for the Re-election of Jim Thompson "tries to give the impression that Adlai is unquestionably anti-Israel." Thompson's political director, Philip O'Connor, denied there was a smear campaign and disavowed the Friedman flyer.

Thompson himself said of Stevenson, "I don't think he is an anti-Semite, [but he is] no particular friend of Israel." The *Chicago Sun-Times* published an editorial rebuke to this remark: "That's like saying, 'No, I don't think Stevenson beats his wife, but she did have a black eye last week.'"[33] The editorial continued:

> Far more important, the statement is not true; Stevenson as a Senator may have occasionally departed from positions advocated by the Israeli government, but out of well-reasoned motives and a genuine desire to secure a lasting peace for the area. Thompson's coy phrasing was a reprehensible appeal to the voter who measures a candidate's worth by a single, rubbery standard.

The only Jews who tried to counter the attack were those close to Stevenson. Philip Klutznick, prominent in Jewish affairs and chairman of the Stevenson Dinner Committee, said, "It is beneath the dignity of the Jewish community to introduce these issues into a gubernatorial campaign."[34] Stevenson campaign treasurer Milton Fisher said: "Adlai's views are probably consistent with 40 percent of the Knesset [Israeli parliament]."

Stevenson was ultimately defeated in the closest gubernatorial election in the state's history. The margin was 5,074 votes—one-seventh of one percent of the total 3.5 million votes cast.

The election was marred by a series of mysterious irregularities, which *Time* magazine described as "so improbable, so coincidental, so questionable that it could have happened only in Wonderland, or the Windy City."[35] On election night ballot boxes from fifteen Chicago precincts inexplicably disappeared, and others turned up in the homes or cars of poll workers. Stevenson asked for a recount—past recounts had resulted in shifts of 5,000 to 7,000 votes—but the Illinois Supreme

Court denied his petition by a 4-to-3 vote.[36] Judge Seymour Simon, a Democrat, joined the three Republicans on the court in voting against Stevenson's request.

A post-election editorial in a suburban Chicago newspaper acknowledged the impact of the concerted smear campaign on the election outcome:

> An intense last-minute effort among Chicago-area Jews to thwart Adlai Stevenson's attempt to unseat Illinois Governor James Thompson in last Tuesday's election may have succeeded. The weekend before the election many Chicago and suburban rabbis spoke out against Stevenson and there were thousands of pamphlets and leaflets distributed in Jewish areas . . . all attacking the former Senator.

After describing the attack, the editorial concluded,

> The concentrated anti-Stevenson campaign, particularly since it went largely unanswered, almost surely cost him thousands of votes among the 248,000 Chicago-area Jews—266,000 throughout the state—who traditionally have leaned in his direction politically.[37]

Campaign manager Joseph Novak agreed: "If that effort hadn't happened, Stevenson would be governor."[38] In the predominantly Jewish suburban Chicago precincts of Highland Park and Lake County "We just got killed, just absolutely devastated." Press secretary Rick Jasculca adds, "What bothers me is that hardly any rabbis or Jewish leaders beyond Phil [Klutznick] were willing to speak up and say this is nonsense to call Adlai anti-Israel."[39]

Thomas A. Dine, then executive director of the American Israel Public Affairs Committee, gloated, "The memory of Adlai Stevenson's hostility toward Israel during his Senate tenure lost him the Jewish vote in Illinois—and that cost him the gubernatorial election."[40] Stevenson, too, believed that the effort to discredit him among Jews played a major role in his defeat: "In a race that close, it was more than enough to make the difference."[41] Asked about the impact of the Israeli lobby on the U.S. political scene, he responded without hesitation:

> There is an intimidating, activist minority of American Jews that supports the decisions of the Israeli government, right or wrong. They do so very

vocally and very aggressively in ways that intimidate others so that it's their voice—even though it's a minority—that is heard and felt in American politics. But it still is much louder in the United States than in Israel. In other words, you have a much stronger, more vocal dissent in Israel than within the Jewish community in the United States. The prime minister of Israel has far more influence over American foreign policy in the Middle East than over the policies of his own government generally.

The former senator reported a profound change within the Jewish community in recent years:

The old passionate commitment of Jewish leaders to civil liberties, social welfare—in short, to liberalism has to a large extent dissipated. The issue now is much more Israel itself. If given a choice between the traditional liberal commitment and the imagined Israeli commitment, they'll opt now for the Israeli commitment.

Reflecting on his career and the price he has paid for challenging Israeli policies, Stevenson concluded:

I will have no hesitation about continuing. I wish I had started earlier and been more effective. I really don't understand the worth of public office if you can't serve the public. It's better to lose. It's better not to serve than to be mortgaged or compromised.

Stevenson followed the tradition of a colleague, a famous senator from Arkansas who eloquently criticized Israeli policy and American foreign policy over a period of many years.

The Dissenter

"When all of us are dead, the only one they'll remember is Bill Fulbright."[42] The tribute by Idaho Senator Frank Church, a fellow Democrat, was amply justified. As much as any man of his time, J. William Fulbright shaped this nation's attitudes on the proper exercise of its power in a world made acutely dangerous by nuclear weapons. Dissent was a hallmark of his career, but it was dissent with distinction. The fact was that Fulbright was usually right.

He first gained national attention by condemning the "swinish blight" of McCarthyism.[43] In 1954, while many Americans cheered the crusade of the Wisconsin senator's Permanent Investigations Subcommittee, Fulbright cast the lone vote against a measure to continue the subcommittee's funding. Because of this vote, he was accused of being "a communist, a fellow traveler, an atheist, [and] a man beneath contempt."[44]

Fulbright opposed U.S. intervention in Cuba in 1961 and in the Dominican Republic four years later, and was ahead of his time in calling for détente with the Soviet Union and a diplomatic opening with China. When he proposed a different system for selecting presidents, an offended Harry Truman called him "that overeducated Oxford s.o.b." Twenty-five years later, in 1974, the *New York Times* recognized Fulbright as "the most outspoken critic of American foreign policy of this generation."[45]

His deepest and most abiding interest was the advancement of international understanding through education, and thousands of young people have broadened their vision through the scholarships that bear his name.[46] But Fulbright also became well known for his outspoken opposition to the Vietnam War as "an endless, futile war . . . debilitating and indecent"—a stand that put him at odds with a former colleague and close friend, President Lyndon B. Johnson.[47] President Johnson believed that America was embarked on a noble mission in Southeast Asia against an international communist conspiracy. Fulbright put no stock in the conspiracy theory, feared the war might broaden into a showdown with China, and saw it as an exercise in "the arrogance of power."[48]

In 1963 Fulbright chaired an investigation that brought to public attention the exceptional tax treatment of contributions to Israel and aroused the ire of the Jewish community.[49] The investigation was managed by Walter Pincus, a journalist Fulbright hired after reading a Pincus study of lobbying. Pincus recalls that Fulbright gave him a free hand, letting him choose the ten prime lobbying activities to be examined and backing him throughout the controversial investigation.[50] One of the groups chosen by Pincus, himself Jewish, was the Jewish Telegraph Agency, which was at that time a principal instrument of the Israeli lobby. Both Fulbright and Pincus were accused of trying to destroy the Jewish Telegraph Agency and of being anti-Semitic.[51]

Pincus remembers, "Several senators urged that the inquiry into the Jewish operation be dropped. Senators Hubert Humphrey and Bourke

Hickenlooper [senior Republican on the Foreign Relations Committee] were among them. Fulbright refused."

The Fulbright hearings also exposed massive funding illegally channeled into the American Zionist Council by Israel.[52] More than five million dollars had been secretly poured into the council for spending on public relations firms and pro-Israel propaganda before Fulbright's committee closed down the operation.

Despite his concern over the pro-Israeli lobby, Fulbright took the exceptional step of recommending that the United States guarantee Israeli's borders.[53] In a major address in 1970 he proposed an American–Israeli treaty, under which the United States would commit itself to intervene militarily if necessary to "guarantee the territory and independence of Israel" within the lands it held before the 1967 war. The treaty, he said, should be a supplement to a peace settlement arranged by the United Nations. The purpose of his proposal was to destroy the arguments of those who maintained that Israel needed the captured territory for its security.

Fulbright saw Israel's withdrawal from the Arab lands it occupied in the 1967 war as the key to peace: Israel could not occupy Arab territory and have peace too. He said that Israeli policy in establishing settlements on the territories "has been characterized by lack of flexibility and foresight." Discounting early threats by some Arab leaders to destroy the state of Israel, Fulbright noted that both President Nasser of the United Arab Republic and King Hussein of Jordan had in effect repudiated such Draconian threats, "but the Israelis seem not to have noticed the disavowals."

During the 1970s Fulbright repeatedly took exception to the contention that the Middle East crisis was a test of American resolve against Soviet interventionism. In 1971 he accused Israel of "communist-baiting humbuggery" and argued that continuing Middle East tension, in fact, only benefited Soviet interests.[54]

Appearing on CBS television's *Face the Nation* in 1973, Fulbright declared that the Senate was "subservient" to Israeli policies that were inimical to American interests.[55] He said that the United States bore "a very great share of the responsibility" for the continuation of Middle East violence. "It's quite obvious [that] without the all-out support by the

United States in money and weapons and so on, the Israelis couldn't do what they've been doing."

Fulbright said that the United States failed to pressure Israel for a negotiated settlement, because:

> The great majority of the Senate of the United States—somewhere around 80 percent—are completely in support of Israel, anything Israel wants. This has been demonstrated time and time again, and this has made it difficult for our government.

The senator claimed that "Israel controls the Senate" and warned, "We should be more concerned about the United States' interests." Six weeks after his *Face the Nation* appearance, Fulbright again expressed alarm over Israeli occupation of Arab territories.[56] He charged that the United States had given Israel "unlimited support for unlimited expansion."

His criticism of Israeli policy caused stirrings back home.[57] Jews who had supported him in the past became restless. After years of easy election victories, trouble loomed for Fulbright in 1974. Encouraged, in part, by the growing Jewish disenchantment with Fulbright, on the eve of the deadline for filing petitions of candidacy in the Democratic primary Governor Dale Bumpers surprised the political world by becoming a challenger for Fulbright's Senate seat. Fulbright hadn't expected the governor to run, but recognized immediately that the popular young governor posed a serious challenge: "He had lots of hair [in contrast to Fulbright], he looked good on television, and he'd never done anything to offend anyone."[58]

There were other factors. Walter Pincus, who later became a *Washington Post* reporter, believed that Fulbright's decision to take a golfing holiday in Bermuda just before the primary deadline may have helped convince Bumpers that Fulbright would not work hard for the nomination.[59] It was also the year of Watergate—a bad year for incumbents. In his campaign, Bumpers pointed with alarm to the "mess in Washington" and called for a change. The *New York Times* reported that he "skillfully exploited an old feeling that Mr. Fulbright . . . spent all his time dining with Henry Kissinger and fretting over the Middle East."[60]

The attitude of Jewish voters, both inside Arkansas and beyond, was also a significant factor. "I don't think Bumpers would have run without that encouragement," said Fulbright.[61] Following the election, a national Jewish organization actually claimed credit for the young governor's stunning upset victory. Fulbright had a copy of a memorandum circulated in May 1974 to the national board of directors of B'nai B'rith. Marked "confidential," the memo from Secretary-General Herman Edelsberg, announced that ". . . all of the indications suggest that our actions in support of Governor Bumpers will result in the ousting of Mr. Fulbright from his key position in the Senate."[62] Edelsberg later rejected the memorandum as "phony."

Following his defeat, Fulbright continued to speak out, decrying Israeli stubbornness and warning of the Israeli lobby. In a speech just before the end of his Senate term, he warned, "Endlessly pressing the United States for money and arms—and invariably getting all and more than she asks—Israel makes bad use of a good friend."[63] His central concern was that the Middle East conflict might flare into nuclear war.[64] He warned somberly that "Israel's supporters in the United States . . . by underwriting intransigence, are encouraging a course which must lead toward her destruction—and just possibly ours as well."

Pondering the future from his office three blocks north of the White House on a bright winter day in 1983, Fulbright saw little hope that Capitol Hill would effectively challenge the Israeli lobby:

> It's suicide for politicians to oppose them. The only possibility would be someone like Eisenhower, who already feels secure. Eisenhower had already made his reputation. He was already a great man in the eyes of the country, and he wasn't afraid of anybody. He said what he believed.[65]

Then he added a somewhat more optimistic note: "I believe a president could do this. He wouldn't have to be named Eisenhower." Fulbright cited a missed opportunity:

> I went to Jerry Ford after he took office in 1975. I was out of office then. I had been to the Middle East and visited with some of the leading figures. I came back and told the president, 'Look, I think these [Arab] leaders are willing to accept Israel, but the Israelis have got to go back to the 1967 borders. The problem can be solved if you are willing to take a position on it.

Fulbright predicted that the American people would back Ford if he demanded that Israel cooperate. He reminded him that Eisenhower was reelected by a large margin immediately after he forced Israel to withdraw after invading Egypt:

> Taking a stand against Israel didn't hurt Eisenhower. He carried New York with its big Jewish population. I told Ford I didn't think he would be defeated if he put it the right way. He should say Israel had to go back to the 1967 borders; if it didn't, no more arms or money. That's just the way Eisenhower did it. And Israel would have to cooperate. And politically, in the coming campaign, I told him he should say he was for Israel, but he was for America first.

Ford, Fulbright recalled, listened courteously but was noncommittal. "Of course he didn't take my advice," said Fulbright.

Yet his determination in the face of such disappointment echoes through one of his last statements as a U.S. senator:

> History casts no doubt at all on the ability of human beings to deal rationally with their problems, but the greatest doubt on their will to do so. The signals of the past are thus clouded and ambiguous, suggesting hope but not confidence in the triumph of reason. With nothing to lose in any event, it seems well worth a try.[66]

Fulbright died on February 9, 1995, ending one of the most illustrious careers in American politics. Reared in the segregationist South, he left an imposing legacy as a fearless, scholarly, and determined champion of human rights at home and abroad.

Warning Against Absolutism

James G. Abourezk of South Dakota came to the Senate in 1973 after serving two years in the House of Representatives. The son of Lebanese immigrants, he was the first person of Arab ancestry elected to the Senate. He spoke up for Arab interests and quickly became a center of controversy.

Soon after he took office, Abourezk accepted an invitation to speak at Yeshiva University in New York, but anxious school officials called almost immediately to tell him of rising student protests against his appearance.[67] A few days later, the chairman of the dinner committee asked Abourezk to make a public statement calling for face-to-face negotiations between Israel and its Arab neighbors, assuring Abourezk that this proposal, identical to the one being made by Israel's prime minister, Golda Meir, would ease student objections and end the protest. Although Abourezk favored such negotiations, he refused to make the requested statement. He explained, "I do not wish to be in the position of placating agitators." Rabbi Israel Miller, vice president of the school, came to Washington to urge Abourezk to reconsider. When Abourezk refused, the dinner chairman telephoned again, this time to report that students were beginning to picket. Sensing that school officials wanted the event canceled, Abourezk offered to withdraw from the obligation. His offer was hastily accepted.

Soon after, Abourezk was announced as the principal speaker at a rally to be held in Rochester, New York, to raise money for victims of the Lebanese civil war. The rally's organizing committee was immediately showered with telephoned bomb threats. In all, twenty-three calls warned that the building would be blown up if Abourezk appeared on the program. With the help of the FBI, local police swept the building for bombs and, finding none, opened it for the program. A capacity crowd, unaware of the threats, heard Abourezk speak, and the event proceeded without incident.

After making a tour of Arab states in December 1973, Abourezk sympathized with Arab refugees in a speech at the National Press Club in Washington. Covering his speech for the AIPAC newsletter *Near East Report* Wolf Blitzer wrote, "If [Abourezk's] position were to prevail, Israel's life would be jeopardized." Blitzer's report was sent to Jews who had contributed to Abourezk's campaign, accompanied by a letter in which I. L. Kenen, AIPAC director, warned that Abourezk was "going to great lengths" to "undermine American friendship for Israel."[68] The mailing, Abourezk recalled, began an "adversary relationship" with AIPAC. He added, "I doubt that I would have spent so much time on the Middle East had it not been for that particular unfair personal attack."[69]

On one occasion in the Senate, Abourezk turned lobby pressure to his advantage. Wishing to be appointed in 1974 to fill a vacancy on the Senate Judiciary Committee, he warned David Brody, lobbyist for B'nai B'rith's Anti-Defamation League, that if he did not secure the appointment he would seek a seat on the Foreign Relations Committee. He recalls, with a chuckle, "This warning had the desired effect. The last thing Brody wanted was to see me on Foreign Relations, where aid to Israel is decided. Thanks to the help of the lobby I received the appointment to Judiciary, even though James Allen, a Senator with more seniority, also wanted the position." The appointment enabled Abourezk to chair hearings in 1977 on the legality of Israel's occupation of the West Bank and Gaza. "They were the first—and last—hearings on this subject," Abourezk recalled. "And not one of my colleagues attended. I was there alone."

In 1975 Abourezk invited the head of the PLO's Beirut office, Shafiq al-Hout, to lunch in the Senate and learned that PLO-related secrets are hard to keep. On Abourezk's assurance that the event would be kept entirely private, eleven other senators, including Abraham Ribicoff of Connecticut, who is Jewish, attended and heard al-Hout relate the PLO side of Middle East issues. Within an hour after the event was concluded, Spencer Richardson of the *Washington Post* telephoned Abourezk for comment. He had already learned the identity of all senators who attended. The next day Israel's leading English language daily newspaper, the *Jerusalem Post*, reported that Ribicoff and the others had had lunch with "murderer" al-Hout.

A major storm erupted in 1977 when Abourezk agreed on short notice to fill in for Vice President Walter Mondale as the principal speaker at the annual Jefferson–Jackson Day dinner sponsored in Denver by the Colorado Democratic Party.[71] Jewish leaders protested his appearance, and John Mrozek, a labor leader in Denver, attacked Abourezk as "pro-Arab and anti-Israel." Betty Crist, a member of the dinner committee, moved that the invitation be withdrawn. When the Crist motion was narrowly rejected, the committee tried to find a pro-Israeli speaker to debate Abourezk, with the intention of canceling the event if a debate could not be arranged. This gave the proceedings a comic twist, as Abourezk at no point had intended to mention the Middle East in his remarks. Unable to find someone to debate their guest, the committee reconsidered and let the invitation to Abourezk stand in its original form.

Arriving at the Denver airport, Abourezk told reporters, "As a United States Senator, I have sworn to uphold the government of the United States, but I never dreamed that I would be required to swear allegiance to any other government." In his remarks to the dinner audience of 700, he warned of the "extraordinary influence of the Zionist lobby." He said the United States "is likely to become, if it has not already, a captive of its client state."

He said, "The point of the controversy surrounding this dinner has been my refusal to take an absolutist position for Israel. There is extreme danger to all of us in this kind of absolutism. It implies that only one position—that of being unquestionably pro-Israel—is the only position."

The *Rocky Mountain News* reported that his speech received a standing ovation, "although there were pockets of people who sat on their hands." The Denver newspaper editorialized, "James Abourezk is not a fanatic screaming for the blood of Israel. Colorado Democratic leaders should be proud to have him as their speaker. He is better than they deserve." In 1980, after retiring from the Senate, Abourezk founded the American-Arab Anti-Discrimination Committee, which has grown into the Arab American civil rights organization with the largest membership in the country. Its purpose, Abourezk says, "is to provide a countervailing force to the Israeli lobby."

Sins of Omission

The Israeli lobby's long string of Capitol Hill victories has been broken only a few times in the past forty-two years.[72] Two setbacks occurred in the Senate and involved military sales to Saudi Arabia. In 1978 the Senate approved the sale of F-15 fighter planes by a vote of 54–44, and in 1981 it approved the sale of AWACS (Airborne Warning and Control System) intelligence-gathering planes and special equipment for the F-15s by a vote of 52–48. Curiously, both controversies entangled the American Israel Public Affairs Committee in the politics of the state of Maine.

This involvement began on the Senate floor one afternoon in the spring of 1978 when Senator Edward "Ted" Kennedy received a whispered message that brought an angry flush to his face.[73] AIPAC had forsaken a Senate Democrat with a consistently pro-Israel record. Senator William Hathaway of Maine, who had, without exception, cast his vote in behalf of Israel's interests, was being "dropped" by the lobby in favor of William S. Cohen, his Republican challenger. Kennedy strode to the adjoining cloakroom and reached for a telephone.

Kennedy demanded an explanation from Morris J. Amitay, then executive director of AIPAC. Flustered, Amitay denied that AIPAC had taken a position against Hathaway. The organization, he insisted, provides information on candidates but makes no endorsements. Pressed by Kennedy, Amitay promised to issue a letter to Hathaway complimenting him on his support of Israel.

The letter was sent, but the damage had already been done.[74] While Amitay was technically correct—AIPAC does not formally endorse candidates for the House or Senate—the lobby has effective ways to show its colors, raise money, and influence votes. In the Maine race, it was making calls for Cohen and against Hathaway. The shift, so astounding and unsettling to Kennedy, arose from a single "failing" on Hathaway's part. It was a sin of omission, but a cardinal sin nonetheless.

Over the years, Hathaway had sometimes refused to sign letters and resolutions that AIPAC sponsored.[75] The resolutions were usually statements of opinion by the Senate ("sense of the Senate" resolutions) and had no legislative effect. The letters were directed to the president or a cabinet officer, urging the official to support Israel. In refusing to sign, Hathaway did not single out AIPAC projects; he often rejected such requests from other interest groups as well, preferring to write his own letters and introduce his own resolutions. Nor did he always refuse AIPAC. Sometimes, as a favor, he would set aside his usual reservations and sign.

Hathaway cooperated in 1975 when AIPAC sponsored its famous "Spirit of 76" letter.[76] It bore Hathaway's name and those of seventy-five of his colleagues and carried this message to President Gerald R. Ford: "We urge that you reiterate our nation's long-standing commitment to Israel's security by a policy of continued military supplies and diplomatic and economic support." At another moment, this expression would have caused no ripples. Since the administration of John F. Kennedy, the U.S. government had been following a policy of "continued military supplies." But when this letter was made public in January 1975, it shook the executive branch as have few Senate letters in history.

Ford, dissatisfied with Israel's behavior, had just issued a statement calling for a "reappraisal" of U.S. policies in the Middle East.[77] His statement did not mention Israel by name as the offending party, but his message was clear: Ford wanted better cooperation in reaching a compromise with Arab interests, and "reappraisal" meant suspension of U.S. aid until Israel improved its behavior. It was a historic proposal, the first time since the Eisenhower era that a U.S. president even hinted publicly that he might suspend aid to Israel.

Israel's response came, not from its own capital, but from the United States Senate. Instead of directly protesting to the White House, Jerusalem activated its lobby in the United States, which, in turn, signed up as supporters of Israel's position more than three-fourths of the members of the United States Senate.

A more devastating—and intimidating—response could scarcely be conceived. The seventy-six signatures effectively told Ford he could not carry out his threatened "reappraisal." Israel's loyalists in the Senate—Democrats and Republicans alike—were sufficient in number to reject any legislative proposal hostile to Israel that Ford might make, and perhaps even enact a pro-Israeli piece of legislation over a presidential veto.

The letter was a demonstration of impressive clout. Crafted and circulated by AIPAC, it had been endorsed, overnight, by a majority of the Senate membership. Several senators who at first had said no quickly changed their positions. Senator John Culver admitted candidly, "The pressure was too great. I caved." So did President Ford. He backed down and never again challenged the lobby.

This wasn't the only time Hathaway answered AIPAC's call to oppose the White House on a major issue. Three years later, Ford's successor, Jimmy Carter, fought a similar battle with the Israeli lobby.[78] At issue this time was a resolution to disapprove Carter's proposal to sell F-15 fighters to Saudi Arabia. The White House needed the support of only one chamber to defeat the resolution. White House strategists felt that the House of Representatives would overwhelmingly vote to defeat the sale, so they decided to put all their resources into the Senate.

Lobbying on both sides was highly visible and aggressive.[79] Frederick Dutton, chief lobbyist for Saudi Arabia, orchestrated the pro-sale forces on Capitol Hill. The *Washington Post* reported, "Almost every morning these days, the black limousines pull up to Washington's Madison Hotel to collect their Saudi Arabian passengers. Their destination, very often, is Capitol Hill, where the battle of the F-15s unfolds."[80]

The Israeli lobby pulled out all the stops. It coordinated a nationwide public relations campaign that revived, as never before, memories of the genocidal Nazi campaign against European Jews during World War II. In the wake of the highly publicized television series, *Holocaust*, Capitol Hill was flooded with complimentary copies of the novel on which the TV series was based.[81] The books were accompanied by a letter from AIPAC saying, "This chilling account of the extermination of six million Jews underscores Israel's concerns during the current negotiations for security without reliance on outside guarantees." Regarding the book distribution, AIPAC's Aaron Rosenbaum told the *Washington Post*: "We think, frankly, that it will affect a few votes here and there, and simplify lobbying."[82]

Senator Wendell Anderson of Minnesota at first agreed to support the proposed sale.[83] He told an administration official: "Sure, I'll go for it. It sounds reasonable." But a few days before the vote he called back: "I can't vote for it. I'm up for election, and my Jewish cochairman refuses to go forward if I vote for the F-15s." Furthermore, he said, a Jewish group had met with him and showed him that 70 percent of the contributions to the Democratic Senatorial Campaign Committee the previous year came from Jewish sources.

The pressure was sustained and heavy. Major personalities in the Jewish community warned that the fighter aircraft would constitute a serious threat to Israel. Nevertheless, a prominent Jewish senator, Abraham Ribicoff of Connecticut, lined up with Carter. This was a hard blow to Amitay, who had previously worked on Ribicoff's staff. Earlier in the year Ribicoff, while keeping his own counsel on the Saudi arms question, took the uncharacteristic step of sharply criticizing Israeli policies, as well as the tactics of AIPAC. In an interview with the *Wall Street Journal*, Ribicoff described Israel's retention of occupied territory as "wrong" and unworthy of U.S. support.[84] He said that AIPAC does "a great disservice to the United States, to Israel, and to the Jewish community." He did not seek re-election in 1980.

The Senate approved the sale, 52–48, but in the process Carter was so bruised that he never again forced a showdown vote in Congress over Middle East policy.

Hathaway was one of the forty-eight who stuck with AIPAC, but this was not sufficient when election time rolled around. AIPAC wanted a Senator whose signature—and vote—it could always count on. Searching for unswerving loyalty, the lobby switched to Cohen. Its decision came at the very time Hathaway was resisting pressures on the Saudi issue. The staff at the Democratic Senatorial Campaign Committee was outraged. One of them declared to a visitor: "AIPAC demands 100 percent. If a fine Senator like Hathaway fails to cooperate just once, they are ready to trade in his career."[85] A staff member of a Senate committee commented: "To please AIPAC, you have to be more pure than Ivory soap—99.44 percent purity is not good enough."[86] Lacking the purity AIPAC demanded, Hathaway was defeated in 1978.

Caught in the AWACS Dilemma

William S. Cohen was elected to the Senate, but he soon found himself in a storm similar to the one Hathaway, his predecessor, had encountered. Once again, a proposal to sell military equipment to Saudi Arabia was raising concerns among pro-Israeli forces about a senator from Maine. It occurred soon after Ronald Reagan's inauguration, when the new president decided to approve the same request that the Carter administration had put off the year before. Saudi Arabia would be allowed to purchase its own AWACS planes, along with extra equipment to give Saudi F-15 fighters greater range and firepower. Israeli officials opposed the sale, because, they said, this technology would give Saudi Arabia the capacity to monitor Israeli air force operations.[87]

As it had in 1978, the Senate became the main battleground, but the White House was slow to organize. Convinced that Jimmy Carter the year before had taken on too many diverse issues at once, the Reagan forces decided to concentrate on tax and budget questions in the early months of the new administration. This left a vacuum in the foreign policy realm, which AIPAC skillfully filled. New director Thomas A. Dine orchestrated a bipartisan counterattack against arms transfers to Saudi Arabia. Even before Reagan sent the AWACS proposal to Capitol Hill for consideration, the Associated Press reported that the Israeli lobby had lined up "veto-strength majorities."[88]

AIPAC's campaign against AWACS began in the House of Representatives with a public letter attacking the proposal, which was sponsored by Republican Norman Lent of New York and Democrat Clarence

Long of Maryland. Ultimately, in October, the House rejected the proposed sale by a vote of 301–111, but the real battleground was the Senate. Earlier in the year, before the Senate took up the question, Senator Bob Packwood of Oregon, always a dependable supporter of Israel, announced that fifty-four senators, a majority, had signed a request that Reagan drop the idea. Needing time to persuade the senators to reconsider, the White House put off the showdown. By September, fifty senators had signed a resolution to veto the sale, and six more promised to sign if necessary. Once more, the White House had no choice but to delay.

This time, the Saudis were testing their relationship with the new president, and they left more of the lobbying to the White House than was true in 1978. Their case relied heavily on the personal efforts of Howard Baker, Republican Senate leader; Senator John Tower, chairman of the Armed Services Committee; and Senator Charles Percy, chairman of the Foreign Relations Committee. Lobbyist Dutton was instructed to stay in the background, although David Saad, executive director of the National Association of Arab Americans, helped organize the support of U.S. industries that had a stake in the sale.[89]

Dine's team roamed the Senate corridors, while AIPAC's grassroots contacts brought direct pressure from constituents. The *Washington Post* reported that "AIPAC's fountain of research materials reaches a readership estimated at 200,000 people."[90] Senator John Glenn of Ohio said: "I've been getting calls from every Jewish organization in the country. They didn't want to talk about the issues. The big push was to get me to sign this letter and resolution."[91] Glenn did not sign, largely because he hoped to broker a deal with the White House.

Syndicated columnist Carl Rowan wrote that "there is strong evidence" that the AWACS struggle increased "public resentment against the 'Jewish lobby.'"[92] The issue was portrayed by some as a choice between President Reagan and Prime Minister Begin. Bumper stickers appeared around Washington that read, "Reagan or Begin?" When the Senate finally voted, Cohen, who had announced his opposition to the proposal, switched and provided one of the critical votes supporting the AWACS sale.[93] He explained his reversal by declaring that Israel would have been branded the scapegoat for failure of the Middle East peace process if the proposal were defeated.

Aside from this "sin," one of "commission" in the eyes of AIPAC, Cohen's behavior was exemplary. Never once did he stray from the fold, and in 1984 AIPAC did not challenge his bid for re-election.

Standing Up for Civility

One of the most popular members of the Senate, Charles "Mac" Mathias of Maryland was something of a maverick—a trait that was probably necessary for his political survival. He was a Republican in a state where Democrats outnumber Republicans by three to one.

During the Nixon administration especially, he frequently dissented from the Republican party line. His opposition to the war in Vietnam and his staunch advocacy of civil rights and welfare initiatives earned him a place on the Nixon administration's "enemies list" of political opponents.[94] In a December 1971 speech, before the Watergate break-in at Democratic headquarters that led to Nixon's downfall, and while the country was angrily divided by domestic tensions and the war in Vietnam, Mathias advised Nixon to work to "bind the nation's wounds."[95] He urged the president to "take the high road" in the 1972 campaign and to disavow a campaign strategy "which now seems destined, unnecessarily, to polarize the country even more." In the same message, Mathias criticized Nixon's advisers for "divisive exploitation of the so-called social issues [through] . . . the use of hard-line rhetoric on crime, civil rights, civil liberties, and student unrest." Mathias was alarmed at what he saw as the Republican drift to the right.[96]

In 1975 and 1976 he considered running for president as an independent "third force" candidate in an effort to forge a "coalition of the center." The late Clarence Mitchell, director of the Washington office of the NAACP, said: "He's always arrived at his position in a reasoned way."[97] In fact, early in his career Mathias marked himself as a progressive and a champion of civil rights, and his constituency took his liberalism on social issues in stride.[98] A resident of Frederick, Mathias's home town, told the *Washington Post,* "Why, a lot of people around here think he's too liberal. But they seem to vote for him. The thing is, he's decent. He's got class."[99]

He also had flashes of daring. In the spring of 1981, he wrote an article in the quarterly *Foreign Affairs* that he knew would put him in hot water with some of his Jewish constituents. In it, Mathias criticized the role played by ethnic lobbies—particularly the Israeli lobby—in the formation of U.S. foreign policy. The controversial article upset Maryland's influential Jewish community, which had consistently supported Mathias's campaigns for office.[100] Mathias had voted to sell fighter planes to the Saudis in 1978, and his vote helped President Reagan get Senate clearance for the AWACS sale in 1981.

The same year the controversial article appeared, just after voters elected him to his third term in the Senate, Mathias took another step that appeared so politically inexpedient that many people assumed he had decided to retire from Congress in 1986.[101] At the urging of Senators Howard Baker and Charles Percy, who wanted another moderate Republican on the Foreign Relations Committee, Mathias gave up a senior position on the Appropriations Committee in order to take the foreign policy committee assignment.

His committee decision shook the leadership of Baltimore, the largest city in the state and a competitor for federal grant assistance. As the *Baltimore Sun* noted in an article critical of the move, "Had he remained on the Appropriations Committee, Mr. Mathias almost certainly would have become chairman of the subcommittee that holds the purse strings for the Department of Housing and Urban Development, an agency of great importance to the 'renaissance' of Baltimore."[102]

Contrary to the assumptions of Maryland political observers, Mathias was not planning to retire. He had left a committee that was important to his constituents, but the senator welcomed the opportunity to help shape the issues that come before the Foreign Relations Committee. He was exhibiting a political philosophy admired by former Senator Mike Mansfield, who once called Mathias "the conscience of the Senate," and by former Secretary of State Henry Kissinger, who recognized Mathias as "one of the few statesmen I met in Washington."[103]

These qualities led Mathias to write his controversial *Foreign Affairs* article, which called for "the reintroduction of civility" into the discussion of "ethnic advocacy" in Congress.[104] He acknowledged that ethnic groups have the right to lobby for legislation, but he warned, "The affirmation of a right, and of the dangers of suppressing it, does not . . . assure that the right will be exercised responsibly and for the general good."

Mathias cited the Israeli lobby as the most powerful ethnic pressure group, noting that it differs from others in that it focuses on vital national security interests and exerts "more constant pressure." Other lobbying groups "show up in a crisis and then disappear" and tend to deal with domestic matters. Mathias continued:

> With the exception of the Eisenhower administration, which virtually com-
> pelled Israel's withdrawal from the Sinai after the 1956 war, American pres-
> idents, and to an even greater degree Senators and Representatives, have
> been subjected to recurrent pressures from what has come to be known as
> the Israel lobby.

He added an indictment of his colleagues: "For the most part they have been responsive [to pro-Israel lobbying pressure], and for reasons not always related either to personal conviction or careful reflection on the national interest."

Mathias illustrated his concern by reviewing the "spectacular" success of AIPAC in 1975 when the group promoted the "Spirit of 76" letter: "Seventy-six of us promptly affixed our signatures, although no hearings had been held, no debate conducted, nor had the administration been invited to present its views."

The Maryland Republican felt that the independence of Congress was compromised by the intimidating effect of AIPAC's lobbying. He wrote that "Congressional conviction" in favor of Israel "has been immeasurably reinforced by the knowledge that political sanctions will be applied to any who fail to deliver" on votes to support high levels of economic and military aid to Israel.

Although he signed AIPAC's letter to President Ford in 1975, Mathias resisted AIPAC's 1978 lobbying against the Carter administration's proposal to sell sixty F-15 fighter planes to Saudi Arabia. In the Senate debate before the vote, he said that both Israel and Saudi Arabia were important friends of the United States and that "both need our support."

Despite this attempt to balance American interests with those of Israel and Saudi Arabia, Mathias said an "emotional, judgmental atmosphere" surrounded the arms sale issue. He quoted from a letter, written to a New York Jewish newspaper, condemning his vote:

Mr. Mathias values the importance of oil over the well-being of Jews and the state of Israel. . . . The Jewish people cannot be fooled by such a person, no matter what he said, because his act proved who he was.

Yet Mathias had already responded to such criticism in his *Foreign Affairs* article:

Resistance to the pressures of a particular group in itself signals neither a sellout nor even a lack of sympathy with a foreign country or cause, but rather a sincere conviction about the national interest of the United States.

He appealed to both the president and the Congress to "help to reduce the fractiousness and strengthen our sense of common American purpose." The president's national constituency, he wrote, afforded him a unique opportunity to work toward this end, but Congress, "although more vulnerable to group pressures," must also be active.

Mathias asserted that it is not enough simply to follow public opinion: "An elected representative has other duties as well—to formulate and explain to the best of his or her ability the general interest, and to be prepared to accept the political consequences of having done so." He warned that ethnic advocacy tends toward excessiveness and can thwart the higher good of national interests.

The Baltimore *Jewish Times* reported that Jewish leaders faced "a delicate dilemma" as they considered how to respond to the article:

Basically, they're damned if they do and damned if they don't. If they keep a low profile and do not challenge Mathias's assertions, they feel they will be shirking their duty and giving in. Yet if they "go after" the Senator, they will be falling into a trap by proving his point about excessive pressure.[105]

Some Jews decided to take the latter course. Arnold Blumberg, a history professor at Towson State University, charged that Mathias "is in the mainstream of a tradition which urged Americans to pursue trade with Japan and Nazi Germany right up to the moment when scrap metal rained on the heads of American GIs from German and Japanese planes."[106] A prominent Jewish community official charged that the article was "malicious" and expressed hurt that Mathias had the "poison in him to express these views."[107] Congressman Benjamin S. Rosenthal, a Democrat from New York and a senior member of the House Foreign

Affairs Committee, charged that Mathias was "standing on the threshold of bigotry" and denying "to the ethnic lobbies alone the right to participate in shaping the American concensus on foreign policy."[108] Other critics expressed the fear that the article would encourage anti-Semitism.[109]

A spokesperson for the Maryland Jewish War Veterans organization said Mathias had "sold" himself "to the cause of the Saudis," while a letter to the *Baltimore Sun* chided, "I wish that [Mathias] had had the integrity to express those views one year prior to his re-election rather than one year after."[110]

One critic, identified as "a former lobbyist," told the *Jewish Times* of Baltimore,

> Mathias is a bright, well-respected legislator who's been effective on Soviet Jewry, but when it comes to Israel he was always the last to come on board. He was always reluctant, and was pressured by Jewish groups, and he resented the pressure. He sees himself as a statesman above the fray. Now he obviously feels he's in a position to say what he really believes.[111]

The Jewish Community Relations Council in San Francisco criticized Mathias in its August 3, 1981, "Backgrounder" newsletter for raising the issue of "dual loyalty" within the "Jewish lobby." Mathias dismissed the charge as a false issue.[112] In Maryland, the article was denounced by some rabbis, and Rabbi Jacob Angus of Baltimore publicly defended Mathias.

Two journalist friends, Frank Mankiewicz and William Safire, warned Mathias that his article would "cause trouble." Two years later, Mankiewicz assessed the senator's future and said he felt the article had created serious problems.

Ethnic lobbying still worried Mathias. Pondering each word over a cup of tea one afternoon in the fall of 1983, he told me,

> Ethnic ties enrich American life, but it must be understood they can't become so important that they obscure the primary duty to be an American citizen. Sometimes the very volume of this kind of activity can amount to an excessive zeal.

Some of his critics had not even read his article, Mathias recalls with a smile. "In a way, they were saying, I haven't read it, but it's outrageous." At breakfasts sponsored by Jewish groups, Mathias was regularly challenged. "When this happened, I would ask how many had actually read my article. In a crowd of 200, maybe two hands would be raised."

Did the article close off communication with Jewish constituents? "I can't say it closed off access, but I have noticed that invitations have fallen off in the past two years," said Mathias.

Mathias did not seek a fourth term in the Senate. He told a friend that controversy in the Jewish community was a factor in his decision.

$3.1 Million from Pro-Israel Sources

Boy wonder of industry, self-made millionaire, tireless Republican campaigner for progressive causes—Charles H. Percy was a bright prospect for the presidency in the late sixties. He skyrocketed to prominence during his first term in the Senate, which began in 1967 after he won an upset victory over Paul Douglas, the popular but aging liberal Democrat.

In his first bid for election, 60 percent of Jewish votes—Illinois has the nation's fourth largest Jewish population—went to Douglas.[113] But over the next six years Percy supported aid for Israel, urged the Soviet Union to permit emigration of Jews, criticized PLO terrorism, and supported social causes so forcefully that Jews rallied to his side when he ran for re-election. In 1972 Percy accomplished something never before achieved by carrying every county in the state. Even more remarkable for an Illinois Protestant Republican, he received 70 percent of the Jewish vote.

His honeymoon with Jews was interrupted in 1975 when he returned from a trip to the Middle East to declare, "Israel and its leadership, for whom I have a high regard, cannot count on the United States in the future just to write a blank check."[114] He said that Israel had missed some opportunities to negotiate, and he described PLO leader Yasser Arafat as "more moderate, relatively speaking, than other extremists such as George Habash." He urged Israel to talk to the PLO, provided the organization renounced terrorism and recognized Israel's right to exist behind secure defensible borders, noting that David Ben Gurion, Israel's first prime minister, had said that Israel must be willing to swap real estate for peace.

A week later Percy received this memorandum from his staff: "We have received 2,200 telegrams and 4,000 letters in response to your Mideast statements. . . . [They] run 95 percent against. As you might imagine, the majority of hostile mail comes from the Jewish community in Chicago. They threaten to withhold their votes and support for any future endeavors."

That same year, Percy offended pro-Israel activists when he did not sign the famous "Spirit of 76" letter, through which seventy-six of his Senate colleagues effectively blocked President Gerald R. Ford's intended "reappraisal" of Middle East policy. This brought another flood of protest mail.[115]

Despite these rumblings, the pro-Israel activists did not mount a serious campaign against Percy in 1978. With the senator's unprecedented 1972 sweep of the state fresh in their minds, they did not seek out a credible opponent either in the primary or the general election. In fact, when the Democratic nomination went largely by default to an unknown lawyer, Alex Seith, Jews took little interest. Even Percy's vote to approve the sale of F-15 planes to Saudi Arabia during the campaign year caused him no serious problem at that time.

In fact, only about one hundred Chicago Jews, few of them prominent, openly supported Seith. The challenger's scheduler, who is Jewish, called every synagogue and every Jewish men's and women's organization in the state, but only one agreed to let Seith speak. His campaign manager, Gary Ratner, concludes, "Most Jews felt there was no way Percy would lose, so why get him mad at us." Of the $1 million Seith spent, less than $20,000 came from Jews. Encouraged by Philip Klutznick, a prominent Chicago Jewish leader, Illinois Jews contributed several times that amount to Percy. Of seventy Jewish leaders asked to sign an advertisement supporting Percy, sixty-five gave their approval. On election day, Jewish support figured heavily in Percy's victory. He received only 53 percent of the statewide vote, but an impressive 61 percent of the Jewish vote.

The 1984 campaign was dramatically different. Pro-Israel forces targeted him for defeat early and never let up. Percy upset Jews by voting to support the Reagan administration sale of AWACS planes to Saudi Arabia, a sale also supported by the Carter administration. These developments provided new ammunition for the attack already underway against Percy. His decision was made after staff members who had visited Israel said they had been told by an Israeli military official that the strategic military balance would not be affected, but that they did not want the symbolism of the United States doing business with Saudi Arabia.

Early in 1984, AIPAC decided to mobilize the full national resources of the pro-Israel campaign against Percy. In the March primary, it encouraged the candidacy of Congressman Tom Corcoran, Percy's challenger for the nomination. One of Corcoran's chief advisers and fundraisers was Morris Amitay, former executive director of AIPAC. Corcoran's high-decibel attacks portrayed Percy as anti-Israel. His fundraising appeals to Jews cited Percy as "Israel's worst adversary in Congress." A full-page newspaper advertisement, sponsored by the Corcoran campaign, featured a picture of Arafat and headlined, "Chuck Percy says this man is a moderate."[116] A letter to Jewish voters defending Percy and signed by fifty-eight leading Illinois Jews made almost no impact.

Although Percy overcame the primary challenge, Corcoran's attacks damaged his position with Jewish voters and provided a strong base for AIPAC's continuing assault.[117] Thomas A. Dine, executive director of AIPAC, set the tone early in the summer by attacking Percy's record at a campaign workshop in Chicago. AIPAC encouraged fund-raising for Paul Simon and mobilized its political resources heavily against Percy. It assigned several student interns full time to the task of anti-Percy research, and it brought more than one hundred university students from out-of-state to campaign for Simon.

Midway through the campaign, AIPAC took a devious step to make Percy look bad. The key votes that were selected by AIPAC and used to rate all senators showed Percy supporting Israel 89 percent of the time during his career. This put him only a few points below Simon's 99-percent rating in the House of Representatives—hardly the contrast AIPAC wanted to cite in its anti-Percy campaign. The lobby solved the problem by changing its own rule book in the middle of the game. It added to the selected list a number of obscure votes that Percy had cast in the subcommittee, as well as letters and resolutions that Percy had not signed. The expanded list dropped the senator's rating to only 51 percent, a mark that Simon used when he addressed Jewish audiences.

While most financial support from pro-Israel activists came to Simon from individuals, political action committees figured heavily. By mid-August these committees had contributed $145,870 to Simon, more than to any other Senate candidate.[118] By election day, the total had risen to $235,000, with fifty-five committees participating.

In addition, California Jewish activist Michael Goland, using a loophole in the federal law, spent $1.6 million for billboard, radio, and television advertising that urged Illinoisans to "dump Percy" and called him a "chameleon." Percy undertook vigorous countermeasures. Former Senator Jacob Javits of New York, one of the nation's most prominent and respected Jews, and Senator Rudy Boschwitz, chairman of the Senate subcommittee on the Middle East, made personal appearances for Percy in Chicago, and one hundred Illinois Jews, led by former Attorney General Edward H. Levi, sponsored a full-page advertisement declaring that Percy "has delivered for Illinois, delivered for America, and delivered for Israel." The advertisement, in an unstated reference to Goland's attacks, warned, "Don't let our U.S. Senate race be bought by a Californian."

Except for charging in one news conference that Simon incorrectly proclaimed that he had a 100-percent voting record for the pro-Israel lobby, Percy tried to avoid the Israel–Jewish controversy in the campaign.

These precautions proved futile, as did his strong legislative endeavors. His initiatives as chairman of the Senate Foreign Relations Committee brought Israel $425 million more in grant aid than Reagan had requested in 1983 and $325 million more in 1984, but these successes for Israel seemed to make no difference. A poll taken a month before the election showed a large majority of Jews supporting Simon. The Percy campaign found no way to stem the tide.

When the votes were counted, Percy lost statewide by 89,000 votes.[119] One exit poll indicated that Percy had won 35 percent of the Jewish vote. In the same balloting, Illinois Jews cast only 30 percent of their votes for the re-election of President Ronald Reagan—evidence of their unhappiness with the chief executive's views on the separation of church and state, abortion, and other social issues, not to mention his insistence on selling AWACS planes to Saudi Arabia.

In an election decided by so few votes, any major influence could be cited as crucial. Although broadly supportive of Reagan's program, Percy was remembered by many voters mainly as a moderate, progressive Republican. Some conservative Republicans rejoiced at his defeat. The "new right," symbolized by the National Conservative Political Action Committee, withheld its support from Percy, and early in the campaign indicated its preference for Simon, despite the latter's extremely liberal record in Congress.

The Middle East controversy alone may have been sufficient to cost Percy his Senate seat. Thousands of Jews who had voted for Percy in 1978 left him for the Democratic candidate six years later. And these votes fled to Simon mainly because Israel's lobby worked effectively throughout the campaign year to portray the senator as basically anti-Israel. Percy's long record of support for Israel's needs amounted to a repudiation of the accusation, but too few Jews spoke up publicly in his defense. The senator found that once a candidate is labeled anti-Israel, the poison sinks so swiftly and deeply it is almost impossible to remove.

The Middle East figured heavily in campaign financing as well as voting.[120] Simon's outlay for the year was $5.3 million, Percy's about $6 million. With Goland spending $1.6 million in his own independent attack on Percy, total expenditures on behalf of the Simon candidacy came to $6.9 million.

Forty percent—$3.1 million—of Simon's campaign financing came from Jews who were disgruntled over Percy's position on Arab–Israel relations. Indeed, Simon was promised half this sum before he became a candidate. While he was still pondering whether to vacate his safe seat in the House of Representatives in order to make the race, he was assured $1.5 million from Jewish sources. The promise came from Robert Schrayer, Chicago area businessman and leader in the Jewish community, whose daughter, Elizabeth, was helping to organize anti-Percy forces in her job as assistant director of political affairs for AIPAC.

Reviewing the impact of the Middle East controversy on his defeat, Percy says, "Did it make the difference? I don't know. But this I believe: I believe Paul Simon would not have run had he not been assured by Bob Schrayer that he would receive the $1.5 million."[121] Simon acknowledges, "This assurance was a factor in my decision."

AIPAC's Thomas A. Dine told a Canadian audience: "All the Jews in America, from coast to coast, gathered to oust Percy. And American politicians—those who hold public positions now, and those who aspire—got the message."[122]

"Leave the Grandstanding to Others"

The message came through so loud, so clear, that some senators now find it necessary to confer with AIPAC executives before introducing legislation related to the Middle East. One such politician is Senator Dianne Feinstein (D-CA), who in the 2000 elections won out over her challenger, former Representative and critic of Israel Tom Campbell. Feinstein went on to sponsor, along with Mitch McConnell (R-KY), every blatantly pro-Israel piece of legislation in the 107th Senate. These senators reportedly conferred with Howard Kohr, executive director of AIPAC, before drafting their legislation. Kohr claims to receive "dozens of calls" from lawmakers asking what they can do to help Israel.

On May 2, 2002, Feinstein and McConnell introduced Senate Resolution 247 which, like Tom DeLay's "Israel First" resolution in the House, criticized the Palestinian Authority, condemned suicide bombings, and made no mention whatsoever of Israeli aggression. Senator Robert C. Byrd (D-WV), was appalled:

> Nowhere in this resolution is Israel called upon to fulfill its role in working for peace in the Middle East. . . . If the Senate is serious about promoting peace in the Middle East—and I believe to the depths of my soul that we are—then we should leave the grandstanding to others. We should support the real work of peacekeeping. . . . This is not the time for the United States Senate to wade into the fray waving a sledgehammer in the form of an ill-timed, ill-advised, and one-sided resolution, and I intend to vote against it.[123]

5

The Lobby and the Oval Office

ON A SUNDAY afternoon, just a few days before the 1960 presidential election, John F. Kennedy, the Democratic candidate, parked his car in front of the residence at 4615 W Street, just off Foxhall Road in a fashionable section of Washington, D.C. He was alone, unencumbered by the Secret Service officers who would soon be a part of his life.

Kennedy wanted to get away from campaign pressures and have a chat with Charles Bartlett, a journalist and a close friend of many years. Their friendship had remained firm since they became acquainted in Florida immediately after World War II, and it was Bartlett who introduced Kennedy to his future bride, Jacqueline Bouvier.

The night before, Kennedy had gone to dinner with a small group of wealthy and prominent Jews in New York City. An episode of the evening troubled him deeply. Describing it to Bartlett as an "amazing experience," he said one man at the dinner party—he did not identify him by name—told him that he knew Kennedy's campaign was in financial difficulty and, speaking for the group, offered "to help, and help significantly" if Kennedy as president "would allow them to set the course of Middle East policy over the next four years." It was an astounding proposition.[1]

Kennedy told Bartlett that he reacted to the offer less as a presidential candidate than as a citizen. "He said he felt insulted," Bartlett recalls,
"that anybody would make that offer, particularly to a man who even
had a slim chance to be president. He said if he ever did get to be president, he would push for a law that would subsidize presidential campaigns out of the U.S. Treasury. He added that whatever the cost of this
subsidy, it would insulate future presidential candidates from this kind
of pressure and save the country a lot of grief in the long run."

Just what Kennedy said at the dinner in response to the proposition,
Barlett did not know. "Knowing his style, he probably made a general
comment and changed the subject."

After learning of the event from Bartlett, I talked with one of the
people attending the dinner.[2] Myer Feldman, a Washington attorney, had
worked closely in the 1960 Kennedy campaign and would later become
assistant to the president, with special responsibilities for liaison with
the Jewish community. I hoped he could supply further details about
the dinner party conversation. As a freshman congressman in 1961–62,
I had had several friendly encounters with Feldman over wheat sales to
the Soviet Union.

He recalled the gathering. It was held, he said, at the apartment of
Abraham Feinberg, chairman of the American Bank and Trust Company in New York and influential in national Jewish affairs and the Democratic Party. Those attending, Feldman recalled, were "ambiguous about
Kennedy." They weren't sure "which way he would go" on Middle East
policy and were therefore not sure they would support him. The candidate was "peppered with tough and embarrassing questions." Asked for
his opinion about moving the U.S. embassy in Israel from Tel Aviv to
Jerusalem, Kennedy replied, "Not under present circumstances." Feldman said that Kennedy answered all questions directly and made a good
impression on his hosts. Feldman said he was unaware of the proposition
that "insulted" the future president.

It was not the first time Middle East politics intruded forcibly into
presidential campaigns. Bartlett says that when he related the episode to
Roger L. Stevens, founding chairman of the John F. Kennedy Center for
the Performing Arts in Washington, D.C., Stevens responded, "That's
very interesting, because exactly the same thing happened to Adlai [for-
mer UN Ambassador Adlai E. Stevenson] in Los Angeles in 1956."

Stevenson was then the Democratic candidate for president, opposing the re-election of Dwight D. Eisenhower.

Ethnic group pressure is an ever-present part of U.S. partisan politics, and because the president of the United States is the executor of all foreign policy, and the formulator of most of it, pressures naturally center on the people who hold or seek the presidency. When the pressure is from friends of Israel, presidents—and presidential candidates—often yield.

Lobby pressure on the White House is applied at several different levels. The most direct—person-to-person—varies greatly, depending on the inclinations of the person who is president at the time.

Some of those applying pressure are close personal friends whose influence is limited to just one presidency, an example being Harry S Truman's close friendship with Ed Jacobson, his former haberdashery partner and an ardent Zionist. Mr. and Mrs. Arthur Krim, Jewish leaders from New York, maintained a close relationship with Lyndon B. Johnson.[3] A White House official of the period recalls: "Arthur Krim stayed at the LBJ Ranch during crucial moments before the 1967 war, and his wife, Mathilde, was a guest in the White House during the war." White House logs show that Mrs. Krim talked frequently by telephone with Johnson.

Other Jewish leaders maintain a relationship from one administration to another. Abraham Feinberg of New York, who hosted the dinner for Kennedy in October 1960, kept close White House ties over a period of years. He was a frequent visitor at the White House during the Johnson years, and, as late as 1984, during the pre-convention presidential campaigning, brought the leading Democratic contenders, Walter Mondale and Gary Hart, together for a private discussion at his New York apartment. Philip Klutznick of Chicago, former president of B'nai B'rith, kept close relations throughout the Truman, Eisenhower, Kennedy, Johnson, and Carter administrations.

Sometimes Israeli diplomats have a personal relationship that gives them direct access to the president. Ephraim Evron, then deputy chief in the Israeli embassy and a friend of Lyndon B. Johnson's since his Senate days, sometimes talked privately with Johnson in the Oval Office.

The second level of pressure comes through officials close to the president—his adviser on relations with the Jewish community or others among his top aides. President Kennedy told a friend, with a chuckle, that he learned that when he was away from Washington, Myer Feldman, his adviser on Jewish matters, would occasionally invite Jewish leaders to the White House for a discussion in the Cabinet Room.

The third level of pressure is within the top tiers of the U.S. departments—the State Department, Defense Department, and National Security Council—where Israeli officials and groups of U.S. citizens who are pro-Israeli activists frequently call to present their agendas to cabinet officers or their chief deputies.

"The Votes Are Against You"

Zionists began pressing their case early in Harry S. Truman's administration and intensified their efforts in 1947, when Truman initially expressed opposition to the establishment of a Jewish state in Palestine.[4] Jewish leaders bought newspaper advertising designed to transform public shame and outrage over the Holocaust into popular support for the idea of a Jewish national homeland. Both Houses of Congress passed resolutions urging presidential support.

When Truman continued to resist and publicly urged citizens to avoid inflaming "the passions of the inhabitants of Palestine," a group of New Jersey Jews wired: "Your policy on Palestine . . . has cost you our support in 1948."[5] With election day approaching, it was a reminder of the grim political facts of life. Two-thirds of American Jews lived in New York, Pennsylvania, and Illinois, and these states would cast 110 electoral votes in the presidential voting.[6] Considered the underdog in the upcoming election despite his incumbency, Truman knew he must have those votes to win.

With a proclamation announcing the new state of Israel expected soon, Truman assembled his Middle East ambassadors to get their views. Their spokesman, ambassador to Egypt Pinkerton "Pinky" Tuck, advised against the United States' immediate recognition of the state.[7] He told Truman that the decision to recognize Israel should be delayed long enough to allow a consultation with Arab states, which Truman's predecessor, Franklin D. Roosevelt, had promised the king of Saudi Arabia.

Truman replied, "Mr. Tuck, you may be right, but the votes are against you." In deciding to recognize Israel immediately, Truman rejected not just Tuck's advice but that of all his military and diplomatic advisers. He chose instead the recommendation of his close friend Ed Jacobson. In fact, pro-Israeli partisans today generally view Truman's immediate recognition of Israel as a prime example of effective lobbying through a "key contact" rather than via the usual pressure tactics.[8] Jacobson's pro-Zionist view was shared by Truman's political advisers, particularly his legal counsel, Clark Clifford.

Secretary of State George C. Marshall opposed the decision so strongly that he bluntly told Truman soon after his recognition announcement that if the election were held the next day he would not vote for him.[9] Sentiments were, of course, much different in Israel. During a 1949 White House visit, the chief rabbi of Israel told the president, "God put you in your mother's womb so you would be the instrument to bring about the rebirth of Israel after 2,000 years."[10]

In partisan political terms, Truman's decision paid off. On election day he received 75 percent of the nation's Jewish vote, which helped him win a razor-thin upset victory—and a permanent place of honor on the face of Israeli postage stamps, as well as in the hearts of Zionists.

Dismayed by Partisan Considerations

Presidential behavior toward the state of Israel took a turn in the opposite direction when Truman's successor, Dwight D. Eisenhower, assumed office. He resisted pressures from the Israeli lobby, and on three occasions forced Israel to abandon major policies to which it was publicly and strongly committed.

In September 1953, Eisenhower ordered a cancellation of all aid—amounting to $26 million—until Israel stopped work on a diversion canal being constructed on the Jordan River, a violation of the 1949 ceasefire agreements.[11] The diversion canal would help Israel assume control of water resources that were important to all nations in the region. It was the first time a president actually cut off all aid to Israel. Eisenhower also instructed the Treasury Department to draft an order removing the tax-deductible status of contributions made to the United Jewish Appeal and other organizations that raised funds for Israel in the United States.

Predictably, Eisenhower's decision kicked up a major storm.[12] Dr. Israel Goldstein told an audience of 20,000 celebrating Jerusalem's 3,000th birthday at New York's Madison Square Garden: "Peace will not be helped by withholding aid as an instrument of unwarranted duress."[13] New York members of Congress joined the bandwagon. Senator Robert Wagner called the decision "cruel and intemperate," and Congressman

Emanuel Celler denounced it as a "snap judgment." All major Jewish organizations condemned the action.

Eisenhower stood firm in withholding aid, and less than two months later Israel announced it was ceasing work on the river diversion project. The president had won a first round, the confrontation was postponed, aid to Israel was resumed, and the order ending the privileged tax status enjoyed by Zionist groups was not issued.

Eisenhower faced the lobby again in October 1956, just days before his re-election as president.[14] Israel had negotiated a secret deal with Britain and France under which the three nations would coordinate a military attack on the Nasser regime in Egypt, which had just taken over the Suez Canal. Israel would strike across the Sinai Desert and move against the canal, while British and French forces would deploy an air bombardment and then invade from the north.

The allied governments assumed that the United States would not interfere; France and Britain believed that Eisenhower would avoid a public showdown with his wartime allies. With the U.S. presidential election just days away, Israel counted on partisan pressures from its American lobby to keep candidate Eisenhower on the sidelines. They all miscalculated.

Israel's invasion of Egypt began on October 29. Eisenhower immediately canceled all aid to Israel. He permitted only the delivery of food already in transit, stopping all other forms of assistance, both economic and military. These measures created such pressure that Israel halted its attack. The British and French, also under heavy U.S. pressure, abandoned their invasion from the north. Despite partisan assaults on his Middle East policy, the president was easily reelected.[15] In fact, more U.S. Jews (40 percent) voted for Eisenhower in 1956 than in 1952 (36 percent).

But Eisenhower's problems with Israel were far from over. Even after the invasion was halted, Israel decided to keep occupying forces in the Egyptian-administered Gaza Strip, as well as the strategic village of Sharm el-Sheik at the access to the Gulf of Aqaba. Despite protests by the United States and six resolutions by the United Nations, Israel refused to withdraw.[16] As weeks passed, lobby pressure against Eisenhower's position received support from Eleanor Roosevelt, former President Truman, and the leaders of both parties in the Senate, Democrat Lyndon Johnson of Texas, and Republican William Knowland of California.

Informed that the United States might support UN sanctions against Israel, Knowland threatened to resign as a member of the UN delegation and warned Secretary of State John Foster Dulles, "This will mean a parting of the ways."[17] Dulles was firm: "I think you should study this. We cannot have all our policies made in Jerusalem." Dulles told Henry Luce, owner of Time, Inc. and a supporter of Israel's position, "I am aware how almost impossible it is in this country to carry out a foreign policy not approved by the Jews. [But] I am going to try to have one. This does not mean I am anti-Jewish, but I believe in what George Washington said in his farewell address, that an emotional attachment to another country should not interfere."

Eisenhower considered the issue vital. He summoned the bipartisan leadership of Congress to the White House to request their support. Unwilling to tangle with pro-Israeli activists, the group refused. That night the president wrote in his diary: "As I reflected on the pettiness of the discussion of the morning, I found it somewhat dismaying that partisan considerations should enter so much into life-or-death, peace-or-war decisions."[18]

A determined president took his case to the American people in a televised address in the spring of 1957:

> Should a nation which attacks and occupies foreign territory in the face of the United Nations' disapproval be allowed to impose conditions on its own withdrawal? If we agreed that armed attack can properly achieve the purposes of the assailant, then I fear we will have turned back the clock of international order.[19]

Letters and telegrams poured into the White House. Almost all of the communications came from Jews, 90 percent of which supported Israel's position. Dulles complained, "It is impossible to hold the line, because we get no support from the Protestant elements in the country.[20] All we get is a battering from the Jews."

Eisenhower persisted, declaring that the United States would support a UN resolution imposing sanctions if Israel did not withdraw from all of the Sinai peninsula and from Gaza and threatening to take away the tax privilege enjoyed by donors to Israeli causes.[21] Faced with that prospect, Israel finally capitulated and withdrew from the occupied territory.

"Armed Shipments Are . . . Ready to Go"

Israel fared better at the hands of the next occupants of the White House. Presidents John F. Kennedy and Lyndon B. Johnson began to help Israel in its military activities.

Although there is no evidence to suggest that Kennedy accepted the dinner party proposition—to exchange control of Middle East policy for campaign contributions—he fared well on election day in 1960, receiving 82 percent of the Jewish vote, topping even Harry Truman's 75 percent, and, as president, he made a decision that was vital to Israel's military plans.[22] He approved, for the first time in history, the U.S. sale of weapons to Israel.[23]

But Israel's military fortunes received a still greater boost with the arrival in the Oval Office of President Lyndon B. Johnson, whose sympathy for the underdog—in his view, Israel—made him responsive to the demands of Israel and its lobby in the United States.[24] Friends of Israel with special influence included Arthur Goldberg, U.S. ambassador to the United Nations; Philip Klutznick of Chicago; and three New Yorkers, Abraham Feinberg and Arthur and Mathilde Krim.[25] The Krims often worked through the Rostow brothers, Walt Rostow, Johnson's national security adviser, and Eugene Rostow, assistant secretary of state for political affairs.[26]

In a September 1966 letter to Feinberg, Klutznick called for an improved relationship between Johnson and the U.S. Jewish community.[27] He did not want Jewish differences with Johnson over the Vietnam War or aid to private schools, for example, to complicate American support for Israel. He called on Feinberg to help establish a "sense of participation." The elements of a deal were present. At the time, Johnson desperately wanted public support for the war in Southeast Asia, and the Jewish leaders wanted assurance that the United States would stand by Israel in a crisis. Aid levels were increased, clearances for almost any military item were issued, and extensive credit was extended.

Lobby pressure may not have been needed to persuade Johnson to support Israel, but the pressure came nevertheless. Harold Saunders, a member of the National Security Council staff who would later become Carter's assistant secretary of state for the Near East and South Asia, recalls the avalanche of telegrams and letters that urged President Johnson to stand behind Israel when Egypt's President Nasser closed the Strait of Tiran in May 1967: "I had 150,000 telegrams and letters from the Jewish community in boxes in my office. I do not exaggerate. There were 150,000 pieces of paper sitting there. They all said the same thing. And Johnson decreed that every one of them should be answered."

In early June, on the day that Israel attacked Egypt, the president received this urgent message from Walter Rostow: "Arthur Krim reports that many armed shipments are packed and ready to go to Israel, but are being held up. He thinks it would be most helpful if these could be released."[28]

Israel was at war, and this time the president of the United States would cause no problems. Aid would go forward without interruption, and calls for sanctions against Israel in the United Nations would face adamant U.S. opposition. The United States would actively support Israel's military endeavors. Powerful new ties with Israel would lead the president of the United States to cover up the facts concerning one of the most astonishing disasters in the history of the United States Navy, the Israeli attack on the USS *Liberty*.

Saunders recalls that after the Arab–Israeli war, pro-Israeli interests blanketed the White House with the basic demand that Israel not be forced to withdraw from territory it occupied until the Arab states agreed to a "just and lasting peace" with Israel. Under this demand, Israel could use occupied Arab territory as a bargaining chip in seeking Arab recognition, an option that President Eisenhower refused after the Suez crisis in 1957.

Saunders adds, "This Israeli demand was accepted by President Johnson without discussion in the National Security Council or other policy institutions. It has had a profound impact on the course of events in the Middle East since that time." According to another high official of that period, the policy was adopted because the lobby succeeded in "pervading the very atmosphere of the White House."

Nixon's Order Ignored

Although Johnson's successor, Richard M. Nixon, came to office with little Jewish help, he supported Israel so heavily in his first term as president that in the 1972 re-election campaign Israel's ambassador to Washington, Yitzhak Rabin, openly campaigned for him. Nixon won 35 percent of the Jewish vote in 1972, up twenty points from four years before.[29]

In 1973 Nixon came powerfully to Israel's defense when Arab states tried to recover territory seized in 1967 by the Israelis. During the conflict, the weapons and supplies that Nixon ordered airlifted to Israel proved to be Israel's lifeline. His decision to order forces on a high state of alert worldwide may have kept the Soviet Union from undertaking a larger role in the conflict.

Privately, Nixon criticized Israel for failing to cooperate in a comprehensive settlement of issues with its Arab neighbors.[30] On several occasions, he ordered Henry Kissinger, national security adviser (and later, secretary of state), to suspend aid to Israel until it became more cooperative. Three days before he resigned the presidency, Nixon instructed Kissinger to disapprove an Israeli request for "long-term military assistance." Kissinger writes in his memoirs: "He would cut off all military deliveries to Israel until it agreed to a comprehensive peace. He regretted not having done so earlier. He would make up for it now. His successor would thank him for it. I should prepare the necessary papers." Kissinger adds that Nixon did not return to the subject. Although "the relevant papers were prepared," according to Kissinger, they were "never signed." Nor did Kissinger see fit to carry out the orders. (In July 1984, Nixon verified the Kissinger account, saying it was accurate and adding that he "still believes that aid to Israel should be tied to cooperation in a comprehensive settlement."[31])

Assuming the presidency in 1975, Gerald R. Ford took no action on the cutoff papers prepared for Nixon. (In 1983, while taking part in a conference sponsored by the American Enterprise Institute, a Washington think tank, I asked Ford's former chief of staff, Richard Cheney, who had been my colleague in the House of Representatives, if he knew what happened to the papers Kissinger had drafted. He said he was totally unaware of the papers. They seemed to have disappeared without a trace.) Nevertheless, Ford confronted Rabin, who by then had become the Israeli prime minister, over the same comprehensive peace issue. In an effort to elicit greater Israeli cooperation, Ford announced in 1975 that he would "reassess" U.S. policy in the Middle East. Under lobby-organized pressure from the Senate, Ford dropped the reassessment, but this retreat did not win him votes when he sought a full term as president the next year. In 1976, 68 percent of the Jewish vote went to Democrat Jimmy Carter.

Uncritical Support Is No Favor to Israel

During the period between Carter's election in 1976 and his inauguration in January 1977, the Israeli lobby played a role in his decision on who would manage foreign policy. Carter decided to nominate as Secretary of State Cyrus Vance, a man of decency and fairness who possessed the right impulses regarding Middle East policy. In doing so, however, he passed over George W. Ball, a man who had all these same important qualities but who also possessed the experience, personal force, and worldwide prestige Carter would need in upcoming crises in the Middle East and elsewhere.

When I visited Ball at his Princeton, New Jersey, residence during the summer of 1983, he was well into writing his fourth major book. I found him in a room at the end of a narrow corridor that was lined with cartoons and photographs of the political past. The large high-ceilinged room bustled with the activity of a city newsroom just before press time.

At the center of it all, pecking away at a word processor keyboard and surrounded by papers stacked high on a U-shaped table, sat the man who had been deputy secretary of state under two presidents, the U.S. ambassador to the United Nations, and an executive with one of Manhattan's largest investment banking firms. At 73, he was still busy trying to bring order to a world in disarray. The *Manchester Guardian* characterized him as "an idealist facing chaos with dignity."[32]

I was armed with questions. What price had Ball paid for speaking out on Middle East issues? Had it hurt his law practice, or spoiled his chances to serve in higher office? Ball took time to talk, but he was busy. He had just addressed the cadets at West Point and was midway through preparing an editorial piece for the *Washington Post* in which he would warn the Reagan administration of immense pitfalls ahead in its Lebanese policy. Ball was one of my heroes, especially for his courage on Vietnam policy, and I admired his brilliance as a writer. Eloquent and witty, he reminded me of his colleague in the Johnson administration, former Secretary of State Dean Rusk, although their views on Vietnam were sharply at odds.

"I'll be with you in a minute," Ball said, glancing up from the keyboard. He gave the computer keys a few more whacks, stood up, whipped out a diskette and told his assistant, Lee Hurford, "Print it all."

His six-foot two-inch frame exuded confidence and power. Making his way through the array of books and papers, he explained, "I'm addicted to this machine. I would never go back to a typewriter. I quit commuting to Manhattan," he added, gesturing down the corridor, "because I can slip down here evenings if I have some ideas to put down."

Put them down he has. Over the years many diplomats have firmly criticized Israeli policies, but most have confined their advice to private circles. Those who have spoken out publicly usually have done so in muted tones. Close friends doubt that Ball has any muted tones. He has never pulled any punches. But while on government assignments Ball dutifully kept his advice private.

Ball has paid a price for such candor on Israeli policy. He was one of only three people considered for appointment as secretary of state under President Carter. Had it not been for his outspoken views on Middle East affairs, his nomination would have seemed inevitable.

His political and professional credentials were immaculate. A lifelong Democrat, he twice campaigned vigorously for Adlai E. Stevenson for president. In 1959 he became a supporter of John F. Kennedy's presidential ambitions. His diplomatic experience and prestige were diverse and unmatched. He had served as number two man in the State Department under Presidents John F. Kennedy and Lyndon Johnson. In those assignments he dealt intimately with the Cuban missile crisis and most other major issues in foreign policy for six years. He took the job as ambassador to the UN, a job he did not want, because, in his words, "LBJ had surrounded me."[33]

Ball challenged military policies forcefully within administration circles. Deliberating a proposed policy, Johnson would frequently go around the cabinet room for advice, then say, "Now let's hear what Ball has to say against it." Ball consistently argued against the buildup in Vietnam. The *Washington Post* described him as "the consistent dove in a hawkish administration." Journalist Walter Lippman, a close friend, urged him to resign in protest: "Feeling as you do, you should resign and make your opposition public." Ball declined, believing it important that criticism of the war be heard directly from within the administration, although Johnson usually rejected his advice.[34]

Ball was one of America's best-known and most admired diplomats, but he probably spiked his prospects of becoming Carter's secretary of state when he wrote an article entitled "The Coming Crisis in Israeli–American Relations" for the Winter 1975–76 issue of *Foreign Affairs*.[35] It provoked a storm of protest from the Jewish community.

In the article, Ball cited President Eisenhower's demand that Israel withdraw from the Sinai as "the last time the United States ever took, and persisted in, forceful action against the strong wishes of an Israeli government." He saw the event as a watershed. "American Jewish leaders thereafter set out to build one of Washington's most effective lobbies, which now works in close cooperation with the Israeli embassy."

He lamented the routine leakage of classified information:

> Not only do Israel's American supporters have powerful influence with many members of the Congress, but practically no actions touching Israel's interests can be taken, or even discussed, within the executive branch without it being quickly known to the Israeli government.

He bemoaned Israel's rejection of U.S. advice at a time when Israel's dependence on U.S. aid had "reached the point of totality." Yet he was not surprised that Israel pursued an independent course:

> Israelis have been so long conditioned to expect that Americans will support their country, no matter how often it disregards American advice and protests and America's own interests.

Despite such sharp criticism, for a time candidate Carter considered Ball his principal foreign policy adviser, and selected him as one of three finalists for secretary of state. The other two finalists were Paul Warnke, former assistant secretary of defense, and, of course, Cyrus Vance. Zbigniew Brzezinski, Carter's national security adviser, wrote in his book *Power and Principle* that Ball was his preference for secretary of state during the period preceding election day (he later shifted his preference to Vance). Asked for his views during the post-election process at Plains, Georgia, Brzezinski told Carter that Ball would be "a strong conceptualizer but probably a poor organizer, an assertive individual but probably somewhat handicapped by his controversial position on the Middle East." He said Ball's appointment as secretary of state would be received "extremely well in Western Europe and Japan, probably somewhat less so in the developing countries, and negatively in Israel." A number of

Jewish leaders urged Carter not to name Ball to any significant role in his administration. The characteristic that made Ball unacceptable to the Israeli lobby was his candor; he wasn't afraid to speak up and criticize Israeli policy. Carter dropped Ball from consideration.

With Carter's cabinet selection process completed, Ball continued to speak out. Early in 1977 he wrote another article for *Foreign Affairs*, titled "How to Save Israel in Spite of Herself," in which he urged the new administration to take the lead in formulating a comprehensive settlement that would be fair to the Palestinians as well as Israel. For a time Carter moved in this direction, even trying to communicate with the Palestine Liberation Organization through Saudi Arabia. When this approach floundered, Carter shifted his focus to attempting to reach a settlement between Egypt and Israel at Camp David, where Ball believes Carter was double-crossed by Begin. "I talked with Carter just before Camp David," said Ball. "We had a long dinner together. He told me he was going to try to get a full settlement on Middle East issues, and he seemed to understand the significance of the Palestinian issue. On this I have no doubt, and I think he desperately wanted to settle it." After the Camp David meeting, Israel frustrated Carter's goals, continuing to build settlements in occupied territory and blocking progress toward autonomy for Palestinians in the West Bank.

Although not a part of the Carter administration, Ball continued to be an all-time favorite on television interview shows. One of these appearances led to a public exchange with a Jewish leader. On a panel interview in late 1977, Ball said he felt the Jewish community in the United States had put U.S. interests "rather secondary in many cases." To Morris B. Abram, Manhattan lawyer and former president of the American Jewish Committee, these were fighting words. Enlisted the year before in support of the effort to make Ball the secretary of state, Abram wrote him a public letter, published in the *Washington Post*, charging that these comments established Ball "as one who is willing to accept and spread age-old calumnies about Jews."[36]

Responding in the *Washington Post*, Ball denied that he was suggesting that "even the most ardent Zionist consciously choose Israel over America." He explained, "I suggest rather that the effect of their uncritical encouragement of Israel's most excessive actions is not wholly consistent with the United States' interests." His correspondence with Abram was published in the *Washington Post*. Ball concluded:

> When leading members of the American Jewish community give [Israel's] government uncritical and unqualified approbation and encouragement for whatever it chooses to do, while striving so far as possible to overwhelm any criticism of its actions in Congress and in the public media, they are, in my view, doing neither themselves nor the United States a favor.

During the Reagan administration, Ball became one of the few Democrats who attempted to take his party back to the Middle East morality of Eisenhower. Of Reagan, he said:

> He did not demand, as he should have done under the law, that we would exact the penalties provided unless the Israelis stopped murdering civilians with the weapons we had provided them solely for self-defense. Instead he bought them off by committing our own marines to maintain order while we persuaded the PLO leaders to leave rather than face martyrdom.

Ball did not let his business career, any more than his public career, soften his public expressions. He admitted that his plain talk about the Middle East "certainly hasn't helped" him as a businessman:

> I'm sure that my partners at Lehman Brothers had to absorb a certain amount of punishment. But they were tolerant and understanding people. I never felt I lost anything very much by speaking out. I'm politically untouchable, but I am sure certain groups would rather shoot me than deal with me.[37]

While he was never shot for his views, Ball's encounters with the Israeli lobby were numerous, and they began early in his career. He recalls the day, during the 1952 presidential race, when a pro-Israel emissary visited Adlai Stevenson's presidential campaign headquarters in Springfield, Illinois. The emissary told Ball that his friends had gathered a "lot of money" but wanted to "discuss the Israeli question" before turning it over. Ball says Stevenson met with the group—"he met with any group"—but he "never made any of the promises expected."

In more recent presidential campaigns, Ball experienced lobby pressure of a different kind. In early 1979, impressed with the early pronouncements of Republican John B. Anderson, Ball announced that he planned to vote for the maverick, who was running for president as an independent. Upon hearing the news, an elated Anderson called Ball and promised to visit him at Princeton "soon." Anderson soon changed his mind. He never came. Convinced by his campaign staff that he had to cultivate the pro-Israeli community if he hoped to make progress as a candidate, Anderson made a ritual visit to Israel. He issued statements fully supporting Israel. He shunned Ball.

Being shunned was not a new experience for the elder statesman. In 1983, after testifying to the Senate Foreign Relations Committee one morning, Ball was approached by Senator John Glenn, who was already testing the presidential waters. Glenn invited Ball to call because he wanted his advice on foreign policy issues. After trying unsuccessfully to get calls through, Ball wrote to him. He stated his willingness to help Glenn set up a panel of scholars and former diplomats who could help the candidate with ideas, statements, and speeches during the hectic days of campaigning. Ball had done the same thing for Adlai Stevenson in 1956. Several weeks later, a letter arrived from Glenn stating that he would take up the suggestions with his campaign staff. That was the end of Ball's relationship with Glenn.

Despite the intimidating factors that led candidates Carter, Anderson, and Glenn to avoid linkage with the former ambassador, Ball feels the lobby is overrated in the power it can deliver. While it controls many votes in strategically important states and provides generous financial support to candidates, he contends that these are not the principal factors of its influence. Ball believes the lobby's instrument of greatest power is its willingness to make broad use of the charge of anti-Semitism: "They've got one great thing going for them. Most people are terribly concerned not to be accused of being anti-Semitic, and the lobby so often equates criticism of Israel with anti-Semitism. They keep pounding away at that theme, and people are deterred from speaking out." In Ball's view, many Americans feel a "sense of guilt" over the extermination of Jews by Nazi Germany. The result of this guilt is that the fear of being called anti-Semitic is "much more effective in silencing candidates and public officials than threats about campaign money or votes."

He Was Not Consistent

Jimmy Carter, for a fleeting moment, gave every indication of being a president who would stand up to Israel and pursue policies based on U.S. interests in the Middle East. He came to the presidency determined to be fair to Arab interests as well as to those of Israel, and once in office even advocated a homeland with secure borders for the Palestinians.

While this endeavor soon faded, Carter made great strides in foreign policy elsewhere. In addition to organizing the Camp David Accords, his administration marked the consummation of the treaty with Panama, normalization of diplomatic relations with China, a major reform in international trade policy, and the initial agreement with the Soviet Union on strategic arms limitation. In overall Middle East policy, however, he lacked consistent purpose and commitment.

Carter was dismayed when Jews in the United States remained disgruntled with his administration despite his major role in achieving a long-sought Israeli goal, the peace treaty between Egypt and Israel. A senior diplomat, whose career stretches over thirty years, remembered the pressures Jewish groups brought to bear following the joint U.S.–Soviet communique of October 1977.[38] Carter was trying to revive the Geneva conference on the Middle East in order to get a comprehensive settlement of the Arab–Israeli dispute. The American Jewish community strongly objected. The diplomat recalled, "I remember I really had my hands full meeting with protesting Jewish groups. I figured up one day, totaling just the people the groups said they represented, that I must have met with representatives of half the entire U.S. Jewish community."

The groups came well briefed. All, he says, used the same theme:

What a terrible unpatriotic act it was to invite the Russians back into the Middle East; it was anti-Israel, almost anti-Semitic. I would spend part of my time meeting Jewish groups on Capitol Hill in the offices of Senators and Congressmen. Other times I would meet with groups of twenty to forty in my conference room at the State Department. Meanwhile, Secretary of State Vance would be meeting with other groups, and the President with still others.

The pressure was too much. Carter yielded to the lobbies and quickly dropped the proposal. But he learned, like Ford had before him, that yielding to the lobby on relations with Israel did not pay dividends on election day. Many Jews deserted him when he sought re-election in 1980.

"They Wouldn't Give Him a Dime"

The same year, the pressures of pro-Israeli activists became decisive in the fortunes of a renegade Texas Democrat who turned Republican because he wanted to succeed Jimmy Carter as president.

In October 1979, John Connally, who had been Democratic governor of Texas, came to Washington to give the first major foreign policy speech of his campaign for the presidency. The field of Republican aspirants to the White House was already crowded. Although Ronald Reagan had not yet formally entered the race, seven other Republicans had announced their candidacy.

Connally's campaign theme was "leadership for America," and television advertisements showed him as the "candidate of the forgotten American who goes to church on Sunday."[39] America, Connally believed, was looking for leadership. His speech to the Washington Press Club contained a section outlining a plan to resolve the Arab–Israeli conflict. It was part of a campaign strategy designed to present the former governor of Texas and secretary of the treasury as a decisive leader who was capable of talking man to man with powerful foreigners. He had served in several cabinet positions under President Nixon. With his wide-ranging political experience, he should have known the sensitivity of the Arab–Israeli question.

Several Middle East peace plans had been advanced by presidents, but the plan Connally outlined in his speech was the most ambitious ever presented by a candidate for the office. He argued that the Carter initiative at Camp David had stalled because of failed diplomatic leadership and that it was time for the United States to pursue a new Middle East policy, one "based not on individual Arab or Israeli interests, but on American interests."[40]

American interests demanded peace and stability in the region, Connally said, and this could best be achieved by a program whereby the Israelis withdrew from occupied Arab territories in return for Arab acceptance of Israeli sovereignty and territorial integrity. The Arabs would be obligated to "renounce forever all hostile actions toward Jews and give up the use of oil supply and prices to force political change." This would ensure an uninterrupted supply of Middle East oil, which, Connally said, "is and will continue to be the lifeblood of Western civilization for decades to come." The United States would guarantee the stability of the region by greatly expanding its military presence there.

Connally became the first prominent presidential candidate to declare his support for Palestinian self-determination.[41] He said that the Palestinians should have the option of establishing an independent state on the

West Bank and Gaza or an autonomous area within Jordan. Palestinian leaders who were willing to work for a compromise peace settlement with Israel should be welcomed to discussions, he added, but "those extremists who refuse to cooperate and continue to indulge in terrorism should be treated as international outlaws by the international community."

Connally also suggested that future American aid be conditioned on Israeli willingness to adopt a more reasonable policy on the West Bank. Noting the strain imposed upon the Israeli economy by the need for constant military preparedness, he said, "Without billions of dollars in American economic and military aid, Israel simply could not survive. Yet it is only candid to say that support for this level of aid, in the absence of greater willingness by Israeli leadership to compromise with their neighbors, is eroding." He criticized the Begin government's "policy of creeping annexation of the West Bank," quoting a group of American Jewish leaders who earlier in the year had denounced Israeli policy regarding the West Bank as "morally unacceptable and perilous for the democratic character of the Jewish state."

Connally knew his speech would stir controversy, and indeed the criticism came quick and hard. Rabbi Alexander Schindler, president of the Union of American Hebrew Congregations, said Connally's call for withdrawal from the territories "is a formula for Israel's liquidation." The *Washington Star* quoted unnamed Israeli officials in Washington as calling his plan "a total surrender to blackmail by Arab oil-producing countries." Henry Siegman, executive director of the American Jewish Congress, said Connally's criticism of the Camp David peace process "gives encouragement to the Arab confrontation states who urge a violent solution to the Arab–Israeli conflict. It is disappointing, although perhaps not surprising, that Mr. Connally should emerge as the candidate of the oil interests."[42] Connally's campaign manager later accused the Israeli embassy of orchestrating the attack.

Few news commentators praised his speech. *Christian Science Monitor* columnist Joseph C. Harsch found Connally's peace plan remarkable for its candor.[43] Harsch wrote that Connally "broke with and, indeed, defined the pro-Israel lobby." He "said things about Israel which no prominent American politician has dared to say for a long time, with the exception of Senator J. William Fulbright." Agreeing that the peace plan was really nothing new, Harsch pointed out that it "comes out of the book of official American foreign policy as stated since the 1967 war." What was unusual, Harsch wrote, was that this policy should be articulated by a candidate for president:

> The immediate question is whether Mr. Connally can demonstrate that it is possible to take the official government position on Middle East policy and still survive in the present political climate.

Writing in the *Nation*, Arthur Samuelson called Connally's plan "both wrong and dangerous," but went on to say that "Connally's candor is praiseworthy":

> For all too long, public debate over the Middle East has been characterized by a marked dishonesty on the part of aspirants for public office. Rather than put forward how they plan to break the impasse in American–Israeli relations that has remained constant since 1967, they fall over one another in praise of Israel's virtues.[44]

The *Washington Post* called Connally's speech "a telling measure of how American debate on this central issue is developing":

> No previous candidate for a major party's presidential nomination has staked out a position so opposed to the traditional line. Mr. Connally offers no deference to the "Jewish lobby," attacking the current Israeli government's policies head-on.[45]

Within a few days of the speech, however, less friendly voices were heard.[46] A Jewish Republican running for mayor of Philadelphia snubbed Connally by refusing to be photographed with him. Two Jewish members of Connally's national campaign committee resigned in protest. One of them, Rita Hauser, chairman of the Foreign Affairs Council of the American Jewish Committee, called the speech "inexcusable" and said it represented "the straight Saudi line." The second, attorney Arthur Mason, said he was fearful that Connally's speech might stir anti-Semitism.

The bad news kept coming. The New York Republican Committee withdrew its invitation for Connally to speak at its annual Lincoln Day dinner, and traditional big givers boycotted a fund-raiser in New York that was to feature Connally.[47] The *Washington Post* quoted an unnamed source who said the speech had robbed Connally of the support that his pro-business positions had won among some Jews: "Now they wouldn't give him a dime."[48]

Certainly the Connally candidacy suffered problems that were unrelated to his positions on the Middle East: the campaign experienced organizational difficulties; the forceful Texan came across to some as too "hot" on the "cool" medium of television; and he was undoubtedly hurt by his switch from the Democratic to the Republican party in 1973. But Winton Blount, Connally's campaign chairman, believes that none of these factors equalled the "devastating" effect of the controversial speech. Connally himself says there is "no question" that the speech hurt. Columnist William Safire, an admirer of Connally but also a pro-Israeli hard-liner, made a pained assessment of the speech's effect on the presidential race:

> Supporters of Israel—along with many others concerned with noisy U.S. weakness in the face of Soviet military and Arab economic threats—made a reassessment of Ronald Reagan and decided he looked ten years younger.[49]

Succumbing to Israeli Dictates

In 1984 it was no contest at all on the Republican side of the presidential race, either for the nomination or in respect to policy toward Israel. Ronald Reagan had the field to himself, and he was not about to risk a confrontation like the one that had proved fatal to the candidacy of John Connally four years before.

In late 1983, certain to be a candidate for re-election, Reagan was in a position to deliver, not just promise. He encountered Israeli pressures in opposition to his September 1982 peace plan and his delay in delivering fighter aircraft in the wake of Israel's bombing of the Iraq nuclear plant. But he avoided a major showdown with Israel, and, beginning in 1983, Reagan went all-out for the Jewish vote, pandering to the Israeli lobby while trying to keep the Middle East crisis on hold until after the election.[50]

Polls showed the need for repair work.[51] In 1980 Reagan had received 40 percent of the Jewish vote—the largest ever for a Republican presidential candidate—but half of this support had since drifted away. In

April 1983 Albert A. Spiegel, a longtime Reagan supporter, quit as a special adviser to Reagan on Jewish affairs.[52] Spiegel was upset over a newspaper story that said that Reagan intended to press his Middle East peace plan despite Jewish opposition, and that he felt he could be reelected without Jewish votes.

In December, Reagan launched a broad bid for Jewish support. The first action was upgrading the position of the White House liaison with the Jewish community, but his changes on the policy front were even more significant. After meeting with Israeli Prime Minister Yitzhak Shamir in December 1983, Reagan announced a dramatic increase in the level of aid to Israel.[53] Instead of the old formula, under which Israel was required to pay back some of the funds advanced, the administration requested that in the future all aid be in the form of a grant. In addition, in a gesture to Israel's sagging industry, he agreed that $250 million in U.S. aid funds could be spent in Israel to help finance the manufacture of a new Israeli warplane.[54] United States aircraft firms were dismayed, because they receive no similar government aid.

Reagan proposed a new, higher level of "strategic cooperation" in the military field and a free trade relationship that would make Israel the only nation with tariff-free access to both the European community and the United States. All of this won applause from the Israeli lobby. *Near East Report*, the AIPAC newsletter, declared editorially: "[Reagan] has earned the gratitude of all supporters of a strong United States–Israel relationship."[55]

In March, Reagan made further concessions to the lobby.[56] He refused to intercede with Israel at the request of King Hussein of Jordan, whom he had been pressing to join the peace process. Aiming both to strengthen Yasser Arafat against more radical elements within the Palestine Liberation Organization and to improve his own influence over the Palestinian cause, Hussein asked the president for help. He wanted Reagan to press Israel to permit Palestinians living on the West Bank and Gaza to attend the upcoming session of the Palestine National Council. In another message, Hussein asked the United States to support a UN resolution declaring illegal the settlements Israel had built in the Arab territory it occupied, a position maintained for years by previous presidents. Reagan rejected both requests. Hussein told a reporter for the *New York*

Times that "the United States is succumbing to Israeli dictates," and that he saw no hope for future improvement.[57]

The leading contenders for the Democratic nomination never missed an opportunity to pledge allegiance to Israel. The 1984 presidential contest often focused on the competition between former Vice President Walter Mondale and Senator Gary Hart on the question of who was more loyal to Israel. Mondale accused Hart of being weak in supporting the removal of the U.S. embassy from Tel Aviv to Jerusalem.[58] Hart accused Mondale of trying to "intimidate and coerce Israel into taking unacceptable risks" while he was vice president under President Carter.[59]

Cy Vance Took the Blame

Actually, Mondale was the principal pro-Israel force within the Carter Administration. During the 1980 campaign, he responded to lobby pressure by helping to engineer a diplomatic maneuver that proved costly to the United States. When Donald McHenry, the U.S. ambassador to the United Nations, cast a vote on March 1 in favor of rebuking Israel publicly for its settlements policy—the first such rebuke of an Israeli action since the Eisenhower administration—Jewish circles were furious, and so was Mondale.[60] McHenry's vote supported a resolution that offended the pro-Israel lobby on two fronts: it was critical of Israeli settlements on the West Bank, and it referred to East Jerusalem as "occupied territory."

Mondale organized an immediate counterattack within White House circles. He persuaded Carter that the State Department had wrongly advised him. Late in the evening of the controversial vote the White House announced a "failure in communications" between Washington and New York. It explained that McHenry had misunderstood his instructions and should have abstained. Three days later, Secretary of State Cyrus Vance personally took the blame for the "failure." Few believed him.[61]

Both the nation and the Carter–Mondale ticket would have been better off had Carter ignored Mondale's demand for a vote reversal.[62] For Carter, the episode was an unrelieved diplomatic disaster. Arabs were outraged by what they viewed as a shameless withdrawal in the face of Jewish pressure.[63] American Jews, urged to action by Israeli Defense

Minister Ariel Sharon, doubted the honesty of the explanation and felt betrayed. Sharon told Jews in New York, "I do not like to interfere with internal United States affairs, but the question of Israeli security is a question for Jews anywhere in the world."[64] To the world, the administration appeared out of control.

Senator Edward Kennedy was the main beneficiary of Carter's embarrassment. Calling the UN vote a "betrayal" of Israel, he won the Massachusetts primary by two to one. He also carried New York and Connecticut, where earlier polls had shown Carter ahead. In New York, Jews voted four-to-one for Kennedy. A member of the Israeli parliament said: "The American Jewish community showed itself to have the leverage to swing a vote over the issue of whether the president is good to Israel."

Mondale's measures did not placate the Jewish vote. In November, Carter–Mondale became the first Democratic presidential ticket to fail to win a majority of the Jewish votes cast. Exit polls showed it received, at the most, 47 percent.[65]

After losing to the Reagan–Bush ticket, Mondale devoted himself full-time to campaigning for the presidency, with his uncritical support of Israel becoming a principal plank in his platform. Early in the campaign, he dismissed the idea that Saudi Arabia would "become a strong assertive force for moderation" and urged the prepositioning of high-technology U.S. military equipment in the custody of Israeli "technicians, an arrangement that would eliminate any possibility that the equipment could be used for purposes independent of Israeli wishes."

Later, Mondale and his campaign team carefully avoided any relationship with Arab interests, or even Arab American interests. In June 1984 this zeal led Thomas Rosenberg, Mondale's finance director in Illinois, to return five $1,000 checks to Chicagoans of Arab ancestry who had presented them as campaign donations.[66] He explained that some of the comments they had made in a personal meeting with Mondale amounted to "an anti-Israeli, anti-Semitic diatribe." One of the five, Albert Joseph, a lifelong Democrat and owner of Hunter Publishing, denied the accusation, recalling, "We passed forty-five minutes with [Mondale] in the utmost friendliness and respect."

Joseph said that when the checks were returned he was informed by Joseph Gomez, at the time a member of the Mondale finance committee in Illinois, that Mondale's organization had decided to "take no more money from Arab Americans in the future." The Chicago publisher said he felt "insulted, betrayed, and shocked." He told a reporter that Mondale was "disenfranchising a whole group of Americans." Upset by the decision to return the funds, Gomez, a Chicago banker and Hispanic leader, withdrew from the Mondale campaign. Gomez said the Mondale campaign decision confirmed his view that "people of Arab ancestry are the most persecuted group in America today."

Candidate Gary Hart's record of support for Israel was as unblemished as Mondale's, and his campaign organization displayed a similar indifference to Arab American sensibilities. Upon learning that the First American Bank in Washington, D.C.—where he had done his personal banking for years—had been purchased by a group of Middle East investors in 1982, Hart immediately closed out a campaign loan of $700,000 and severed all ties with the bank.[67] His special counsel explained, "We didn't know it was an Arab bank. We got [Hart] out of it as soon as we knew." Hart's competitor for the nomination, Jesse Jackson, denounced the move as a "serious act of racism."[68]

As a senator, Hart voted for every pro-Israeli measure, opposed every initiative intended to provide arms to Arab states, and put his signature on every major letter and resolution helpful to the Israeli cause.[69] When a few colleagues, such as Senator John Glenn, condemned Israel's raid on the Iraqi nuclear installation, he deplored the condemnation.

"Intimidation is So Great"

Senators Ernest Hollings of South Carolina and Alan Cranston of California and former Florida governor Reuben Askew—early dropouts in the Democratic competition—were similarly uncritical in their support of Israel.[70] So was Senator John Glenn of Ohio, who had been expected by many observers to take a middle road position on Middle East policy. In the past he had criticized Israeli military actions, supported the sale of F-15 aircraft to Saudi Arabia, and even suggested talks with the PLO.[71]

Bitten by the presidential bug, Glenn shifted ground in 1983, effectively ruling out such talks and excusing his vote for the F-15 sale on the grounds that Saudi Arabia would otherwise have bought planes from France with "no strings attached."[72]

In a speech to the Foreign Policy Association in New York, Glenn went much further, saying that the United States should recognize Jerusalem as the official capital of Israel once the terms of Camp David were completed or if negotiations broke down completely.[73] He characterized the PLO as "little more than a gang of thugs" and said the biggest obstacle to peace in the Middle East was Arab refusal to accept the legitimacy of Israel.

Although the speech did not allay Jewish suspicion, it cost him the support of citizens who felt that the next president must respond to Arab as well as Israeli concerns. One of Glenn's closest colleagues, an Ohio congressman, reacted with alarm and distress: "Glenn caved in, and he didn't have to do it. I was so demoralized by that statement I delayed making some calls to labor people in his behalf."[74] The speech caused a veteran diplomat of the Johnson administration, former Ambassador Lucius Battle, to refuse to serve as a Glenn foreign policy adviser.[75]

Only two candidates spoke up for a balanced policy in the Middle East: black civil rights activist Jesse L. Jackson and George McGovern, the 1972 Democratic presidential nominee. McGovern called for the creation of an independent Palestinian state and criticized Israeli military and settlement actions.[76] His proposals were even more precise than those that brought John Connally's campaign to an end four years before.

In a speech at a Massachusetts synagogue in February, McGovern asked, "Is it not both bad politics and bad ethics to brand as anti-Israel an American politician who is willing to apply the same critical standards to Israeli policies that are applied to United States policies?"[77] McGovern said that even though during his twenty-two years in Congress he had voted "100 percent" for measures providing economic and military aid to Israel, he nevertheless opposed Israel's invasion of Lebanon: "I don't think one sovereign nation has the right to invade another."

Neither McGovern nor Jackson had a serious prospect for nomination. In different ways, each presented himself in the role of "party conscience." The "Super Tuesday" primaries in March eliminated McGovern, and only Jackson's conscience remained in the campaign.[78]

Jackson had become controversial with U.S. Jews four years before his presidential bid, when he carried his human rights activism abroad to Lebanon and there met PLO leader Yasser Arafat.[79] Until then, the former disciple of the Reverend Martin Luther King, Jr., worked mainly for black rights through his organization, People United to Save Humanity (PUSH), a Chicago-based group that received substantial Jewish financial support. In Lebanon, he came face-to-face with the misery of Palestinians, describing them as "the niggers of the Middle East."

Early in 1983, Jackson began traveling around the country as a "non-candidate" but already drumming up interest in a "rainbow coalition" of interest groups. At a time when prospective candidates often try to blur controversial statements made in the past, Jackson reiterated his recommendation that the United States open a dialogue with the Palestine Liberation Organization. In a televised statement in New York, he said the United States could best help Israel by supporting the creation of a Palestinian homeland. Until that happened, he said, Palestinians would engage in "more acts of terrorism, more acts of desperation." He urged direct U.S. talks with the PLO to get the peace process moving, but he said that our diplomats could not even discuss this option, because "intimidation is so great" in the United States. These statements put him at odds with most Jewish leaders.

By the time Jackson became a candidate in October 1983, *Washington Post* editorial editor Meg Greenfield had called him one of the nation's two greatest political orators (sharing the honor with President Reagan).[80] Jackson immediately enlivened the political scene by flying to Syria, where he negotiated the release of a U.S. Navy pilot held captive there.[81] He proclaimed, "The temperature has been lowered somewhat between Syria and America. The cycle of pain has been broken."[82]

In the critical primaries beginning in March, Jackson received impressive support in Illinois, New York, and Pennsylvania, as well as in southern states. In televised debates with Mondale and Hart, Jackson called for compassion in dealing with all people in the Middle East and rejected the "terrorist" labels so often attached to all Palestinians.[83] While Mondale and Hart rejected Jackson's plea for a comprehensive Middle East peace involving a Palestinian homeland in the West Bank, the exchange was moderate in terms and expression. It was the first time that Palestinian rights had been discussed with civility in a presidential campaign.

Jackson found himself on the defensive when a reporter disclosed that, in a private conversation, he had referred to Jews as "Hymies" and New York as "Hymietown," a slip that led many to charge him with being anti-Semitic.[84] He was encumbered by the endorsement of controversial black leader Louis Farrakhan, who called Judaism a "dirty religion" and Hitler a "wickedly great man." Inspired by attacks from Jewish leaders, the press never let up in pressing him about the allegations of anti-Semitism and his relationship with Farrakhan.[85] Even in his press conference in Cuba, where his endeavors brought the release of several U.S. citizens, the anti-Semitic theme dominated the questioning. In advance of the Democratic convention, the American Jewish Committee organized a campaign to keep Jackson from attaining prominence in the campaign of the expected nominee, Walter Mondale.[86]

Despite these problems, Jackson rallied support broadly enough to remain a major factor throughout the convention. While no one expected Jackson to be on the presidential ticket, he emerged a winner even before the convention. He proved that a black man could be a credible candidate for the nation's highest office, even while supporting positions strongly opposed by the Israeli lobby. In doing so, he lifted the self-esteem of two ethnic groups often abused or neglected in U.S. society: blacks and Arab Americans.

The winner of the presidential sweepstakes, Ronald Reagan, was left to wonder if his heroic endeavors for Israel had paid off at the polls. He received 31 percent of the Jewish vote, down from the 40 percent he received in 1980.

"One Lonely Little Guy"

Reagan's successor, President George H. W. Bush, did slightly worse than his former boss in the 1988 elections, receiving an even smaller percentage of the national Jewish vote. Two years later, Bush got involved in what one author calls "the most noteworthy showdown with Israel and the American–Israeli lobby of any American president."[87] It began in March 1990, when Israel submitted a request to the United States for more than $1 billion in loans, gifts, and donations. The money was going to pay to resettle Soviet Jews in the occupied territories—in clear violation of international law. Bush's response was simple and straightforward: There should be no new settlements in the West Bank or East Jerusalem."

This reiteration of American policy would open the floodgates to a tidal wave of criticism. Eighteen months later in September 1991 the request was repeated—except this time, Israel asked for a $10 billion loan guarantee. Again, the purpose was to build and expand settlements in the occupied territories. The request was made despite U.S. Secretary of State James Baker's suggestion five months earlier that Israel cease settlement expansion, which Baker called "an obstacle" to peace. Adding to the Oval Office's concerns were Bush's plans to convene an Arab–Israeli peace conference in Madrid—plans that would have been significantly undermined had the president agreed to subsidize further illegal Israeli settlements.

Bush asked Congress to delay the loan guarantees for four months. Immediately, almost one thousand pro-Israel lobbyists swamped Capitol Hill, insisting that the United States dispense the guarantees at once. Congress, not surprisingly, was inclined to listen. Sensing that both his authority and plans for peace were at risk, President Bush made the following complaint:

> I heard today there were something like a thousand lobbyists on the Hill working the other side of the question. We've got one lonely little guy doing it.[88]

When Congress realized that the "lonely little guy" was their president, and that he was serious about delaying the loan guarantees, they quickly approved his request. American Jews were indignant, labeling Bush an anti-Semite for his criticisms of lobby pressure and accusing him of denying them the right to practice citizen advocacy. Bush quickly apologized, but to many it was a case of too little, too late. According to one author, "The showdown led to a strain in United States–Israel relations, and some Republicans say Bush lost Jewish votes." Of course, this overlooks an important factor of the episode: during the showdown, polls showed that more than 80 percent of the American public supported Bush, a tide of support members of Congress could not ignore.[89]

While his stance in 1991 may have cost Bush Jewish votes, he lost the votes of those critical of Israel the next summer when, despite continued construction of the controversial settlements, the U.S. president finally caved to pressure and approved the loan guarantees. Bush also exhibited strong—and strongly biased—support for Israel in October of 1991 when, after U.S. intelligence determined that Israel had exported missile components to South Africa, the president waived U.S.-mandated sanctions against Israel.

Nevertheless, this support was not enough to erase the memory of the Bush–Israel showdown from the minds of Israel's American supporters. While campaigning for the presidency in 2000 against Bush's son, Democratic candidate Al Gore mentioned the incident—and Bush's 1992 loss at the polls—in a speech to AIPAC:

> I vividly remember standing up against a group of administration foreign policy advisers who promoted the insulting concept of linkage. . . . We defeated them.[90]

It was a lesson well learned by American politicians, as no U.S. president since has openly threatened to withhold funds to ensure Israeli compliance with international law. Indeed, according to *USA Today*, current President George W. Bush "says he believes his father, the first President Bush, made a political mistake that helped cost him re-election when he threatened to withhold some U.S. aid" from Israel.[91]

6

Penetrating the Defenses at Defense and State

The Pentagon—that enormous, sprawling building on the banks of the Potomac—houses most of the Department of Defense's central head-quarters. It is the top command for the forces and measures that provide Americans with security in a troubled world. Across the Potomac is the Department of State, a massive eight-story building on Washington's Foggy Bottom, the nerve center of our nation's worldwide diplomatic network. These buildings are channels through which flow thousands of messages dealing with the nation's top secrets each day. No one can enter either building without special identification or advance clearance. Armed guards seem to be everywhere, and in late 1983 concrete embankments and strategically placed heavy trucks were added to provide extra buffers should a fanatic launch an attack. These buildings are fortresses, where the nation's most precious secrets are carefully guarded by the most advanced technology.

147

But how secure are the secrets?

The leaks to Israel are fantastic.[1] If I have something I want the secretary of state to know but don't want Israel to know, I must wait till I have a chance to see him personally.

This declaration came from an ambassador, still on active duty in a top assignment, while he reviewed his long career in numerous posts in the Middle East. Although hardly a household name in the United States, his is one of America's best-known abroad. Interviewed in the State Department, he spoke deliberately, choosing his words carefully: "It is a fact of life that everyone in authority is reluctant to put anything on paper that concerns Israel if it is to be withheld from Israel's knowledge," said the veteran. "Nor do such people even feel free to speak in a crowded room of such things."

The diplomat offered an example from his own experience. "I received a call from a friend of mine in the Jewish community who wanted to warn me, as a friend, that all details of a lengthy document on Middle East policy that I had just dispatched overseas were 'out.'" The document was classified "top secret," the diplomat recalled. "I didn't believe what he said, so my friend read me every word of it over the phone."

His comments will upset pro-Israel activists, many of whom contend that both the State Department and Defense Department are dominated by anti-Israeli "Arabists." Such domination, if it ever existed, occurs no longer. In the view of my diplomat source, leaks to pro-Israel activists are not only pervasive throughout the two departments, but "are intimidating and very harmful to our national interest." He said that, because of "the ever-present Xerox machine," diplomats proceed on the assumption that even messages they send by the most secure means will be copied and passed on to eager hands. "We just don't dare put sensitive items on paper." A factor making the pervasive insecurity even greater is the knowledge that leaks of secrets to Israel, even when noticed—which is rare—are almost never investigated.

Whatever intelligence the Israelis want, whether political or technical, they obtain promptly and without cost at the source. Officials who normally would work vigilantly to protect our national interest by identifying leaks and bringing charges against the offenders are demoralized.

In fact, they are disinclined even to question Israel's tactics for fear this activity will cause the Israeli lobby to mark them as troublemakers and take measures to nullify their efforts, or even harm their careers.

The lobby's intelligence network, having numerous volunteer "friendlies" to tap, reaches all parts of the executive branch where matters concerning Israel are handled. Awareness of this seepage keeps officials—no matter what rung of the ladder they occupy—from making or even proposing decisions that are in the United States' interest.

If, for example, an official should state opposition to an Israeli request during a private interdepartmental meeting—or worse still, put it in an intra-office memorandum—he or she must assume that this information will soon reach the Israeli embassy, either directly or through AIPAC. Soon after, the official should expect to be criticized by name when the Israeli ambassador visits the secretary of state or another prominent U.S. official.

The penetration is all the more remarkable because much of it is carried out by U.S. citizens on behalf of a foreign government. The practical effect is to give Israel its own network of sources, through which it is able to learn almost anything it wishes about decisions or resources of the U.S. government. When making procurement demands, Israel can display better knowledge of Defense Department inventories than the Pentagon itself.

Israel Finds the Ammunition—in Hawaii!

In its 1973 Yom Kippur war against Egypt and Syria, Israel sustained heavy losses in weapons of all kinds, especially tanks. It looked to the United States for the quickest possible resupply. Henry Kissinger was their avenue. Richard Nixon was entangled in the Watergate controversy and would soon leave the presidency, but under his authority the government agreed to deliver substantial quantities of tanks to Israel.

Tanks were to be taken from the inventory of U.S. military units on active duty, reserve units, even straight off production lines. Nothing was held back in the effort to bring Israel's forces back to its desired strength as quickly as possible.

Israel wanted only the latest-model tanks, which were equipped with 105-millimeter guns. But a sufficient number could not be found even by stripping U.S. forces. The Pentagon met the problem by filling part of the order with an earlier model fitted with 90-millimeter guns. When these arrived, the Israelis grumbled about having to take "second-hand junk." Then they discovered they had no ammunition of the right size and sent an urgent appeal for a supply of 90-millimeter rounds.

The Pentagon made a search and found none. Thomas Pianka, an officer then serving at the Pentagon with the International Security Agency, recalled: "We made an honest effort to find the ammunition. We checked everywhere. We checked through all the services—Army, Navy, Marines. We couldn't find any 90-millimeter ammunition at all."[2] Pianka said the Pentagon sent Israel the bad news: "In so many words, we said, 'Sorry, we don't have any of the ammunition you need. We've combed all depots and warehouses, and we simply have none.'"

A few days later the Israelis came back with a surprising message: "Yes, you do. There are 15,000 rounds in the Marine Corps supply depot in Hawaii." Pianka recalled, "We looked in Hawaii and, sure enough, there they were. The Israelis had found a U.S. supply of 90-millimeter ammunition we couldn't find ourselves."

Richard Helms, director of the CIA during the 1967 Arab–Israeli war, recalled an occasion when an Israeli arms request had been filled with the wrong items.[3] Israeli officials resubmitted the request complete with all the supposedly top-secret code numbers and a note to Helms that said the Pentagon perhaps had not understood exactly which items were needed. "It was a way for them to show me that they knew exactly what they wanted," Helms said. Helms believed that during this period no important secret was kept from Israel.

Not only are the Israelis adept at getting the information they want—they are masters at the weapons procurement game. Les Janka, a former deputy assistant secretary of defense who is a specialist in Middle East policy, recalled Israeli persistence:

> They would never take no for an answer. They never gave up. These emissaries of a foreign government always had a shopping list of wanted military items, some of them high technology that no other nation possessed, some of it secret devices that gave the United States an edge over any adversary. Such items were not for sale, not even to the nations with whom we have our closest, most formal military alliance—like those linked to us through the North Atlantic Treaty Organization.[4]

Yet Janka learned that military sales to Israel were not bound by the guidelines and limitations that govern U.S. arms supply policy elsewhere. "Sales to Israel were different," he said. "Very different."

Janka has vivid memories of a military liaison officer from the Israeli embassy who called at the Defense Department and requested approval to purchase a military item that, because of its highly secret advanced technology, was on the prohibited list: "He came to me, and I gave him the official Pentagon reply. I said, 'I'm sorry, sir, but the answer is no. We will not release that technology.'"

The Israeli officer took pains to observe bureaucratic courtesies and not antagonize lower officials who might devise ways to block the sale. He said, "Thank you very much, if that's your official position. We understand that you are not in a position to do what we want done. Please don't feel bad, but we're going over your head." And that of course meant he was going to Janka's superiors in the office of the secretary of defense, or perhaps even to the White House.

Asked if he could remember an instance in which Israel failed to get what it wanted from the Pentagon, Janka paused to reflect, then answered, "No, not in the long run."

Janka had high respect for the efficiency of Israeli procurement officers:

> You have to understand that the Israelis operate in the Pentagon very professionally, and in an omnipresent way. They have enough of their people who understand our system well, and they have made friends at all levels, from top to bottom. They just interact with the system in a constant, continuous way that keeps the pressure on.

The Carter White House tried to establish a policy of restraint. In an interview with Zbigniew Brzezinski, Carter's assistant for national security, Brzezinski remembered Defense Secretary Harold Brown's efforts to hold the line on technology transfer.[5] "He was very tough with Israel on its requests for weapons and weapons systems. He often turned them down." But Brown's was not the final word. For example, Brzezinski cited as the most notable example Brown's refusal to sell Israel the controversial antipersonnel weapon known as the cluster bomb. Despite written agreements restricting the use of these bombs, Israel had used them twice against populated areas in Lebanon, causing death and injury to civilians. Brown responded by refusing to sell Israel replacements. But even on that request,

Israel eventually prevailed. President Reagan reversed the administration policy, and cluster bombs were returned to the approved list.

Others who have occupied high positions in the executive branch were willing to speak candidly, but, unlike Janka, they did so with the understanding that their names would not be published. As one explained, "My career is not over. At least, I don't want it to be. Quoting me by name would bring it to an end." With the promise of anonymity, he and others gave details of the astounding process through which the Israeli lobby is able to penetrate the defenses at the Defense Department—and elsewhere.

Sometimes the act is simple theft. One official says, "Israelis were caught in the Pentagon with unauthorized documents, sometimes scooping up the contents of 'in boxes' on desk tops." He recalls that, because of such activity, a number of Israeli officials were told to leave the country. No formal charges have ever been filed against an Israeli official involved in such activities, and Israel has covered each such exit with an excuse such as family illness or some other personal reason: "Our government never made a public issue of it." He added, "There is a much higher level of espionage by Israel against our government than has ever been publicly admitted."

The official recalled one day when he received a list of military equipment that Israel wanted to purchase. Noting that "the Pentagon is Israel's 'stop and shop,'" he took it for granted that the Israelis had obtained clearances. So he followed usual procedure by circulating it to various Pentagon offices for routine review and evaluation:

> One office instantly returned the list to me with a note: 'One of these items is so highly classified you have no right to know that it even exists.' I was instructed to destroy all copies of the request and all references to the particular code numbers. I didn't know what it was. It was some kind of electronic jamming equipment, top secret. Somehow the Israelis knew about it and acquired its precise specifications, cost, and top secret code number. This meant they had penetrated our research and development labs, our most sensitive facilities.

Despite that somber revelation, no official effort was launched to discover who had revealed the sensitive information.

"They Always Get What They Want"

Israel's agents are close students of the U.S. system, and they work it to their advantage. Besides obtaining secret information by clandestine operations, they thoroughly and effectively apply open pressure on executive branch offices. A weapons expert explains their technique:

> If promised an answer on a weapons request in thirty days, they show up on the thirty-first day and announce: "We made this request. It hasn't been approved. Why not? We've waited thirty days." With most foreign governments, you can finesse a problem. You can leave it in the box on the desk. With Israel, you can't leave anything in the box.

He said the Israeli embassy knows exactly when things are scheduled for action:

> It stays on top of things as does no other embassy in town. They know your agenda, what was on your schedule yesterday, and what's on it today and tomorrow. They know what you have been doing and saying. They know the law and regulations backward and forward. They know when the deadlines are.

He admired the resourcefulness of the Israelis in applying pressure:

> They may leak to Israeli newspapers details of their difficulty in getting an approval. A reporter will come in to State or Defense and ask a series of questions so detailed they could be motivated only by Israeli officials. Sometimes the pressure will come, not from reporters, but from AIPAC. If things are really hung up, it isn't long before letters or calls start coming from Capitol Hill. They'll ask, "Why is the Pentagon not approving this item?" Usually, the letter is from the congressman in whose district the item is manufactured. He will argue that the requested item is essential to Israel's security. He probably will also ask, "Who is this bad guy in the Pentagon— or State—who is blocking this approval? I want his name. Congress would like to know."

The American defense expert paused to emphasize his point: "*No* bureaucrat, no military officer likes to be singled out by anybody from Congress and required to explain his professional duty."

He recalled an episode involving President Carter's secretary of defense, Harold Brown:

> I remember once Israel requested an item on the prohibited list. Before I answered, I checked with Secretary Brown and he said, "No, absolutely no. We're not going to give in to the bastards on this one." So I said no. Lo and behold, a few days later I got a call from Brown. He said, "The Israelis are raising hell. I got a call from [Senator Henry] 'Scoop' Jackson, asking why we aren't cooperating with Israel. It isn't worth it. Let it go."

When Jimmy Carter became president, the Israelis were trying to get large quantities of the AIM 9-L, the most advanced U.S. air-to-air missile at the time. A former Pentagon official said his colleagues objected. One of them said, "No, no, no. It isn't yet deployed to U.S. troops. The production rate is not enough to supply even U.S. needs. It is much too sensitive to risk being lost." Yet, early in his administration, Carter overruled the Pentagon, and Israel got the missiles.

A former administration official recalled a remarkable example of Israeli ingenuity:

> Israel requested an item of technology, a machine for producing bullets. It was a big piece of machinery, weighed a lot, and it was exclusive. We didn't want other countries to have it, not even Israel. We knew if we said no, the Israelis would go over our heads and somehow get approval. So, we kept saying we were studying the request. Then, to our astonishment, we discovered that the Israelis had already bought the machinery and had it in a warehouse in New York.

The Israelis did not have a license to ship the equipment, but they had nonetheless been able to make the purchase. When they were confronted by the Defense official, they said, "We slipped up. We were sure you'd say yes, so we went ahead and bought it. And if you say no, here's the bill for storage, and here's what it will cost to ship it back to the factory." Soon after, the official recalled, someone in the State Department called and said, "Aw, give it to them," adding an earthy expletive.

This sense of futility sometimes reaches all the way to the top. Unrestricted supplies to Israel were especially debilitating in the 1974–77 period, when U.S. military services were trying to recover from the 1973

Arab–Israeli war. In that conflict, the United States had stripped its own army and air forces in order to supply Israel.

During this period of U.S. shortage, Israel kept bringing in its shopping lists. The official recalls that the Pentagon would insist, "No, we can't provide what you want now. Come back in a year or so." In almost every one of those cases, he said, the Pentagon position was overruled by a political decision out of the White House. This demoralized the professionals in the Pentagon. Still worse, it handicapped national security: "Defense Department decisions made according to the highest professional standards went by the board in order to satisfy Israeli requests," said the official.

"Exchanges" That Work Only in One Direction

The Israelis are particularly adept at exploiting sympathetic officials, as a former Pentagon officer explained:

> We have people sympathizing with Israel in about every office in the Pentagon. A lot of military personnel have been in Israel, and some served there, making friends—and, of course, a number of Israeli personnel study in U.S. military schools. The guts, the energy, the skill of the Israelis are much admired in the Pentagon. Israelis are very good at passing back to us their performance records using our equipment. Throughout our military schools are always a large number of Israeli students. They develop great professional rapport with our people.

For years, the United States and Israel have exchanged military personnel. On paper, it works both ways. In practice, Israel is the major beneficiary. The reason is more one of culture than anything clandestine. Israeli officers generally speak English, so it's no problem for them to come to the United States and quickly establish rapport with U.S. officers. On the other hand, hardly any U.S. officers speak Hebrew.

Language disparity is not the only problem. Of equal gravity is the American laxity in enforcing its security regulations. Many Israeli officers spend a year in a sensitive area—one of the U.S. training commands, or a research and development laboratory. At the start they are told they cannot enter certain restricted areas. Then, little by little, the rules are relaxed. A former Defense Department official explained:

The young Israeli speaks good English. He is likeable. You know how Americans are: they take him in, and he's their buddy. First thing you know, the restrictions are forgotten, and the Israeli officers are admitted to everything in our laboratories, our training facilities, our operational bases.

The former official quickly added that rules are seldom relaxed in Israel:

This means that the officer training exchange is really a one-way street. Israel does not permit our officers, whether they speak Hebrew or not, to serve in sensitive military facilities in Israel. Many areas are totally off limits. They are very strict about that. Our officers cannot be present even when U.S.-supplied equipment and weapons are being delivered for the first time. U.S. officers on exchange programs in Israel are, more often than not, given a desk in an office down the hall, and assigned just enough to do to keep them busy and prevent them from being too frustrated. Without knowledge of Hebrew, they have almost no way to know what is going on.[6]

Camaraderie is also an element. Many employees in the executive branch, Jewish and non-Jewish, feel that the United States and Israel are somehow "in this together" and therefore cooperate without limit. Many also believe that Israel is a strategic asset and that weapons and other technology provided to Israel serve U.S. purposes. These feelings sometimes cause official restrictions on sharing of information to be modified or conveniently forgotten. As one Defense official put it, the rules get "placed deeper and deeper into the file":

A sensitive document is picked up by an Israeli officer while his friend, a Defense Department official, deliberately looks the other way. Nothing is said. Nothing is written. And the U.S. official probably does not feel he has done anything wrong. Meanwhile, the Israelis ask for more and more.

"Like Sending a Weather Report"

Despite such openhanded generosity by the United States, the flow of information—like the unbalanced U.S.–Israel officer "exchanges"—is a one-way exchange. The September 1990 publication of Victor Ostrovsky's *By Way of Deception* did much to broaden awareness of what goes on in the realm of Israeli perfidy.

The shocking exposé, written by a former Israeli spy, reports that the Mossad, Israel's intelligence agency, failed to relay to the United States early data about the 1983 suicide bombing that killed 241 U.S. Marines who were asleep in a barracks at the Beirut airport.

An informant had told the Mossad that a large truck was being fitted by Shi'ite Muslims with spaces that could hold bombs of exceptional size. Local agents concluded that the marine barracks was among the most likely targets, but, according to Ostrovsky, the Mossad chief in Tel Aviv made a conscious decision not to warn the U.S. government, declaring: "We're not there to protect Americans." Accordingly, only a routine notice went to the CIA, which Ostrovsky writes "was like sending a weather report."

In an attempt to cover up this and other damning information, the government of Israel requested—and a New York judge ordered—that Ostrovsky's book be banned in the United States. The *New York Post* headlined: "Israelis muzzle spy author." The *New York Times* summed up the book's allegation: the Mossad failed to warn the CIA because it wanted "to poison American relations with Arab countries." When the ban was overturned by a higher court the next day, the book enjoyed a second round of nationwide publicity. Overnight, it became a bestseller.

In addition to withholding valuable intelligence information from its number one benefactor, Israel does not hesitate to obtain United States classified information through all-out espionage, a process that the American government has been unable to halt.

The Mossad's Role in the Network

Exactly three U.S. government employees have been punished for leaking classified information to Israel. The first was Fred Waller, a career foreign service officer in charge of the Israel–Jordan desk at the State Department, who in 1954 read in a classified document that revealed that a friend on the staff of the Israeli embassy—under suspicion for espionage—was being recommended by the FBI for expulsion from the United States.

Waller told associates that he considered the charges "unjustified" and, according to allegations, tipped off his friend at the Israeli embassy. For this, Waller was the first person ever marked for dismissal, but he was later permitted simply to retire. "They wanted to throw him out without a nickel," states Don Bergus, who succeeded Waller in the State Department assignment. During those years of McCarthyism, Bergus recalls, "the FBI was recommending that a lot of people be declared *persona non grata*. They were so happy with themselves in doing this. They knew damned well their recommendations wouldn't be acted upon."

Bergus recalled that Israel obtained a lot of information without resorting to espionage: "A lot of the information was volunteered. The apples were put on the table, and I don't blame Israel for taking them."

The investigation of Waller occurred during the high point of our government's concern over Israeli intelligence activities in the United States. Because the Eisenhower administration was trying to withhold weapons from Israel, as well as other states in the Middle East, a major attempt was made to bring leaks of classified information under control. A veteran diplomat recalled the crisis: "Employees in State and Defense were being suborned and bribed on a wide scale, and our government went to Israel and demanded that it stop."

After high-level negotiations following the Waller affair, the United States and Israel entered into an unwritten agreement to share a larger volume of classified information and, at the same time, to sharply restrict the clandestine operations each conducted in the other's territory. The diplomat explained that it was supposed to be a two-way street: "The deal provided that we would get more from them too, and it was hoped the arrangement would end the thievery and payoff of U.S. employees."

The understanding with Israel did not end the problem, however, as the Israelis were not content to let the United States decide what classified information it would receive. Israel did not live up to the terms of the agreement and continued to broadly engage in espionage activities throughout the United States.

This was still true more than twenty years after the Waller episode, during the tenure of Atlanta mayor Andrew Young as U.S. ambassador to the United Nations during the Carter administration. Young recalled, "I operated on the assumption that the Israelis would learn just about everything instantly. I just always assumed that everything was monitored, and that there was a pretty formal network."[7]

Young resigned as ambassador in August 1979 after it was revealed that he had met with Zuhdi Terzi, the PLO's UN observer, in violation of the U.S. pledge to Israel not to talk to the PLO.[8] Press reports on Young's episode said Israeli intelligence learned of the meeting and that Israeli officials then leaked the information to the press, precipitating the diplomatic wrangle that led to Young's resignation.

Israel denied that its agents had learned of the Young–Terzi meeting. The press counselor at the Israeli embassy went so far as to tell the *Washington Star*, "We do not conduct any kind of intelligence activities in the United States." This denial must have been amusing to U.S. intelligence experts, one of whom talked with *Newsweek* magazine about the Mossad's activities here: "They have penetrations all through the U.S. government.[9] They do better than the KGB," said the expert, whom the magazine did not identify.

The *Newsweek* article continued:

> With the help of American Jews in and out of government, the Mossad looks for any softening in U.S. support and tries to get any technical intelligence the administration is unwilling to give to Israel. "The Mossad can go to any distinguished American Jew and ask for his help," says a former CIA agent. The appeal is a simple one: "When the call went out and no one heeded it, the Holocaust resulted." The United States tolerates the Mossad's operations on American soil partly because of reluctance to anger the American Jewish community.

Another reason cited: the Mossad is often a valuable source of information for U.S. intelligence.

Penetration by Israel continued at such a high level that a senior State Department official who has held the highest career positions related to the Middle East confides, "I urged several times that the United States quit trying to keep secrets from Israel. Let them have everything. They always get what they want anyway. When we try to keep secrets, it always backfires."

An analysis prepared by the CIA in 1979, twenty-five years after the U.S.–Israeli espionage agreement, gives no hint that the Mossad had in any way restricted its operations within the United States. According to the forty-eight-page secret document, titled *Israel: Foreign Intelligence and Security Services*, the United States continued to be a focus of Mossad operations:

> In carrying out its mission to collect positive intelligence, the principal function of the Mossad is to conduct agent operations against the Arab nations and their official representatives and installations throughout the world, particularly in Western Europe and the United States. . . . Objectives in Western countries are equally important (as in the USSR and East Europe) to the Israeli intelligence service. The Mossad collects intelligence regarding Western, Vatican, and UN policies toward the Near East; promotes arms deals for the benefit of the IDF; and *acquires data for silencing anti-Israel factions in the West* [emphasis added].

Under "methods of operation," the CIA booklet described the way in which the Mossad makes use of domestic pro-Israeli groups. It states that "the Mossad over the years has enjoyed some rapport with highly placed persons and government offices in every country of importance to Israel." It adds, "Within Jewish communities in almost every country of the world, there are Zionists and other sympathizers who render strong support to the Israeli intelligence effort." It explained:

> Such contacts are carefully nurtured and serve as channels for information, deception material, propaganda, and other purposes. . . . Mossad activities are generally conducted through Israeli official and semiofficial establishments—deep cover enterprises in the form of firms and organizations, some especially created for, or adaptable to, a specific objective—and penetrations effected within non-Zionist national and international Jewish organizations. . . . Official organizations used for cover are: Israeli purchasing missions and Israeli government tourist offices, El Al, and Zim offices. Israeli construction firms, industrial groups and international trade organizations also provide nonofficial cover. Individuals working under deep or illegal cover are normally charged with penetrating objectives that require a long-range, more subtle approach, or with activities in which the Israeli government can never admit complicity. . . .
>
> The Israeli intelligence service depends heavily on the various Jewish communities and organizations abroad for recruiting agents and eliciting general information. The aggressively ideological nature of Zionism, which emphasizes that all Jews belong to Israel and must return to Israel, had had its drawbacks in enlisting support for intelligence operations, however, since there is considerable opposition to Zionism among Jews throughout the world.
>
> Aware of this fact, Israeli intelligence representatives usually operate discreetly within Jewish communities and are under instructions to han-

dle their missions with utmost tact to avoid embarrassment to Israel. They also attempt to penetrate anti-Zionist elements in order to neutralize the opposition.

The theft of scientific data is a major objective of Mossad operations, which is often attempted by trying to recruit local agents:

> In addition to the large-scale acquisition of published scientific papers and technical journals from all over the world through overt channels, the Israelis devote a considerable portion of their covert operations to obtaining scientific and technical intelligence. This had included attempts to penetrate certain classified defense projects in the United States and other Western nations.
>
> The Israeli security authorities (in Israel) also seek evidence of illicit love affairs which can be used as leverage to enlist cooperation. In one instance, Shin Bet (the domestic Israeli intelligence agency) tried to penetrate the U.S. Consulate General in Jerusalem through a clerical employee who was having an affair with a Jerusalem girl. They rigged a fake abortion case against the employee in an unsuccessful effort to recruit him. Before this attempt at blackmail, they had tried to get the Israeli girl to elicit information from her boyfriend.

Israel's espionage activities, according to the CIA, even included "crude efforts to recruit marine guards [at the United States Embassy at Tel Aviv] for monetary reward." It reports that a hidden microphone "planted by the Israelis" was found in the office of the U.S. ambassador in 1954, and that two years later, telephone taps were found connected to two telephones in the residence of the U.S. military attache. Retired diplomat Don Bergus recalls the episode: "Our ambassador, Ed Lawson, reported the bug in a telegram to Washington that went something like this: 'Department must assume that all conversations in my office as well as texts of my telegrams over the last six months are known to the Israelis.' Ed had dictated all telegrams to his secretary."

During the Iranian hostage crisis in 1980, columnist Jack Anderson quoted "U.S. intelligence reports," actually supplied by the Israeli embassy, by way of the American Israel Public Affairs Committee, that the PLO had mined the embassy to frustrate any rescue attempt by the United States. The intelligence reports proved to be bogus.

Asked about the present activities of the Mossad in the United States, a senior official in the Department of State, was candid:

> We have to assume that they have wiretaps all over town. In my work I fre-
> quently pick up highly sensitive information coming back to me in con-
> versations with people who have no right to have these secrets. I will ask,
> "I wonder who has the wiretaps out to pick that up," and usually the answer
> is, "I don't know, but it sure isn't us."

The same official said he never gives any highly sensitive information
over his office phone. "You have to respect their ingenuity. The Mossad
people know how to get into a system."

"No One Needs Trouble Like That"

Leaks of classified information remain a major problem for policy makers. An official whose identity I promised to withhold says that during
the Carter administration his colleagues feared even to speak up even in
small private meetings. When Israeli requests were turned down at interagency meetings attended by, at most, fifteen people—all of whom knew
the discussions were to be considered top secret—within hours "the
Israeli military attaché, the political officer, or the ambassador—or all
of them at once—were lodging protests. They knew exactly who said
what, even though nothing had been put on paper." He adds, "No one
needs trouble like that."

He said that David McGiffert, assistant secretary of defense for international security affairs, was often subjected to pressure. Frequently, the
Israeli embassy would demand copies of documents that were still in the
draft stage and had not reached his desk.

To counteract these kinds of leaks, some officials have taken their
own precautions.

Although no charges are ever brought, those suspected of leaking
information to Israel are sometimes bypassed when classified documents
are handed out. The word is forwarded discreetly to drop their names
from the distribution list. One such official served during both the Carter
and Reagan administrations. When he occupied a senior position in the
Carter administration, his superiors were instructed to "clear nothing" in
the way of classified documents related to the Middle East through his
office and to use extreme caution when discussing such matters in his pres-

ence. One of his colleagues says, admiringly, "He is brilliant. He belongs in government, but he has a blind spot where Israel is concerned."

To strike back at government officials considered to be unsympathetic to Israeli needs, the pro-Israel lobby singles them out for personal attack and even the wrecking of their careers. In January 1977 a broad-scale purge was attempted immediately after the inauguration of President Carter. The perpetrator was Senator Richard Stone of Florida, a Democrat, a passionate supporter of Israel.[10] When he was newly installed as chairman of the Senate Subcommittee on the Middle East, he brought along with him a "hit list." In his view, fifteen officials were not sufficiently supportive of Israel and its weapons needs, and he wanted them transferred to positions where their views would create no problems for Israel. Marked for removal were William Quandt, Brzezinski's assistant for Middle East matters, and Les Janka, who had served on the National Security Council under Ford. The others were career military officers, most of them colonels. Stone's demands were rejected by Brzezinski. According to a senior White House official, "after pressing reasonably hard for several days," the senator gave up. Although unsuccessful, his demands caused a stir. One officer says, "I find it very ironic that a U.S. senator goes to a U.S. president's national security adviser and tells him to fire Americans for insufficient loyalty to another country."

Leaks Disrupt American Foreign Policy

At least four times in recent years, major leaks of information to Israel caused serious setbacks in our relations with Israel's neighbors. The first destroyed an arrangement with Jordan that had been serving U.S. security interests successfully for years.

Under a long-standing secret agreement, Jordan's King Hussein received secret financial support from the CIA. This was a carryover of a normal support system developed by the British. Under it, moderate leaders such as Hussein received payments in exchange for helpful services, which enabled them to maintain their political base without having to account to anyone locally.

Early in the Carter administration, a White House review was ordered of all covert operations, including, of course, the CIA payments to the Middle East. Nineteen people attended the review meeting in early February 1977. One of the senior officials who attended recalled: "I feared at the time that leaks were certain to occur." A few days later, the *Washington Post* headlined a story "CIA Paid Millions to Jordan's King Hussein."[11] Written by Bob Woodward, the article said that over a period of twenty years the CIA had made "secret annual payments totaling millions of dollars" to Hussein. It said the payment in 1976 was $750,000. The disclosure provoked wide international controversy.

When he read Woodward's *Washington Post* article, Senator James G. Abourezk of South Dakota called in Harold Saunders, then an official of the National Security Council, and received confirmation that Israel, as well as Jordan, was receiving secret payments from the CIA.[12] Abourezk recalled that Saunders estimated that during the same period Hussein received about $10 million, more than $70 million went to Israel. The payments helped Israel support its own burgeoning foreign aid program in Africa, and Abourezk believed that the payments still continued. Hussein used the funds to maintain a strong relationship with the Bedouin tribes of his desert kingdom.

After confirming the information, Abourezk called Woodward and asked if he was aware of the CIA's aid to Israel when he wrote about the payments to Jordan. Abourezk recalls, "Woodward admitted knowledge of the payments to Israel, but said he thought the circumstances were different, and that was why he did not write about them." Abourezk recalls being so outraged at this explanation and Woodward's "selective" coverage of the news that he shouted over the phone, "It seems to me that sort of judgment is better left up to the readers of the *Post.*"

Abourezk tried unsuccessfully for several months to interest Washington journalists in the news that Israel too received CIA payments.[13] Months later, after the furor over Jordan had died down, Jack Anderson mentioned the payments to Israel in his syndicated column. There was no public outcry.

The CIA arrangement with Jordan was viewed by Zbigniew Brzezinski, Carter's national security adviser, as "very valuable" to the United States. But as a result of the publicity, he recalls, the arrangement had to be canceled, Hussein was embarrassed, and the United States suffered a setback in its relations with the Arab world.

The next leak so embarrassed U.S.–Saudi relations that a career intelligence officer was ordered out of Saudi Arabia. After the fall of the Shah of Iran in 1979, there was speculation that the Saudi regime also might fall. The CIA station chief in Saudi Arabia reported this information to Washington in a secret cable, citing it as only a rumor, not a forecast. On the basis of this and other reports and analysis in Washington, the CIA produced a paper that was given restricted circulation in the official policy community. That paper discussed the stability of the Saudi regime. A report was leaked to news services, which erroneously stated that the CIA station chief in Saudi Arabia predicted the fall of the Saudi government within six months.

John C. West, former governor of South Carolina, was the U.S. ambassador to Saudi Arabia at the time. West recalls the CIA story: "Of course, there was no such prediction that the Saudi government would fall, but that's the way it was printed." The episode caused deep resentment in the Saudi capital, and the station chief was asked to leave.[14]

West had other problems with leaks. On another occasion, this time in 1980, a government employee's leak of secret information destroyed a sensitive mission to Saudi Arabia and, in West's opinion, led to a costly confrontation between the president and the Senate. The leak came from a secret White House meeting, where West and a small group of high officials discussed several Saudi requests to buy military equipment. "The arms package was of very, very great concern to the Saudis," West recalled:

> It was essential that they, as serious customers, not be embarrassed. As we went over the items, I said, "Whatever we do, we must not say no to the Saudis on any of these. It's very important that we avoid a flat turndown."

The group agreed to approve four of the requests, but found the other two highly controversial. The Saudis wanted to buy high technology AWACS intelligence-gathering aircraft and special bomb racks for F-15 fighter planes they already owned. These sales would cause an uproar in neighboring Israel, and the Carter administration did not want to offend either government.

West worked out solutions to both problems. "Let's do this," he advised the group:

The bomb racks haven't yet been adopted as a part of the U.S. system. There are still some bugs that need to be worked out. Let's explain that we won't make a decision until we decide the bomb racks are right and meet our own requirements. Given that explanation, the Saudis will go along.

Regarding the AWACS dilemma, West predicted that the Saudis would withdraw their request to buy the planes if the United States would resume a practice that had been initiated during the tense period following the fall of the Shah of Iran. At that time, he says, "The United States met Saudi intelligence needs by operating AWACS planes from Saudi bases and supplying to the Saudi government the information accumulated on these flights." West told the group, "I will explain to the Saudis that the United States can't deliver the new planes until 1985, and by then the technology will probably be outdated."

West's recommendations were accepted. The Saudis would be permitted to buy the four noncontroversial items, and the other two requests would be set aside in a way that would cause no offense. West says, "I was instructed to explain the decisions personally when I returned to Saudi Arabia."

But once again, sensitive information was leaked in a twisted form. West recalled:

> The very day I left for Saudi Arabia, the *New York Times* published a story headlined: "Carter Is Said to Refuse Saudi Request for Arms." Other news services reported that at a high level meeting the White House decided to turn down the Saudi request, and after debating for several days on how to break the news, West was instructed simply to tell them no.[15]
>
> I knew nothing of the leak until I landed in Saudi Arabia, ready to meet Saudi officials in appointments already scheduled. The news story hit me in the face when I got off the plane. It was terrible.

The *Times* story delivered the blunt negative answer that West had warned must be avoided at all cost. "It destroyed all chance of success in my diplomatic mission."

West does not know how the newspapers got the damaging report. Only a few had attended the meeting in the White House, but notes were taken, memos prepared. He speculates that the story, with deliberate inaccuracies, was leaked by "someone determined to worsen relations between the United States and Saudi Arabia."

A few months later, the Carter administration resumed AWACS operations based in Saudi Arabia. Nonetheless, embarrassed by the earlier headlines, Saudi officials decided to insist on buying their own AWACS planes and launched a public relations campaign in the United States that culminated in a costly, bruising showdown two years later in the U.S. Senate. Without the leak, West believed, the Saudis would have accepted the Carter administration decision, and the AWACS controversy would never have surfaced. If so, the U.S. taxpayers might have been spared an extra $1.2 billion in aid to Israel—the price Israel's lobby demanded as compensation when it lost the AWACS vote in the Senate.[16]

West recalled that leaks to Israel were so frequent that he imposed strict rules on communications:

> I would never put anything in any cable that was critical of Israel. Still, because of the grapevine, there was never any secret from the government of Israel. The Israelis knew everything, usually by the time it got to Washington. I can say that without qualification.

West added that if he wanted to communicate any information that was in any way critical of Israel, he felt more confident using an open telephone line than a top-secret cable.

West's problems with the lobby did not end with his departure from diplomatic service. Before leaving his post in 1981, in an interview in Jeddah, he told a reporter that the "most difficult question" he encountered during his work as ambassador was trying to explain why talks between the United States and the PLO were not permitted.[17]

This mild comment caused trouble when West returned to private life. His appointment as distinguished professor of Middle East studies at the University of South Carolina brought a strong protest from a group of South Carolina Jews, led by State Senator Hyman Rubin. "The group charged bias," West recalls, "and the protest so disturbed the university administration that public announcement of my appointment was delayed for more than a year." When he learned of the protest, West asked Rubin to arrange a meeting with his group. The result was a candid two-hour discussion between twenty critics and the ambassador-turned-professor. In its wake, West said, "The controversy subsided," and he assumed his post.

In 1983 the Israeli embassy itself directly arranged a news leak that effectively blocked U.S. support for a Jordanian rapid deployment force, although the embassy concealed its own role in the event. The White House was privately considering a proposal under which the United States would help Jordan establish an airborne unit that would be able to provide swift help if nearby Arab states were threatened. A White House official explained:

> When the Bahrainis asked for help during the Iranian crisis, Jordan wanted to help but had no way to get there. The Jordanian force idea is sound. Arabs need to be able to defend their own territory. Instead of having an American rapid deployment force going to the Persian Gulf, it would be better for Arabs to do the job themselves. Better to have Muslims defending Muslim territory than American boys.

L. Dean Brown, former ambassador to Jordan, says the proposal would have been a "godsend" to the small countries of the gulf.[18] "What Jordan needed was C-130 transport planes in order to move light weapons by air."

At first, Israel raised no objection. Told of the plan while he was still Israel's ambassador to the United States, Moshe Arens simply listened. A White House official close to the project recalled, "We told Arens that we were going to have Israeli interests in mind, but we were going ahead. We would proceed in a way that would not harm Israel."

The noncommittal Israeli reaction was mistaken as a green light, and, after getting clearance from the intelligence committees of Congress, the Reagan administration proceeded with secret negotiations.

After Arens left to become Israel's defense minister, the proposal ran into trouble. Briefed on the progress of the project by Secretary of State George Shultz, Meir Rosenne, Israel's new ambassador, suddenly raised objections. The Israeli embassy tipped off a reporter for an Israeli radio station about the issue, suggesting he go to Congressman Clarence Long, chairman of the House Appropriations Subcommittee that handles aid to Israel, saying "he will tell you the whole story." Long cooperated, Israeli radio broke the story, and with controversy swirling in Israel, AIPAC joined the fray with its own salvos.

A White House official recalled the effect. "Once this became public," he said, "King Hussein of Jordan backed away too. He didn't want to be seen as a tool of the Americans." The official says his colleagues at the White House were convinced that the whole thing was a carefully engineered leak by the Israeli embassy. It was delayed only until Arens left Washington. "It was a carom shot, bounced through Doc Long and Israeli radio in such a way that it would not be traced back to the embassy." Former U.S. Defense Secretary Harold Brown described the leak by the Israelis as "purposeful."

"The State Department Leaks Like a Sieve"

A leak got Talcott Seelye, ambassador to Syria, in hot water in 1981 when he sent a classified cable from Syria to the State Department protesting a resolution just introduced in the House of Representatives by Stephen Solarz, a member of the Foreign Affairs Committee. Solarz represents a New York district in which Jews of Syrian origin are numerous, and his resolution criticized Syria for not permitting more Jews to leave that country.

In the cable Seelye warned that approval of the resolution would make Syria less cooperative, not more. Seelye explained, "My cable said that if Solarz was sincere and serious about getting the Jews out of Syria, he would not go ahead with this resolution; on the other hand, if he merely wanted to make points with the voters, he should do something else." The cable was leaked to Solarz, who called Secretary of State Vance and demanded, "Look, you've got to get Seelye out of there." Vance was furious over the leak.

Seelye kept his job, but the State Department did little to defeat the resolution. When the resolution was taken up in the House, only one "no" vote was heard.

The employee guilty of leaking the cable to Solarz worked under Ed Sanders, Carter's official liaison with the Jewish community, who then had an office in the State Department as well as in the White House. No punishment was imposed; the employee was simply transferred to a different job. The leak confirmed the fears of diplomats who had strongly opposed locating a Jewish liaison office in the State Department. One diplomat of the period describes Sanders as "a very decent human being, and he was there to do his job at the request of the president. At the same time, some of the stuff we were doing should not get out of the building to anybody."

Harold Saunders, a scholarly career Middle East specialist who occasionally got in hot water by noting Arab concerns, was then assistant secretary of state.[19] He voiced his feelings to Vance: "How would you like having somebody from U.S. Steel sitting in our Economic Bureau's tariff office?" Vance, too, opposed the arrangement, but Sanders's State Department office was not closed for months.

Seelye pinpointed a very mundane reason for the wave of leaks: the prevalence of copying machines.[20] He says that, as ambassador to Syria, he operated on the assumption that the Israelis would learn everything he sent to Washington. He said, "The trouble with our system of classification is that even when we limit distribution, say, to just twenty copies for the whole government, one of the offices on the list will make a dozen extra copies for their own use, and so on. It's hard to control."

Veterans in government lay the blame for much of the leaking on political appointees holding important positions in the State Department and not on career diplomats. In the early months of the Reagan Administration, National Security Adviser Richard Allen was viewed as highly sympathetic to Israeli interests and, in fact, as the de facto clearance officer, encouraging the placement of personnel who were acceptable to the state of Israel in key positions. After Allen's departure from government, a senior officer of the State Department recalled, "No one was needed to replace him, as people with pro-Israeli interests—we call them mail carriers—are spotted in every important office."

A senior diplomat, now on leave, says: "The leaks are almost never traced to professional foreign service officers. In my experience, leaks are normally by staff members brought in by political appointees, and every administration brings in a lot of them. They seem to be all over the place." He says these "loose-tongued amateurs" are prominent on the seventh floor, where offices of senior State Department officials are located, and on the staff for policy planning, as well as in the White House. This gives them ready access to sensitive material. "Unfortunately," he added, "they do not have the same idea of discipline and sense of loyalty as the professionals."

Some leaks originate from a few members of Congress and their staff. A former Defense Department official recalled:

> There were individuals on Capitol Hill that the Pentagon viewed as conduits to Israel. No question about it. A number of times we would get requests from congressmen or senators for intelligence materials. We knew damn well that these materials were not for their own edification. The information would be passed to Israel. For example, we would get a letter from a congressman, stating he had heard the Pentagon had done a study on the military balance between Israel and its Arab neighbors. He would like to have a copy of it. We would respond, "We can't give you a copy, but we can give you an oral briefing." The usual answer is, "Sorry, we are not interested in an oral briefing."

The Case of Stephen Bryen

In the opinion of all these sources, Israeli penetration of State and Defense departments reached an all-time high during the Reagan administration. In 1984 people known to have intimate links with Israel were employed in offices throughout the bureaucracy, particularly in the Defense Department, where top-secret weapons technology and other sensitive matters are routinely handled.

The bureaucracy was then headed by Fred Ikle, undersecretary of defense for international security. The three personalities of greatest importance in his area were Richard Perle, Ikle's assistant for international security policy; Stephen Bryen, Perle's principal deputy, whose assigned specialty was technology transfer; and Noel Koch, principal deputy to Richard Armitage, assistant secretary for international security affairs. Koch was formerly employed by the Zionist Organization of America. Perle previously served on the staff of Democratic Senator Henry Jackson of Washington, one of Israel's most ardent boosters, and had the reputation of being a conduit of information to the Israeli government. Stephen Bryen came to the administration under the darkest cloud of all.

Bryen's office had representatives on the interagency unit, known as the National Disclosure Policy Commission, which approves technology transfers related to weapons systems. The commission includes representatives of the State and Defense departments, National Security Council, and the intelligence services. Bryen was publicly accused in 1978 of offering a top-secret document on Saudi air bases to a group of visiting Israeli officials.[21]

The accusation arose from an incident reported by Michael Saba, a journalist and former employee of the National Association of Arab Americans. Saba, who readily agreed to a lie detector test by the FBI, said he overheard Bryen make the offer while having breakfast in a Washington restaurant. At the time, Bryen was on the staff of the Senate Foreign Relations Committee. A senior career diplomat expressed the problem that State Department officials encountered during that period: "Whenever Bryen was in the room we always had to use extreme caution." During the controversy, Bryen was suspended from the committee staff, but he was later reinstated.[22] He later left the committee position and became executive director of the Jewish Institute for National Security Affairs (JINSA), an organization founded—according to *The Jewish Week*—to "convince people that the security of Israel and the United States is interlinked."[23] When Bryen moved to a position in the Defense Department, his wife, Shoshona, replaced him at JINSA.

After nine months, the investigating attorneys recommended that a grand jury be impanelled to consider the evidence against Bryen. According to the Justice Department, other witnesses testified to Bryen's Israeli contacts. Indeed, a Justice Department memorandum dated January 26, 1979, discussed "unresolved questions thus far, which suggest that Bryen is (a) gathering classified informations for the Israelis, (b) acting as their unregistered agent and (c) lying about it. . . ."[24] The Justice Department studied the complaint for two years. Although it found that Bryen had an "unusually close relationship with Israel," it made no charges, and in late 1979 it closed the file. Early in 1981 Bryen was hired as Richard Perle's chief deputy in the Pentagon. He remained in that highly responsible position for several years, and was twice awarded the Defense Department's highest civilian honor, the Distinguished Public Service Medal. Apparently forgetting (or ignoring) the suspicions surrounding Bryen, President Ronald Reagan once insisted that Bryen "made lasting contributions to our national defense that have earned him the respect and admiration of his colleagues and the gratitude of all Americans."[25]

Bryen's former boss, Richard Perle, was also the subject of an Israel-related controversy. An FBI summary of a 1970 wiretap described Perle discussing classified information with someone at the Israeli embassy.[26] He came under fire in 1983 when newspapers reported he received substantial payments to represent the interests of an Israeli weapons company. Perle denied a conflict of interest, insisting that, although he received payment for these services after he had assumed his position in the Defense Department, he was between government jobs when he worked for the Israeli firm.

Because of these controversies, both Perle and Bryen were given assignments in the Reagan administration that—it was expected—would keep them isolated from issues relating to Israel. But, observed a State Department official, it did not work out that way. Sensitive questions of technology transfer, that affect Israeli interests, were often settled in the offices of Perle and Bryen.

Despite the investigation, Bryen held one of the highest possible security classifications at the Department of Defense. It is a top secret code word classification, which gave him access to documents and data anywhere in the government, almost without limit. A high official in the Department of State explained the significance of Bryen's access: "With this classification, Bryen can keep up to date not only on what the United States has in the way of technology, but on what we hope to have in the future as the result of secret research and development."

"I'll Take Care of the Congress"

Admiral Thomas Moorer recalls a dramatic example of Israeli lobby power from his days as chairman of the Joint Chiefs of Staff.[27] At the time of the 1973 Arab–Israeli war, Mordecai Gur, the defense attaché at the Israeli embassy who later became commander-in-chief of Israeli forces, came to Moorer demanding that the United States provide Israel with aircraft that were equipped with a high technology air-to-surface anti-tank missile called the Maverick. At the time, the U.S. had only one squadron so equipped. Moorer recalled telling Gur:

> I can't let you have those aircraft. We have just one squadron. Besides, we've been testifying before the Congress, convincing them we need this

equipment. If we gave you our only squadron, Congress would raise hell with us.

Moorer looked at me with a steady, piercing gaze that must have kept a generation of ensigns trembling in their boots. "And do you know what he said? Gur told me, 'You get us the airplanes; I'll take care of the Congress.'" Moorer paused, then added, "And he did." America's only squadron equipped with Mavericks went to Israel.

Moorer, speaking in his office in Washington as a senior counselor at the Georgetown University Center for Strategic and International Studies, said he strongly opposed the transfer but was overruled by "political expediency at the presidential level." He notes that President Richard Nixon was then in the throes of Watergate. "But," he added:

> I've never seen a president—I don't care who he is—stand up to them [the Israelis]. It just boggles your mind. They always get what they want. The Israelis know what is going on all the time. I got to the point where I wasn't writing anything down. If the American people understood what a grip those people have got on our government, they would rise up in arms. Our citizens don't have any idea what goes on.

On another occasion, fear of lobby pressure caused a fundamental decision regarding further military sales to Israel to be deliberately pigeonholed. It involved the general consensus of professionals in the Pentagon that Israel had enough military power for any need as of 1975. By then it had reached a level of regional superiority that was overwhelming. In December 1976 the Middle East Arms Transfer Panel wrote a report to Secretary of Defense Donald Rumsfeld, concluding that no additional arms sales to Israel were necessary. Rumsfeld did not send the report to the State Department, however. It was the closing days of the Ford administration, and its transmission as an official document and subsequent leakage would have given the Democrats a partisan edge with the Israeli lobby.

Jewish groups in the United States are often pressed into service to soften up the secretary of state and other officials, especially in advance of a visit to the United States by the Israeli prime minister. A senior Defense Department official explained, "Israel would always have a long shopping list for the prime minister to take up. We would decide which items were worth making into an issue and which were not. We would try to work things out in advance." There was the constant threat that the prime minister might take an arms issue straight to the president, and the tendency was to clear the agenda of everything possible. "We might decide that we don't want this chickenshit electronic black box to be an issue between the president and prime minister, [so] we would approve it in advance."

On one such occasion, Ed Sanders, President Carter's adviser on Jewish affairs, brought a complaint to the National Security Council offices: "I'm getting a lot of flack from Jewish Congressmen on the ALQ 95-J. What is this thing? And why are we being so nasty about it? Shouldn't we let Israel have it? The president is getting a lot of abuse because the Pentagon won't turn it loose." It was a high technology radar jamming device, and soon it was approved for shipment to Israel.

In advance of Carter's decision to provide a high technology missile to Israel, a procession of Jewish groups came, one after another, to say:

Please explain to us why the Pentagon is refusing to sell AIM 9-L missiles to Israel. Don't you know what this means? This missile is necessary so the Israelis will be able to shoot down the counterpart missile on the Mig 21, which carries the Eight Ball 935.

A former high-ranking official in security affairs cited the intimidating effect of this procession on career specialists:

When you have to explain your position day after day, week after week, to American Jewish groups—first, say, from Kansas City, then Chicago, then East Overshoe—you see what you are up against. These are people from different parts of the country, but they come in with the very same information, the same set of questions, the same criticism. They know what you have done even in private meetings. They will say, "Mr. Smith, we understand that in interagency meetings, you frequently take a hard line against technology transfers to Israel. We'd like you to explain yourself." They keep you on the defensive. They treat you as if you are the long pole in the anti-Israeli tent no matter how modest the position you have taken.

Jewish groups in turn press Capitol Hill into action:

We'll get letters from congressmen: "We need an explanation. We're hearing from constituents that Israel's security is threatened by the refusal of the

Pentagon to release the AIM 9-L missile. Please, Mr. Secretary, can you give me your rationale for the refusal?"

The certainty of such lobby pressure can be costly to taxpayers. In one instance, it kept the United States from trying to recover U.S.-supplied arms, which Israel captured from Lebanon. During Israel's invasion of Lebanon in 1982, its forces overran and captured tons of equipment of all sorts, including weapons supplied by the United States to the government forces in that country. Knowledge of this came to light in an unusual way a year later.

During a visit to Lebanon, the Reverend George Crossley of Deltona, Florida, was shown cases of U.S.-made M-16 rifles, which Israeli officials said were captured from Palestinian forces.[28] Crossley noted that they carried a Saudi insignia, and he wrote down the serial numbers. Saudi Arabia, of course, had no forces involved in the fighting in Lebanon, and the clergyman jumped to the conclusion that rifles, sold by the United States to Saudi Arabia, had been turned over to PLO forces in Lebanon, then captured by the Israelis. If true, this would have been a violation of a U.S. law that prohibits transfer of U.S.-supplied weapons to another country without permission.

Crossley wrote to his congressman, Bill Chappell, Jr., who asked the State Department to explain. A check of records showed that the United States had never sold M-16 rifles to the Saudis, who prefer a German make. The rifles in question were provided directly to forces of the Lebanese government.[29]

The episode got public attention at a time when the U.S. government, at great expense, was once again equipping Lebanese forces. A White House official, reading accounts of the Crossley affair, asked the desk officer at the Pentagon why the United States didn't demand that the Israelis give back these rifles and all other equipment they had taken from the Lebanese army. The Pentagon had an accurate list of what the United States had supplied. Surely, he argued, the Israeli government could be forced to cooperate, and this would ease United States' costs substantially.

The desk officer exploded: "Are you kidding? No way in hell! Who needs that? I answer maybe one hundred letters a month for the secretary of defense in reply to congressmen who bitch and complain about our mistreatment of Israel. Do you think that I want to increase my workload answering more shitty letters? Do you think I am going to recommend action that will increase the flow of problem letters to my boss? Be serious."

Every official of prominence in the State and Defense departments proceeds on the assumption—and certainty—that at least once a week he will have to deal with a group from the Jewish community. One of them summarized:

> One has to keep in mind the constant character of this pressure. The public affairs staff of the Near East Bureau in the State Department figures it will spend about 75 percent of its time dealing with Jewish groups. Hundreds of such groups get appointments in the executive branch each year.

In acting to influence U.S. policy in the Middle East, the Israeli lobby has the field virtually to itself. Other interest groups and individuals who might provide some measure of counterbalancing pressure have only begun to get organized. Americans of Arab ancestry, for example, remain divided. A diplomat who formerly served in a high position in the State Department gave this example:

> When a group concerned about U.S. bias favoring Israel would come in for an appointment, more often than not those in the group start arguing among themselves. One person will object to a heavy focus on Palestinian problems. Another will want Lebanon's problems to be central to the discussion. I would just sit back and listen. They had not worked out in advance what they wanted to say.

Les Janka had similar experiences.[30] In a commentary at a gathering sponsored by the American Enterprise Institute, he recalled visits by groups who were sympathetic to Arab problems:

> Their complaints tended to be fairly general. They would say, "We want the United States to be more evenhanded, more balanced," or "We want you to be more interested in the Palestinians." Nothing specific. In contrast, the Jewish groups come in with a very specific list of demands.
>
> On all kinds of foreign policy issues the American people just don't make their voices heard. Jewish groups are the exceptions. They are prepared, superbly briefed. They have their act together. It is hard for bureaucrats not to respond.

Aid Dollars Into the Pockets of Traitors

The first nationwide shockwave that revealed Israel in an untrustworthy posture emanated from a bizarre spy case, one of the most extraordinary in American history. Jonathan Jay Pollard, Jr., thirty-one, a navy counterintelligence analyst, was arrested in November 1985 for stealing classified documents as a paid spy for Israel.

"We have a moral problem," a former Mossad member said when he learned of the arrest. "You can't take the money of the United States, and then use that money to buy information about that country." Immoral or not, that is exactly what happened.

Before the arrest, the prosecution of those involved in Israeli espionage had been taboo at the Federal Bureau of Investigation, despite long-standing evidence that placed other federal employees under suspicion. Like officials at the State Department, where a senior diplomat describes as "fantastic" the level of spying for Israel, FBI officials habitually chose to look the other way, viewing pro-Israel political influence as great enough to make attempted prosecution an exercise in futility.

The FBI "knew of at least a dozen incidents in which American officials transferred classified information to the Israelis," according to Raymond W. Wannal, Jr., a former assistant director of the FBI. None was prosecuted. The files gathered dust.

John Davitt, a career official and former chief of the Justice Department's internal security section, said: "When the Pollard case broke, the general media and public perception was that this was the first time this had ever happened. No, that's not true at all." He adds that, during his tenure, only the Soviet Union did more spying in the United States than Israel.

Pollard's thievery, however, was so gross and frequent it could not be ignored. On several occasions he took large boxes of classified documents from the Pentagon, flagrantly abusing his "courier" clearance.

In the wake of Pollard's arrest, William Safire, a columnist who rarely criticizes Israel, warned, "The stark fact is that if the espionage charges hold up in court, American aid dollars will have been channeled by Israel into the pockets of American traitors. That will blow up, not over." From the day of his arrest until the present, aspects of the scandal have appeared frequently in nationwide headlines and newscasts.

As it came to light, the Pollard case had all the trappings of a fiction thriller—free luxury trips to faraway places, expensive gifts for the spy's wife, shady spymasters who handled the cash and stolen documents, dashes to elude surveillance teams, and finally, arrest just steps away from political asylum—in the Israeli embassy.

The spy deal was cut in the summer of 1984 when Pollard, an ardent Zionist, met Aviem Sella, an Israeli aviation hero who doubled as an espionage agent. He promised Sella military secrets in return for $1,500 a month. The process began with a flourish. Pollard and his wife, Anne, twenty-six, traveled first class to Paris for a luxury holiday and meetings with Sella, as well as with Rafael Eitan, the famous Israeli Nazi-hunter and spymaster, who gave the Pollards $10,000 to cover expenses. Anne received a sapphire ring worth $7,000 from their hosts. They were also introduced to Joseph Yagur, a member of the Israeli embassy staff in Washington who subsequently became Pollard's main "handler."

Returning to Washington, Pollard stole documents from U.S. military files about three times a week and delivered them for copying to either Yagur or Irit Erb, another embassy employee.

The next spring, the Pollards enjoyed another $10,000 luxury trip—this time to Israel, where Jonathan received an Israeli passport under a new name, a raise in pay to $2,500 a month, and a promise that the pay would continue for the next nine years. He was informed that a Swiss bank account had been established in his name.

Six months later—just over a year after the espionage began—the operation fell apart. FBI agents stopped Pollard for questioning in the parking lot near his Washington work station. Pollard broke away long enough to telephone his wife and, with the code word "cactus," warned her to remove all stolen documents from their apartment. While he returned for further questioning by the agents, Anne gathered up the papers and took them in a suitcase to Erb's residence.

Shaken by the interview, Pollard asked Yagur for guidance. He suggested that the Pollards "lay low" for a while, elude FBI surveillance, and then find political asylum at the Israeli embassy. On November 21, 1985, they made the break, but failed to shake their surveillance. They were refused asylum just inside the embassy gates and arrested as they left the property. Meanwhile, Yagur and Erb left for Israel.

After Pollard's arrest, embarrassed Israeli officials apologized for the spying. They denounced it as an unauthorized "rogue" operation unknown by anyone at cabinet level, and offered full cooperation in a U.S. investigation. They pledged that "those responsible will be brought to account."

Secretary of State George Shultz warmly accepted the apology, and the State Department quickly attempted a cover-up. Shultz sent a team headed by legal adviser Abraham Sofaer, an ardent Zionist who maintained a home in Israel, on a brief investigation there. Returning, Sofaer falsely reported that Israel had provided "full access" to all persons with knowledge of the facts. Within a month of the arrest, the department announced that Israel had returned all stolen documents and that the United States had resumed sharing intelligence with Israel "in all fields." The matter, for the State Department, was now closed.

More Damage Than Terrorists Could Dream Of

Elsewhere, the matter was far from closed. At the Justice Department, U.S. Attorney Joseph E. DiGenova pressed the prosecution vigorously, and the case remained in the headlines for more than three years, giving the American people frequent reason to question Israel's cooperation and reliability, especially since the Pollard spy ring—far from being a "rogue" operation—had reported to the highest levels of the Israeli government, including the Defense Ministry.

In addition, the "return" of stolen documents was a mockery. Of the thousands copied by the Pollards, Israel bothered to return only 163 and, given its appetite for top secrets, surely retained extra copies of these as well.

Instead of cooperating, Israel stonewalled attempts by the U.S. Justice Department to investigate the spy ring, refusing to permit key officials to be interviewed in either the United States or Israel. One U.S. official, reflecting on the Sofaer mission, said, "The question is whether we got the truth. Quite frankly, we didn't."

The two Israelis who had the most prominent roles in the spy episode were "brought to account" by the Israeli government in a curious way: each won a higher position. Colonel Aviem Sella, identified by Pollard as his first principal "handler" and later indicted by a U.S. court for complicity with Pollard, was promoted to commander of Israel's Tel

Nof air base, usually the last rung in the command ladder before becoming air force commander. As a further reward, Israel refused to permit Sella to return to the United States for prosecution. Rafael Eitan, the man who headed the spy program, received similar "punishment"—appointment as the chief executive officer of Israel's largest state-owned company.

The promotions inspired embarrassing headlines, and a delegation of American Jews flew to Israel, urging the government to rescind the decisions. In the face of these protests, Sella resigned as air base commander but later quietly assumed a posh job at Electro-Optic, a major defense corporation. When they learned of this latest salute to Sella, the outraged editors of *Defense News* called for a $200 million cut in Israeli aid each year until the U.S. government recovered the full cost of the Sella–Pollard espionage.

The case returned to prime news coverage on June 4, 1986, when Jonathan Pollard, after engaging in extensive plea-bargaining interviews, pleaded guilty to conspiring to provide U.S. military secrets to the Israelis, and his wife, Anne, pleaded guilty to conspiring to receive and embezzle government property.

In return for Jonathan Pollard's cooperation, the prosecution did not ask for a life sentence. Judge Aubrey Robinson, impressed by a forty-six-page memorandum from Secretary of Defense Caspar Weinberger, selected that punishment anyway. He sentenced Anne Pollard to five years.

Weinberger wrote that the thievery caused "substantial and irrevocable harm," risked the lives of U.S. agents, and created the danger that "U.S. combat forces, wherever they are deployed in the world, could be unacceptably endangered through successful exploitation of this data." He added that Pollard had "both damaged and destroyed policies and national assets which have taken many years, great effort, and enormous national resources to secure."

In the wake of sentencing, Israel doubled Pollard's pay. The same government that had earlier denounced the affair as an unauthorized "rogue" operation began depositing in Pollard's bank account $5,000 each month, assuring him a comfortable life in Israel if he is ever released for good behavior.

Pollard became a cause célèbre in both the United States and Israel, where public protests against his sentence were organized and legal defense funds raised. These funds were only a pittance; the Israeli government provided most of the $200,000 that American lawyers for the two Pollards collected.

Alan Dershowitz, a Harvard professor and an attorney for Pollard, cited Weinberger's assessment of U.S. security damage as the main reason the court ordered a life sentence. Dershowitz considered the sentence excessive, and he challenged Weinberger to prove that Pollard's thievery actually harmed U.S. security.

It was a limp challenge, as the public record already disclosed overwhelming evidence of damage. Items stolen by Pollard included photographs of security-related installations taken by high-flying U.S. surveillance planes, sensitive data on laser technology and U.S. weapons, secret information on naval forces, mines, and port facilities in the Middle East, and the text of a large handbook, nicknamed the "bible," which contained strategies the U.S. Navy would use if attacked. The stolen documents were voluminous enough, the court was told, to fill a box six by six by ten feet in dimension.

Israel made quick use of the secrets. Information provided by Pollard enabled Israeli warplanes to evade U.S. naval and air surveillance in the Mediterranean during their October 1985 air strike against the Tunis headquarters of the Palestine Liberation Organization. The precision-like attack, dismissed by President Ronald Reagan as "legitimate self-defense" but later denounced by other administration officials, left nearly one hundred dead, mostly Tunisian civilians, and the PLO headquarters in shambles.

The gravest harm to U.S. interests at the time occurred when the Soviet Union acquired documents stolen by Pollard, perhaps all of them. The Soviets acquired the data through two separate secret channels. Israel opened one of them directly, offering U.S. secrets in an attempt to influence Moscow's policy on Jewish emigration. Using some of these same contacts, the KGB, Moscow's intelligence service, opened the other channel without the knowledge of Israeli leadership, establishing a spy network within the Mossad.

These shocking revelations came in a news report distributed by United Press International on December 13, 1987. The author, Richard Sale, reported that the Soviet Union had breached Israeli intelligence and that information stolen by Pollard "was traded to the Soviets in return for promises to increase emigration of Soviet Jews to Israel." A State Department source told Sale, "It began as a straight data-for-people deal," but through it the Soviets "penetrated the Israeli defense establishment at a high level."

This new scandal belied Pollard's excuse that, in helping Israel, he did not hurt the United States. U.S. intelligence sources said stolen documents reaching Moscow by this route included "sensitive U.S. weapons technology and strategic information about the defense forces of Turkey, Pakistan, and moderate Arab countries, including Saudi Arabia."

Soviet acquisition of documents stolen by Pollard was discussed during an urgent review of the scandal by the CIA, FBI, and other U.S. intelligence officials: "One of the guys was commenting that if Pollard had stolen the stuff, at least it was going to a U.S. ally, but a CIA guy spoke up and said that if the Mossad was involved it meant that copies of everything were going to [the KGB's] Moscow center."

The Israel–Moscow spy link enabled highly placed Soviet moles to penetrate the Mossad, the most serious blow to Israeli intelligence in twenty years. One U.S. intelligence analyst fixed the blame on "right-wing Jews" in Israel. U.S. agents first learned of the Israeli–Moscow spy link when information stolen by Pollard was "traced to the Eastern bloc."

The reported diversion of stolen documents to Moscow made headlines in nine newspapers, but competing news services and television networks ignored it. The *New York Times* and the *Washington Post* printed not a word.

In yet another episode, Israel used data stolen by Pollard as the basis for a proposed military strike. Alarmed by the possibility that Pakistan might be building its own nuclear weapons—a concern that was shared by India—and armed with satellite photographs, stolen by Pollard, that showed a secret nuclear facility, Israel officials approached New Delhi in June 1985 with a daring plan. They urged that the two governments destroy the facility in a joint air attack. India refused.

The Pollard case continued to make headlines: In April 1988, Israel refused to let Howard Katz, an Israeli lawyer who had been associated with Pollard, visit the United States for questioning. In June, two committees of the Israeli parliament, previously citing "lies, whitewash, and contradictions," closed their official report on the Pollard affair by blaming senior officials of both the Labor and Likud parties, but recommended no action. On several occasions in the 1990s, President Bill Clinton was approached with proposals to grant Pollard clemency—proposals the president greeted with warmth until drastic actions by senior staff members (such as the threatened resignation of CIA director George Tenet) convinced him otherwise.

By 1995, CNN correspondent and former AIPAC employee Wolf Blitzer estimated that the Pollards were due around $600,000 in deferred payments from Israel—or would be, had Jonathan not divorced Anne immediately after she served her five years in prison, hence cutting her off from further payments. The money, therefore, is all Jonathan's, although Anne, who lives in Israel, continued to profit from the incident by opening a nightclub in Tel Aviv called "Pollard's Place."[31]

Finally, despite Israel's claims that the Pollard affair was part of a "rogue operation," on the tenth anniversary of his arrest Israel granted Jonathan Pollard full Israeli citizenship. In May 1998, after denying for thirteen years that Pollard was an Israeli spy, Israel officially recognized Pollard as its agent, in an unsuccessful attempt to negotiate his release. From all this, columnist Safire concludes, "The Pollards, in America, and their spymasters in Israel, have done more damage to their respective countries than any terrorists could dream of doing."

"All I Can Tell You..."

The imprisonment of the Pollards did not end Israeli espionage in the United States. In 1997, forty-year-old U.S. Army Tank Automotive and Armaments Command (TACOM) engineer David Tenenbaum was suspended from his employment without pay and had his credentials confiscated by U.S. authorities after admitting to divulging "non-releasable classified information to every Israeli liasion officer assigned to TACOM over the last ten years."

Widespread speculation that the Tenenbaum case might develop into another Pollard affair caused the FBI to make very little information about the new incident public. The *Detroit Jewish News* reported in June 1998 that Tenenbaum had been cleared of all charges; however, FBI agents refused to confirm that report. Instead, said one:

> All I can tell you is a two-sentence statement. The case is closed. No criminal charges have been filed.

Of course, the question that remains is whether Tenenbaum was charged and formally acquitted or if, as the FBI agent's statement suggests, the investigation was dropped entirely. A spokesman for TACOM noted that Tenenbaum was back at work, although not at his previous job—a fact that caused some to seriously question Tenenbaum's innocence. "If the FBI investigation found that Tenenbaum is innocent," one colleague asked, "why isn't he back at his previous job?"[32]

An Unofficial Network

In a 1986 statement to the press, Israeli Embassy spokesman Yossi Gal said:

> The Pollard affair was an unauthorized deviation from the clear-cut Israeli policy of not conducting any espionage activity whatsoever in the United States or activities against the interests of the United States, given that the United States is a true friend of Israel.[33]

Numerous bits of evidence suggest otherwise, as time and again individuals accused of passing classified information to Israel are allowed to disappear, or worse, receive promotions and financial compensation. Still, most of the secret information passed onto Israel is furnished by U.S. citizens without compensation of any kind. As one official complains, "The Mossad is the most active foreign intelligence service on U.S. soil."

For years, Israel has been able to learn virtually every secret about U.S. foreign policy in the Middle East. Reporter Charles Babcock of the *Washington Post,* basing his estimate on a 1979 CIA report and recent interviews with more than two dozen active or former U.S. intelligence officials, concluded, "This remarkable intelligence harvest is provided largely not by paid agents, but by an unofficial network of sympathetic American officials who work in the Pentagon, the State Department, congressional offices, the National Security Council, and even the U.S. intelligence agencies." A 1996 U.S. government report stated the problem more explicitly: Israel "conducts the most aggressive espionage operation against the United States of any U.S. ally."[34]

7

The Assault on *Assault*

ALTHOUGH ISRAEL's lobby seems able to penetrate our nation's strongest defenses at will in order to gain the secret information it wishes, when the lobby's objective is to keep U.S. information secret from the world, our defenses suddenly become impenetrable.

After thirty-five years, James M. Ennes, Jr., a retired officer of the U.S. Navy, is still having difficulty prying loose documents that shed light on the worst peacetime disaster in the history of our navy. In this quest, he has encountered resistance by the Department of Defense, the Anti-Defamation League of B'nai B'rith, the American Israel Public Affairs Committee, the book publishing industry, the news media, and the Israeli Foreign Ministry. The resistance, seemingly coordinated on an international scale, is especially perplexing because Ennes's goal is public awareness of an episode of heroism and tragedy at sea that is without precedent in American history.

As the result of a program of concealment supported by successive governments in both Israel and the United States, hardly anyone remembers the miraculous survival of the USS *Liberty* after a devastating assault by Israeli forces on June 8, 1967, left 34 sailors dead, 171 injured, and the damaged ship adrift with no power, rudder, or means of communication.

The sustained courage of Captain William L. McGonagle and his crew in these desperate circumstances earned the *Liberty* a place of honor in the annals of the U.S. Navy. But despite energetic endeavors, including those of Ennes, who was officer of the deck that day, awareness of the incident remains dim and obscure. His stirring book-length account of the attack, *Assault on the* Liberty, itself continues to be under heavy assault twenty-two years after its publication.

The episode and its aftermath were so incredible that Admiral Thomas L. Moorer, who became chairman of the Joint Chiefs of Staff a month after the attack, observes, "If it was written as fiction, nobody would believe it."[1]

Certain facts are clear. The attack was no accident. The *Liberty* was assaulted in broad daylight by Israeli forces who knew the ship's identity.[2] The *Liberty,* an intelligence-gathering ship, had no combat capability and carried only light machine guns for defense. A steady breeze made its U.S. flag easily visible. The assault occurred over a period of nearly two hours—first by air, then by torpedo boat. The ferocity of the attacks left no doubt: the Israeli forces wanted the ship and its crew destroyed.

The public, however, was kept in the dark. Even before the American public learned of the attack, U.S. government officials began to promote an account of the assault that was satisfactory to Israel. The American Israel Public Affairs Committee worked through congressmen to keep the story under control. The president of the United States, Lyndon B. Johnson, ordered and led a cover-up so thorough that sixteen years after he left office, the episode was still largely unknown to the public— and the men who suffered and died have gone largely unhonored.

The day of the attack began in routine fashion, with the ship first proceeding slowly in an easterly direction in the eastern Mediterranean, later following the contour of the coastline westerly about fifteen miles off the Sinai Peninsula. On the mainland, Israeli forces were winning smashing victories in the third Arab–Israeli war in nineteen years. Israeli Chief of Staff Yitzhak Rabin, announcing that the Israelis had taken the entire Sinai and broken the blockade on the Strait of Tiran, declared: "The Egyptians are defeated."[3] On the eastern front, the Israelis had overcome Jordanian forces and captured most of the West Bank.

At 6:00 A.M. an airplane, identified by the *Liberty* crew as an Israeli Noratlas, slowly circled the ship, then departed. At 9:00 A.M., a jet appeared at a distance, then to the left of the ship.[4] At 10:00 A.M., two rocket-armed jets circled the ship three times. They were close enough for their pilots to be observed through binoculars. The planes were unmarked. An hour later the Israeli Noratlas returned, flying not more than 200 feet directly above the *Liberty* and clearly marked with the Star of David. The ship's crew members and the pilot waved at each other. The plane returned every few minutes until 1:00 P.M. By then, the ship had changed course and was proceeding almost due west.

At 2:00 P.M., all hell broke loose. Three Israeli Mirage fighter planes headed straight for the *Liberty*, their rockets taking out the forward machine guns and wrecking the ship's antennae. The Mirages were joined by Mystere fighters, which dropped napalm on the bridge and deck and repeatedly strafed the ship. The attack continued for more than twenty minutes. In all, the ship sustained 821 holes in her sides and decks. Of these, more than 100 were rocket-sized.

As the aircraft departed, three torpedo boats took over the attack, firing five torpedoes, one of which tore a forty-foot hole in the hull, killing 25 sailors. The ship was in flames, dead in the water, listing precariously, and taking on water. The crew was ordered to prepare to abandon ship. As life rafts were lowered into the water, the torpedo boats moved closer and shot them to pieces. One boat concentrated machine gun fire on rafts that were still on deck as crew members there tried to extinguish the napalm fires. Petty Officer Charles Rowley declares, "They didn't want anyone to live."

At 3:15 P.M., the last shot was fired, leaving the vessel a combination morgue and hospital. The ship had no engines, no power, no rudder. Fearing further attack, Captain McGonagle, despite severe leg injuries, stayed at the bridge. An Israeli helicopter, its open bay door showing troops in battle gear and a machine gun mounted in an open doorway, passed close to the deck, then left. Other aircraft came and went during the next hour.

U.S. air support never arrived. The USS *Saratoga* was only thirty minutes away, and, with a squadron of fighter planes on deck ready for a routine operation, it was prepared to respond to an attack almost instantly. But the rescue never occurred. Without approval by Washington, the planes could not take aggressive action, even to rescue a U.S. ship confirmed to be under attack. Admiral Donald Engen, then captain of the USS *America*, a second U.S. carrier in the vicinity, later explained: "President Johnson had very strict control. Even though we knew the *Liberty* was under attack, I couldn't just go and order a rescue."[5] The ship's planes were hardly in the air when the voice of Secretary of Defense Robert S. McNamara was heard over Sixth Fleet radios: "Tell the Sixth Fleet to get those aircraft back immediately."[6] They were ordered to have no part in destroying or driving off the attackers.

Shortly after 3:00 P.M., nearly an hour after the *Liberty*'s plea was first heard, the White House gave momentary approval to a rescue mission, and planes from both carriers were launched. At almost precisely the same instant, the Israeli government informed the U.S. naval attaché in Tel Aviv that its forces had "erroneously attacked a U.S. ship" after mistaking it for an Egyptian vessel, and offered "abject apologies." With the apology in hand, Johnson once again ordered U.S. aircraft back to their carriers.

When the second launch occurred, there were no Israeli forces to "destroy or drive away." Fifteen hours of lonely struggle to keep the wounded alive and the vessel afloat were ahead for the *Liberty* and its ravaged crew. Not until dawn of the next day would the *Liberty* see a U.S. plane or ship. The only friendly visit was from a small Soviet warship. Its offer of help was declined, but the Soviets said they would stand by in case need should arise.

The next morning, two U.S. destroyers arrived with medical and repair assistance. Soon the wounded were transferred to the carrier hospital by helicopter. The battered ship then proceeded to Malta, where a navy Court of Inquiry was to be held. The inquiry itself was destined to be a part of an elaborate program to keep the public from knowing what had really happened.

In fact, the cover-up began almost at the precise moment that the Israeli assault ended. The apology from Israeli officials reached the White House moments after the last gun fired at the *Liberty*. President Johnson accepted and publicized the condolences of Israeli Prime Minister Levi Eshkol, even though readily available information showed the Israeli account to be false; the CIA had learned a day before the attack that the Israelis planned to sink the ship.[7] Nevertheless, congressional comments largely echoed the president's interpretation of the assault, and the nation was caught up in euphoria over Israel's stunning victories over the Arabs. The casualties on the *Liberty* got scant attention. Smith Hempstone, foreign correspondent for the *Washington Star,* wrote from Tel Aviv, "In a week since the Israeli attack on the USS *Liberty,* not one single Israeli of the type which this correspondent encounters many times daily—cab drivers, censors, bartenders, soldiers—has bothered to express sorrow for the deaths of these Americans."[8]

The Pentagon staved off reporters' inquiries with the promise of a "comprehensive statement" once the official inquiry, conducted by Admiral Isaac Kidd, was finished.[9] Arriving at Malta, Kidd gave explicit orders to the crew: "Answer no questions. If somehow you are backed into a corner, then you may say that it was an accident and that Israel has apologized. You may say nothing else." Crew members were assured they could talk freely to reporters once the summary of the Court of Inquiry was made public. This was later modified. They were then ordered not to provide information beyond the precise words of the published summary.

The court was still taking testimony when a charge that the attack had been deliberate appeared in the U.S. press.[10] An *Associated Press* story filed from Malta reported that "senior crewmen" on the ship were convinced the Israelis knew the ship was American before they attacked. "We were flying the Stars and Stripes and it's absolutely impossible that they shouldn't know who we were," a crew member said. The navy disputed the story, saying the United States "thoroughly accepted the Israeli apology."

With the testimony completed, Admiral Kidd handcuffed himself to a huge box of records and flew to Washington where they were examined by Chief of Naval Operations Admiral McDonald, as well as by congressional leaders before the long-awaited summary statement was issued.[11] When it was finally released, it was far from comprehensive.[12] It made no attempt to fix blame, focusing instead almost entirely on the actions of the crew.

The censored summary did not reveal that the ship had been under close aerial surveillance by Israel for hours before the attack, or that during the preceding twenty-four hours Israel had repeatedly warned U.S. authorities to move the *Liberty.*[13] It contained nothing to dispute the notion of mistaken identity. The navy erroneously reported that the attack lasted only six minutes instead of seventy minutes, and falsely asserted that all firing stopped when the torpedo boats came close enough to identify the U.S. flag. The navy made no mention of napalm or of life rafts being shot up. It even suppressed records of the strong breeze that made the ship's U.S. flag plainly visible.

The report did make one painful revelation: Before the attack, the Joint Chiefs of Staff had ordered the *Liberty* to move farther from the coast, but the message "was misrouted, delayed, and not received until after the attack."[14]

Several newspapers criticized the Pentagon's summary. The *New York Times* said it "leaves a good many questions unanswered."[15] The *Washington Star* used the word "cover-up," called the summary an "affront," and demanded a deeper and wider probe.[16] Senator J. William Fulbright, chairman of the Senate Foreign Relations Committee, after a closed briefing by Secretary of State Dean Rusk, called the episode "very embarrassing." The *Star* concluded: "Whatever the meaning of this, embarrassment is no excuse for disingenuousness."

In early July, the Associated Press quoted Micha Limor, identified as an Israeli reservist who had served on one of the torpedo boats, as saying that Israeli sailors noticed three numbers on the ship as they circled the *Liberty*, but insisted that the numbers meant nothing to them.[17] Lieutenant James M. Ennes, Jr., a cypher officer recovering in a hospital from shrapnel wounds, was incredulous when he read the Limor story.[18] He had been officer of the deck. He knew that the ship's name appeared in large letters on the stern and that the hull number was plainly visible on the bow. He knew also that a breeze made the ship's U.S. flag easily visible during the day. He had just ordered a new 5- by 8-foot flag displayed early on the day of the attack. By the time the torpedo boats arrived, that flag had been shot down, but an even larger (7- by 13-foot) flag was mounted in plain view from a yardarm. He knew that the attackers, whether by air or surface, could not avoid knowing it was a U.S. ship. Above all, he knew that *Liberty*'s intercept operators had heard the Israeli reconnaissance pilots reporting to Israeli headquarters that the ship was American.

Disturbed by the Limor account and the exchange of public messages concerning the assault, Ennes determined to unravel the story. During the four months he was bedridden at Portsmouth, Virginia, he collected information from his shipmates. Later, while stationed in Germany, he recorded the recollections of other crew members. Transferred to Washington, D.C., he secured government reports under the Freedom of Information Act, and he also obtained the full Court of Inquiry report, which was finally, after nine years, declassified from being top secret in 1976.

The result was Ennes's book, *Assault on the* Liberty, published in 1980, two years after he retired from the navy. I first read the book while crossing the Atlantic as a member of a congressional delegation. Amazed by its contents, I shared it with several colleagues, who were equally astounded. Ennes discovered "shallowness" in the court's questioning, and a failure to follow up "on evidence that the attack was planned in advance," as well as evidence that interceptors from two radio stations heard an Israeli pilot identify the ship as American.[19] He wrote that the court ignored the ship's log, which recorded a steady breeze blowing and included confirming testimony from crewmen, and erroneously concluded that attackers may not have been able to identify the flag's nationality: the flag, according to the court, "hung limp at the mast on a windless day."

Concerning Israeli motives for the attack, Ennes wrote that Israeli officials may have decided to destroy the ship because they feared its sensitive listening devices would detect Israeli plans to invade Syria's Golan Heights. (Israel invaded Syria the day after the *Liberty* attack, despite Israel's earlier acceptance of a ceasefire with its Arab foes.) A BBC television documentary titled *Dead in the Water* was broadcast several times in England and in several European markets—but not in the United States. The documentary reported a different theory: Israel wanted to destroy the *Liberty*, confident that Egypt, not Israel, would be blamed. Israel hoped this would provoke sufficient American outrage against Egypt that the United States would enter the war in alliance with Israel.

Ennes learned that crewmen sensed a cover-up even while the Court of Inquiry was taking testimony at Malta.[20] He identified George Golden, the *Liberty*'s engineering officer and acting commanding officer, as the source of the Associated Press story that charged that the attack was deliberate. Golden, who is Jewish, was so outraged at the prohibition against talking with reporters that he ignored it—risking his future career in the navy to rescue a vestige of his country's honor.

The U.S. embassy at Tel Aviv relayed to Washington the only fully detailed Israeli account of the attack—the Israeli Court of Inquiry report known as "Israeli Preliminary Inquiry 1/67." The embassy message also contained the recommendation that, at the request of the Israeli government, the account not be released to the American people.[21] Ennes believes this is probably because both governments knew the mistaken identity excuse was too transparent to believe.[22]

Another request for secrecy was delivered by hand to Eugene Rostow, undersecretary of state for political affairs.[23] It paralleled the message from the embassy at Tel Aviv, imploring the Department of State to keep the Israeli Court of Inquiry secret because "the circumstances of the attack [if the version outlined in the file is to be believed] strip the Israeli navy naked."[24] Although Ennes saw that message in an official file in 1977, by 1984 it had vanished from all known official files. Ennes believes that Israeli officials decided to make the Israeli navy the scapegoat in the controversy. With the blame piled on its navy, the orphan service that has the least clout in Israel's military hierarchy, Israel then asked the United States to keep the humiliation quiet. United States officials agreed not to release the text of the Israeli report.

Legal Adviser's Report Becomes Top Secret

During this same period, in the weeks immediately following the assault on the *Liberty*, an assessment of "Israeli Preliminary Inquiry 1/67" was prepared by Carl F. Salans, legal adviser to the secretary of state. It was prepared for the consideration of Eugene Rostow. The report, kept top secret until 1983 and apparently given only cursory examination by Secretary of State Dean Rusk, examines the credibility of the Israeli study and reveals as has no other single document the real attitude of the U.S. government toward the Israeli attack on the USS *Liberty*. It was a document too explosive to release.

Item by item, Salans demonstrated that the Israeli excuse could not be believed. Preparing the report immediately after the attack, he relied mainly on the limited information in Admiral Isaac Kidd's Court of Inquiry file. Kidd never interviewed Ennes, Golden, or any of the other principal witnesses, but he found enough evidence to thoroughly discredit the Israeli document. The factors that Salans examined were the speed and direction of the *Liberty*, aircraft surveillance, identification by Israeli aircraft, identification by torpedo boats, flag and identification markings, and the time sequence of attacks. In each instance, eyewitness testimony or known facts disputed Israel's claims of innocent error.

For example, the Israeli report contended that the *Liberty* was traveling at a speed of twenty-eight to thirty knots, hence behaving suspiciously. Its actual speed was five knots. Israeli reconnaissance aircraft claimed to have carried out only two overnight missions, at 6:00 A.M. and 9:00 A.M. Aircraft actually flew over the *Liberty* eight times before opening fire, the first at 6:00 A.M. and the last at 1:00 P.M. The Israeli report charged that the *Liberty*, after refusing to identify itself, opened fire. Captain McGonagle testified that the only signals by the torpedo boats came from a distance of 2,000 yards when the attack run was already launched and torpedoes were on their way. The Israeli torpedo boats' blinker signals could not be seen because of intermittent smoke and flames. Not seeing them, the *Liberty* did not reply. The Israeli report contended that the *Liberty* did not display a flag or identifying marks. Five crewmen testified that they saw the U.S. flag flying the entire morning. When the flag was shot away during the air attack, another, larger, flag was hoisted before the torpedo onslaught began. Hull markings were clear and freshly painted. The Israelis tried to shift responsibility by asserting that the attack originated because of reports that the coastal area was being shelled from the sea. Salans said it should be clear to any trained observer that the small guns aboard the *Liberty* were incapable of shore bombardment.

The Salans report was forwarded September 21, 1967, to Undersecretary of State Rostow. This means that high officials of the administration knew the falsity of Israeli claims about the *Liberty* soon after the assault itself.

With a document in hand that so thoroughly refuted Israel's claims, the next logical step obviously would be its presentation to the Israeli government for comment, followed by publication of the findings. Instead, it was stamped "top secret" and hidden from public view, as well as from the attention of other officials of our government and its military services, along with the still-hidden Israeli report. Dean Rusk, secretary of state at the time, says that he has "no current recollection" of seeing the Salans report. He adds, however, that he "was never satisfied with the Israeli purported explanation of the USS *Liberty* affair."

The cover-up of the Salans report and other aspects of the episode soon had agonizing implications for U.S. security. If the navy had been candid about the *Liberty* episode even within its own ranks, the nation might have been spared the subsequent humiliation of an ordeal that began five months later when North Korean forces killed a U.S. sailor and captured the USS *Pueblo* and its entire crew. The agony ended when the crew was released after experiencing a year of captivity under brutal conditions.

Pueblo commander Lloyd M. Bucher later concluded that, had he been armed with the facts of the disaster in the Mediterranean, he might have prevented the *Pueblo* episode.[25] In the late summer of 1967, still ashore but preparing to take command of the ill-fated ship, Bucher learned of the *Liberty*'s misfortune. Headed for hostile waters near North Korea, he believed his mission would profit from the experience and asked for details. Bucher recalls how his request was brushed aside: "I asked my superiors about the disaster and was told it was all just a big mistake, that there was nothing we could learn from it."[26] When he later read Ennes's book, Bucher discovered that the *Liberty* crew had encountered many of the same problems his ship faced just before its capture. Both ships had inadequate means for destroying secret documents and equipment, and, in a crisis, even the ship itself. Both had serious shortcomings in control procedures. Bucher blames "incompetency at the top" and "lack of response to desperate calls for assistance during the attack." He speaks bitterly of the *Pueblo*'s ordeal:

> We had a man killed and fourteen wounded. Then a year of pretty damned severe brutality, which could have been prevented had I been told what happened to the *Liberty*. It's only because that damned incident was covered up as thoroughly as it was.

The cover-up of the attack on the *Liberty* had other, more personal consequences. On recommendation of the U.S. Navy, William L. McGonagle, captain of the *Liberty*, was approved by President Johnson for the nation's highest award, the Congressional Medal of Honor. According to Ennes, the captain "defied bullets, shrapnel, and napalm" during the attack and, despite injuries, stayed on the bridge throughout the night. Under his leadership, the eighty-two crewmen who survived death and injury had kept the ship afloat despite a forty-foot hole in its side, and managed to bring the crippled vessel to safe harbor.

McGonagle was an authentic hero, but he was not to get the award with the customary style, honor, ceremony, and publicity. It would not be presented personally by the president, nor would the event be at the White House. The navy got instructions to arrange the ceremony elsewhere. The president would not take part. It was up to the navy to find a suitable place. Admiral Thomas L. Moorer, who had become chief of naval operations shortly before the order arrived, was upset.[27] It was the only Congressional Medal of Honor that, in his experience, would not be presented at the White House. He protested to Secretary of Defense Robert S. McNamara, but the order stood. No voice of protest came from the legislature for which the medal is named.

The admiral would have been even more upset had he known at the time that the White House delayed approving the medal until it was cleared by Israel. Ennes quoted a naval officer as saying: "The government is pretty jumpy about Israel. The State Department even asked the Israeli ambassador if his government had any objection to McGonagle getting the medal. 'Certainly not,' Israel said."[28] The text of the accompanying citation gave no offense: it did not mention Israel.

The secretary of the navy presented the medal in a small, quiet ceremony at the navy yard in Washington. Admiral Moorer said later that he was not surprised by the extraordinary arrangements.[29] "They had been trying to hush it up all the way through." Moorer added, "The way they did things, I'm surprised they didn't just hand it to him under the 14th Street Bridge."

Even tombstone inscriptions at Arlington National Cemetery perpetuated the cover-up.[30] As with McGonagle's citation, Israel was not mentioned. For fifteen years, the marker over the graves of six *Liberty* crewmen read simply, "died in the Eastern Mediterranean." There was no mention of the ship, the circumstances, or Israel. Visitors might have concluded that they died of natural causes. Finally, survivors of the ship banded together to form the USS *Liberty* Veterans Association and launched a protest that produced a modest improvement. The cover-up was lifted ever so slightly in 1982, when the cemetery marker was changed to read, "Killed USS *Liberty*." The dedication event at grave site was as quiet as the McGonagle ceremony had been years before. The only civilian official of the U.S. government attending, Senator Larry Pressler, promised further investigation of the *Liberty* episode, but did nothing.

"We get lots of promises," Ennes says, "but no action." He relates the following example:

> Senator Kennedy once promised to look into the issue and spent a year sup-
> posedly reviewing my book and files we sent. Eventually he wrote to say,
> "Everything humanly possible must be done to find the truth about the
> USS *Liberty*." Fine, we said, so conduct an investigation. You can do that
> alone as a U.S. senator. He never answered that or several follow-up letters.

The national cover-up of the event went so far as to dictate the phrasing of letters of condolence to the survivors of those killed in the assault. In such circumstances, next of kin normally receive a letter from the president setting forth the facts of the tragedy and expressing profound feelings over the hardship, sacrifice, and bravery involved in the death. In fact, letters by the hundreds were then being sent to next of kin as the toll in Vietnam mounted.

To senior White House officials, however, death by Israeli fire was different from death at the hands of the Vietcong. A few days after the assault on the *Liberty*, the senior official in charge of President Johnson's liaison with the Jewish community, Harry McPherson, received this message from White House aide James Cross:

> Thirty-one navy personnel were killed aboard the USS *Liberty* as the result
> of the accidental attack by Israeli forces. The attached condolence letters,
> which have been prepared using basic formats approved for Vietnam War
> casualties, strike me as inappropriate in this case. Due to the very sensitive
> nature of the whole Arab–Israeli situation and the circumstances under
> which these people died, I would ask that you review these drafts and pro-
> vide me with nine or ten different responses which *will* adequately deal
> with this special situation.[31]

The "special situation" led McPherson to agree that many of the usual paragraphs of condolence were "inappropriate." He suggested phrases that de-emphasized combat, and that ignored the Israeli role and even the sacrifice involved. Responding to the "very sensitive nature" of relations with Israel, the president's staff set aside time-honored traditions in recognizing those killed in combat.[32] McPherson suggested that the letters express the president's gratitude for the "contribution to the cause of peace" made by the victims and state that Johnson had tried to avert the Israeli–Arab war.

While Washington engaged in this strange program of cover-up, *Liberty* crewmen could remember with satisfaction a moment of personal pride, however brief.[33] On the afternoon of June 10, 1967, as the battered ship and its crew prepared to part company with the USS *America* for their journey to Malta and the Court of Inquiry, Captain Donald Engen ordered a memorial service for those who had died during the assault. Held on the deck of the *America*, where more than 2,000 sailors were gathered, the service was an emotional moment. Afterward, as the ships parted, Engen called for three cheers for the *Liberty* crew. Petty Officer Jeffery Carpenter, weakened from loss of blood, occupied a stretcher on the *Liberty*'s main deck. Crewman Stan White lifted one end of the stretcher so Carpenter could see as well as hear the tribute being paid by the carrier. "Such cheers!" Engen told me. "Boy, you could hear the cheers echo back and forth across the water. It was a very moving thing."

It was the only "moving thing" that would be officially bestowed in tribute to the heroic crew.

"This Is Pure Murder"

Books have perpetuated myths about the *Liberty*. Yitzhak Rabin, military commander of Israeli forces at the time, declared in his memoirs, published in 1979, that the *Liberty* was mistaken for an Egyptian ship: "I must admit I had mixed feelings about the news [that it was actually a U.S. ship]—profound regret at having attacked our friends and a tremendous sense of relief [that the ship was not Soviet]."[34] He wrote that Israel, while compensating victims of the assault, refused to pay for the damage to the ship "since we did not consider ourselves responsible for the train of errors."

Lyndon Johnson's own memoirs, titled *Vantage Point*, continued the fiction that the ship had been "attacked in error."[35] Although his signature had appeared on letters of condolence to thirty-four next of kin, his memoirs reported the death toll at only ten.[36] He cited 100 wounded; the actual count was 171. He added, "This heartbreaking episode grieved the Israelis deeply, as it did us." Johnson wrote of the message he had sent on the hotline to Moscow, in which he assured the Soviets that carrier aircraft were on their way to the scene and that "investigation was the sole purpose of these flights." He did not pretend that protection and rescue of the ship and its crew were among his objectives, nor did he record that the carrier aircraft were never permitted to proceed to the *Liberty* even for "investigation." The commander in chief devoted only sixteen lines to one of the worst peacetime naval disasters in history.

Israeli Defense Minister Moshe Dayan, identified in a CIA report as the officer who personally ordered the attack, made no mention of the *Liberty* in his lengthy autobiography.[37] According to the CIA document, Dayan had issued the order over the protests of another Israeli general who said, "This is pure murder."

The cover-up also dogged Ennes in the marketing of his book.[38] Despite high praise in reviews, book orders routinely got "lost," wholesale listings disappeared mysteriously, and the Israeli lobby launched a far-flung campaign to discredit the text. The naval base in San Diego returned a supply of books when a chaplain filed a complaint. Military writer George Wilson told Ennes that when the *Washington Post* printed a review, "It seemed that every phone in the building had someone calling to complain about our mention of the book." The *Atlanta Journal* called Ennes's *Assault on the* Liberty a "disquieting story of navy bungling, government cover-up and Israeli duplicity that is well worth reading."[39] The *Columbus Dispatch* called it "an inquest of cover-up in the area of international political intrigue." Journalist Seymour Hersh praised it as "an insider's book by an honest participant," and the prestigious Naval Institute at Annapolis called it "probably the most important naval book of the year."[40]

Israel took swift measures to warn U.S. readers to ignore the reviews. The Israeli Foreign Office charged, "Ennes allows his very evident rancor and subjectivity to override objective analysis," and that his "conclusions fly in the face of logic and military facts." These charges, Ennes later said, were "adopted by the Anti-Defamation League of B'nai B'rith for distribution to Israeli supporters throughout the United States." A caller to the American Israel Public Affairs Committee was told that the book was "a put-up job, all lies and financed by the National Association of Arab Americans."[41] Ennes said the "emotional rhetoric" caused "serious damage to sales and a marked reluctance of media executives to allow discussion of this story."

As the result of radio talk shows and lecture platforms on which Ennes appeared, he heard from people "all over the country" who had been frustrated in efforts to buy his book.[42] Several retail book stores, seeking to order the book from the publisher, Random House, were given false information—they were told the book did not exist, or that it had not been published, or that it was out of print, or that it was withdrawn to avoid a lawsuit.

Talk show host Ray Taliaferro caused a stir one Sunday night in 1980 when he announced over San Francisco radio station KGO that he would interview Ennes the following Sunday.[43] More than 500 protest letters poured into the station, but the program went on as scheduled. Public response was overwhelming, as listener calls continued to stream in for a full hour after the two-hour show with Ennes had ended. Two phone calls arrived threatening Taliaferro's life—one on a supposedly private line.

At the invitation of Paul Backus, editor of the *Journal of Electronic Defense*, Ennes wrote a guest editorial in 1981 on the implications of the *Liberty* incident, stating that friendly nations sometimes feel compelled to take hostile actions.[44] In the case of the *Liberty*, he added:

> Because the friendly nation . . . is the nation of Israel, and because the nation of Israel is widely, passionately, and expensively supported in the United States, and perhaps also because a proper inquiry would reveal a humiliating failure of command, control, and communications, an adequate investigation . . . has yet to be politically palatable.

Backus was stunned when the owners of the magazine, an organization of military- and defense-related executives known as the Association of Old Crows, ordered him not to publish the Ennes editorial. Association spokesman Gus Slayton wrote to Backus that the article was "excellent," but said "it would not be appropriate to publish it now in view of the heightened tension in the Middle East." Backus, a retired navy officer, resigned. "I want nothing more to do with organizations which would further suppress the information," he stated. The Ennes piece was later given prominent play in a rival magazine, *Defense*

Electronics, and the issue became a popular reprint, selling for three dollars a copy.

As Ennes lectured at universities in the Midwest and West in 1981 and 1982, he encountered protests in different form. Although most reaction was highly favourable, hecklers called him a liar and an anti-Semite, and protested to administrators against his appearance on campus. Posters announcing his lectures were routinely ripped down. Wording, identical to that used by the Israeli Foreign Office and B'nai B'rith in their attacks on the book, appeared in flyers distributed by local "Jewish student unions" as Ennes spoke to college audiences.

Criticism of Ennes's book seemed to be coordinated on a national— even international—scale. After National Public Radio broadcast the full text of the book over its book-reading network, local Anti-Defamation League spokesmen demanded and received the opportunity for a ten-minute rebuttal at the end of the series.[45] The rebuttal in Seattle was almost identical to the wording of a document attacking the book that was issued by the Israeli Foreign Office in Jerusalem. Both rebuttals matched verbatim a letter criticizing Ennes that had appeared in the Jacksonville, Florida, *Times-Union*.

Ennes's misfortunes took an ironic turn in June 1982 when ABC's *Nightline* canceled the broadcast of a segment it had prepared on the fifteen-year reunion of the *Liberty* crew. The show was preempted by crisis coverage of Israel's invasion of Lebanon, which had begun the day before. In early 1983, *Nightline* rescheduled the segment, but once again Israel intruded, this time when Moshe Arens, Israel's new ambassador to the United States, took the allotted time. Subsequently, the edited tape and fifteen reels of unedited film disappeared from the studio library.

Ennes's book may have cost the former captain of the ill-fated *Pueblo* an appearance on ABC's *Good Morning America* television show in 1980.[46] Bucher was invited to New York for a post-captivity interview. Suddenly the invitation was withdrawn. A studio official told Bucher only that he had heard there were problems "upstairs," but then he asked Bucher, "Did you have a book review published recently in the *Washington Post*?" He had indeed. The review had heaped praise on Ennes's book.

Later in 1983, the Jewish War Veterans organization protested when the Veterans of Foreign Wars (VFW) quoted Ennes to support its call for "proper honors" for those killed on the *Liberty*, and again when James R. Currieo, national commander of the Veterans of Foreign Wars, referred to the "murderous Israeli attack."[47] Currieo excited Jewish wrath even more when he published in the VFW magazine a letter to President Reagan inviting the White House to send a representative to the cemetery to help honor the men who died. There was no reply.

Twenty-two years after publication of *Assault on the* Liberty, Ennes is still receiving a steady flow of correspondence about the episode, particularly through the book's official Web site at www.ussliberty.org. Elected by his shipmates as their official historian, he became editor of *The USS* Liberty *Newsletter.* Another retired officer, Admiral Thomas L. Moorer, applauds Ennes's activities and still wants an investigation.[48] He scoffs at the mistaken identity theory, and says he hopes Congress will investigate. If it does not, he favors reopening the navy's Court of Inquiry. He adds, "I would like to see it done, but I doubt seriously that it will be allowed."

Asked why the Johnson administration ordered the cover-up, Moorer is blunt: "The clampdown was not actually for security reasons but for domestic political reasons. I don't think there is any question about it. What other reasons could there have been? President Johnson was worried about the reaction of Jewish voters." Moorer maintains that the attack was "absolutely deliberate" and adds, "The American people would be goddamn mad if they knew what goes on." Indeed: Ennes learned from a U.S. Air Force intelligence analyst that "the Israelis not only knew we [on the *Liberty*] were American but were deeply frustrated and angry when the *Liberty* did not sink quickly as intended."[49]

Beyond *Assault*

Thirty-five years after the assault, Ennes has written a new edition of his book and finds glimmers of hope:

> Every attempt to hide this story seems to bring more attention. This past year brought a sixty-minute documentary, produced by CBS News Productions, that was broadcast by The History Channel—much to the dismay and over the heated objections of the Israeli Embassy and various spokesmen for Israel, who did all in their power to block it. CAMERA,

a leading pro-Israel propaganda arm, produced an extended and angry critique of the film, accusing survivors and CBS of producing a "propaganda-laden bogus history" that is deliberately distorted and anti-Semitic. The History Channel's report was aired as scheduled and rebroadcast later. Although CAMERA urged The History Channel not to sell a video version, it was made available anyway. In June 2002 London's BBC released a new documentary called *Dead in the Water*. It reveals secret collaboration between Washington and Tel Aviv during the Six-Day War. A new book, called *Operation Cyanide*, argues that carefully laid plans were made to sink the *Liberty*, and that the United States was as much to blame as Israel for what happened.[50]

A number of other authors have also released in-depth analyses of the crisis and subsequent cover-up. In his Ph.D. dissertation *The USS* Liberty*: Dissenting History vs. Official History*, John E. Borne painstakingly compares two versions of the *Liberty* attack—those of official U.S. history and the testimony of the *Liberty* crew—and refutes, point by point, the erroneous claims of the former, noting also the often contradictory explanations offered by various Israeli sources. Most striking to Borne is the extent to which the American government involved itself in a cover-up of the truth:

> Above all, the [Johnson] administration had the power to silence the crewmen and even to order them to make statements agreeing with the official version of the event. The crewmen hoped to somehow attract attention to their claims, but their hope was in vain. All factors seemed to combine to silence the crewmen, to make their story, even if heard, seem unbelievable, and to favor the administration view of the matter.[51]

Donald Neff's *Warriors for Jerusalem* uses government records released through the Freedom of Information Act to add historical detail to the *Liberty* tragedy. Of the painful revelations Neff makes, especially tragic is the fact that *Liberty* captain McGonagle, upon hearing of the outbreak of hostilities and well before approaching Israel, requested protection from the U.S. Sixth Fleet commander, Vice Admiral William I. Martin. The request was denied, according to Admiral Martin, because the *Liberty* was "a clearly marked United States ship in international waters, not a participant in the conflict and not a reasonable subject for attack by any nation."[52] Neff also mentions the fact that, when U.S. officials were having second thoughts and decided to order the *Liberty* away from the area of fighting, two messages conveying that order were not delivered.

James Bamford's *Body of Secrets* also mentions the failed correspondences, noting that U.S. government inquiries immediately following the episode "dealt principally with such topics as the failure of the naval communications system and how the crew of the ship performed during the crisis. No American investigators ever looked into the 'why' question or brought the probe to Israel, the scene of the crime." The details uncovered by Bamford, including President Johnson's cover-up in order to preserve Jewish votes, were simply lying in a box in the back of the National Security Agency Museum—no one had bothered to check for them before.[53]

Response to Bamford's book has been varied. Ambassadors and Middle East experts have spoken with knowledge of the event, one noting that the evidence Bamford and others have provided is "strong evidence that this was a deliberate attack." Supporters of Israel are less forthcoming about the actual event: Thomas Neumann, executive director of the Jewish Institute for National Security Affairs (JINSA), claimed that— "though I have not personally read the book"—Bamford's allegations were nonetheless clearly anti-Semitic.[54]

He Wanted to Avoid "Hurt Feelings"

I occasionally return to Capitol Hill, where I am always on the lookout for a member of Congress who might be brave enough to seek hearings, at long last, on the Israeli assault on the USS *Liberty*. The surviving crew members richly deserve the official, public recognition the hearings would bring. Mrs. Findley and I, both navy veterans, have attended several of their annual reunions, each a bittersweet experience with neglected military heroes. A hearing should be conducted while survivors of the tragedy are still alive to provide details. The cover-up is an indignity that keeps from the history books a record of rare heroism.

One day in early 1990 I stopped to see Charles Bennett of Florida, who was just starting his twenty-first and final two-year term in the House of Representatives. Over the years he had become a congenial symbol of rectitude, dignity, and diligence, and was much respected by his colleagues. Never fully recovered from a leg injury during army service in World War II, he was a familiar sight, scurrying, with the aid of a cane, to take part in every vote and quorum call. He declined to take part in congressional study missions, better known as junkets, because he considered them a waste of taxpayer money.

I believed it a perfect moment to seek Bennett's leadership for hearings on the *Liberty*. He was in his final term in Congress, meaning that Israel's lobby could do him no harm in the next election; he served as chairman of the seapower subcommittee of the House Committee on Armed Services; and he knew he would never achieve his long-standing ambition to be chairman of the full committee, as his Democratic colleagues in the House had recently discarded the seniority system for choosing committee leadership by elevating Les Aspin to the chairmanship. This decision passed over several more senior colleagues, including Bennett.

I reasoned that Bennett would welcome the responsibility of chairing hearings that would fully disclose, on public record, what actually happened to the *Liberty* and its crew. I was wrong. He welcomed me to his office with warmth, but when I stated my mission, he displayed the first anger I had ever observed in this usually quiet, reserved colleague. He stood and said: "I won't do it. All the hearings would do is hurt the feelings of some of my good Jewish friends in my district." He spoke with such vehemence that I knew the interview was over. I excused myself, astounded that this highly patriotic colleague with a long record of loyalty to the armed services would fiercely reject hearings for navy heroes out of concern for the embarrassment the truth might cause a few of his constituents. Their feelings, it seems, rated higher than the pain that the *Liberty* survivors have suffered for thirty-five years.

A Call for Justice

Despite the awesome power of Israel's U.S. lobby, *Liberty* survivors have a voice in the House of Representatives, thanks to Democrat Cynthia McKinney, Georgia's first African American congresswoman. Long a supporter of civil and human rights, she was the only member of Congress to attend a massive rally held April 20, 2002, on Washington's National Mall to express solidarity with the Palestinian people. Two months later, she introduced the following speech into the Congressional Record, a fitting testimonial to the determination of the *Liberty* crew:

> Mr. Speaker, I speak to commemorate and recognize the tragic attack that took place against the USS *Liberty* on June 8, 1967. Although thirty-five years have come and gone since this historic event, the survivors of the USS *Liberty* are still struggling with the fact that their story has never been heard. While there has never been an official investigation into this event, we have

learned from survivor accounts that for over seventy-five minutes the Israeli defense forces attacked the USS *Liberty*, killing 34 American soldiers and wounding an additional 171. With over 85 percent of the crew either dead or wounded, they somehow managed to keep the ship afloat after being hit by over a thousand rounds of rocket, cannon, machine gun, napalm hits, and even a direct hit from a torpedo. This unprovoked attack took place in international waters, and by a trusted ally. The only explanation given to the survivors and their families as to why this attack took place was that it was an accident and that their ship was not identified as being American, regardless of the fact that our flag was proudly flown throughout the attack. Unfortunately, that explanation is not good enough for those whose lives have been impacted by this attack, and it should not be good enough for the American people. Let's not wait another thirty-five years before we provide the survivors an official investigation into why this attack took place and allow them to tell their story. We owe them more than a debt of gratitude for their sacrifice; we owe them the truth.

The navy's official Court of Inquiry was a sham. Both the admiral who headed the inquiry and his legal counsel knew it was phony. In retirement, U.S. Navy Captain Ward Boston, who served as court counsel, admitted that they privately disputed the court's official conclusion that the assault was a case of mistaken identity. Boston told a reporter for the *Navy Times* that both he and Rear Admiral Isaac Kidd, who served as president of the court, privately agreed that the Israeli forces knew they were attacking a U.S. Navy ship. In explaining why he participated in the sham, Boston said, "In military life, you accept the fact that if you're told to shut up, you shut up. We did what we were told." Former CIA director Richard Helms said, "It was no accident."[55]

It is a pity that Senator John McCain, a prisoner-of-war survivor and an authentic hero of the U.S. Navy during the Vietnam War, was duped into publicly endorsing the phony findings of the Court of Inquiry. After reading *The* Liberty *Incident*, the latest attempt to cover up Israel's perfidy, written by a former navy pilot who is a federal judge, McCain wrote: "After years of research for this book, Judge A. Jay Cristol has reached a similar conclusion to one my father [then chief of Naval Operations] reached in his June 18, 1967, endorsement of the findings of the Court of Inquiry. I commend Judge Cristol for his thoroughness and fairness, and I commend this work."[56]

The episode leaves one wondering if someone ordered the federal judge to write the book-length whitewash of the Court of Inquiry whitewash.

Subverting Academic Freedom

THE ISRAELI LOBBY pays special attention to the crucial role played by American colleges and universities in disseminating information and molding opinion on the Middle East. Lobby organizations are concerned not only with academic programs dealing with the Middle East, but also with the editorial policies of student newspapers and with the appearance on campus of speakers who are critical of Israel. In all three of these areas of legitimate lobby interest and activity, as in its dealings on Capitol Hill, pro-Israeli organizations and activists frequently employ smear tactics, harassment, and intimidation to inhibit the free exchange of ideas and views.

As government, academic, and public awareness of the Middle East increased following the 1973 OPEC oil price hike, organizations such as the American Israel Public Affairs Committee and the American Jewish Committee developed specific programs and policies for countering criticism of Israel on college campuses.

Making It "Hot Enough" on Campus

In 1979 AIPAC established its Political Leadership Development Program (PLDP), which trains student activists on how to increase pro-Israeli influence on campus. In 1984, coordinator Jonathan Kessler recently reported that "AIPAC's program has affiliated over 5,000 students on 350 campuses in all 50 states":

> They are systematically monitoring and comprehensively responding to anti-Israeli groups on campus. They are involved in pro-Israel legislative efforts, [and] in electoral campaign politics as well.[1]

Kessler's assessment seems generous, as the official PLDP Web site, in 2002, cites the number of PLDP campuses at only 200—just over half the supposed 1984 total.[2] However self-serving and perhaps exaggerated such statements may be, AIPAC works closely with the B'nai B'rith Hillel Foundation on many campuses. When Kessler was introduced to campus audiences, it was as one who has "trained literally thousands of students." His campus contacts sent him tapes or notes from talks that were considered to be "pro-Palestinian" or "anti-Israeli" and alerted him to upcoming speaking engagements. Kessler kept the notes on file and when he learned that a particular speaker was coming to a campus, he sent summaries of the speaker's usual points and arguments, his question-and-answer style, and potentially damaging quotes—or purported quotes—from other talks. Kessler specialized in concocting questions with which the speaker would have difficulty and in warning the campus organizers away from questions the speaker could answer well.

If the student union or academic senate controlled which groups were allowed to reserve halls, Kessler worked to get supporters of Israel into those bodies. If the control was with the administration, undesirable speakers who were booked were accused of advocating violence, either by "quoting" earlier speeches or by characterizing them as pro-PLO. AIPAC students also argued that certain forums such as memorial lectures should not be "politicized." While this may not have always eliminated certain speakers, Kessler advised that "if you make it hot enough" for the administrators, future "anti-Israel" events would be discouraged and even turned down rather than scheduled.

Kessler's students received training—including role-playing and "propaganda response exercises"—in how to counter anti-Israel arguments. These exercises simulated confrontations at pro- and anti-Israel information tables and public forums. Once a solid AIPAC contingent was formed, it took part in student conferences and tried to forge coalitions with other student groups. AIPAC then had pro-Israel resolutions passed in these bodies. It also placed pro-Israel advertisements, which included signatures of members of, for example, the (liberal) Americans for Democratic Action and the (conservative) Young Americans for Freedom rather than just by AIPAC. The PLDP workshop handout said: "Use coalitions effectively. Try finding non-Jewish individuals and groups to sign letters to the editor, for it is far more effective and credible."

In 1983 AIPAC distributed to students and faculty around the country a ten-page questionnaire on political activism on their campuses. Its instructions included: "Please name any individual faculty who assist anti-Israel groups. How is this assistance offered? What are the propaganda themes?" The survey results formed the body of the *AIPAC College Guide: Exposing the Anti-Israel Campaign on Campus,* published in April 1984. While AIPAC claimed to respect the right of all to free speech, number eight on its list of ten suggested "modes of response" to pro-Palestinian events or speakers on campus reads: "Attempt to prevent."

Number ten on the same list is "creative packaging." Edward Said, a professor of comparative literature at Columbia University who frequently speaks on campuses in support of the Palestinian cause, described a case of "creative packaging" at the University of Washington, where he spoke in early 1983:

> They stood at the door of the auditorium and distributed a blue leaflet that seemed like a program, but it was in fact a denunciation of me as a "terrorist." There were quotations from the PLO, and things that I had said were mixed in with things they claimed the PLO had said about murdering Jews. The idea was to intimidate me and to intimidate the audience from attending.[3]

Said reported another experience at the University of Florida, where the group protesting Said's talk was led by a professor of philosophy:

They tried to disrupt the meeting and [the professor] finally had to be taken out by the police. It was one of the ugliest things—not just heckling, but interrupting and standing up and shouting. It's pure fascism, outright hooliganism.

Another episode involving Said occurred at Trinity College in Hartford, Connecticut. In the fall of 1982 Said spoke at the invitation of the college's Department of Religion on the subject of Palestine and its significance to Christians and Muslims as well as Jews. As the day of the talk approached, the department began to get letters of protest from prominent members of the Hartford Jewish community and from Jewish faculty members. Said, said the protesters, was pro-Palestinian and had made "anti-Israel" statements. One writer asked the organizers of the talk: "How could you do this, given the fact that there are two Holocaust survivors on the faculty?" After Said spoke, more letters of protest arrived at the religion department. The uproar died down after several months, but the protests had their effect. Asked whether the department would feel free, given the reaction of the Jewish community, to invite Edward Said again, a department spokesperson responded, "No, I don't think we would."

The *AIPAC College Guide* also includes profiles of 100 U.S. campuses and the anti-Israel campaign "unprecedented in scope and magnitude" that supposedly pervaded them. Anti-Semitism was cited as a major influence on some campuses. For example, Colorado State University's campus newspaper, the *Collegian,* was said to have printed anti-Semitic letters to the editor; but only a letter which "sought to draw attention to the 'Jewish lobby and the true extent of its influence over the U.S. media'" was cited as evidence.

An example of how the lobby works on campus came in the spring of 1982, when the American Indian Law Students Association (AILSA) at Harvard Law School hosted a conference on the rights of indigenous peoples in domestic and international law. They invited Deena Abu-Lughod, an American of Palestinian origin who worked as a researcher at the PLO mission to the United Nations, to participate in the conference. The Harvard Jewish Law Students Association (HJLSA), which according to one source had an active membership of only about twenty, asked AILSA to remove Abu-Lughod from the program.[4] When this failed, the Jewish group vehemently protested to the dean of the law school, and it asked the dean of students to consider withdrawing all funding for the conference.[5] The latter refused, saying she was "not in the business of censoring student conferences." But the dean of the law school, who was slated to give the opening address at the conference, backed out. Several members of the AILSA and the director of the Harvard Foundation, which cosponsored the conference, received telephoned death threats.[6] One came from callers who identified themselves as Jewish Harvard students. Told of these calls, a member of the HJLSA said, "We were contacted by the JDL [Jewish Defense League], but we didn't want to have anything to do with any disruption of the conference."

The conference took place as scheduled, but, as one organizer recalls:

> The atmosphere was incredibly tense. We were really very concerned about Deena's physical safety and about our own physical safety. We had seven policemen there. We had many, many marshals and very elaborate security. We had searches at the door, and we confiscated weapons, knives—not pocket knives, but butcher knives. We also had dogs sniff the room for explosives. The point is that the event did occur, but in a very threatening atmosphere.

The following spring, a group of Third World student organizations at Harvard invited Hassan Abdul-Rahman, the director of the PLO Information Office in Washington, to speak on the theme "Palestine: Road to Peace in the Middle East." Again the Harvard Jewish Law Students Association organized a demonstration, but this time the protesters packed the hall and actively disrupted the meeting. "It was just an absolute madhouse inside," recalls one student who was present. "Abdul-Rahman spoke for probably an hour and a half to virtually constant taunting, jeering, insults, screams, shouts, cursing." According to the *Harvard Law Record*, a representative of the Harvard Arab Students Society "struggled" simply to relate a biographical sketch of the speaker and provide an introduction to his talk.[7] "It was an extremely intimidating atmosphere," recalls the student:

> We just barely kept the lid on things. I think the fact that these events occurred is a testimony to our perseverance, not to the lack of intimidation. Because the intimidation is really very overt and very strong.

In both cases, the protesters used material provided by the Anti-Defamation League of B'nai B'rith.

AIPAC is not the only pro-Israel organization to keep files on speakers. The Anti-Defamation League of B'nai B'rith (ADL) keeps its own files. Noam Chomsky, world renowned professor of linguistics at MIT and author of two books on the Middle East, was leaked a copy of his ADL file, which contained about a hundred pages of material.[8] Says Chomsky: "Virtually every talk I give is monitored and reports of their alleged contents (sometimes ludicrously, even comically distorted) are sent on to the [Anti-Defamation] League, to be incorporated in my file." Says Chomsky:

> When I give a talk at a university or elsewhere, it is common for a group to distribute literature, invariably unsigned, containing a collection of attacks on me spiced with "quotes" (generally fabricated) from what I am alleged to have said here and there. I have no doubt that the source is the ADL, and often the people distributing the unsigned literature acknowledge the fact. These practices are vicious and serve to intimidate many people. They are, of course, not illegal. If the ADL chooses to behave in this fashion, it has a right to do so, but this should also be exposed.

Student publications are also monitored. When the monthly *Berkeley Graduate*, a magazine of news and opinion intended for graduate students at the University of California at Berkeley, published in its April 1982 issue several articles that were critical of Israeli Prime Minister Menachem Begin and his government's policies, the office of the magazine began to receive anonymous phone calls, generally expressing in crude terms the caller's opinion of the magazine.[9] One caller suggested that the editor, James Schamus, "take the next train to Auschwitz." According to Schamus, these calls continued for several weeks.

The campus Jewish Student Board circulated a petition protesting the content of the April issue and characterized the *Graduate* as anti-Semitic—until it discovered that editor James Schamus was himself Jewish.[10] Schamus met with Jewish Student Board members and agreed to furnish space in the following issue of the magazine for a 4,000-word rebuttal, but they were not satisfied.

The following week, members of the Jewish Student Board introduced a bill in the Graduate Assembly expressing "regret" at the content of the April issue and stipulating that if an oversight committee was not formed "to review each issue's content before it goes to press," steps would be taken to eliminate the *Graduate*.[11] The assembly voted down the resolution, but agreed to revive a moribund editorial oversight committee to set editorial policy. Opponents of the bill, including editors of several campus publications, defended the right of the *Graduate* to print "without prior censorship."

The next day, the Student Senate narrowly defeated a bill that would have expressed "dissatisfaction" with the *Graduate* magazine.[12] An earlier draft of the bill, amended by the Senate, would have asked the Senate to "condemn" the publication. An editorial in *The Daily Californian*, the university's main student newspaper, said that such "meaningless censures" came not out of intelligent consideration of an issue, but out of "irrational urgings to punish the progenitor of an idea with which one disagrees."

The May issue of the *Graduate* did contain a response to Schamus's original article. The author concluded his piece by calling the April issue of the *Graduate* "simple, unvarnished anti-Semitism in both meaning and intent." Later in May, Schamus left for a two-month vacation. While he was gone, the Graduate Assembly leadership decided by administrative fiat to cut the amount of student funds allocated to the *Graduate* by 55 percent and to change the accounting rules in such a way that the magazine could no longer survive.[13] Schamus resigned, as did his editorial and advertising staffs. In an interview with the *San Francisco Examiner*, Schamus said that the series on Begin "directly precipitated our silencing."[14] He told *The Daily Californian*, "This whole situation was a plan by student government censors to get rid of the magazine and create a new one in its own image next year."[15] The chairman of the Graduate Assembly denied any conspiracy. "The Israel issue had absolutely nothing to do with it," he said. He acknowledged, however, that the controversy over the issue "brought up the question of content in the *Graduate*." For a few years the *Graduate* reverted to little more than a calendar of events. It no longer exists today.

Student Editor Under Fire

Another student newspaper editor who learned to think twice before criticizing Israel is John D'Anna, editor of the *Arizona Daily Wildcat* at the University of Arizona in Tucson during the 1982–83 academic year.

In February of 1983, twenty-two-year-old D'Anna wrote an editorial entitled "Butcher of Beirut Is Also a War Criminal," in which he decried the fact that former Israeli Defense Minister Ariel Sharon was permitted to remain a member of the Israeli cabinet after he had been found "indirectly responsible" for the massacre of Palestinian civilians at the Sabra and Shatila camps in Lebanon. If Nazi war criminal Klaus Barbie, the infamous "butcher of Lyon" was to be tried for his crimes against humanity, asked D'Anna, "shouldn't those responsible for the Beirut massacre be tried for theirs?"

D'Anna was shocked by the reaction to his editorial:

> My grandparents were the only John D'Annas listed in the phone book, and they were harassed with late night phone calls. I personally got a couple of the type "If we ever catch you alone. . . ." There were threats on my life. I also got hate mail. Some of the letters were so vitriolic it makes me shudder.[16]

There followed a series of letters to the newspaper accusing D'Anna of "irresponsible polemic," "fanning hatred," and "inciting violence." The director of the local B'nai B'rith Hillel Foundation wrote that D'Anna's editorial "merely inflames passions, draws conclusions on half-truths, and misleads."

The uproar prompted D'Anna to write an apology in a subsequent issue. He said that while he stood by his beliefs, "I just wish I had expressed those beliefs differently."[17] He agreed with some of his critics that it was a bad editorial and that he could have made the same points "without arousing passions and without polemic."

Nevertheless, the day after D'Anna's apology appeared, members of twenty local Jewish groups wrote to the university president demanding that the *Wildcat* editor resign or be fired for his "anti-Semitic" and "anti-Israel" editorial.[18] If he was not fired by noon the following Monday, said the letter, the group would tell *Wildcat* advertisers that the newspaper was "spreading hatred," in the hope that the advertisers would cancel their ads. The group's spokesman was Edward Tennen, head of the local Jewish Defense League, a group founded by Rabbi Meir Kahane, who advocated the forcible expulsion of Arabs from Israel. Because of its extremist reputation, the JDL is shunned by AIPAC and other Jewish groups.

When the deadline passed without D'Anna's removal, the group call-ing for a boycott, having dubbed itself "United Zionist Institutions," distributed a letter to local businesses and ad agencies urging them to stop supporting the *Wildcat's* "anti-Semitic editor" and his "consciously orchestrated bigotry."[19] Calling D'Anna "an accomplice to PLO aims," the letter asked the advertisers to "search your consciences and do what you know must be done." D'Anna noted that the group's acronym was UZI, the name of the standard-issue Israeli machine gun. Meanwhile, about twenty-five members of local Jewish groups, mostly from the cam-pus Hillel organization, attended a meeting of the university's Board of Publications, during which they confronted D'Anna with their com-plaints. As the former editor recalls it:

> I was on the hot seat for about two hours. And I tried to deal with all their questions and they kept demanding that steps be taken. I asked them what steps, and they said they wanted a review board. And I said "That's fine, you can review anything you want after it comes out in the paper," and they said "No, we want to review it before it comes out in the paper," and I said that was totally unacceptable.

In the end, the boycott effort was ineffective, as only two businesses canceled their advertising. Moreover, D'Anna received firm support from the newspaper staff and from the head of the university's journal-ism department, who was Jewish. Yet the former editor recalled that the campaign against him had an impact: "It was effective to a certain extent. I was gun-shy, and it was quite a while before I touched any interna-tional issue."

"It Seemed to Be Politics"

The Hartford Seminary in Hartford, Connecticut, has the oldest Islamic studies program in the United States. Beginning in the early 1970s, the president of the seminary began to receive complaints from members of the Hartford Jewish community that the program was anti-Jewish.[20] One person said the program was in fact an "al-Fatah support group." More recently, Willem A. Bijlefeld, director of the seminary's Center for the Study of Islam and Christian–Muslim Relations, was asked by the local daily *Hartford Courant* to write a piece about PLO leader Yasser Arafat.

On New Year's Eve, 1983, the day following publication of his article, Bijelfeld received a phone call from a man who identified himself only as Jewish. The caller said that the seminary had a long tradition of "anti-Jewish propaganda" and accused Bijelfeld of supporting "the killing of Jews and the destruction of Israel." He then expressed his joy at the "extremely painful death" of NBC news anchorwoman Jessica Savitch, killed in an automobile accident, which he said was a "manifestation of divine justice" since she had "lied" about the number of Lebanese forced out of their homes during the 1982 Israeli invasion. The caller said that he was fully confident that this kind of punishment awaited "any enemy of Israel." Said Bijelfeld, "The implications for me were clear."

Ostracism is another weapon of the lobby. Eqbal Ahmad was an American scholar of Pakistani origin who held two Ph.D. degrees from Princeton University, one in political science and one in Islamic studies. He was also a fellow at Washington's Institute for Policy Studies. Ahmad wrote widely on the Middle East and had a number of articles published on the op-ed page of the *New York Times.* He said that, as a critic of Israeli policies and a supporter of the rights of the Palestinians, he was ostracized by the academic community:

> It is not only the material punishments that people encounter, but the extraordinary environment of conformity that is imposed upon you and the price of isolation that individuals have to pay for not conforming on this issue.[21]

Ahmad joined the faculty of Cornell University in 1965. "I was a young assistant professor, generally liked by my colleagues," he recalled. "And they continued to be very warm and civil to me despite the fact that many of them were conservative people and I had already become fairly prominent in the anti–Vietnam War movement."

After the Arab–Israeli war of June 1967, Ahmad made a speech at Cornell criticizing Israel's conquest and retention of Arab territory. He also signed petitions supporting the right of the Palestinians to self-determination. Throughout his two remaining years at Cornell, said Ahmad, no more than four members of the entire faculty spoke to him. "I would often sit at the lunch table in the faculty lounge, which is generally very crowded, and I would have a table for six to myself." Ahmad noted that of the four who remained his friends, three were Jews:

The issue is not one of Jew versus gentile. There is a silent covenant within the academic community concerning Israel. The interesting thing is that the number of prominent Jews who have broken the covenant is much larger than the number of gentiles.

In 1983, Ahmad's name appeared in the B'nai B'rith publication *Pro-Arab Propaganda in America: Vehicles and Voices.* "This they are doing to somebody who has not to date received any form of support from an Arab government or an Arab organization," said Ahmad. He noted that about a quarter of his income came from speaking engagements, mainly university-endowed lectures. Since the publication of the B'nai B'rith "enemies list," his speaking invitations dropped by about 50 percent. "These invitations come from my reputation as an objective, independent scholar," said Ahmad. "By putting me under the rubric of propagandist, they have put into question my position as an objective scholar."

After leaving Cornell in 1969, Ahmad had difficulty obtaining a regular teaching appointment. He spent a few years as a visiting professor at one college or another, and was considered for appointment near the end of his 1982–83 term at Rutgers University in Newark, New Jersey. At the last minute, the appointment fell through. Said Ahmad:

I have been told privately that it was because Zionist professors objected to my appointment. The dean was told that I would not get the vote of the faculty because accusations had been made that I was anti-Semitic and had created an anti-Semitic atmosphere on a campus while I was teaching there. All this was told to me in private; I have nothing in writing.

S. C. Whittaker, former chairman of the Political Science Department at Rutgers University and the man who originally hired Ahmad as a visiting professor, was away when the question of a full professorship for Ahmad came up.[22] "When I got back," said Whittaker, "I was told that he'd been a great smash as a teacher and that his enrollments were terrific. But when the proposal to have him stay on permanently came up, it was shot down, and it seemed to be politics." Politics were not enough to keep the scholar out of academia for long: in 1982 Ahmad became a full professor at Hampshire College in Massachusetts. Ahmad taught there until 1997, when he took on the role of professor emeritus and began an intensive worldwide travel and lecture tour. He died on May 10, 1999, in Islamabad, Pakistan, following surgery.

Ahmad's good friend and noted professor Edward Said wrote a eulogy, in which he said of Ahmad:

> He was an epic and poetic one, full of wanderings, border crossings, and an almost instinctive attraction to liberation movements, movements of the oppressed and the persecuted, causes of people who were unfairly punished. He was that rare thing, an intellectual unintimidated by power or authority, a sophisticated man who remained simply true to his ideals and his insight till his last breath.

Arab Funding Too Hot to Handle

In 1977, three of America's most prestigious small colleges—Swarthmore, Haverford, and Bryn Mawr—proposed to seek funds from a private Arab foundation for a joint Middle East studies program. The three "sister schools," located in the affluent "mainline" suburbs of Philadelphia, already shared a Russian studies program.

The idea for the joint program originated in conversations between college officials and Swarthmore alumnus Willis Armstrong, a former assistant secretary of state who had recently become secretary-treasurer of the Triad Foundation. The Washington-based foundation had been established by wealthy Saudi entrepreneur Adnan Khashoggi in order to finance, in his words, "programs with long-range goals for building bridges of understanding between countries."[23] Khashoggi was a flamboyant multimillionaire who made his fortune by serving as a middleman to foreign companies, including several major defense contractors, seeking business in Saudi Arabia.

The three-year, $590,000 program worked out by Armstrong and the colleges was exemplary by everyone's account. The plan would provide foreign student scholarships to needy Arab students, expand the colleges' collections of books and periodicals dealing with the Middle East, and strengthen existing Middle East–related courses. In addition, about one-fourth of the grant would be used to finance a rotating professorship. The visiting professors would teach courses on the Middle East and its relation to disciplines including anthropology, art history, economics, history, political science, and religion.

"It was as innocuous and rich as a proposal could be," recalled Swarthmore Vice President Kendall Landis five years later.[24] Haverford President Stephen Cary had described it at the time as "promising in terms of academic enrichment."[25] The program would serve to "raise the consciousness of students about the Middle East situation," commented Haverford's associate director of development, John Gilbert.[26] Perhaps the most enthusiastic supporter of the plan was Bryn Mawr President Harris Wofford. A former Peace Corps director, Wofford was known for his long-standing interest in promoting international understanding. He called the Middle East studies proposal "a good prospect for something we badly want."

The grant proposal included a guarantee of absolute academic freedom. "This was to be done in accordance with the highest academic standards," explained Armstrong.[27] "The colleges would choose the visiting professors, *they'd* buy the books, and *they'd* pick out the students to whom to give scholarships." Moreover, the rotating professorship meant that no one professor would be around long enough to develop roots. "We really bent over backward to be completely fair," said Landis. "Jewish professors would be employed as well as others."

"There was never any pressure from Triad in any discussions we had with them," said Haverford's Cary, "nor any indication from them that it couldn't be a study that would include Israel.[28] So I never had any criticism of the Triad Foundation people at all." The agreement with Triad was all but concluded by the three colleges. All that remained was to formally present the grant proposal to the Triad Foundation, which, Armstrong assured the college officials, would accept it and write out the check.

Some, however, such as Ira Silverman of the American Jewish Committee, saw dangers in the plan. Silverman had received a telephone call from Swarthmore political science professor James Kurth alerting the AJC to the grant proposal. In a confidential memorandum he prepared for the AJC's National Committee on Arab Influence in the United States, Silverman wrote:

> Professor Kurth, who is not Jewish, believed that the proposed program should be of concern to the AJC inasmuch as it would not only expand study of the contemporary Arab world, but would explicitly seek to bring the Arab political message to those campuses.

Professor Kurth brought these facts to our attention and asked for AJC help in blocking the implementation of the program. We discussed the matter and agreed that it would make the most sense to try to kill the program through quiet, behind-the-scenes talks with college officials before "going public," and that protests against the program need not be based solely or particularly on Jewish opposition to Arab influence. Instead, we thought it should be possible to generate concern about the program based on its sponsorship by Khashoggi and its evident public relations aims, [which were] not appropriate for colleges of the stature of these three schools.

Silverman went right to work orchestrating a campaign to discredit Khashoggi and Triad:

I immediately sent Professor Kurth a folder of information on Khashoggi, the Triad Corporation, and Triad Foundation, which was compiled by the AJC Trends Analysis division. I also notified the AJC Philadelphia chapter of these developments so that they could be in touch with Professor Kurth to assist in getting some local Philadelphia Jewish community leaders, alumni of the schools or otherwise, associated with them, to raise questions about the proposed grant."

The effect of the AJC's efforts to "kill the program" was stunning. Using material provided by Silverman, the Swarthmore student newspaper, the *Phoenix*, published an article that falsely stated that Khashoggi was "under indictment by a federal grand jury" in connection with certain payments to Lockheed.[29] Asked later about the role this article played in the controversy, James Platt, who had edited the student newspaper, said: "The *Phoenix* got things out there publicly, at least for students and certain alums who probably hadn't heard about it beforehand, to make their phone calls and be upset and so forth."[30] Where had he gotten his information? He refused to say. "I'd prefer to talk to the people first just to make sure they have no problem with that. At the time, it was to remain confidential."

Before the *Phoenix* article appeared, Swarthmore President Theodore Friend called a meeting of department representatives to obtain the concurrence of faculty on the tentative grant proposal. Some of the faculty were reported to have objected to the plan. On the evening after the *Phoenix* article appeared, a petition was circulated in the college dining hall calling Khashoggi a "munitions monger" and referring to "kickbacks" in the Middle East. The petition, which called on the administration to drop the proposal, was signed by 230 students and faculty. Almost at the same time, the Philadelphia Jewish Federation had a letter on the president's desk. "Speaking from memory," says one observer close to the Swarthmore scene, "it all happened in about eighteen and a half minutes. It was like the Great Fear sweeping across France during the French Revolution."

On November 3, 1977, articles appeared in the *Philadelphia Inquirer* and in another Philadelphia paper, the *Evening Bulletin*. The latter was headlined: "Colleges Hesitate in Scandal." By November 4, the student newspaper published jointly by Bryn Mawr and Haverford had also published an article detailing both the grant proposal and Khashoggi's background. The same issue included an editorial entitled "Say No to Triad." The Jewish Community Relations Council, the American Jewish Committee and the Anti-Defamation League of B'nai B'rith issued a joint statement: "It is altogether appropriate that the schools should seriously question the wisdom of accepting any grant from such a tainted source and one which is dominated by a figure like Adnan Khashoggi."[31]

Finally, the Washington office of the AJC put Professor Kurth in touch with Congressman James Scheuer, who was Jewish and a Swarthmore alumnus.[32] According to Armstrong, Scheuer called President Friend and requested the telephone numbers of the members of the college's board of managers "so he could call them at once and get them to put a stop to this outrageous thing." Various groups tried to enlist faculty intervention. Harrison Wright, a professor of history at Swarthmore, recalled later that there were "memos to the whole faculty and to the department chairmen by different groups.[33] It was a fairly short but quite sharp exchange of different points of view."

The first of the three colleges to publicly withdraw from the joint effort was Haverford. In a prepared statement, President Cary said the college was "grateful to Triad for its willingness to consider an application," but "because of Haverford's Quaker background, it has decided it shouldn't apply for funds derived so directly from arms traffic, which it deplores."

Swarthmore's withdrawal followed immediately. President Friend announced the college's decision in these words: "At a time of rigorous financial planning and examination of curriculum, our lack of a significant existing base in Middle Eastern studies at Swarthmore does not in our view warrant what at present could only be a temporary experiment."

Peter Cohan, a leader of student protest against the Triad grant, complained later to a *Phoenix* reporter that the statement "did not establish principles, but spoke only to the immediate situation."[34] In the same *Phoenix* article, Swarthmore Vice President Landis pointed out that the decision on the Triad grant was made "amid a whirlwind of protest that arose from 'more than just Khashoggi.'" According to Landis, "There were other concerns within the protest."

In a letter to *The Phoenix*, Ben Rockefeller, another student, agreed with Landis:

> Jewish students are not disturbed about the Rockefellers' business conduct because they aren't truly contesting anybody's business conduct: the alleged concern about Mr. Khashoggi's professional character is a ruse to conceal an anti-Arab prejudice.[35]

Only Bryn Mawr continued to pursue the grant. "I think the question of judging the source of money is not a simplistic one," said President Wofford.[36] He defended the college's decision in an article published in the Bryn Mawr–Haverford student newspaper, *The News*, which was on record as opposing the grant: "No one at Bryn Mawr has suggested that Mr. Khashoggi's record is irrelevant or that we don't care about it. We explored that record in the three-college discussions last summer and circulated information we found. If there is new information we should consider it carefully. But instead of simply saying 'No' to Triad, as *The News* proposes, I think we should examine all the facts and together think about the issues raised. In deciding our next steps, we need to guard against prejudice, against misinformation, and against the politics of purely personal psychic satisfaction. Wouldn't it be prejudice to accept a donation from Lockheed, for example, which was found guilty of improper practices, while refusing it from Triad, whose donor (contrary to the Swarthmore *Phoenix*'s allegation) has not been indicted, let alone convicted, of anything?"

The *Philadelphia Inquirer* supported Bryn Mawr's position. In an editorial titled ". . . But Money Has No Smell," the newspaper said it did not believe it necessary that Haverford, Swarthmore, and Bryn Mawr "look with revulsion" at the source of the $590,000 grant.[37] "We believe they would do well to follow the counsel of the celebrated American philosopher Woody Allen, and take the money and run." Like Wofford, the newspaper pointed out that "quite a few sources of donations to higher education would not bear close scrutiny."

The American Jewish Committee memo noted with satisfaction that, although Bryn Mawr pursued the grant proposal, it did so "on a substantially reduced scale." In fact, Bryn Mawr's request for funds ultimately went unanswered. Khashoggi had been badly burned. He gave up the foundation and with it the offer to the three colleges. Reflecting on the controversy and on Bryn Mawr's decision to stay with the proposal, Wofford said: "We were in a relatively strong position because that same year we had started a program of inviting people who wanted to contribute to Bryn Mawr's Judaic Studies program to donate Israel bonds." The Jewish community was pleased by this. "In fact," said Wofford, "I was awarded the Eleanor Roosevelt Award of the Israeli Bonds Organization."

Asked how he felt about the withdrawal of the other colleges, Wofford said, "We felt sort of run out on by both of them. In the first place, they publicly withdrew without any real consultation. And secondly, it was something we had thought through and it seemed an unfair flap at a potential donor."

In a letter to President Friend, Willis Armstrong said: "Swarthmore seems to me to have taken leave of its principles and to have yielded all too quickly to partisan and xenophobic pressure from a group skilled in the manipulation of public opinion.[38] I am at a loss to think how the United States can promote peace in the Middle East unless we can gain Arab confidence in our understanding and objectivity. For a Quaker institution to turn its back on an opportunity to contribute to this understanding is profoundly depressing."

Haverford President Cary, like Swarthmore's President Friend, denied that his decision to withdraw from the grant proposal was influenced by pressures from the Jewish community. Said Cary: "I did have some letters from some of our Jewish alumnae who thought that we should have no part of such a thing. But that had nothing to do with my decision."

Haverford's provost at the time, Tom D'Andrea, assessed the importance of Jewish opposition differently: "One of the big issues, of course, had to do with very strong opposition from Jewish organizations. I think a lot of it had to do with Arab influence and the whole Middle East situation. But then, of course, you get into really serious questions about academic freedom. The freedom of expression. Well, one way you can avoid that is to find another peg to hang the protest on, and the arms one is a little cleaner given the Quaker factor."[39]

In concluding his memo describing the success of the American Jewish Committee's efforts to foil the Middle East studies program at the three colleges, Ira Silverman wrote: "Our participation was not widely known on the campuses and not reported in the public press, as we wished. This is a good case history of how we can be effective in working with colleges to limit Arab influence on campuses, although in view of the schools' Quaker background and Khashoggi's cloudy reputation as an arms merchant, its happy ending is not likely to be replicated easily in other cases."

Swarthmore, Haverford, and Bryn Mawr did nothing in the immediate wake of the 1977–78 events to improve their offerings in a field that became too hot for many colleges to handle. Another college about a hundred miles away showed more courage, although it, too, nearly faltered.

Returning Solicited Gifts

Georgetown University's Center for Contemporary Arab Studies (CCAS) was the first academic program in the United States devoted exclusively to the study of the modern Arab world. Established in 1975, the center is a functional part of the Georgetown University School of Foreign Service. As such, CCAS not only offers an academic program leading to a master's degree in Arab studies, but also provides opportunities for students with other international interests to learn about the 22 political systems and 170 million people in North Africa, the Nile valley, the Fertile Crescent, and the Arabian Peninsula.

Since federal funding for a traditional Middle East center at Georgetown had twice been sought and denied, the directors of the new center decided early on to seek support from private sources. They hoped to obtain about half the needed funds from Arab governments. The dean of Georgetown University's School of Foreign Service, Peter F. Krogh, explained the original plan: "It was our view that we should not play favorites among the Arab states and seek support from some but not from others. This would then suggest that the academic program would also play favorites."[40]

After obtaining approval of the plan from the university's development office and from Georgetown's president at the time, the Reverend R. J. Henle, Dean Krogh visited all the Arab embassies and missions in Washington. He told them about the center's plans and asked for their assistance. "I went to all of them," says Krogh, "whether they had diplomatic relations with the United States or not, whether they were moderate or radical, whatever their stripe." The director of the center's Master of Arts in Arab Studies program, John Ruedy, recalled the fund-raising philosophy in similar terms: "We were going to be sure that we weren't labeled as being in anybody's pocket."[41]

The first country to contribute was Oman, soon followed by grants from United Arab Emirates, Egypt, and Saudi Arabia. Then, in May 1977, Libya committed $750,000, payable over five years, to endow a professorial chair in Arab culture. The Libyan gift aroused controversy. According to one faculty member, there was "considerable consternation" among faculty, students, and some administrators and trustees. The protest included a letter to the student newspaper, the *Georgetown Voice*, from columnist Art Buchwald, who called the gift "blood money from one of the most notorious regimes in the world today."[42] But Georgetown's executive vice president for academic affairs, the Reverend Aloysius P. Kelley, told the *Washington Post* at the time that the Libyan gift "contributes to the fulfillment of the main purpose of the center . . . which is to increase knowledge of the Arab world in the United States."[43] Says Dean Krogh, "Libya was responding to the blanket request to all Arab countries to take an interest in our work and to help us where they could. It was an endowment. They sent the check; we deposited it. They never inquired, never asked for an accounting. They didn't even ask for a stewardship report." Center Director Michael Hudson stressed in press interviews that no conditions were attached to the gift regarding who could occupy the chair or what the chosen professor could teach. "We don't mix politics and education," Hudson told the *Washington Post*.[44]

The next governmental contributors were Jordan, Qatar, and Iraq. The Iraqi gift of $50,000 came in the spring of 1978. It was an unrestricted contribution, which the center subsequently decided to use to hire a specialist in Islamic ethics.

In the meantime, Henle had been replaced as president of George-town by the Reverend Timothy S. Healy. In July 1978 Healy took the unusual step of returning Iraq's $50,000 gift without advising the center of his intentions. The official reason given for the action was that another donor had come forward to provide funds for the same purpose. In his letter to the director general of Iraq's Center for Research and Information, Healy wrote: "I feel obliged in conscience to return to Your Excellency the generous check that you have sent us. I hope that in doing this, we can continue our conversations and that it will be possible for the university to return to the generosity of the Iraqi government in the future and ask for a gift for which full credit can be given to the gov-ernment which gave it. I am sure you will understand the delicacy of the university's position in this matter."[45]

But faculty members at the Center for Contemporary Arab Studies said they did not understand "the delicacy of the university's position." Arab Studies Director John Ruedy commented at the time: "Acting as agents of the university, we solicited money from Iraq. The president of this university returned it without ever seeking our approval. His inter-vention into this is really extraordinary."[46] Dean Krogh told the press, "This is the first time we've given back a grant as long as I've been here," adding that the issue had been "taken out of my hands." According to the *Washington Star*, both supporters and opponents of the Iraqi grant agreed that "the decision was politically motivated."[47] Ruedy told the *Star*, "I don't know what other basis there would be for refusing the money." CCAS fac-ulty members charged that Healy's own support for Israel, combined with pressure from pro-Israeli members of the university's community and from influential Jewish leaders, led him to return the gift.

John Ruedy recalls the incident: "The timing was appalling. We were just shocked. We had been arguing with [Healy] over that for a couple of months. He said he didn't like it. We knew he was distressed about it. But we thought that we had convinced him that he must quietly accept the gift because we had asked for it under the mandate given to us by his predecessor." According to one member of the CCAS faculty, the center's problems really began with the arrival of Healy: "His whole political socialization regarding the Middle East took place within the context of New York City [where Healy grew up]. He told us early on that if he had been here in our formative days, we wouldn't exist. He was a vulnerable instrument for these [Jewish] people and they kept pushing and pushing and pushing. He was under enormous pressure."

Healy refused to comment to the press on his decision to return the gift, saying that to do so "would only harm the institution."[48] The university's executive vice president for academic affairs and provost, Reverend Aloysius P. Kelley, declined to comment directly on whether the university had considered any other use for the general purpose grant.

Despite Healy's return of the Iraqi gift, Georgetown's new Arab studies center came under attack. In June 1979 the *New Republic*, a liberal weekly that has become a staunchly pro-Israeli magazine under owner Martin Peretz, ran an article by Nicholas Lemann on Georgetown's Center for Contemporary Arab Studies insinuating that the center was "nothing but a propagandist for the Arabs." Wrote Lemann, "Unlike the older Middle Eastern studies centers at other universities, the Georgetown center makes no attempt to achieve balance by studying Israel along with the Arab nations or by hiring Israeli scholars." Center Director Michael Hudson and Dean Peter Krogh answered this charge in a reply that was prepared but never published: "Since when was it required, for example, that a center for Chinese studies study the Soviet Union and employ Soviet scholars? . . . The center studies the Arabs, and it employs scholars recruited through normal University departmental and school procedures, which provide for appointments without discrimination of any kind. If this country is not allowed by particular interest groups to pursue the study of the Arabs by the same standards applied to the study of other major peoples and cultures, this country's knowledge of, and international relations with, a significant group of countries is going to be deeply, perhaps tragically, flawed."

The *New Republic* article added that the Georgetown center "is constantly charged with violating standards of scholarly objectivity," but it did not say by whom. Author Lemann referred to the center's critics, "who, in the cloak and dagger spirit, like to remain anonymous."

Hudson and Krogh, in their unpublished reply, wrote:

Detective Lemann, to his credit, discovers "an informal network of people," operating in the "cloak and dagger spirit," who are busy trying to embarrass the center in some way. To his discredit, he associates himself with this undercover group by borrowing upon these anonymous accusations in criticizing an open, legitimately constituted academic program. A more worthy

approach would have been to investigate and reveal the composition, operations, and motivations of this "informal network." We think the public
should be deeply concerned about an underground group that seeks to
undermine the imparting of knowledge and understanding about the Arab
world; certainly we would be interested in any findings Mr. Lemann (or his
publisher, Mr. Martin Peretz) could provide on this question.

Despite the return of the Iraqi grant, Georgetown continued to
receive Arab funds, including grants of $1 million each from Kuwait
and Oman in the fall of 1980. An article in the *Washington Post* reporting the Kuwaiti gift quoted Ira Silverman of the American Jewish Committee as saying that Georgetown's Arab studies center "has a clearly
marked pro-Arab, anti-Israel bias in its selection of curriculum material,
its faculty appointments, and speakers."[49] By accepting money from
"political sponsors of one point of view," said Silverman, Georgetown
might be "selling something very precious to Americans—the integrity
of its universities."

Georgetown officials rejected criticism of the Arab gifts, pointing
out that if it had pro-Arab scholars in the Arab studies center, it had pro-
Israel scholars elsewhere on its faculty, particularly in its Center for
Strategic and International Studies.

Then, in February 1981, President Healy returned another Arab
donation that had been solicited and received by the Arab studies center. This time it was the grant from Libya received four years earlier. Of
the $750,000 pledged over five years, $600,000 had been received.
Healy personally took a check for that amount, plus about $42,000 in
interest earned, to the Libyan embassy. Healy said that Libya's "accent on
violence as a normal method of international policy and its growing support of terrorism made [keeping the money] . . . incompatible with
everything Georgetown stands for."[50]

Once again, many doubted the official reason given. As one professor in the Arab studies program put it: "If it was strictly an ethical judgment, it certainly was a long time in coming." John Ruedy added: "If you
ask around here, you'll probably find nobody in our center who approves
of the policies of [Iraqi President] Saddam Hussein. But we have tried
to maintain cooperative relationships with the government and, to the
extent that we can, with the Iraqi people. We think that this is our mission. And I feel the same way about Libya. I find [Libyan President]

Gadhafi very objectionable in most instances. This was a gift, as far as I'm concerned, from the Libyan people."[51] "This whole thing is something out of the blue," Professor Hisham Sharabi told the *Washington Post.* "It's very strange."

Dean Krogh opposed returning the money but did not make an issue of it. He declined to comment to the press, except to say, "We never felt any pressure from the Libyan government" on how the money was to be spent. But, he observed: "Deans are deans and presidents are presidents. Presidents do pretty much what they please."

Ira Silverman of the American Jewish Committee was "delighted that Georgetown has made this decision." Moreover, the day after the return of the Libyan money, the New York City investment banking firm Bear, Stearns & Co., donated $100,000 to the university.[52] Said senior managing partner Alan Greenberg, "We admire them, and this is our little way of saying thank you."

Healy told the *Post* that in returning the money to Libya, "I was under absolutely no heat and pressure, but it worried me. I guess I'm just kind of slow to move, but I came to a growing realization that what Libya is up to is incompatible with Georgetown."[53] In an interview with *Washingtonian* magazine, however, he was more candid.[54] Originally, he had approved the Libyan gift despite some misgivings. He told the magazine the Libyan money "had been a huge nuisance and had kept him entangled in a verbal version of the Arab–Israeli war." Reported the *Washingtonian:*

> His Jewish friends screamed at him privately, and the American Jewish Committee issued a statement publicly condemning the university. Even his gestures of appeasement and balance—a goodwill trip to Israel, an honorary degree for the Israeli ambassador to the United States, refusal of a gift from Iraq, wearing a yarmulke at a Jewish service on campus—did little to offset Jewish anger over the Libyan money.

In fact, pressure on Healy had been intense before his return of the Libyan grant. One expression of Jewish anger took the form of a visit to Healy's office by a delegation of rabbis.[55] Max Kampelman, an influential Jewish member of Georgetown University's Board of Trustees, also interceded with Healy directly. As a former ambassador to the Helsinski Accords, Kampelman was "a major factor," observed Dean Krogh.

Former ambassador to the United Nations Arthur Goldberg reportedly added his weight to the pressure. In addition, Healy received, according to John Ruedy, "loads of letters." Another Georgetown professor called it "hate mail."

Indeed, controversy over the Arab studies program largely subsided after the return of the Libyan grant. As one professor at the center put it, "If returning the Libyan money has brought us some breathing space and gotten the monkey off our backs, maybe it was worth it." But since then, Arab governments have been less forthcoming with contributions. Said Ruedy, "We know that in some cases it has specifically to do with a sense of affront. Returning a gift in one donor's face is seen as an attack on all of them."[56]

On the other hand, Georgetown University has committed itself and its own financial resources to Arab studies. In the spring of 1983, Arab studies was one of nine graduate programs that the university "designated for excellence." "I feel that this may mean we have crossed the Rubicon," said Ruedy.

One reason that Georgetown's Arab studies center has been able to survive, and even prosper despite the controversy, is that it is affiliated with a private university. Ruedy said: "You could probably not have an Arab studies program in a public institution. You can have a Jewish studies program, of course. In fact, that is politically very advantageous. . . . Georgetown and the Jesuits are as far from dependency on Jewish support as you could be."

"That Was the Buzzword, 'Arab'"

The second U.S. university to create an Arab studies program, Villanova University in Pennsylvania, is also Catholic. In 1983, Villanova set up the Institute for Contemporary Arab and Islamic Studies, naming the Reverend Kail Ellis, an Augustinian priest of Lebanese origin, as its director. Villanova's was a modest program that originated without the involvement of outside funds. It offered certificates in Arab studies to undergraduates majoring in other fields. The institution also sponsored conferences, lectures, and cultural events. Father Ellis said, "Our goal is to familiarize the students with the history, language, politics and culture of the Arab Islamic world."

Despite the program's modest scope and the absence of Arab funding, there was considerable opposition to it from within the university, mainly from the political science department. "The pressure wasn't really overt as such," says Ellis. "It was always behind the scenes. There are a couple of faculty people who were the most vocal against it and they organized the opposition."

The political science department was originally asked to comment on the proposal for establishing the institute. In a minority report attached to the department's comments, one professor warned about the effect of such a program on the Jewish community:

> Villanova exists in a larger community on which it depends for both financial and political support. This larger community is made up of Protestants, Catholics, Jews, and very few Muslims. If Villanova creates an Islamic Studies Institute, it will have no effect, positive or negative, on its Catholic and Protestant constituencies. But because this issue has high emotional content, it will in my view have strong negative effects on the Jewish community in the Villanova area who, though relatively few in number, are financially and politically influential. Such an institute might reflect on Villanova University's president in such a way as to affect his ability to function on the Holocaust Committee, where his efforts have provided great credibility for Villanova among the Jewish Committee. It is my opinion that the existence of such an institute might dry up possible Jewish financial and political support.

Another professor commented:

> Israel is the single most important United States ally in the Middle East politically, it has extensive and close economic and business ties with the United States, [and] it is the cultural and religious homeland of millions of Americans. To exclude the study of Israel from the proposed program is a mistake and may affect potential enrollment.

Ellis explains: "The idea was to broaden the program from Arab studies. That was the buzzword, 'Arab.'" Georgetown's John Ruedy was invited to Villanova as a consultant to participate in the preparations for the Arab studies proposal. "The opposition was very interesting," said Ruedy: "It was the Zionist issue but nobody said it. I could just tell, because I'd been there before. The first line of opposition is on academic grounds. But when you get around all these and answer all the questions, then they bare their fangs and say, 'This is anti-Israel, this is anti-Semitic, and it will be against the interests of the university. And we have to relate to Jewish donors and so on.' This is precisely what happened at Villanova."

After the institute opened, Father Ellis received a letter from American Professors for Peace in the Middle East, a national pro-Israeli organization. The executive director, George Cohen, took issue with a map that appeared in the institute's brochure. The map, clearly labeled "The Arab and Islamic World," shows only the Arab countries of the Middle East and Africa in dark green and the non-Arab Islamic countries (namely, Turkey, Afghanistan, and Pakistan) in light green. Cohen noted that the map did not identify Israel. "Is this an error," he asked, "or is it intended to make a political statement, excluding Israel?"

Ellis wrote back that the purpose of the map was to identify the Arab and Islamic countries with which the program dealt: "It was not our intention to make a political statement about Israel or any other country, such as Ethiopia, Cyprus, Mali, Chad, or even the Turkmen, Uzbek, and Tajik Republics of the Soviet Union, all of which are located in the area and have substantial Muslim populations but which were excluded from the map."

Cohen was not satisfied and wrote another letter, saying he did not accept Ellis's response and asking him to "present this issue to your department before I take it further." Cohen did not specify what measures he might employ in "taking it further," and Ellis did not respond to his second letter. Meanwhile, the Institute for Contemporary Arab and Islamic Studies continued to gain acceptance within the Villanova scholarly community.

Attacks against the academic community in Middle East studies were, in the view of a leading scholar, continuing and "perhaps getting even stronger." He added, "They are not directed just at one or two institutions, but appear to have a nationwide basis."

Think Tank Under Pressure

Of the many think tanks that have sprung up around the country in the past two decades, Georgetown University's Center for Strategic and International Studies (CSIS) is one of the most prestigious. Established in 1965, CSIS had grown by 1984 to comprise a staff of 150, a budget of $6 million, and a publications list of nearly 200 titles.[57] Among the eminent names on the Center's roster were Henry Kissinger, Howard K. Smith, Lane Kirkland, and John Glenn. CSIS is a nonprofit, tax-exempt organization that, though known to be conservative in outlook, included both Democrats and Republicans on its advisory board.

Based in Washington, the center viewed the provision of expert research and analysis to government leaders as one of its most vital functions. As part of Georgetown University, CSIS considered itself an "integral part of the academic community." Scholarly participation in all center activities "insures that the widest and most rigorous thinking is brought to bear on issues."[58]

The center, said its brochure, is "well equipped to function in a true interdisciplinary, nonpartisan fashion." Yet a report completed in 1981 by the director of the center's Oil Field Security Studies Project was suppressed on the eve of congressional action on the sale of AWACS planes to Saudi Arabia. Supporters of Israel from outside the center were opposed to the sale and did not want the contents of the report known because they feared it could be used effectively in winning congressional approval. Six months later, the author of the offending study was fired by the center and urged to leave town.

The victim was Mazher Hameed, a native of Saudi Arabia, a graduate of the Fletcher School of Law and Diplomacy, and a specialist on international security affairs. Former U.S. ambassador to Saudi Arabia James Akins wrote of Hameed in 1983, "I know of no one else in this country with his insight, his honesty, his analytical ability and his profound knowledge of the Middle East, particularly the Arabian Peninsula."[59] Hameed was hired by the center in November 1980 as a research fellow "with responsibilities for research on a project on Saudi oil field security."[60] In the letter of appointment, CSIS Executive Director Amos Jordan wrote: "This letter also constitutes a formal approval of the oil field security project."

The scope of the project was outlined in a memorandum to Jordan that had been prepared a month earlier by Wayne Berman, who was responsible to Jordan for fund-raising. That memo stated that the project would focus on the political and military analysis of oil field vulnerabilities in the Middle East, the likelihood of attacks from various sources, an examination of security planning, and technical defense profiles.[61] Amos Jordan himself brought up with Hameed the need to evaluate the AWACS–F-15 enhancement package before it became an issue on Capitol Hill.

For the next nine months, Hameed carried out his research and wrote a series of drafts of a report on his results. These drafts were shown to Amos Jordan, who had become vice chairman of the center, and to David Abshire, the chairman, as well as to several experts outside the center. The final report was to be published by CSIS. Jordan told Hameed, after reading one of the earlier drafts, that his work was "brilliant" and that he wanted to see more work of that caliber emerging from the center. Abshire concurred with this view. Jordan personally gave copies of one of the earlier drafts to William Clark, who at that time was deputy secretary of state, and who would subsequently become President Reagan's national security advisor. Other Middle East experts who praised the report were Anthony Cordesman, international editor of the *Armed Forces Journal*, and William Quandt, director of the Energy and National Security Project of the Brookings Institution.

In August 1981, Abshire and Jordan left together for a trip to Tokyo. They took Hameed's final draft with them. Jordan sent back a telex praising the study: "On plane I read Hameed's Saudi security paper," read the telex, "which is informative and beautifully written."[62] The telex went on to suggest that the report should be edited to tone down its strong advocacy of the AWACS–F-15 package. "Paper makes strong case without overkill," wrote Jordan. "Careful edit to meet above point needed before CSIS publishes in house by about 10 or 15 September. Suggest 300 copies."

In accordance with these instructions, Hameed met with Jean Newsom, a senior editor at the center, and William Taylor, director of political and military studies, and the three of them set to work on the final editing. At the same time, Newsom initiated talks with McGraw-Hill concerning publication of the report. Jean Newsom, when asked to confirm that the center had negotiated publication of the report with McGraw-Hill, demurred.[63] She said in a telephone interview: "We were not negotiating with McGraw-Hill, just seeing whether they were interested." But Trish Wilson, a research assistant for Hameed at the time, said, "They were talking about what the price was. They gave McGraw-Hill an estimate of how much they could sell the book for."[64]

The editing proceeded simultaneously with the negotiations through September and into October when, without warning, the center's comptroller, David Wendt, told Hameed that David Abshire had called from California, where he was vacationing on his way back from Japan. The message from Abshire was that the report was not to be released. Upset, Hameed pursued the matter with Jordan and others at the center: "They told me that many very large contributors to the center would be upset if they saw a report that was, as they described it, 'lacking in objectivity.'" Research assistant Paul Sutphin recalled: "I remember that it came as quite a surprise that suddenly there was going to be a problem with the center's putting out the report. Everything fell apart at the last moment. Hameed said that suddenly the 'powers on high' had decided to nix the center's support of the publication."[65]

Trish Wilson also remembers the incident: "They didn't want him to publish it at all, even privately." Another of Hameed's research assistants, George Smalley, who had been hired at the beginning of October on a salary basis, was told before the month was over that his status would be changed.[66] "Due to budget problems," he was to work on a fee basis and would no longer be granted any of the benefits initially agreed upon. These included social security, a paid vacation, sick leave, and free tuition at Georgetown University after one year. Smalley was convinced there was a direct link between the fate of Hameed's report and the fate of his own position with the center.

At that point, Hameed decided to take the initiative: "I wanted the report out before the AWACS issue came up in Congress . . . this was a document that was relevant to what was being discussed on the Hill, and I want my work to be looked at." He sent copies of the eighty-five-page report to major corporations that contributed to the center. He told them: "I understand you people would be upset if you saw this report coming out of the center." Until that time, says Hameed, he had no relationship with these companies. The center had asked him specifically not to go to any of these corporations for funding as it had long-standing relationships with most of them and didn't want these disturbed.

"These people," said Hameed, "for the first time heard about me, saw the report, got excited, and started calling the center to ask what was going on. They said that not only was the document interesting, not only did it have a unique point of view, but it had something very timely to say." Some of these companies, acknowledged Hameed, were engaged

in the lobbying effort on behalf of the AWACS sale. "They found something that they liked very much," he recalls, "and they wanted to use it.
So I used some influence of that sort to get a compromise." The compromise was that the center permitted Hameed to release the report as
a private document. "But they didn't want me to indicate my designation
at the center. I could just say I was a research fellow and program director without mentioning the name of the project." Naming the project
would have given the report additional credibility. "They didn't want
him to say that it was under the research auspices of the center," confirmed Paul Sutphin.

Hameed complied with the request. "For me, the primary interest
was to get the document out and to get it read. What the document had
to say was more important than these other matters." So Hameed had
the report printed at his own expense and released it himself. The
response to the report in government circles was immediate. Recalls
Hameed: "People at the State Department asked for copies, people on the
Hill asked for copies, NSC [the National Security Council] asked for
copies." After Egyptian President Anwar Sadat was assassinated the following month, William Clark gave copies of Hameed's report to former
Presidents Nixon, Ford, and Carter to help them update themselves on
the Middle East while en route to Cairo for Sadat's funeral. Clark called
CSIS Vice Chairman Amos Jordan specifically to tell him about it. Jordan conveyed this information to Hameed and assured him that the center's chairman, David Abshire, concurred in praising the report.

On October 28, the U.S. Senate voted 52–48 against a resolution
that would have blocked the AWACS sale to Saudi Arabia. Although the
House had passed such a resolution two weeks earlier, a majority in both
chambers was required to prevent the sale from going through. The Senate vote represented a rare defeat for the pro-Israeli lobby and one it was
not about to forget. In November Amos Jordan received a visit from
Steven Emerson, an aide in former Senator Frank Church's law firm,
who had earlier assisted Church on the Senate Foreign Relations Committee.[67] Emerson asked Jordan probing questions about the center's
activities, some of them concerning Hameed's project. He told Jordan he
was writing an article for the *New Republic* about the influence of
petrodollars. Emerson said he was interested in Hameed's report and

wanted to know who had funded it. After the interview, Jordan called Hameed, cautioned him that there might be some "turbulence," and advised him to "fasten your seatbelt." To Jordan, the interview was "something threatening." He later told Hameed: "It was clear that Emerson's questions were hostile, and we were concerned that we would be subject to some unwarranted charges."

In early December, Emerson and his associates returned to the center and brought with them the draft of the Emerson article for the *New Republic*.[68] It was part of a series Emerson was writing for the magazine on alleged Arab attempts to manipulate U.S. public opinion. The suggestion was that policy think tanks receiving money from oil corporations with Arab business were under obligation to serve the political interests of those companies. But the draft fell short of singling out CSIS, and center officials continued to feel they could safely weather the storm caused by Hameed's report.

Hameed, exhausted physically and emotionally, left in December for a vacation, but only, he said, after receiving assurance from Jordan that there was "nothing to worry about." "I came back in January," said Hameed, "to learn that these gentlemen had returned once more to the center with another draft of the *New Republic* article. This time the draft appeared to compromise the center in a more specific way."

Nevertheless, another member of the center's senior staff, Jon Vondracek, had been in touch with the publisher of the *New Republic*, Martin Peretz. He told Hameed that he thought the center had enough clout to prevent the magazine from doing any harm. During the same period, Emerson phoned Hameed's office, asking questions about the report and, more specifically, about how Hameed's project was funded. When Hameed declined to reveal his sources of funding, Emerson threatened to expose an alleged petrodollar connection at CSIS. Hameed wished him luck. In addition to calling Hameed and his staff, Emerson had also contacted several corporations in his attempt to find out who had funded the research.

"What was funny," says Hameed, "was that my project had some funding, but not from any of the companies you would expect. I felt I shouldn't go to companies that had an obvious interest in influencing my work. What I had to say didn't need influence from other groups, particularly those that were funding it. But beyond that, I didn't want the appearance of such influence. Having been meticulous about all this, I was especially irked to have this problem at the end."

On February 17, 1982, the first of Steve Emerson's series of articles appeared in the *New Republic.* Entitled "The Petrodollar Connection," the article was to be followed, according to the magazine, by future articles dealing with "strings-attached donations to policy think tanks, universities, and research institutions."[69]

The very next day, the center found itself under the spotlight. *Platt's Oilgram News,* a respected newsletter owned by McGraw-Hill, published an article on February 18 about Hameed's report, saying the document had been "kept under wraps" by CSIS. Titled "Georgetown Study: Israel Could 'Create' a Saudi Oil Embargo to Pressure U.S.," the article quoted from the section of the report that discussed threats to Saudi Arabia from its neighbors.[70] This was one of the sections that the CSIS directors were most nervous about, because it made the point that since Israel considered Saudi Arabia a "confrontation state" in the Arab–Israeli conflict, the Israelis might make preemptive strikes against Saudi military and economic assets.

"The study notes," said the *Platt's* article, "that Israel already occupies Saudi territory (the islands of Tiran and Sanafir) and that since 1976, Israeli aircraft have been making practice bombing runs over the Saudi air base of Tabuk, dropping empty fuel tanks on several occasions. In addition, Israel has pointed out that its air force has the capability to create an 'oil embargo' of its own by destroying Saudi oil installations."

The editor of *Platt's Oilgram News,* Onnik Maraschian, did not know who had written the report or that it had been released privately months earlier.[71] "All we knew was that there was a report," says Maraschian. "It was distributed as a draft, as a CSIS report, and then it got pulled back, but we ran it nevertheless because it started as a project of CSIS." After the *Platt's* article appeared, CSIS began to receive phone calls from people wanting copies of the study. This created an embarrassing situation for the center. Should they admit that they had suppressed the report? How could they explain the fact that they had never published it? Vice Chairman Amos Jordan attempted a solution in the form of a memorandum to "concerned staff" that deserves a prize for obfuscation. The memo called the staff's attention to the publication of the *Platt's* article and suggested they use the following paragraph to answer all inquiries:

> The center has not "completed last fall" a study entitled "Saudi Security and the Evolving Threat to U.S. Interests." We have had underway for over a year a project on oil field security and research and that study continues. The project has produced several research fragments, including a partial draft with the title cited, but that does not represent a center study—rather, it is only a small piece of the problem; and that at an early stage. When the study is completed later this year and becomes a CSIS report, it will be made public.[72]

"They were quite taken aback when they saw that we used the story," recalls Maraschian. "Obviously when they commissioned the man to do this study they knew what his qualifications were. So why did they go with it for a year and then pull it back?" Maraschian had an idea: "You see, what they got mad at was the possibility of a preemptive strike by Israel." Hameed was not the only one who thought that Israel might make a preemptive strike against Saudi Arabia. In the secret version of a government report titled "U.S. Assistance to the State of Israel," which was leaked to the press in June 1983, the CIA is cited as warning that, in reaction to the modernization of Arab armies, Israel might launch "preemptive attacks in future crises."[73] In fact, over the years Israeli military officials have talked openly about such strikes against Saudi Arabia.

Embarrassed by the *Platt's* article and worried about efforts by the Israeli lobby to discredit the center, Jordan and Abshire—despite their own inclination to support the sale of AWACS to Saudi Arabia—apparently finally decided that Hameed was too great a liability. A week later, the center's comptroller, David Wendt, told Hameed he would have to pay an additional surcharge on his office space amounting to $1,570 a month.[74] As project director, Hameed was already paying 24 percent of his project funds to cover office overhead costs and another 20 percent to help cover the center's general operations. The new charge would come on top of what he was already paying.[75]

"I grumbled a bit but finally agreed," recalls Hameed. "Then came the bombshell. They made it retroactive back eighteen months!" Wendt told Hameed that, with the new charges, his project was $40,000 in deficit.[76] Wendt said he would have to report the deficit and that it was likely that Hameed's project would be terminated.

The stunned Hameed called John Shaw, a member of the senior staff. Shaw confided to Hameed that David Abshire was furious, although Shaw wouldn't say why. Committee meetings were held throughout that day in order, Hameed believed, to discuss how to deal with the "problem." The answer reached, said Hameed, was to offer up his head. In April Hameed met with Jordan, whom he found uncharacteristically cold and distant. Jordan said he was concerned about the "deficit" and warned that Hameed's project was in an unsustainable financial position.

A few days later, Jordan sent Hameed a letter stating that the project would have to be terminated by the end of the following month. Jordan added that he would be happy to review his decision and that Hameed might be hired back if he could raise "especially large amounts of money." After receiving the letter, Hameed met again with Jordan. He still hoped there was something he could do to prevent the imminent collapse of his project. He still saw Jordan as a friend, a man who had supported him personally and professionally. He thought that Jordan had been given a distorted picture of his project's finances. But Jordan was unmoved. He responded that the new surcharge had been decided formally and that the matter was beyond his control. Hameed pleaded with Jordan to give him at least three or four months in which to wind things up, but his request was to no avail.

Hameed spoke to other prominent people at the center in a desperate attempt to save his project. One told him, "Just lie low and once this thing blows over, we can probably arrange to have you come back." But, recalled Hameed with some bitterness, "Basically, no one stood up for me. They all looked the other way. They let it happen. The knives were out."

Then, on March 5, shortly after learning that his job was to be terminated, Hameed arrived at his office to find that it had been burgled during the night.[77] Someone had managed to penetrate three locked doors and had then pried open the file cabinet next to Hameed's desk. The burglar first had to have entered the office building, which was equipped with an electronic surveillance system using card readers, then the locked door to the office suite, and finally, the locked door to Hameed's office. There were no signs of forced entry. But the file cabinet was bent and the drawer had been wrenched open. Adds Paul Sutphin, "This bore no signs of a common burglary. There were other valuable things that were not taken." In fact, nothing was taken at all. "It was such a lousy job, so obvious," says Trish Wilson, "that we concluded it was there to scare us."

The next day Hameed found that the post office box he used for some of his correspondence had been broken open. A few days later, the mailbox at his home was broken open. "Other weird things started to happen as well," recalls Hameed. "For example, I'd leave for the weekend and come back and find things in my house that didn't belong there . . . like contact lenses." These incidents were particularly frightening to Hameed—and the contact lens prank needlessly cruel—because he is blind.

Hameed left the center at the end of March. In May and June, the *New Republic* published the second and third parts of its series on petrodollar influence in the United States. The promised exposé of "strings-attached donations to policy think tanks" was missing from the series.

The last episode in Hameed's relations with CSIS occurred in May 1982, some weeks after he had left the center. Officers of the center contacted a number of Hameed's friends as well as corporate executives in an effort to discredit him. In one case, a senior administration official's help was sought to encourage Hameed to "leave town." Several corporations, after learning that Hameed had been fired, cut back their contributions to Georgetown University and made it clear that the reason was the treatment accorded Mazher Hameed.[78]

Amos Jordan, asked to comment on Hameed's charges, insisted that these various circumstances were coincidental and that Hameed's departure related only to his performance. He denied that the center responded to lobby pressure: "I went out of my way to protect and sponsor Hameed despite the deficits. I am concerned that the center not have a reputation for being a Zionist foil."

It was an unsettling, traumatic time for the scholar. In a short space of weeks, people from the *New Republic* magazine had descended on the center, threatening an exposé of petrodollar influence, warning about the center's tax status under IRS regulations, and questioning the funding of Hameed's project. Preceding and following these events were the center's suppression of the report and the personal harassment of

Hameed, his associates and his friends—and his dismissal. If these events were purely coincidental, it was a remarkable happenstance.

Recalling what he knew of Hameed's tenure at CSIS, William Quandt, senior fellow at the Brookings Institution and a personal friend of Hameed, said: "The way they terminated his whole relationship there was rather strange. He was very shabbily treated, to say the least." Les Janka, former special assistant for Middle East affairs in the White House, said: "CSIS did not have the courage to put out under its own name a paper that made a significant contribution to public debate."

"Blaming the Victim"[79]

Dangers to academic freedom became more pronounced following the 9/11 terrorist attacks on the United States. Swept up in the national hysteria was Dr. Sami Al-Arian, a Palestinian-born veteran champion of Arab and Muslim human rights, who became the first tenured professor in American history to be fired for exercising the right of free speech.

Al-Arian acquired the distinction in December 2001 when University of South Florida (USF) President Judy Genshaft dismissed him from his faculty position as a professor of computer sciences. His offense: In an appearance on the television program, *The O'Reilly Factor* a few days after 9/11, host Bill O'Reilly accused him of associating with terrorists, quoting statements that Al-Arian had made thirteen years before in a speech off campus.

In the 1989 speech, Al-Arian, speaking to an audience consisting largely of Arab Americans, quoted in the Arabic language slogans then in use by Palestinians protesting Israel's occupation of Palestinian land, the most inflammatory being "Death to Israel. Revolution until victory." Al-Arian responded to O'Reilly's accusations: "When you say, 'Death to Israel,' you mean death to [Israeli] occupation, death to apartheid, death to oppression." He denied that the slogan meant death to any human being, or to the actual state of Israel.

During the weeks following 9/11, Al-Arian spoke to several audiences of Christians and Jews in the Tampa area, denouncing the attacks on America, noting that Islam opposes violence and suicide, and declaring that the perpetrators of 9/11 could not have been "truly religious" men. Dr. Harry E. Vanden, a professor of political science at the University of South Florida who writes and lectures on terrorism, denies that Al-Arian supports terrorism: "I've heard Sami speak in my church. He talked about how 9/11 is wrong, an evil act. He went on *The O'Reilly Factor* to show that American Muslims weren't in favor of this." Vanden notes that Al-Arian "never had the chance" to express himself in the interview, which was dominated by O'Reilly's frequent and numerous interruptions.

As the result of the *O'Reilly* appearance, Al-Arian received death threats, and harsh protests poured into the university from donors and alumni. Genshaft announced the suspension of Al-Arian with pay until she met with trustees to receive their recommendation on what to do. At the meeting, only Connie Mack, a trustee and former U.S. senator, voiced concern over the wisdom of denying academic freedom on the basis of criminal and threatening actions of others. When the discussion ended, Mack nevertheless joined other trustees in recommending dismissal. Only one trustee voted no.

Later, explaining her historic decision against academic freedom, Genshaft offered this excuse: "The fundamental question [is] how much disruption the university must endure because of the manner in which a professor exercises his right to express political and social views that are outside the scope of his employment." When Florida Governor Jeb Bush, the brother of President George W. Bush, supported Genshaft's decision, a *New York Times* editorial denounced both Bush and the university president: "Wartime is precisely the moment when unpopular views and the role of a university as an open forum for ideas must be most vigorously defended." Even O'Reilly opposed Al-Arian's dismissal, and he called for Genshaft's resignation.

The USF episode was not the first time Al-Arian had been unfairly targeted. Self-styled terrorism expert Steven Emerson had mounted a decade-long campaign against Al-Arian and his associates. In a 1996 speech in St. Petersburg, Florida, Emerson accused "Palestinian radicals" at the university of being involved in the 1993 World Trade Center bombing. He did not reveal sources for the charge, and federal investigations yielded no evidence of any "Palestinian radical" wrongdoing. Arab American Institute president James Zogby, who has long defended the human rights of Arab Americans and challenged Emerson's credentials as a terrorism expert, said that Emerson "[has] made his life's work discrediting Arab American and Muslim groups, and his obsession makes me uncomfortable."

Despite his many setbacks, Al-Arian is tireless in his campaign for political and social justice. Much of his focus is on the plight of his brother-in-law, Dr. Mazen Al-Najjar, who is also Palestinian, who spent three years and seven months in a Florida jail on the basis of secret "evidence" and alleged ties to terrorism. Al-Najjar was released from jail on December 15, 2000, when a federal judge ruled his detention unconstitutional. He was arrested again on November 24, 2001, after another court refused to overturn an order to deport Al-Najjar due to an expired visa. U.S. authorities said that, while he had nothing to do with 9/11 events, Al-Najjar's detention nevertheless demonstrated the Justice Department's "commitment to address terrorism."

Randall Marshall, an American Civil Liberties Union (ACLU) attorney who is working on behalf of Al-Najjar, remonstrated: "Al-Najjar has never been accused of a crime, yet he is being detained in solitary confinement under conditions more severe than those imposed on many convicted murderers." *New York Times* columnist Anthony Lewis decried Al-Najjar's treatment: "Could that happen in America? In John Ashcroft's America it has happened. . . . At a time of national anxiety about Arabs and Muslims, Mr. Al-Najjar is a useful target: a Palestinian Muslim."[80] While serving in the U.S. House of Representatives, David Bonior (D-MI) was an outspoken opponent of secret evidence. Of the Al-Najjar case, Bonior could only say, "I've been in this business for thirty years, and I've never seen an injustice like this."[81]

"No Such Thing as Academic Integrity"

An early champion of Palestinian statehood, Francis A. Boyle is a professor of international law at the University of Illinois and a prolific writer on international legal issues, particularly those dealing with human rights. He lectures widely and frequently and often appears before international courts, sometimes representing clients there on a pro bono basis.

He is controversial at the university because of his outspoken and long-standing support of Palestinian rights and his sharp criticism of U.S. and Israeli policies in the Middle East. Friends believe he has paid a price for this advocacy, because he has been passed over several times for what would normally be routine increases in salary. He served as advisor to the PLO from 1987 to 1989, and he advised the Palestinian delegation to the Middle East peace negotiations in Washington, D.C., from 1991 to 1993.

During that time, Boyle urged the Palestinians to reject the proposal that eventually became the Oslo Accords. He warned: "They are offering you a Bantustan. As you know, the Israelis had very close relations with the Afrikaner Apartheid regime in South Africa. It appears they have studied the Bantustan system quite closely. So it is a Bantustan that they are offering you." A decade after Boyle's analysis, protesters around the world began making the same Israel–South Africa comparison. "Israel is an Apartheid State" has become a mantra for Palestinian sympathizers worldwide.

Boyle's sharp analytical mind produced this indictment of Israel's scofflaw conduct: "There are 149 substantive articles of the Fourth Geneva Convention that protect the rights of almost every one of these Palestinians living in occupied Palestine. The Israeli government is currently violating, and has been since 1967, almost each and every one of these."[82] He is equally critical of the United States' role as peace broker in the region: "It can be fairly said that U.S. Middle East policy has not shown one iota of respect for international law."

Boyle has maintained these positions for thirty years. He noted with dismay the tendency to stifle Middle East debate in academic and other realms: "I have been accused of being everything but a child molester because of my public support for the Palestinian people. I have seen every known principle of academic integrity and academic freedom violated in order to suppress the basic rights of the Palestinian people. In fact, there is no such thing as academic integrity and academic freedom in the United States when it comes to asserting the rights of the Palestinian people under international law."

9

Paving the Way for the Messiah

DWIGHT CAMPBELL, the youthful clerk of Shelby County, Illinois, sat quietly through the meeting in a Shelbyville restaurant. It was fall 1982, the campaign season in Illinois, and during the session I discussed foreign policy issues with a group of constituents. Only when the gathering had begun to break up did Campbell call me aside to voice his deep concern over remarks I had made criticizing Israeli policy in Lebanon.

He identified himself as a Christian and, speaking very earnestly and without hostility, warned me that my approach to the Middle East was wrong from a political standpoint and, more important, was in conflict with God's plan. He concluded with a heartfelt injunction: "I would not advocate anything to interfere with the destiny of Israel as set forth in the Bible."

The urgency in his voice was striking. It seemed clear that this public official, who was well respected in his community, was not compelled to support Israel by external pressure. Nor was he motivated by a desire for professional or social advancement. As with many evangelical Christians, his support came from deep conviction.

Americans like Dwight Campbell comprise a natural constituency for Israel and add enormous strength to the manipulations of the Israeli lobby. Democratic Congressman Lee H. Hamilton, chairman of the Middle East Subcommittee, hears similar comments when he visits his district in rural Indiana. At town meetings, which Hamilton conducts, constituents frequently speak up. Identifying themselves as Christians, they urge that he support Israel's needs completely and without reservation.[1]

Many U.S. Christians, both conservative and mainline, support Israel because of shared cultural and political values and in response to the horror of the Holocaust.[2] Many conservatives feel, as did the young official in Shelbyville, that the creation of Israel in 1948 came in fulfillment of biblical prophecy, and that the Jewish state will continue to play a central role in the divine plan.

Religious affiliation also tends to influence members of the mainstream denominations, particularly Protestants, toward a pro-Israeli stance. An exclusive focus on biblical tradition causes many Christians to see the Middle East as a reflection of events portrayed in the Bible: twentieth century Israelis become biblical Israelites, Palestinians become Philistines, and so on, in a dangerous, albeit usually unconscious, chain of historical misassociation. The distinction between Jewish settlers on the occupied West Bank and the Hebrew nation that conquered the land of Canaan under Moses and Joshua becomes obscured.

Virtually all Christians approach the Middle East with at least a subtle affinity to Israel and an inclination to oppose or mistrust any suggestion that questions Israeli policy. The lobby has drawn widely upon this support in pressing its national programs. More important, fresh perspectives that challenge shibboleths and established prejudices regarding the Middle East are often denounced by both the lobby and many of its Christian allies as politically extremist, anti-Semitic, or even anti-Christian.

The religious convictions of many Americans have made them susceptible to the appeals of the Israeli lobby, with the result that free speech concerning the Middle East and U.S. policy in the region is frequently restricted before it begins. The combination of religious tradition and overt lobby activity tends to confine legitimate discussion within artificially narrow bounds.

Conservative Christians Rally to the Cause

Fundamentalist and evangelical groups have been active in this campaign to narrow the bounds of free speech. Jerry Falwell and Pat Robertson proselytize tirelessly for ever-increasing U.S. backing of Israel, citing scriptural passages as the basis for their arguments. As the membership of conservative Protestant churches and organizations has expanded over the last decade, this "Christian Zionist" approach to the Middle East has been espoused from an increasing variety of "pulpits": local churches, the broadcast media, and even the halls of Congress.

Senator Roger W. Jepsen, a first-term legislator from Iowa, told the 1981 annual policy conference of AIPAC that one of the reasons for his "spirited and unfailing support" for Israel was his Christian faith. He declared that "Christians, particularly Evangelical Christians, have been among Israel's best friends since its rebirth in 1948." That view is hardly unique, even among members of Congress, but his statement on this occasion aptly expressed the near-mystical identification some Christians feel toward Israel:

> I believe one of the reasons America has been blessed over the years is because we have been hospitable to those Jews who have sought a home in this country. We have been blessed because we have come to Israel's defense regularly, and we have been blessed because we have recognized Israel's right to the land. . . .[3]

Jepsen cited his fundamentalist views in explaining his early opposition to the sale of AWACS to Saudi Arabia, but he credited divine intervention as the reason he switched his position the day before the Senate voted on the proposal.[4] On election day, November 6, 1984, Iowans—spurred by the Israel lobby—did their own switching, rejecting Jepsen's bid for a second term.

Jerry Falwell, leader of the Moral Majority and a personal friend of Menachem Begin and Yitzhak Shamir, has been described by *The Economist* of London as "the silk-voiced ayatollah of Christian revivalism." Acclaimed in a *Conservative Digest* annual poll as the most admired conservative outside of Congress (with President Reagan the runner-up), Falwell embodies the growing Christian–Zionist connection.[5] He has declared: "I don't think America could turn its back on the people of

Israel and survive. God deals with nations in relation to how those nations deal with the Jews." He has testified before congressional committees in favor of moving the U.S. embassy from Tel Aviv to Jerusalem. Falwell is perhaps the best known of the pro-Israel fundamentalist spokesmen, but he is by no means the only one.

In the summer of 1983, Mike Evans Ministries of Bedford, Texas, broadcast an hour-long television special called *Israel, America's Key to Survival.* Evangelist Evans used the program to describe the "crucial" role played by Israel in the political—and spiritual—fate of the United States. Since the show was presented as religious programming, it was given free broadcast time on local television stations in at least twenty-five states. It was also broadcast on the Christian Broadcasting Network cable system. Yet the message of the program was by no means entirely spiritual.

Interspersing scripture quotations with interviews of public and military figures and other evangelists, including Pat Robertson, Oral Roberts, and Jimmy Swaggart, Evans made a number of political assertions about Israel. These included the wild contention that, if Israel gave up control of the West Bank and other territories occupied after the 1967 war, the destruction of Israel and the United States would follow. Evans also implied that Israel was a special victim of Soviet pressure in the form of "international terrorism," which, were it not for Israel, would be brought to bear directly against the United States and Latin America.

Evans concluded the broadcast with a climactic appeal for Christians to come to the support of "America's best friend in that part of the world" by signing a "Proclamation of Blessing for Israel." Stating that "God distinctly told me to produce this television special pertaining to the nation of Israel," Evans argued that the proclamation was particularly important since "war is coming, and we must let our president and Prime Minister Begin know how we, as Americans, feel about Israel." He presented the proclamation to both Prime Minister Shamir and U.S. President Ronald Reagan, then proceeded to congratulate his supporters: "You never thought you would be having such an effect upon the two most powerful leaders in the entire world! But, yes, you are!"[6]

Still, Evans was dissatisfied with Reagan's response. In an August 1984 fund-raising appeal, Evans blamed the United States for Israel's economic woes: "Because of America's encouraging Israel to give up the Sinai and its oil [they lost, he said, $1.7 billion] and because of Israel's assistance to America through defense of the Middle East, Israel is on the verge of economic collapse." He said Reagan was "hesitant" to "alleviate Israel's great pressures."

The Evans theme linking America's survival to Israel was echoed in a full-page ad for the National Political Action Committee, a pro-Israel fund-raising organization, in the December 18, 1983, *New York Times.* It proclaimed that "Israel's survival is vital to our own," and "faith in Israel strengthens America."

Radio and television broadcasts by Jim Bakker, Kenneth Copeland, Oral Roberts, Jimmy Swaggart, and others routinely proclaim the sanctity of Israel through scriptural quotation, usually from the Old Testament, and then reinforce it with political and strategic arguments supplied by the broadcaster.

The arguments find a considerable audience. Most estimates place the number of Evangelical Christians in the United States in the neighborhood of thirty million. Jerry Falwell's "Old Time Gospel Hour" is aired on 392 television stations and nearly 500 radio stations each week. Former Israeli Prime Minister Menachem Begin described Falwell as "the man who represents twenty million American Christians."

Nor is the American style of evangelistic programming confined to U.S. shores. Its pro-Israeli message is now broadcast from the Middle East itself. The High Adventure Holyland Broadcasting Network of George Otis has maintained the Voice of Hope radio station in southern Lebanon since the first Israeli invasion of Lebanon in 1978. He describes it as an effort "to bring the Word of God to an area that has not had the Word of God in many centuries." Otis named his broadcast ministry after his personal conviction that "Jesus [is] high adventure"; but over the past several years the station has been actively involved in adventure of a more secular sort.

The late Major Saad Haddad, the Lebanese commander of the Israeli-backed militia that controlled southern Lebanon prior to the Israeli invasion in 1982, frequently used the Voice of Hope to broadcast his military objectives, including threats against civilians. Evangelist Otis, overlooking grim aspects of Haddad's rule, described Haddad as a "born-again" Christian who was a "good spiritual leader" to the people of southern

Lebanon. The U.S. State Department confirms that Haddad often carried out threats to shell civilian areas, including the city of Sidon, "without previous warning." Haddad rationalized these attacks as reprisals against the Lebanese government for not meeting his demands for salary payment. (The Lebanese government ceased paying the salaries of Haddad's forces after he was dishonorably discharged from the Lebanese army.)

In the spring of 1980, Haddad forces used five U.S.-built Sherman tanks in an attack on a Boy Scout Jamboree near the city of Tyre, killing sixteen boys. Haddad's gunners also shot down a Norwegian medevac helicopter that arrived to help the wounded. The scout gathering, which was sponsored by the Christian Maronite Church, was just beyond the limits of "Free Lebanon," or "Haddadland," the area controlled by Haddad's Israeli-backed army. Haddad announced at the time that such attacks would continue until the Lebanese government provided more electricity to this area and recognized Haddad schools.

In the late 1970s, with the support of both Israel and the remaining Christian forces in the south, High Adventure Ministries established the Star of Hope television station in southern Lebanon. Otis himself described the Israeli support as "a miracle": "Did you ever think we would see the day when the Jews would push us for a Christian station?"[7] Yet since the television station assured more effective communication with the public—for military and other purposes—Israeli approval seemed more the product of sound strategic thinking than of divine intervention. Like the Voice of Hope before it, the new Star of Hope was financed through tax-deductible contributions of money and equipment from donors in North America.

In 1982, Star of Hope was presented to Pat Robertson's Christian Broadcasting Network as a gift. Robertson upgraded the facility and renamed it Middle East Television (METV). The Christian separatist World Lebanese Association—which is affiliated with AIPAC—describes METV as "generally sympathetic to the Christian Maronites of the region and to Israel." It adds that, for years, METV was accused of links to Israel and the now-defunct Israel-allied Christian militia, the South Lebanese Army (SLA).[8]

Through endeavors such as METV, American evangelical broadcasting supported the Israeli government indirectly by emphasizing the moral and religious commitment to the Jewish state that many Americans already feel, and directly by broadcasting in the Middle East messages that promote the military objectives of Israel and its Lebanese allies.

Jerry Falwell periodically conducts tours of Israel for born-again Christians. Although Falwell is careful to avoid the appearance of money flowing from Israel to the Moral Majority, former Israeli Prime Minister Menachem Begin demonstrated his commitment by arranging for a jet plane to be sold to Falwell's organization at a substantial discount.

Besides Falwell's, there are many other Christian groups offering Israel their support. In eastern Colorado, more than ten churches coordinate an annual "Israel Recognition Day" involving films, lectures, cultural exhibits, and sermons reaching more than 25,000 parishioners. The National Christian Leadership Conference for Israel (NCLCI) holds an annual conference in Washington that is attended by more than 200 delegates representing Christian groups from all over the United States. As Dr. Franklin H. Littell, president of NCLCI, has noted, "Concern for Israel's survival and well-being [is] the only issue that some of the organizations ever cooperated on."[9]

Other publicized events have included an October 1982 "Solidarity for Israel Sabbath" at Washington's Beth Shalom Orthodox Synagogue, in which evangelical leaders and local rabbis joined to "build bridges" and coordinate their efforts in behalf of Israel, and the "National Prayer Breakfast in Honor of Israel," which has become an annual event in the nation's capital.

The third such breakfast conference, given February 1, 1984, attracted more than 500 supporters of Israel, most of them Christians. The setting was brightly decorated with Israeli flags and symbols, including apples bearing Star of David stickers. The printed program for the affair boasted an impressive list of political and evangelical leaders, including Edwin Meese III (who was unable to attend, it was announced, because of his just-announced nomination as attorney general); Meir Rosenne, Israeli ambassador to the United States; and representatives from the National Religious Broadcasters and other conservative Protestant groups. Congressman Mark Siljander of Michigan, a member of the Middle East Subcommittee, delivered a stirring reaffirmation of evangelical solidarity with Israel: "It's not that we are anti-Arab. We seek peace in God's plan."

The breakfasts were coordinated by the Religious Roundtable, a group that describes itself as "a national organization dedicated to religious revival and moral purpose in America," yet maintains as one of its primary purposes the advancement of the Israeli cause. Edward E. McAteer, president of the group, was known in the Washington area as a partisan speaker and editorial writer on behalf of Israel. He used the religious format of his organization to back such political stands as closer U.S.–Israeli strategic cooperation, restriction of U.S. arms sales to Arab states, and transfer of the United States embassy in Israel from Tel Aviv to Jerusalem. In 1984 McAteer was an unsuccessful candidate for the Senate in Tennessee.

Writing in the *Washington Post* on January 2, 1984, McAteer supported the Israeli intervention in Lebanon, likening opponents of the invasion to "the premed student who proposed removing only half a cancerous growth [the PLO] because of the blood generated by surgery." Considering the fact that the invasion led to staggering civilian casualties, this crusading knight of the Religious Roundtable certainly cannot be accused of fear of blood.

Perhaps inspired by Mike Evans Ministries, the prayer breakfast committee created its own "Proclamation of Blessing" for Israel. Issued in the name of "America's 50-million-plus Bible-believing Christians," it included a curious mixture of religious, political, and military points: a call for "strategic cooperation" with Israel is followed by an appeal to "the God of Israel, Who through the Jewish people, gave to the world of Scriptures, our Savior, Salvation, and Spiritual blessings"; scriptural selections affirming the divine right of the Jews to the Holy Land, followed by language rejecting the "dual loyalty" charges against American Jewish supporters of Israel; and a call for the transfer of the U.S. embassy to Jerusalem, accompanied by an exhortation that "the Scripturally-delineated boundaries of the Holy Land never be compromised by the shifting sands of political and economic expediency."

Cooperation between Jewish and conservative Protestant groups has an important impact in the political sphere. In a 1983 Jerusalem press conference, Jerry Falwell declared that "The day is coming when no candidate will be elected in the United States who is not pro-Israel."[10] Although the Moral Majority has not had 100 percent success in putting its favorites in power, many candidates for high office, regardless of their own religious inclinations, now often feel compelled to address the issues that are on the evangelical political agenda.

Many conservative Christians see a theological basis for this support, as they ascribe to Israel a prominent role in the interpretation of Christian doctrine. On the one hand, it is maintained that Israel deserves Christian support because it exists as the fulfillment of biblical prophecy. Old Testament passages are most often quoted in defense of this view. On the other hand, many Christians back Israel because they believe that the Jewish people remain, as they were in biblical times, the chosen people of God. The same advocate will often cite both arguments. The prophecy argument is held by the most conservative fundamentalist groups, such as the Moral Majority, and has received more public attention, but the covenantal view is probably held by a larger segment of America's 40 million conservative Christians.[11]

Dr. Dewey Beegle of Wesley Theological Seminary commented on the differing views of Israel held by American Christians in his 1978 book, *Prophecy and Prediction*: "All Christian groups claim to have the truth, but obviously some of these views cannot be true, because they contradict other intepretations which can be verified."

Like many biblical scholars, Beegle has concluded that the scriptural basis that pro-Zionist Christians often cite for the establishment of modern Israel does not withstand close scrutiny. The issue, however, is not whether the scholarship of Beegle or that of the Moral Majority is the more sound, but the importance of open debate of such difficult issues. Here again, the experience of a published author is revealing. Because his book dealt with the controversial issue of modern Israel and its relations to biblical tradition, many publishers, even those who had handled previous works by this scholar, declined to publish it. One of these told him bluntly: "Your early chapters on the biblical matters of prophecy and prediction are well done. The only chapter that seriously disturbs us is 'Modern Israel Past and Present.'" Beegle was informed that his views on Israel, which accept the legitimacy of the modern Jewish state—albeit not on biblical grounds—would be "bound to infuriate" many readers.

Yet the fact that a book or a point of view is controversial is not, at least in the United States, usually grounds for rejection. Dr. Beegle viewed Christians and Jews who disagree with him in this way: "We know that these people think alike and feel alike and are going to help each other. It's perfectly natural. All I'm saying is we ought to have just as much right on the other side to speak out openly and put the information out there."[12] His book finally was published by Pryor Pettengill, a small firm in Ann Arbor, Michigan.

Many Christians who are neither fundamentalist nor evangelical are also inclined to accept the supposed counsel of prophecy as justification for Israel's dominant role in the Middle East. One former American president appears to be among their number. President Reagan, in his October 1983 telephone conversation with AIPAC executive director Thomas A. Dine, turned a discussion of Lebanon's present-day problems into a discourse on biblical prophecy:

> I turn back to your ancient prophets in the Old Testament and the signs foretelling Armageddon and I find myself wondering if . . . we're the generation that's going to see that come about. I don't know if you've noted any of those prophecies lately but, believe me, they certainly describe the times we're going through.[13]

Reagan's views are not unprecedented, even in the Oval Office. His views reflect the wide credence given to biblical prophecy—and its use to justify Israel's existence. George W. Bush, despite his membership in the mainline Methodist Church, has identified himself as born-again.

A Puzzling Paradox

Recognizing Israel as the fulfillment of biblical prophecy implicates the Christian—and, even more so, the Jew—in several paradoxes. First, conservative millennialist Protestants have traditionally sought to convert Jews to Christianity, and relations between the two groups have often been less than cordial. Jews instinctively mistrusted Southern Baptist Jimmy Carter because, as Jewish author Roberta Strauss Feuerlicht writes, "In Jewish history, when fundamentalists came, Cossacks were not far behind."[14]

Ironically, the Christian groups most likely to accept a biblical basis for supporting Israel are also those most likely to feel the necessity of Jewish conversion to Christianity, an extremely sensitive issue to Israelis. Dan Rossing, director of the Department for Christian Communities in the Israeli Ministry of Religious Affairs, states the problem succinctly:

the evangelical "theological scheme clearly implies that Jews have to become Christians—clearly not today, but some day."[15]

Many evangelical organizations carry on missionary activities in the Middle East, particularly in Israel, that are strongly opposed by many Israelis. The evangelists openly proselytize, seeing conversion of the Jews as another precursor of the times that the "recreation" of Israel in 1948 is said to foretell.

The International Christian Embassy in Jerusalem, an organization that works to foster support for Israel in twenty nations, is one of a number of evangelical organizations that have come under fire recently for missionary activity inside Israel. The "embassy" was opened in Jerusalem in October 1980 as a gesture of "international Christian support" for the controversial transfer of the Israeli capital to that city from Tel Aviv.[16]

Despite expressing political support for the state of Israel, the International Christian Embassy devoted some of its efforts to the conversion of Jews to Christianity, an act that made the organization controversial in the eyes of many Israelis. In Israel, Orthodox Jews have been active in pressing for legislation banning foreign missionaries and in organizing opposition against them.[17] Despite the monetary support and goodwill brought to Israel by these organizations, they are widely regarded as Trojan horses. There have even been physical attacks on their members.

The dilemma faced by the Israeli government in dealing with Christian groups such as the International Christian Embassy is essentially the same as that faced by American Jewish groups in forming their relations with conservative Christian groups in the United States.[18] While spokesmen within Israel, such as Rabbi Moshe Berliner, decry the inherent threat to Judaism posed by proselytizing fundamentalists—"Are we so gullible as to take any hand extended to us in friendship?"—the Israeli government under both Begin and Shamir offered an emphatic reply: "Israel will not turn aside a hand stretched out in support of Israel's just cause."[19]

In November 1980 Jerry Falwell was awarded a medal in recognition of his steadfast support of Israel. The award came at a New York dinner marking the hundredth anniversary of the birth of Zionist leader Vladimir Jabotinsky and was made at the behest of Prime Minister Begin. Opposition to the presentation was intense.[20] Henry Siegman, executive director of the American Jewish Congress objected to "the way

[Falwell] conducts his activities and the manner in which he uses religion." In Israel, the *Jerusalem Post* quoted Alexander M. Schindler, former chairman of the Conference of Presidents of Major American Jewish Organizations, as saying that it was "madness and suicide if Jews honor for their support of Israel right-wing evangelists who constitute a danger to the Jews of the United States."[21]

What Schindler meant was illustrated by a remark that Falwell had made at a Sunday service in his own Liberty Baptist Church in Lynchburg, Virginia. He declared that God did not "hear Jewish prayers." He later expressed regret over this remark, but for many Jews, it confirmed their suspicion that Falwell was more interested in their conversion than in the security of Israel. His protestation that "the Jewish people in America and Israel and all over the world have no dearer friend than Jerry Falwell" has not made Jewish leaders forget his fundamentalist religious bias against Judaism, yet they openly continue to cultivate the support of American evangelicals in backing Israel. The paradox is striking.

New View from Mainline Churches

The pro-Israel alliance between American Jews and conservative Protestants emerged at a time of friction between the Jewish community and the mainstream American Christian community. That friction increased with the widespread objection among Christians to the Israeli invasion of Lebanon in 1978.

In September 1981 United Methodist Bishop James Armstrong issued a letter to Indiana United Methodist ministers in which he sharply criticized the "Falwell gospel" and the "Moral Majority mentality." He pointedly observed that:

> Israel was seen as God's "chosen people" in a servant sense. Israel was not given license to exploit other people. God plays no favorites.[22]

Christian concern over events in the Middle East, particularly the suffering of Palestinian refugees, has been a source of tension between Jewish and Christian groups for some time. Although traditional efforts toward ecumenical cooperation between American Judaism and the mainline churches continue—as is reflected in the establishment by the

American Jewish Congress of the Institute for Jewish–Christian Relations—larger denominations have, since the early 1980s, begun to view the Middle East in a new light.[23]

The mainline churches focus more and more on the need to respect the human rights of the Palestinian refugees, as reflected in a series of church policy statements that show more sympathy for the plight of these refugees than many Jewish groups find acceptable.[24] The United States Catholic Conference, United Presbyterian Church, United Methodist Church, American Baptist Churches, United Church of Christ, and others have called for mutual recognition of the Israeli and Palestinian right to self-determination, Palestinian participation in peace negotiations, and Israel's withdrawal from lands occupied in the 1967 war. Several of the churches have identified the PLO as the legitimate representative of the Palestinian people.[25]

As the Reverend Charles Angell, S.A., associate director of Graymoor Ecumenical Institute, observed, for the American churches to commit themselves to such an "evident clash between their position and that of the state of Israel abroad and the majority of the American Jewish organizations at home" represents a break with the past. He feels that the "fundamental shift" occurred after the 1973 war, when Christians responded sympathetically to appeals from the Arab side for a peaceful settlement.

Members of the Jewish community have largely received the statements of the mainline churches as threats to their religious rights. Despite more than forty official statements by Protestant and Catholic organizations in the past two decades condemning anti-Semitism as unchristian, Christian officials who assert the right of all peoples—not just Israelis—to territorial security and a decent standard of living are accused by the Israeli lobby of anti-Semitism.[26]

Christian churches have been accused of "self-delusion" in opposing both anti-Semitism and, at the same time, Israeli government policies that restrict or violate the human rights of Palestinian refugees.[27] Even confirmed humanitarian and pacifist groups such as the Quakers have been branded anti-Semitic for urging greater restraint and mutual understanding upon all of the contending parties of the Middle East. Journalist Ernest Volkmann even sought to pin the anti-Semite label on the Reverend William Howard, president of the National Council of Churches (NCC), for his criticism of the June 1981 Israeli air strike against the Osirak nuclear reactor in Iraq.[28]

The paradox thus becomes compounded: mainline Christians who accept the legitimacy of the Jewish faith but question some policies of the Jewish state are branded anti-Semitic, while evangelical Christians who back Israel but doubt the theological validity of Judaism are welcome as allies. The experience of the NCC is instructive. An NCC insider describes the relationship between the council and the American Jewish community as "the longest case record of Jewish influence, even more than in government." For many years, no one in the Jewish community had serious complaints about the council. Whenever disagreement arose, the Jewish leadership demanded—and usually received—prompt action. As a former NCC official described it, Jewish leaders would come "en masse with the heads of departments of about half a dozen different Jewish agencies and then really lay it out. They felt that they had a special right to get direct input to the council leadership."

The Committee on Christian–Jewish Relations, long a part of the council hierarchy, gave special attention to fostering cooperation and understanding between Christians and Jews in the United States. In addition, Inter-Faith, a division of the NCC devoted to humanitarian programs, was, despite its ecumenical title, for several years composed solely of Jewish and Christian groups.

The Committee on Christian–Jewish Relations has traditionally been known to share whatever information or new council materials it considered important with the American Jewish Committee. This practice was troubling to some council officials, as the committee is not a religious body; although it maintains a religious affairs department, it is mainly a lobbying organization. Jewish organizations of a primarily religious nature, such as the Synagogue Council of America, are not so closely involved in the workings of the council. But because top-level administrators at the NCC are understandably sensitive about the charge of being anti-Israel or insensitive to Jewish concerns in any council actions or publications, the oversight of NCC activities and literature by the American Jewish Committee has been accepted as standard procedure— up to the point of accepting long critiques of proposed materials

A representative of one of the largest Protestant denominations observed that the American Jewish Committee had "much more effect" on the content of NCC study materials than his office, even though his denomination accounted for the purchase and distribution of three-quarters of these publications.

After several years of mounting Jewish criticism—during which the council had debated, but failed to adopt, a number of resolutions on the suffering of Palestinian refugees—the NCC decided in December 1979 to issue a Middle East policy statement. As Allan Solomonow, a frequent commentator on religion, put it, " . . . because of strong Jewish criticism it became apparent that the NCC, which up to that point did not have a clear stand on the Middle East, had to have one." Solomonow also said, "[The consensus was that] the only way to limit criticism was to say exactly what you feel about these issues." But the Middle East policy statement that ultimately appeared was nevertheless unacceptable to many American Jewish groups.

Declaring that "the role of the National Council of the Churches of Christ in the U.S.A. is to seek with others peace, justice, and reconciliation throughout the Middle East," the controversial final section of the statement included a call for control of arms transfers to the Middle East and an appeal for "reciprocal recognition of the right of self-determination" by the government of Israel and the PLO.

The Anti-Defamation League of B'nai B'rith, which had not presented its views in open forum, quickly denounced the statement as "a naive misreading of the contending forces and issues in the Arab–Israeli conflict which can have mischievous consequences."

Pro-Israel writers and commentators seized upon the policy statement as an example of growing anti-Semitism within the NCC—despite the clear emphasis of the text on secure peace for all peoples and denunciation of violent acts on every side. Journalist Ernest Volkmann, in his book *A Legacy of Hate: Anti-Semitism in America*, somehow managed to cite the policy statement as the prime example of "an indifference to American Jews that has occasionally strayed into outright anti-Semitism." *The Campaign to Discredit Israel*, the "enemies list" assembled by AIPAC, goes to the length of claiming that "some segments of the National Council of Churches" are tools of a "systematic effort" to attack Israel's image in the United States. A high-ranking NCC official at the time summed up the matter this way: "For years, no one in the Jewish community had any serious complaints about the National Council; and then, when they started to have political decisions that ran afoul of conventional pro-Israeli opinion, all of a sudden it became anti-Semitic and suspect."

Critics do not like to note, however, that the policy statement recognized the right of Israel to exist as a "sovereign Jewish state" rather than as a "sovereign state," as some on the panel preferred. Butler identified this as "one of the most hotly debated phrases in the policy statement," because some members of the drafting committee refused to vote for the completed document unless it specified the Jewish identity of Israel. The document also explicitly reaffirmed the long and continuing close relationship between the Jewish community and the National Council of Churches.

In April 2002 a delegation of the council, whose general secretary was former Representative Robert Edgar (D-PA), toured the Middle East. Upon its return it issued a statement urging an end to Israel's occupation of the West Bank and Gaza, the establishment of a viable Palestinian state, and "the sharing of Jerusalem by the two peoples and three faiths."[29]

God's Empire Striking Back?

As interest in the Middle East and humanitarian concern for the Palestinian refugees becomes more widespread among Americans of all religious persuasions, many Jewish groups and their pro-Israel allies are more adamant in rejecting open discussion as a means to broader public understanding. Under such pressures, even activist religious groups that are involved in campaigning for social justice and world peace often grow timid when the Middle East becomes a topic of discussion.

In October 1983 the Sacramento Religious Community for Peace (SRCP), a group that works to foster ecumenical cooperation in support of peace and social issues, organized a major symposium, titled "Faith, War, and Peace in the Nuclear Age," at the Sacramento Convention Center. A large number of religious organizations, including the Sacramento Jewish Relations Council, cosponsored the symposium under the auspices of the SRCP. In early September, as publicity for the symposium was being arranged, the Sacramento Peace Center (SPC), another well-established local activist group, asked that a flier publicizing its memorial service for victims of the refugee camp massacres in Lebanon be included in the SRCP mailings for the symposium. Since it is routine for peace organizations in the area to cooperate in this way, Peggy Briggs, codirector of the SPC, was shocked to be informed that the flier would not be included in the promotional mailing.[30]

The SRCP told Briggs that the Sacramento Jewish Community Relations Council—the strongest local Jewish group and a major participant in SRCP activities—had made it known that if the flier appeared in the mailing, Jewish participation in the symposium would be withdrawn. This would have meant not only diminished support from the large local Jewish community, but also the loss of a rabbi who was scheduled as one of the keynote speakers.

Helen Feely, codirector of the SRCP, further informed the SPC that no literature prepared by the SPC Middle East task force could be displayed during the proceedings. In discussing the matter later, Feely was emphatic: "The Middle East task force has absolutely inflamed the Jewish community here, because they do not uphold the right of Israel to exist. That material is just inflammatory."[31]

Greg Degiere, head of the SPC Middle East task force, protested that his group did recognize Israel's right to exist.[32] He pointed out that the SPC called for an end to war in the Middle East, respect for the human rights of all persons in the region, and mutual recognition between Israel and the PLO. The prohibition on discussion of the Middle East, along with the restriction on the center's right to distribute information, was accepted, however, as the cost of Jewish participation in the symposium. Lester Frazen, the rabbi who served as a keynote speaker and thus helped provoke the issue, had unusual credentials for a showdown over free speech. He had boldly asserted his own First Amendment right at the outset of the 1982 Israeli march into Lebanon. He was among the leaders of a Sacramento march, which consisted mainly of fundamentalist Christians, who expressed their joyous support for the invasion with a banner proclaiming: "God's empire is striking back!" Yet Frazen and his backers denied the Sacramento Peace Center the right to memorialize the victims of that invasion or to call for a negotiated end to killing on both sides.

In light of this background, it is not surprising that, although the official title of the gathering was "Faith, War, and Peace in the Nuclear Age," the agenda failed to address conflicts in the Middle East, the region many observers believed to be the most likely center of nuclear confrontation. As Joseph Gerson, peace secretary for the American Friends Service Committee in New England observed, "The Middle East has been the most consistently dangerous nuclear trigger. Presidents Truman,

Eisenhower, Johnson, and Nixon all threatened to use nuclear weapons there. . . ."[33]

The Uproar over Palm Sunday

Despite Jewish–fundamentalist cooperation and the pressures brought to bear against those who publicly advocated negotiation and reconciliation in the Middle East, a few religious leaders had the courage to speak out. Foremost among them was the Very Reverend Francis B. Sayre, who took the occasion of Palm Sunday, 1972, to raise a number of questions to which American Christians are still debating the answers.

Throughout his twenty-seven years as dean of the National Cathedral in Washington, the hearty and dramatic Sayre took controversial stands on a wide variety of public policy issues. In the early fifties he fired some of the first salvos in the campaign to discredit McCarthyism. Declaring the Wisconsin senator's followers "the frightened and credulous collaborators of a servile brand of patriotism" brought Sayre a torrent of hate mail, but the possibility of criticism never caused him to shy away from speaking out on issues that stirred his conscience. He worked as an early advocate of civil rights for blacks, and in the sixties and seventies he stood in the forefront of opposition to the Vietnam War.

Sayre was the grandson of Woodrow Wilson, and his father had been a diplomat, law professor, and eminent Episcopalian layman. Sayre continued the family tradition of leadership, relishing his position as leader of the cathedral's influential congregation. Offered a government post by the newly installed Kennedy administration in 1960, his reply was swift: "No thanks. I already have the best job in Washington."[34]

He once described his role as dean of the cathedral as a "liaison between church and state" and as a platform for "moral guidance" for government leaders. He explained his activism with characteristic candor: "Whoever is appointed dean of a cathedral has in his hand a marvelous instrument, and he's a coward if he doesn't use it."[35]

On Palm Sunday, 1972, Sayre used his prestigious pulpit to deliver a sermon that was perhaps the most powerful—and was certainly one of the most controversial—of his career.[36] He spoke on Jerusalem, identifying the ancient city as a symbol of both the purest yearnings and the darkest anger of the human heart. Historically, he proclaimed, both extremes were embodied in events of the single week between Jesus' triumphal entry into the city and His crucifixion:

> Amidst the pageantry and exultation of Palm Sunday, Jerusalem was the emblem of all man's dreams: a king that will someday come to loose us from every bondage; dream of peace that shall conquer every violence; holiness of heaven driving out the dross of earth.

But just as Jerusalem symbolized "man's yearning for the transcendently good," so did it demonstrate his capacity for "hateful evil":

> Her golden domes are also known as "the Place of the Skull." . . . Jerusalem, in all the pain of her history, remains the sign of our utmost reproach: the zenith of our hope undone by the wanton meanness of men who will not share it with their fellows but choose to kill rather than be overruled by God.

Having recognized Jerusalem as a portrayal of "the terrible ambivalence of the human race about truth, about himself, about God," Sayre spoke compassionately about the meaning of Jerusalem for the people now living in Israel:

> Surely one can sympathize with the loving hope of that little state, which aspires to be the symbol, nay more: the embodiment of a holy peoplehood. For her, Jerusalem is the ancient capital; the city of the temple that housed the sacred Ark of the Covenant. To achieve a government there is . . . the fulfillment of a cherished prayer tempered in suffering, newly answered upon the prowess of her young men and the skill of her generals. Around the world Hosannah has echoed as Jewish armies surged across the open scar that used to divide Arab Jerusalem from the Israeli sector.

Yet Sayre's sermon was fired by a troubled sense that since the military victory of 1967, five years before, something had gone terribly wrong. By 1972 Jerusalem was completely under Israeli control. But, to Sayre, mankind's moral tragedy had been reenacted in Israel's treatment of the city's Arab population. As he saw it, the dream had been tarnished:

> Now oppressed become oppressors. Arabs are deported; Arabs are imprisoned without charge; Arabs are deprived of the patrimony of their lands and

homes; their relatives may not come to settle in Jerusalem; they have neither voice nor happiness in the city that, after all, is the capital of their religious devotion too!

Addressing the moral consequences of the Israeli annexation of Jerusalem, Sayre quoted Dr. Israel Shahak—a Jewish survivor of the Nazi concentration camp at Belsen, a professor at Hebrew University, and a dissenter from Israeli policy—who branded the annexation "an immoral and unjust act," and called for recognition that "the present situation of one community oppressing the other will poison us all, and us Jews first of all."

Sayre explained that Israel's treatment of the Arabs mirrored "that fatal flaw in the human breast that forever leaps to the acclaim of God, only to turn the next instant to the suborning of His will for ours."

He was not the only Washington clergyman to express a theme critical of Israel that day.[37] Dr. Edward Elson, pastor of the National Presbyterian Church and chaplain of the U.S. Senate, chided "those Christians who justify Israel's actions in Jerusalem on the basis that they are the fulfillment of prophecy." And the Armenian Orthodox legate to Washington, Bishop Papken, called on Israel to recognize that "Jerusalem belongs to all men."

But because of his reputation and eminent position in American religion, Sayre was singled out to bear the brunt of the criticism. Rabbi Joshua O. Haberman of the Washington Hebrew Congregation reported to Sayre that the sermon was "so distressing to the Israeli government that there had even been a cabinet meeting on the subject—what to do about this minister who had been friendly always to the Jews but who was so misguided." The response was not long in coming. Two leaders of the Washington Jewish Community Council issued a statement denouncing all three sermons and taking particular exception to the address of Sayre. Drs. Harvey H. Ammerman and Isaac Frank said that Jews, Christians, and Muslims "freely mingle in the reunited city and live and carry on their work in peace." They characterized the Sayre sermon as "an outrageous slander."

The *Washington Post* called Sayre's sermon "an intemperate denunciation of current Israeli policy in Jerusalem."[38] *Washington Post* editors objected to Sayre's assertion that "even as [Israelis] praise their God for the smile of fortune, they begin almost simultaneously to put Him to death." They found the statement "painfully close to a very old, very familiar line of the worst bigotry."

An angry letter to the editor published in the the *Washington Post* dismissed Sayre's sermon as "nonfactual garbage":

> This churchman illustrates well the typical liberal gentile bleeding-heart attitude to the Jews—we'll commiserate with you as long as you're dependent on our goodwill for your survival, and we'll weep for you when you are slaughtered every few years by our coreligionists—but Lordy, don't you start winning and controlling your own destiny! The hell with them, I say.[39]

Several such letters appeared in the Washington press in the weeks after Palm Sunday, yet few challenged Sayre's central contention that Israeli policy did not grant equal treatment to Arabs and Jews living in Jerusalem. The situation in Jerusalem was a matter of fact, subject to relatively easy refutation—or confirmation—through inquiry. Yet Sayre's critics, in the manner of the *Post* editors, largely confined their attacks to the tone and lack of "temperance" in his sermon. Sayre received widespread criticism, not for being wrong, but for being a forthright critic of unjust Israeli policies and therefore, in the eyes of some critics, anti-Semitic. Despite his long career of humanitarian activism, partisans of Israel sought to discredit Sayre himself since they could not discredit his arguments. Writer Ernest Volkmann charged that Sayre demonstrated "mindless pro-Arabism [that] had undone many years of patient effort to improve relations between Christians and Jews."[40]

David A. Clarke of the Southern Christian Leadership Conference wrote to defend Sayre: "I do view with some distrust the emotional rebuttals that follow any question of the propriety of Israeli conduct."[41] He likened such emotionalism to the initial reaction against those who first challenged long-established concepts of racial superiority. Referring to U.S. policy in the Middle East, he expressed gratitude "that one of such intellectual integrity as Dean Sayre has given a differing view so that our perspective will not be one-dimensional."

But influential Christians remained divided in their reaction to the speech. Some shared Sayre's troubled disapproval of Israeli policy in the Holy City. Others continued to invoke the specter of anti-Semitism.

The Reverend Carl McIntire, an outspoken Protestant fundamentalist, took exception to Sayre's sermon in a letter published in the

Washington Star. He and Sayre had clashed previously, when McIntire had sought to disrupt a rally against the Vietnam War at the Washington Cathedral and Sayre had personally ushered him away from the gathering. "The liberals represented by the dean have long since departed from the historic Christian view concerning Israel and Jerusalem," proclaimed McIntire. Describing the 1967 war as "a thrilling example of how to deal with aggressors and the forces backed by Communism," he invoked scriptural justification for Israeli possession of conquered territory:

> It is for those of us who believe the Bible to be the Word of God [to] come now to the assistance of our Jewish neighbors. What God has given them they are entitled to possess, and none of the land that they have won should be bartered away.[42]

Some mainline clergymen joined in the fundamentalist outcry over the Palm Sunday sermon. Two leaders of the Council of Churches of Greater Washington issued a public statement declaring it "distressing and perplexing that men of goodwill should choose the start of this holy week for both Christians and Jews to make pronouncements that would inevitably be construed as anti-Judaic."[43]

Two Catholic clergymen—an official of the secretariat for Catholic–Jewish Relations and a director of the United States Catholic Conference—joined in an attempt to discredit Sayre. First they questioned the propriety of Sayre's quoting Israel Shahak, a dissident, to substantiate his charges of Israeli injustice in Jerusalem: "Is it not too close to the old anti-Semitic stratagem of using passages from the Hebrew prophets in order to scold Jews?"[44] More significant, they asserted that they had "failed to find any evidence of Israeli oppression" during a recent trip to Jerusalem.

Yet an article in *Christianity Today* reported a quite different reaction from the editor of the *United Church Observer,* an official publication of the United Church of Canada. The Reverend A. C. Forrest praised Sayre for "the courage, knowledge, and insight to speak prophetically about one of the most disturbing situations in the world today." Citing UN reports on Jerusalem, he said Sayre's charges "are kind of old stuff to anyone who's done his homework or traveled enough in the Middle East."[45]

Support for Sayre was voiced by Jesuit educator Joseph L. Ryan of Georgetown University.[46] Explaining that he spoke in response to the

injunction of Pope Paul VI—"If you wish peace, work for justice"—
Father Ryan cited statements by the pope and by Catholic leaders in several Middle Eastern countries expressing concern about Israeli actions in
Jerusalem and about the misery of Palestinian refugees. He pointed out
that Israeli oppression of Christians and Muslims in Jerusalem was doc-
umented by publications of the Israeli League for Human Rights and the
United Nations. "There is no dearth of evidence," he wrote. "If the public raising of these cases of oppression is shocking, the reality is incom-
parably more shocking."

Father Ryan reserved his strongest language for criticizing unques-
tioning Christian supporters of Israeli policies:

> Further, a few Catholics and Protestants propagate the insinuation that to
> be anti-Zionist (that is, critical of Israel) is to be anti-Semitic. In their anx-
> iety to wipe out racism, these spokesmen go to extremes. This insinuation,
> which they try to make widespread, hinders instead of helps the develop-
> ment of proper relations between Christians and Jews, and inhibits the free
> and open discussion of fundamental differences [that] for Americans as cit-
> izens of their country and of the world community is essential in the search
> for justice and peace.

Sayre remained largely detached from the tempest he had stirred on
Palm Sunday. His only public action was to state through an aide that
he would not retract any of his comments. Years later he acknowledged
that, while he had given previous sermons on the plight of the Palestinian refugees, the 1972 Palm Sunday address was his first direct criticism
of Israel. "Of course I realized that it would make a big splash," he said.
"But if you put it more mildly, as I had [previously], it made no dent at
all. So what are you going to do?"[47]

Prior to the controversial sermon, Sayre had enjoyed high standing
with the American Jewish community. A local Jewish congregation, at
Sayre's invitation, held services in the cathedral until its synagogue was
built. Jews respected him for the work he had done as president of the
United States Committee for Refugees. In this capacity he had worked
to resettle Jews from Jordan, Syria, and Lebanon. As an Episcopal minister in Cleveland after World War II, he had been head of the dio-
cese's committee to settle refugees, many of them Jews, from Eastern
Europe.

The sermon had personal implications. Sayre and his family experienced a campaign of "very unpleasant direct intimidation" through letters and telephone calls. On a number of occasions, when his children answered the phone they were shouted at and verbally abused. The phone would ring in the middle of the night, only to be hung up as soon as a member of the Sayre family answered. "Even when I went out, I would be accosted rudely by somebody or other who would condemn me in a loud voice," he recalled. Such harassment continued for about six months, Sayre said, "even to the point where my life was threatened over the phone; so much so that I had the cathedral guards around the house for a while."

The ecumenical spirit between Sayre and community rabbis was strained again six months after the sermon. When eleven Israeli athletes were killed at the 1972 Olympic Games in Munich while being held captive by the radical "Black September" guerrillas, Sayre shared the shock and revulsion felt around the world. Together with rabbis and other Jewish leaders in Washington, he immediately began to plan a memorial service in the cathedral.

Three days after the tragedy, Israeli warplanes attacked Palestinian camps in Syria and Lebanon, killing forty people.[48] Sayre then told the rabbis of his intention to "make this a more general service than just for victims of Arab killing" and to memorialize the dead Palestinians as well.

Confronted with this prospect, the rabbis declined to participate. There were, however, a number of Jews among the approximately 500 persons who attended the broadened memorial service. They heard Sayre describe the Arab guerrillas as "misguided and desperately misled" victims "of all the bitterness their lives had been surrounded with since birth, bitterness born of issues left callously unresolved by any international conscience."[49]

He condemned the Israeli retaliation: "An eye for an eye, tooth for tooth is the rationale of that violence, by which I am desolate to think the government of Israel has sacrificed any moral position of injured innocence." The dean invoked the broader historical and humanitarian view that had marked his Palm Sunday sermon in words that might well be repeated for every victim of Middle East violence:

I perceive that the victim of the violence that we mourn today is not only a latter-day Jew upon the blood-stained soil of Germany, nor yet the Arab prisoner of an equally violent heritage. The victim is all of us, the whole human race upon this earth.[50]

Despite these words, Sayre was treated as though he somehow was a preacher of extremism. His career never had quite the shine it had before he uttered his forthright words on the Middle East. Sayre went into semiretirement on Martha's Vineyard, where he served as chaplain at the local hospital but assumed no regular church responsibilities. One morning in 1983, I delayed his project for the morning—digging clams—to ask if the controversial Palm Sunday message had any effect on his career. Still robust in voice and spirit, Sayre answered without hesitation: "Yes, very definitely. I knew it would. It's not popular to speak out. I don't like to speculate about it, because no one knows what would have happened. But I think I was a dangerous commodity from then on, not to be considered for bishop or anything else."

"I Felt I Had to Do Something"

The American religious community has seen few figures of the stature of Francis Sayre willing to speak out forcefully for peace and justice for all Middle East peoples. At the time of the Palm Sunday sermon in 1972, he was one of the most prominent spokesmen of American Christianity—a powerful and intellectually gifted man wielding the authority of Washington Cathedral's prestigious pulpit. Despite the price Sayre paid for his courageous stand, younger voices have emerged that express similar resolve and depth of commitment.

The Reverend Don Wagner, a Presbyterian from Chicago, has risen quickly to the forefront of those within the religious community who seek to educate the public on realities in the Middle East and to counter the religious bias that often obscures awareness of those realities. His experiences have also brought him firsthand acquaintance with the intimidation that such efforts call forth.

Wagner first became involved in public debate over the Middle East while serving as associate pastor of a large Presbyterian church in

Evanston, Illinois. At the time he was, in his own words, "very pro-Israel." In the wake of the first oil crisis, in 1974 the young pastor helped organize a series of speakers within the church, alternating between pro-Israeli and pro-Arab points of view. He felt the series would aid his parishioners to better understand this unprecedented event. Wagner was quite surprised when, halfway through it, he began receiving pressure to stop the series. A barrage of anonymous telephone calls threatened picketing outside the church and more severe, unspecified reprisals if the series continued.

Wagner did not stop. In the end, however, the series was marred by the refusal of two Jewish members of the final panel to take part. They announced a half-hour before the scheduled discussion that the presence of an Arab academic on the panel rendered the event anti-Semitic and that they consequently refused to dignify it with their presence. They implied that Wagner had deceived them about the makeup of the panel and the nature of the discussion, although the topic of the discussion and the list of participants had been publicized well in advance.

Wagner suspected that these men had been pressured by their rabbis to quit the conference. This suspicion was reinforced later when he learned that many of the earlier telephone calls had also been from members of the local Jewish community. One of the callers even told him directly: "I am a Jew, and this kind of activity is very anti-Semitic. For a Christian to be doing this is unconscionable." This experience was an eye-opener for Wagner. He discovered, as have others who have dared to speak out and become involved, that one need not actually criticize the Jewish people or the state of Israel to be labeled anti-Semitic. Simply raising questions about Middle East issues and assuming that the answers may not all be obvious is enough to evoke the charge.

Wagner first traveled to the Middle East in 1977. He paid his own way but traveled with representatives of the Palestine Human Rights Campaign (PHRC), an organization concerned with the protection of Palestinian rights. After spending time with refugees and other residents in Beirut, the West Bank, and Jerusalem, Wagner felt his long-standing sympathy for the displaced Palestinian refugees growing into a strong personal imperative. "I felt I had to do something," he recalled.

After his return to the United States, he learned how difficult it could be to "do something." Shortly before his departure for the Middle East, Wagner had arranged a church speaking engagement for Dr. Israel Shahak, a prominent critic of Israeli government policy. He returned to discover that the senior minister of his church had acceded to pressure from local rabbis to cancel the Shahak engagement without informing either him or Shahak. The senior minister explained that the local rabbis had convinced him that it would be "in the best interests of the church and Jewish relations" if the appearance of such a well-known critic of Israeli policy were canceled.

Undeterred, Wagner became increasingly active in speaking up about the Palestinian plight, offering Sunday morning prayers for the refugees, promoting more educational activities, and even bringing Palestinian Christians to his pulpit to speak. His activities led not only to a continuation of public criticism and pressure, but also to problems within the staff of his own church as well. One associate frequently referred to him as "the PLO pastor," and staff friction grew as Wagner proceeded with plans for the First LaGrange Conference (LaGrange I), named for the Illinois town in which it was held in the spring of 1979.

This conference, like LaGrange II, which would follow in May 1981, was aimed at raising awareness of the Palestinian refugee situation among American church groups and leaders. Both meetings were attended by a broad ecumenical body of Christians, including Evangelical, mainline Protestant, Roman Catholic, and Orthodox. The first conference was jointly sponsored by PHRC and the Middle East task force of the Chicago Presbytery. The second was sponsored by PHRC and the Christian peace groups Pax Christi and Sojourners. The theme of these conferences was summed up in the title of LaGrange II: "Toward Biblical Foundations for a Just Peace in the Holy Land."

After a series of speakers and panels was presented, each conference issued a statement. These two documents have become a topic of debate within the American religious community. The statements stress the common humanity of Arabs, Jews, and Christians and call upon the American Christian churches to be more active in spreading information and promoting reconciliation and peace. Specifically, the churches are enjoined to "encourage dialogue with other Christians as well as Jews and others concerning the priorities of peace in the Holy Land" and to "inform and educate their people of the historical roots of the Israeli–Palestinian conflict."

The participants in LaGrange I and II made a significant step in ecumenical cooperation for greater public understanding of the Middle East. Unfortunately, opponents of cooperation and understanding were also in attendance.

Prior to the convening of LaGrange I, the Chicago Presbytery received pressure from the local chapter of the Anti-Defamation League, led by associate director Rabbi Yechiel Eckstein, to withdraw Presbyterian sponsorship of the conference. There were telephone calls, an extensive letter writing campaign, and, finally, meetings between Jewish leaders and members of the church hierarchy.

The elders of the church stood by Wagner, but the Jewish community promptly passed judgment on the conference. The day before the conference convened, the ADL issued a press release condemning its "anti-Semitic bias."

Efforts to discredit the conference did not end there. The slate of speakers had been planned to include the Reverend John Polakowski, a noted writer on the Holocaust and an active Zionist. On the morning of the conference Father Polakowski sent a registered letter to Wagner announcing his withdrawal from the conference. He had been fully informed as to the nature of the conference and the identity of many of the other speakers, but he denounced the conference as unfairly biased against the Israeli perspective.[51] He fulfilled his own prophecy. His decision to deprive the conference of his own perspective caused the Zionist view to be underrepresented at LaGrange I.

LaGrange II witnessed a virtual repeat of the same tactic. Rabbi Arnold Kaiman had agreed to address a section of the conference entitled "Religious People Talking from Their Perspectives." He had been invited to speak partly because of his long-standing personal friendship with Ayoub Talhami, coconvenor of the conference. Talhami had discussed the planned conference with Rabbi Kaiman in detail and sent him a draft copy of the conference flier, and, of course, the rabbi was aware of the previous conference. On the day of the conference Kaiman sent a special delivery letter to Wagner, Talhami, and others announcing his withdrawal from the conference.[52] The letter denounced Talhami and the convenors of the conference for having "misled" and "deceived" him. Talhami felt that the letter was intended mainly for Kaiman's congregational board, both because the chairman of that board was a coaddressee of the letter and because the accusations of deceit were so preposterous.

Whatever his reasons, Kaiman did more than refuse to speak and repudiate the conference. He provided copies of his letter to reporters so that the withdrawal of a pro-Zionist could be publicized before the conference could issue its statement.

To Wagner, the last-minute withdrawals of Polakowski and Kaiman, each made after it was too late to schedule other pro-Israel speakers, suggested that these supporters of Israel were more concerned with discrediting opposing points of view than with stating their own in an atmosphere of free and open debate. These withdrawals added color to subsequent ADL charges that the LaGrange conferences were "anti-Israel conferences" or "PLO gatherings," despite the balanced character of the statements that emerged from the conferences.

The most disturbing incident to emerge from LaGrange I and II, however, did not involve attempts to discredit the conferences themselves, but were the false charges made against one of the participants.

Sister Miriam Ward, a professor of humanities at Trinity College in Vermont and a Catholic nun, has a long record of humanitarian concern for Palestinian refugees. By her own description, her role in LaGrange II was modest. "I had doubts about whether I could justify the expense of going," she once said. Sister Miriam moderated a panel discussion and received an award for her humanitarian endeavors. Like Mr. Wagner, she knew from experience the price of speaking out on Palestinian questions. Her activities had also attracted hate mail and personal innuendoes. Still, she was not prepared for the smear that resulted from her participation at LaGrange.[53]

Sister Miriam was singled out for a personal attack in *The Jewish Week–American Examiner,* a prominent New York City Jewish publication. The June 21, 1981, issue gave significant coverage to a scheme to disrupt Israeli policy on the occupied West Bank—a scheme that Sister Miriam had supposedly advanced at the conference. The article claimed that she had urged that "churches finance a project with staff in the United States and field-workers in Israel and the West Bank for the purpose of 'spying on the Israelis.' "[54] She was reported saying, "By the time the Israelis caught on to what was going on and expelled a field-worker, they [presumably Sister Miriam and her coconspirators] would have a replacement ready." The *Jewish Week* article added that "the proposal was accepted without dissent, and ways of obtaining church funds for it were discussed."

The report was a complete fabrication. No one at the LaGrange conference had suggested such a plan, least of all Sister Miriam, and she
was stunned when Wagner telephoned from Chicago to inform her of the
printed allegations. She had always shunned publicity for her humanitarian activities, and she felt intimidated and intensely alone at being
singled out for attack. "I was physically ill for some time," she recalls,
"and could not even discuss the matter with other members of my religious community."[55]

After pondering how—and whether—to respond, she finally sought
the advice of a prominent biblical scholar who was lecturing at Trinity
College. He advised her to see an attorney about the possibility of legal
action. The attorney was sympathetic and agreed to take at least preliminary action free of charge. After several letters from the attorney
elicited no response from the newspaper, the scholar, a prominent member of the New York Jewish community, personally telephoned the editor. Sister Miriam feels that it was his call that impelled the editor to act.

In January 1982—more than six months after the original charges
had been asserted—a retraction was finally printed in *The Jewish
Week–American Examiner*.[56] The editors admitted that, "on checking, we
find that there is no basis for the quotations attributed to" Sister Miriam.
They explained that the story had been "furnished by a service" and "was
not covered by any staff member of *The Jewish Week*." In their retraction, the editors added that they were "happy to withdraw any reflection
upon" Sister Miriam.

Yet, as Sister Miriam discovered, the published apology could not
erase the original charge from the minds of all readers. Later the same
year, a Jewish physician from New York was visiting Burlington as part
of a campus program at Trinity College. In a conversation between this
woman and another member of Sister Miriam's religious order, the name
of the biblical scholar involved in Sister Miriam's case came up. The nun
mentioned that he had recently visited Trinity at the invitation of Sister
Miriam. Recognizing the name from the original *Jewish Week* article, the
physician repeated with indignation the accusations made against Sister
Miriam. She had not seen the retraction. The visitor was quickly
informed that the charges were false. Sister Miriam cited this as an example of why she is convinced that the damage to her reputation can never

really be undone. "It's the original thing that does the harm. I just don't want it to happen to anybody else."[57]

"God Will Pour Out His Wrath"

With the September 2000 onset of the Palestinian *intifada*—commonly translated as "uprising"—the tenuous relationship between Zionist Jews and evangelical Christians became even more sharply defined. As reports of Israeli brutality reached Americans, the Christian community divided into two main groups: those whose faith compelled them to work on behalf of Palestinians suffering under occupation, and those who sought the fulfillment of God's prophecy—a Jewish Jerusalem, and the Temple rebuilt. Regardless of the position taken, the Israeli–Palestinian issue came to the forefront of debate in Christian America.

"I don't think anything since Vietnam or apartheid has had the impact [in Christian communities] that this is having," said Stephen Swecker, editor of Zion's *Herald* magazine of Christian opinion. "It hits very close to the heart when you see . . . the Church of the Nativity under siege and sniper fire lighting up the site where Jesus was born."[58]

Despite the danger posed to Christian holy sites by Israeli occupying forces, leaders of the Christian right remained staunch in their support of Israel. One of them, Ralph Reed, former Christian Coalition director, chair of Georgia's Republican Party, and a man previously criticized by the Jewish Anti-Defamation League (ADL) for a perceived lack of tolerance, now writes an op-ed piece that the ADL places in national newspaper advertisements.[59]

Other Jewish groups also welcome Christian support: Toward Tradition, headed by a rabbi, encourages American Jews to recognize "Israel's best friend"—the Christian right. Judy Hellman, in charge of the Kansas City Jewish Committee's Community Relations Board, put it best: "I think it's called pragmatism." National ADL director Abraham Foxman agreed: "Our tradition teaches us to say thank you. We don't need to do more." As long as the Christian right is unflinching in its support of Israel, and as long as that support isn't expected to be returned, Jewish Zionist groups will continue to welcome any help they can get.

As usual, these groups take their cue from the Israeli government. At a New York pro-Israel rally, Israeli consul general Alon Pinkas said that Israelis were "very thankful for the commitment of the Evangelical Christian community." As well they should be. Much of that commitment has its roots in Israeli public relations activity. Suffering a loss of tourism revenues and serious economic damage as a result of the new *intifada*, Israel's Ministry of Tourism hired TouchPoint Solutions, a Colorado consulting agency, to target Christian Zionists and encourage support of Israel. According to Auburn University Professor of Religious Studies Richard Penaskovic:

> Part of the marketing plan involves persuading the top thirty evangelical Zionists to visit and promote Israel. Some of the top evangelical Zionists will receive expense-paid trips to the Holy Land, and the Israeli government has had strategy sessions with the Christian Coalition, headed by Pat Robertson, and other conservative Christian groups.[60]

Israel's efforts in garnering even more support from the Christian right took quick effect. In May 2002, fundamentalist Christians cooperated in several pro-Israel rallies. For example, several hundred people gathered in Nashville to encourage the Tennessee legislature to pass a resolution supporting Israel. One of the Christian sponsors, citing Old Testament scripture, warned the gathering, "God will pour out his wrath among the nations because they are dividing up the land of Israel." About 2,000 attended a similar rally in Memphis.[61]

Despite this outspoken support, many American Jews are hesitant to fully embrace the Christian right as allies in a mutual cause. The question of true intentions comes up again and again. In a speech at a Baptist church, U.S. House of Representatives majority whip Tom DeLay (R-TX), a longtime Israel supporter, said, "Only Christianity offers a comprehensive worldview that covers all areas of life and thought. Only Christianity offers a way to live in response to the realities that we find in this world—only Christianity." The comment prompted a harsh response from the National Jewish Democratic Counsel: "His exclusionist, fundamentalist Christian worldview . . . is indicative of why the American Jewish community will always be uncomfortable with Christian conservative leaders, regardless of their strong support for Israel."[62]

10

Not All Jews Toe the Line

THE FIRST EDITION of this book explained how the U.S. lobby for Israel is able to manipulate U.S. policy in the Middle East, but it did not explain fully why the Israeli government, in the face of worldwide opposition—except in the United States—carried forward its expensive expansionist policies in the occupied territories. It was clear that the settlements were unpopular among many Israelis and a vexing thorn in the side of Israeli officials, as they were costly to subsidize and had become the main focus of international criticism of Israel.

Clearing the Path for the Messiah[1]

A scholarly study by Vincent James Abramo, a veteran federal employee, showed that the settlements are deeply rooted in religion. A little-noted factor in the Middle East imbroglio is the rising power of ultraorthodox Jews in Israeli and U.S. politics. Their core beliefs demand implacable opposition to the establishment of an independent Palestinian state on any part of the West Bank, part of the area seized by Israeli forces in the June 1967 Arab–Israeli war and identified in the Bible as Judea and

Samaria. Ultraorthodox interpretations of Judaic law that are found in the Torah, Talmud, and Halakhah prohibit Jews from sharing power with non-Jews in the "Land of Israel."

In April 2002, a convention of Sharon's Likud Party voted to oppose Palestinian statehood. The vote was seen as an appeal for continued support from ultraorthodox Jews and as an intra-party victory for former Prime Minister Benyamin Netanyahu, who was expected to oppose Sharon in the next Israeli election. Always a factor in Israeli politics, orthodox Jews became a powerhouse in the past decade. In his study of Orthodox Judaism, Abramo wrote: "The success of the religious parties in the 1996 and 1999 Israeli national elections vastly increased the influence of orthodox Jews in the Israeli political process. Politically influential and highly visible orthodox rabbis seek to convince Israel's religiously observant Jews that the Messiah will not arrive until Jews establish themselves as sole rulers in the biblical Land of Israel. They believe that any governmental compromise to return biblical lands to the Palestinians in exchange for a peace agreement is, in the eyes of God, a treacherous and punishable act. The orthodox are committed to derailing all Israeli government and international peace initiatives that would force them to give up any part of Jewish sovereignty, political autonomy, and administrative control over all of Israel's biblical land." Abramo estimated that 20 percent of Israel's Jewish population is committed to these beliefs and ideology. This small percentage has proved adequate to be decisive in close elections.

Orthodox Jews promoted the expansion of settlements and sanctioned violent acts by Jewish extremists. The Orthodox goal is simply the expulsion of the Palestinians from the West Bank. The late Professor Israel Shahak, a survivor of a Nazi concentration camp who became a leading champion of Palestinian rights, wrote of Orthodox leaders: "All were outwardly dovish but employed formulas which could be manipulated in the most extreme anti-Arab sense." In 1993, they mobilized against the Oslo Accords, which contemplated an eventual Palestinian state in the West Bank. They can be expected to marshal all possible resources against U.S. pressure for a Palestine state.

The ruthless tactics employed by Israel's right-wing Orthodox parties assure that they will remain a major factor in Israeli politics for years to come, no matter what Israeli party coalitions may be established.

Abramo warned of possible Jewish violence in the United States: "Continued U.S. pressure to compromise on East Jerusalem, the Temple Mount, and the right of return for an estimated 3.2 million Palestinians creates a scenario that could see the United States as a potential target of Jewish extremism in the future."

Aramo deplored the U.S. tendency to perceive Israel "as a like-minded country with similar democratic values." He warned, "This mirror-imaging has proven to be dangerous and misleading, because it deflects attention away from the powerful undercurrent of [orthodox Jewish] religion as a driving force in Israeli political life."

"It Is Not for Us to Speak Our Minds"

Despite the power of the Orthodox right, a number of Israel's most outspoken critics have been Jews themselves. In its efforts to quell criticism of Israel, the pro-Israel community's first goal is to still Jewish critics. In this quest it receives strong support from the Israeli government.

Every government of Israel gives high priority to maintaining unity among U.S. Jews. This unity is regarded as a main line of Israel's defense—second in importance only to the Israeli army—and essential to retaining the support that Israel must have from the United States government.

American Jews are made to feel guilty about enjoying safety and the good life in the United States while their fellow Jews in Israel hold the ramparts, pay high taxes, and fight wars. As Rabbi Balfour Brickner stated: "We hide behind the argument that it is not for us to speak our minds because the Israelis have to pay the price." One Jewish reporter attributed Jewish silence to an organized enforcement campaign: "I have often been told—verbally, in Jewish publications, and in synagogues—that even if I have doubts about the Israeli government and its treatment of Palestinians, I should keep quiet about it and be steadfast in my support of a nation that needs to exist."[2]

For most Jews, open criticism of Israeli policy is unthinkable. The theme is survival—survival of the Zionist dream, of Judaism, of Jews themselves. The fact that the Jewish community in the United States has produced little debate in recent years on Middle East questions even within its own ranks does not mean that all its members are in agreement.

Trampled to Death

Of the more than 200 principal Jewish organizations functioning on a national scale, only a few, like the New Jewish Agenda and its predecessor, Breira, have challenged any stated policy of the Israeli government

In return for their occasional criticism of Israel's policies, the two organizations were ostracized and kept out of the organized Jewish community. Breira lasted only five years. Organized in 1973, its peak national membership was about 1,000. Named for the Hebrew word meaning "alternative," it called on Jewish institutions to be "open to serious debate," and proposed "a comprehensive peace between Israel, the Arab states, and a Palestinian homeland that is ready to live in peace alongside Israel." Prominent in its leadership were Rabbis Arnold Jacob Wolf, David Wolf Silverman, Max Ticktin, David Saperstein, and Balfour Brickner.

The *National Journal* reports that Briera was "bitterly attacked by many leaders of the Jewish establishment" and that a Breira meeting was "invaded and ransacked" by members of the militant Jewish Defense League. Some members of Breira came under intense pressure to quit either the organization or their jobs. Jewish leaders were warned to avoid Breira or fund-raising would be hurt.[3]

Israeli officials joined rabbis in denouncing the organization. Carolyn Toll, a reporter for the *Chicago Tribune* who had been on the board of directors of Breira, quoted a rabbi: "My bridges are burned. Once you take a position like this [challenging Israeli positions], the organized Jewish community closes you out."[4] Officials from the Israeli consulates in Boston and Philadelphia warned Jews against attending a Breira conference.

Breira came under attack from both right and left within the Jewish community. A pamphlet branding some of its members as "radicals" was quoted by Jewish publications and later distributed by AIPAC. Breira was accused of being allied with the radical U.S. Labor Party. An unsigned "fact sheet" suggested that the organization was really a group of Jewish radicals supporting the PLO.[5] The *Seattle Jewish Transcript* said it was run by a "coterie of leftist revolutionaries" who opposed Israel.[6]

Irving Howe, speaking at the final national conference of Breira in 1977, said that the tactics used to smear the organization were an "outrage such as we have not known for a long time in the Jewish community."[7] At the same meeting, retired Israeli General Mattityahu Peled, who was often boycotted by Jewish groups while on U.S. lecture tours, said, "The pressure applied on those who hold dissenting views here [in the United States] is far greater than the pressure on us in Israel. I would say that probably we in Israel enjoy a larger degree of tolerance than you do here within the Jewish community."[8] Breira disbanded shortly after that conference.

In December 1980, 700 American Jews gathered in Washington, D.C., to found another organization of dissenters, the New Jewish Agenda.[9] Composed mainly of young liberals, it called for "compromise through negotiations with the Palestinian people and Israel's Arab neighbors," and it opposed Israeli policies in the West Bank and Lebanon.

It was soon barred from associating with other Jewish groups. In June 1983, its Washington, D.C., chapter was refused membership in the Jewish Community Council, a group that included 260 religious, educational, fraternal, and social service organizations. The council members voted 98–70 to overturn the recommendation of the group's executive board, which had voted 22–5 for the organization's admission.[10] Irwin Stein, president of the Washington chapter of the Zionist Organization of America, charged that the group was "far out" and "pro-Arab rather than pro-Israel."[11] Moe Rodenstein, representing the New Jewish Agenda, said the group would like to be a part of "the debate" and added, "We're proud of what we're doing."[12]

"It Is a Form of McCarthyism"

Like Jewish organizations, individual Jews rarely express public disagreement with Israel policies, despite the broad and fundamental differences they seem to hold. The handful who have spoken up have had few followers and even fewer defenders. To Carolyn Toll, the taboo against criticism was powerful and extensive:

> I believe even Jews [when they are] outside the Jewish community are affected by internal taboos on discussion—for if one is discouraged from bringing up certain subjects within the Jewish community, think how much more disloyal it could be to raise them outside![13]

Toll lamented the "suppression of free speech in American Jewish institutions—the pressures that prevent dovish or dissident Jews from organizing in synagogues, Jewish community centers, and meetings of major national Jewish organizations." She also lamented the denunciations of American Friends Service Committee representatives as "anti-Semitics" and "dupes of the Palestine Liberation Organization" for insisting that "any true peace must include a viable state for the Palestinians."

A successful Jewish author suffered a different type of "excommunication" when she wrote a book that was critical of Israel.[14] In *The Fate of the Jews,* a candid and anguished history of U.S. Jewry and its present-day dilemma, Roberta Strauss Feuerlicht explained that Zionism has become the "religion" for many Jews. This is why, she wrote, that "opposition to Zionism or criticism of Israel is now heresy and cause for excommunication," adding that the idealism attributed to Israel by most supporters has been marred by years of "patriotism, nationalism, chauvinism, and expansionism." She declared, "Israel shields itself from legitimate criticism by calling her critics anti-Semitic; it is a form of McCarthyism and fatally effective."

A year after its publication in 1983 by Times Books, the book was still largely ignored. The *Los Angeles Times* was the only major newspaper to review it.[15] The publisher undertook no advertising, nor even a minimal promotional tour. Feuerlicht, the author of fifteen successful books, was subjected to what Mark A. Bruzonsky, another Jewish journalist, described as a "combination of slander and neglect." When copies sent to prominent "liberal Jews, Christians, civil libertarians and blacks" brought no response, Feuerlicht concluded, "It would seem that with universal assent, the book is being stoned to death with silence."

Other Jews who dare voice guarded criticism of Israel encounter threats that are far from silent. Threatening phone calls became a part of life for Gail Pressberg of Philadelphia, a Jewish member of the professional staff of the American Friends Service Committee. In her work she was active in projects supporting the Palestinian cause. She reported that abuse calls were so frequent that "I don't pay any attention anymore." One evening, after receiving several calls on her unlisted telephone in which her life was threatened for "deserting Israel," in desperation she left the receiver off the hook. A few minutes later the same voice called on her roommate's phone, also unlisted, resuming the threats.[16]

In my twenty-two years in Congress, I can recall no entry in the *Congressional Record* that discloses a speech that was critical of Israeli policy and was presented by a Jewish member of the House or Senate. Jewish members may voice discontent in private conversation but never on the public record. Only a few Jewish academicians, such as Noam Chomsky, a distinguished linguist, have spoken out. Most of those are, like Chomsky, protected in their careers by tenure and are thus able to become controversial without jeopardizing their positions.

"Dissent Becomes Treason"

Journalism is the occupation in which Jews most often and most consistently voice criticism of Israel. Richard Cohen of the *Washington Post* is a notable example.

During Israel's 1982 invasion of Lebanon, Cohen warned: ". . . The administration can send Begin a message that he does not have an infinite line of credit in America—that we will not, for instance, approve the bombing of innocent civilians."

In a later column, Cohen summarized the reaction to his criticism of Israeli policy: "My phone these days is an instrument of torture. Merely to answer it runs the risk of being insulted. The mail is equally bad. The letters are vicious, some of them quite personal."[17] He noted that U.S. Jews are held to a different standard than Israelis when they question Israel's policies:

> Here dissent becomes treason—and treason not to a state or even an ideal (Zionism), but to a people. There is tremendous pressure for conformity, to show a united front and to adopt the view that what is best for Israel is something only the government there can know.

In a world in which there are plenty of people who hate Jews, it *is* ridiculous to manufacture a whole new category out of nothing more than criticism of the Begin government. Nothing could be worse for Israel in the long run than for its friends not to distinguish between when it is right and when it is wrong.

His reference to anti-Semitism was ironic. In April 2002, Cohen published an editorial in the *Washington Post* entitled "Who's Anti-Semitic?" in which he criticized the tendency in America to automatically portray critics of Israel as anti-Semites:

> Here, criticism of Israel, particularly anti-Zionism, is equated with anti-Semitism. The Anti-Defamation League, one of the most important Jewish organizations, comes right out and says so. "Anti-Zionism is showing its true colors as deep-rooted anti-Semitism," the organization says.

Cohen found this position ridiculous:

> To protest living conditions on the West Bank is not anti-Semitism. To condemn the increasing encroachment of Jewish settlements is not anti-Semitism.

On the other hand, he noted, "To turn a deaf ear to the demands of Palestinians, to dehumanize them all as bigots, only exacerbates the hatred on both sides. The Palestinians do have a case."[18]

Mark Bruzonsky, a persistent journalistic critic of Israeli excesses, once said, "There's no way in the world that a Jew can avoid a savage and personal vendetta if his intent is to write a truthful and meaningful account of what he has experienced."

He may be right. Being Jewish did not spare the foreign news editor of Hearst newspapers from such problems. In early 1981 John Wallach produced a television documentary, *Israel and Palestinians: Will Reason Prevail?* It was funded by the Foundation for Middle East Peace, a nonprofit institute established by Washington lawyer Merle Thorpe, Jr. Wallach's goal was to offer a fair, balanced presentation of the problems confronting Israel in dealing with the Palestinians on the West Bank and Gaza. Before the film was produced, Israeli Ambassador Simcha Dinitz called Wallach, urging him to drop the project. When Wallach persisted, invitations to receptions and dinners at the Israeli embassy suddenly stopped. For a time he was not even notified of press briefings.

Public television broadcast the program without incident in Washington, D.C., New York, and other major cities, but Jewish leaders in Los Angeles demanded an advance showing.[19] Upon seeing the film, they put up such a strong protest that station KCT inserted a statement disclaiming any responsibility for the content of the documentary.

Wallach received many complaints about the presentation, the most common being that it portrayed Palestinian children in a favorable light—some were blond and blue-eyed, and all were attractive—a departure from the frequently negative stereotype of Palestinians.

Wallach found himself in hot water again in 1982, when controversy erupted after a formal dinner he had organized to recognize Ambassador Philip Habib's diplomatic endeavors in Lebanon. Several cabinet officers, congressmen, and members of the diplomatic community attended. During the program, messages from several heads of government were read. Wallach asked Senator Charles Percy, chairman of the Foreign Relations Committee, to read the one from Israel's Prime Minister Menachem Begin to the audience. On Wallach's recommendation, Percy did not read these two sentences:

> In the wake of the Operation Peace in Galilee, Phil Habib made great efforts to bring about the evacuation of the bulk of the terrorists from Beirut and Lebanon. He worked hard to achieve this goal and, with the victory of the Israel Defense Forces, his diplomatic endeavors contributed to the dismantling of that center of international terrorism, which had been a danger to all free nations.

Moshe Arens, the Israeli ambassador, was furious. He sent an angry letter to Percy expressing his shock and stating, "Although I realize that you may not have agreed with its contents, . . . this glaring omission seems to me to be without precedent." He also wrote to Wallach, complaining of "unprecedented discourtesy" and calling the omission an attempt to "cater to the ostrich-like attitude of some of the ambassadors from Arab countries." Arens also wrote protest letters to the management of Hearst Corporation, which had picked up the tab for the dinner.

Wallach told another journalist the next day why he had recommended the omission: "I thought it was insulting to the Arabs [who were present] to have a message about war and terrorism at an evening that was a tribute to Phil Habib and peace."[20] Wallach said, "The irony was that, while I got lots of harsh, critical mail from those supporting Begin, I got no words of support or commendation from the other side. It makes one wonder—when there is no support, only criticism, when one risks his career."[21]

Similar questions were raised by Nat Hentoff, a Jewish columnist who frequently criticizes Israel and challenges the conscience of his fellow

Jews in his column for the *Village Voice*. During the Israeli invasion of
Lebanon in 1982 he lamented:

> At no time during his visit here [in the United States] was [Prime Minister]
> Begin given any indication that there are some of us who fear that he and
> Ariel Sharon are destroying Israel from within. Forget the Conference of
> Presidents of Major American Jewish Organizations and the groups they
> represent. They have long since decided to say nothing in public that is crit-
> ical of Israel.[22]

Hentoff deplored the intimidation that silences most Jewish critics:

> I know staff workers for the American Jewish Congress and the American
> Jewish Committee who agonize about their failure to speak out, even on
> their own time, against Israeli injustice. They don't, because they figure
> they'll get fired if they do.

Indeed, the threat of being fired was forcefully put to a group of
employees of Jewish organizations in the United States during a 1982
tour of Lebanon. Israel's invasion was at its peak, and a number of
employees of the Jewish National Fund (JNF)—a nationwide organization that raises money for the purchase and development of Israeli
land—were touring Lebanese battlefield areas. Suddenly, while the group
was traveling on the bus, Dr. Sam Cohen of New York, the executive vice
president of the JNF, stood up and made a surprising announcement. A
member of the tour, Charles Fishbein, who was at the time an executive
in the Washington office, recalls, "He told us that when we get back to
the United States, we must defend what Israel is doing in Lebanon. He
said that if we criticize Israel, we will be terminated immediately."[23]

Fishbein said the group was on one of several hastily arranged tours
designed to quell rising Jewish criticism of the invasion. In all, more
than 1,500 prominent American Jews were flown to Israel for tours of
hospitals and battlefields. The tours ranged in length from four to seven
days. The more prestigious the group of visitors, the shorter, more com-
pressed the schedule. Disclosing only Israeli hardship, the tours were
successful in quieting criticism within the ranks of Jewish leadership,
and they also inspired many actively to defend Israeli war policies.

"The Time May Not Be Far Off"

Peer pressure does not always muffle Jewish voices. A pioneer in the establishment of the state of Israel, who helped to organize its crucial underpinnings of support in the United States, later became a frequent critic of Israeli policy.

Nahum Goldmann is a towering figure in the history of Zionism. He played a crucial role in the founding of Israel, meeting its early financial problems, influencing its leaders, and organizing a powerful constituency for it in the United States. His service to Zionism spanned nearly fifty years. During World War I, when Palestine was still part of the Ottoman Empire, Goldmann tried to persuade Turkish authorities to allow Jewish immigration. In the 1930s he advocated the Zionist cause at the League of Nations. During the Truman administration, he lobbied for the United Nations resolution calling for partition of Palestine and the establishment of Israel.

After the 1947 UN vote for the partition, unlike most Jews who were eager to proclaim the State of Israel, Goldmann urged delay. He hoped that the Jews would first reach an understanding with the Arab states and thereby avoid war. He lamented the bitter legacy of the war that ensued.[24] He wrote, "The unexpected defeat was a shock and a terrible blow to Arab pride. Deeply injured, they turned all their endeavors to the healing of their psychological wound: to victory and revenge." To the Israelis,

> The victory offered such a glorious contrast to the centuries of persecution and humiliation, of adaptation and compromise, that it seemed to indicate the only direction that could possibly be taken from then on. To brook nothing, to tolerate no attack, cut through Gordian knots, and shape history by creating facts seemed so simple, so compelling, so satisfying that it became Israel's policy in its conflict with the Arab world.

When the fledgling nation was struggling to build its economy, Goldmann negotiated with West German Chancellor Konrad Adenauer the agreement under which the Germans paid more than $30 billion in compensation and restitution to Israel and individual Jews.[25] Yet he was bitterly condemned by some Israelis for his efforts. Philip Klutznick of Chicago, Goldmann's close colleague in endeavors for Israel, recalled the tremendous opposition, particularly from such extreme nationalists as Menachem Begin, to accepting anything from Germany: "At that time, many Jews felt that any act that would tend to bring the Germans back into the civilized world was an act against the Jewish people. Feelings ran deep."

Goldmann's disagreement with Israeli policy toward the Arabs was his central concern. To those who criticized his advocacy of a Palestinian state, he responded,

> If they do not believe that Arab hostility can some day be alleviated, then we might just as well liquidate Israel at once, so as to save the millions of Jews who live there. . . . There is no hope for a Jewish state that has to face another fifty years of struggle against Arab enemies.

Goldmann respected the deep commitment to the Jewish people of Israel's first prime minister, David Ben-Gurion, but he regretted that Ben-Gurion was "organically incapable of compromise" and that his "dominant force" was "his will for power." Goldmann's essential optimism and his instinctive striving to temper hatreds and seek compromise were qualities that distinguished him from so many of his contemporaries—on both the Arab and Israeli sides of the conflict.

"Goldmann might have been prime minister of Israel," Stanley Karnow wrote in 1980, "but he chose instead to live in Europe and act as diplomatic broker, frequently infuriating Israeli officials with his initiatives." Seeking an end to the Arab–Israeli conflict, he attempted to visit Cairo at the invitation of Egyptian President Nasser in 1970. But the Israeli government, headed by Golda Meir, resented his maverick ways and blocked the mission.

Goldmann was sharply critical of the Israeli government of Menachem Begin. He decried what he saw as Israel's denial of the original Zionist vision. He rejected the claim of some Israelis that they must occupy "Greater Israel" because it was promised to them by God. He called this thesis "a profanation." Goldmann understood the need for U.S. support. He lived in the United States for more than twenty years and knew American Jewry well. In 1969 he wrote approvingly of Zionist political action in the United States: "It is not fair to single out Zionist pressure for censure. Democracy consists of a mutiplicity of pressure-exerting forces, each of which is trying to make itself felt."

Near the end of his life, however, Goldmann's views of the pro-Israel lobby changed. In 1980 he warned:

> Blind support of the Begin government may be more menacing for Israel than any danger of Arab attack. American Jewry is more generous than any other group in American life and is doing great things. . . . But by misusing its political influence, by exaggerating the aggressiveness of the Jewish lobby in Washington, by giving the Begin regime the impression that the Jews are strong enough to force the American administration and Congress to follow every Israeli desire, they lead Israel on a ruinous path which, if continued, may lead to dire consequences.

He blamed the Israeli lobby for U.S. failures to bring about a comprehensive settlement in the Middle East. "It was to a very large degree because of electoral considerations, fear of the pro-Israel lobby, and of the Jewish vote." He warned of trouble ahead if the lobby continued its present course. "It is now slowly becoming something of a negative factor. Not only does it distort the expectations and political calculations of Israel, but the time may not be far off when American public opinion will be sick and tired of the demands of Israel and the aggressiveness of American Jewry."

In 1978, two years before he wrote his alarmed evaluation of the Israeli lobby, *New York* magazine reported that Goldmann had privately urged officials of the Carter administration "to break the back" of the lobby: "Goldmann pleaded with the administration to stand firm and not back off from confrontations with the organized Jewish community as other administrations had done." Unless this was done, Goldmann argued, "President Carter's plans for a Middle East settlement would die in stillbirth." His words were prophetic. The comprehensive settlement that Carter sought was frustrated by the intransigence of Israel and its U.S. lobby.

President Ronald Reagan revived the idea of a comprehensive Middle East peace agreement just four days before Goldmann's death in September 1982. A state funeral was conducted in Israel. As Klutznick, Israeli Labor Party leaders Shimon Peres, Yitzhak Rabin, and others stood on Israel's Mount Herzl awaiting the great Zionist leader's burial alongside the five other former presidents of the World Zionist Organization, the conversation centered on the Reagan plan, which Prime Minister Begin had already rejected.

Symbolic of organized Jewry's reaction to Goldmann's life was the response of the Israeli government to his death. Begin gave permission for the burial but did not attend. In a strikingly empty commentary on the life of a man who had done so much to bring Israel into being and give it strength, Acting Prime Minister Simcha Ehrlich said only, "We regret that a man of so many virtues and abilities went the wrong way."[26] It was a callous epitaph for one of Israel's great pioneers.

"You Must Listen When We Speak III"

At 7:45 a.m. the towering John Hancock Building in Chicago's downtown loop area was just beginning to come to life. On the fortieth floor were the offices of Philip Klutznick—attorney, developer, former U.S. secretary of commerce, president emeritus of B'nai B'rith, organizer and former chairman of the Conference of Presidents of Major Jewish Organizations, and president emeritus of the World Jewish Congress. At that hour only Philip Klutznick was at work.

He was on the phone, seated on a sofa at one end of his spacious office, his back to a panoramic view of the building across the street where he and his wife made their home. On the walls were autographed photographs of the seven presidents of the United States under whom he had served.

This morning, in the fall of 1983, he was talking with Ashraf Ghorbal, Egypt's ambassador to the United States and a friend of many years. Ghorbal was preparing for a visit to the United States by his leader, Egyptian President Hosni Mubarak. He wanted to make sure the right people would be available to meet with him. The right people included Klutznick.

Klutznick's vigorous appearance and unrelenting pace belied his seventy-six years. His deep, rich voice echoed around the near-empty offices. His eyes smiled through heavy glasses, and his firm, confident manner was that of a man in the prime of life. But his apparent confidence about the flexibility of U.S. Jews contradicted his own experience working within—and outside—the establishment for sixty years. A visitor sharing coffee and conversation would never guess that this short, handsome, optimistic man—whose persistence and spirit had helped to *create* Israel, pay its bills, and provide its arms—had become, in the eyes of many Jews, a virtual castaway.

Measured by offices held and services rendered, his credentials in the Jewish establishment were impeccable. But in the eyes of most Jewish leaders, he was guilty of a cardinal sin: daring to publicly challenge Israeli government policy. This put him at odds with the very Jewish organizations he did so much to bring into being.

He spoke from a base of confidence that included business success, public office in both Democratic and Republican administrations, and high honors in the Jewish community. After seeing his savings wiped out by the Great Depression, he recovered, became a successful community developer, a millionaire, a leader of the Jewish community, and a diplomat.

In his early years he worked to bring strength and unity to the Jewish community, a quest that took on urgency in 1942 when word arrived of Adolf Hitler's barbaric program to annihilate European Jews. Henry Monsky, an Omaha lawyer and president of B'nai B'rith, convened a meeting in Pittsburgh, inviting the membership of forty-one major Jewish organizations. This gathering, identified as the American Jewish Conference, marked the first serious effort to unite U.S. Jews against the Holocaust.

"You know, we are an unusual group of people," Klutznick chuckled. "We fight over anything." This time the fight was over whether Jews would back the establishment of a national homeland. Monsky, the first committed Zionist to head B'nai B'rith, pulled the organization from its neutral stance into advocacy. When the conference met in early 1943 and cast its lot with Zionism, two of the largest Jewish organizations— the American Jewish Committee and the Jewish Labor Committee— walked out in protest.

"Anyway," Klutznick continued, "that meeting started a movement that stayed alive for four years." It also brought him for the first time in close association with Nahum Goldmann. Klutznick and Goldmann wanted the American Jewish Conference to be permanent. In this effort, Klutznick battled to win the support of B'nai B'rith. "It was an enormous fight, and we lost," Klutznick later recalled.

The bruises were still felt ten years later when Klutznick became president of B'nai B'rith. His first decision put him at odds with Goldmann, who wanted him to help re-create the American Jewish Conference. Despite his earlier effort, Klutznick now felt it would be divisive. "I looked him square in the eye and said, 'I'm not going to do it. If I tried it now it would split B'nai B'rith right down the middle. At this moment B'nai B'rith is too weak. I need these people together.'"

Klutznick told him he would "go all the way" on a program for a Jewish homeland, but he had what he believed to be a better plan for coordination of American Jews: an organization consisting of just the presidents of the major organizations. For one thing, he felt, the leaders needed to get acquainted with each other. "Believe it or not," Klutznick recalled, "many had attained these high positions without even meeting the presidents of other major organizations." Klutznick told Goldmann: "If we really want to do something, the presidents are the powerhouses." Goldmann agreed to the plan.

Klutznick recollected changes: "The fact is, during the 1950s people weren't as intense as they are now." As an example, he cited the Jewish response to the Eisenhower Doctrine, which pledged U.S. help to any nation in the Middle East that was threatened by international communism. Israeli Prime Minister David Ben-Gurion opposed such a sweeping commitment, arguing that it could lead to U.S. support for nations that were hostile to Israel. The Conference of Presidents of Major Jewish Organizations decided to support the United States' position.

Klutznick recalled the confrontation. "I presided at that meeting, and we took the position that we should not oppose the president of the United States, and we didn't. In those days," he said after a long pause, "we could have those arguments. There was mutual tolerance." Dealing with Israeli officials sometimes tested Klutznick's tolerance. In 1955 the United States was horrified by the Israeli massacre of Arab civilians in the Gaza raid, and Klutznick, as president of B'nai B'rith, reported the country's reaction to Jerusalem. He told Israeli Prime Minister Moshe Sharett: "Moshe, it was terrible. It wasn't the fact [that] Israeli forces were defending Israel. It was the overwhelming response. It looked like a disregard for the value of human life."

After a pause, the prime minister answered quietly, "You know, Phil, I did not even know this was taking place. He [Defense Minister David Ben-Gurion] did this on his own. I hope you will tell him what you told me." Klutznick met Ben-Gurion the next day. "It wasn't long before he said, 'Phil, what was the reaction to the Gaza raid?' It was exactly the same question Sharett had asked, and I gave exactly the same answer."

Klutznick was astonished by Ben-Gurion's response:

> He stood up. He looked like an angry prophet out of the Bible and got red in the face. He shouted, "I am not going to let anybody, American Jews or anybody else, tell me what I have to do to provide for the security of my people."

When the prime minister stood up, Klutznick stood up too. Ben-Gurion asked, "Why are you standing up?" Klutznick answered, "Well, obviously I have offended you, and I assume that our discussion is over." Ben Gurion said, "Sit down. Let's talk about something else." Klutznick recalled, "That's the way it happened. So help me God. That's just the way it happened, and we had a wonderful talk." Klutznick said Ben-Gurion could be as "tough or tougher than Begin," but when he had made his point he could go back to "being friends."

Klutznick had a similar experience years later with Prime Minister Begin. In the wake of the Camp David Accords, President Carter called in Klutznick and seven other Jewish leaders. Carter said, "Look, I need some help. I think I can handle [Egyptian President] Sadat. We have an understanding, but I am not sure that I can convince the Prime Minister [Begin]." One of the group interrupted and changed the subject: "Mr. President, Israel is upset because there will be arms sent to Arab countries. There is already a bill pending, as you know." Then the next man said, "Can't you do something to make it more comfortable for Israel?" Several men in a row spoke in a similar vein.

Klutznick noted Carter's irritation and undertook the role of peace-maker:

> Mr. President, I don't think we've quite got your message. There are all of these requests for arms. I think what my colleagues are trying to say, if I

may interpret them, is whether there is some way to defer these requests until the negotiations are over. I don't think it is for us with our limited knowledge to tell you who should get arms and who should not.

He recalled, "I said that if the questions of arms sales had to be answered during the Camp David negotiations, whichever way the president answered them would be difficult." Klutznick said he added, "And I am not here representing anybody except you, Mr. President. Our country has to back you as fairly as it can." Klutznick's remarks got the discussion back on the track Carter wanted, but they were badly twisted in a news report published the next day in Israel, where Klutznick was quoted as having told Carter that he was at the White House meeting representing Egypt, not Israel. He had, of course, said nothing of the kind, and he sent a cable to Begin denying the story. The next day when reporters asked about the incident, Begin said simply, "I have received a cable from President Klutznick of the World Jewish Congress. He denies any such statement was made, and that's the end of it."

But that was not the end of it. Klutznick flew to Israel in a few days for previously scheduled meetings, including an appointment with Begin. Klutznick recalled the frosty scene. It was the first time Begin did not stand up and greet him with an embrace. Klutznick spoke first:

> Look, Menachem, I know you are angry, but I'm the one that's angry and entitled to be. When you told the press you got a cable from Klutznick and he denies it and that's the end of it—is that the right thing to say? I say no. If someone had said that about you to me, I would have said, 'I had a cable from the Prime Minister, and the Prime Minister denies it. And I've known the Prime Minister for a long time, and his word is good enough for me.'

Begin turned to his assistant and said, "Get that cable." He read a cable from his ambassador to the United States that gave an inaccurate account of what Klutznick had told Carter, and asked, "What would you have done?" Klutznick responded, "I would have fired the ambassador. In his cable he wasn't writing about Phil Klutznick. He was writing about the president of the World Jewish Congress. If he had any such information his first duty was to call me, not you. He never called me." Overcome with emotion, Begin stood and embraced his visitor.

Despite such shows of affection, Klutznick did not pull punches in his criticism of Begin's later policies and his recommendations on what the U.S. government should do. In 1981 he deplored the Israeli air attacks, first on the Iraqi nuclear installation and then in Lebanon. Later that year he traveled to the Middle East with Harold Saunders, a former career specialist on the Middle East who served as assistant secretary of state for Near Eastern and South Asian affairs under President Carter; former diplomat Joseph H. Greene, Jr.; and Merle Thorpe, Jr., president of the Foundation for Middle East Peace. Upon returning to the United States, Klutznick joined in the group's conclusion that the Camp David peace process was not enough and that the Palestine Liberation Organization should be brought into negotiations.[27]

Later in the year, when Saudi Arabia announced its "eight-point peace plan," Klutznick called it "useful" and argued that Israel at least "should listen to it."

All of these positions, of course, were violently opposed by Israel and its U.S. lobby. But Klutznick was not deterred. In mid-1982, in an article published in the *Los Angeles Times* and other major newspapers, Klutznick wrote:

> It is up to the Reagan Administration to face the realities of the Middle East as boldly as did the Carter Administration. The first step is to halt the conflict in Lebanon immediately and have Israel's forces withdrawn. This must be followed by an enlarged peace process that includes all parties to the conflict—including Palestinians. Only by doing so without apology and with determination can America pursue its own best interests, promote Israel's long-term well-being and protect world peace.

Despite public condemnation for these statements from the Jewish leadership in the United States, Klutznick privately received praise: "When I opposed the Iraqi raid, my mail from Jews was about four-to-one supportive, and about three-to-one when I proposed dealing directly with the PLO," he recalled. "But, you know, some of that support has to be discounted. There are people in the Jewish community who will assure me of their support even when they think I'm wrong."[28]

Many believed him wrong and said so. Abbot Rosen, Midwest director of the Anti-Defamation League in Chicago, rejected Klutznick's proposal to bring the PLO into the peace process and to establish a state for the Palestinians as "pie in the sky." He reported to the *Chicago Sun-Times* one of the lobby's tired clichés: "Under the present political circumstances, another Palestinian state, adjacent to Israel and Jordan, would provide an additional Soviet foothold in the region."

Robert Schrayer, chairman of the Public Affairs Committee of the Jewish United Fund of Metropolitan Chicago, joined the protest with another shibboleth: "Since no sovereign nation can be expected to negotiate its own destruction, Israel should not be pressured to negotiate with the PLO."[29]

The *Near East Report,* a weekly newsletter published by the American Israel Public Affairs Committee, editorialized against Klutznick's views, and accused him of promoting a "sinister canard" in calling the Palestinians "a special people in the Arab world, in some ways like the Jews were in the West following World War II."[30]

The next year Klutznick took his crusade to Paris, where he joined forces with his old, ailing compatriot, Nahum Goldmann, and Pierre Mendes-France, a Jew and a former prime minister of France, in a plea to end Israel's war in Lebanon. Klutznick's reason for going to Paris was to attend a meeting of the World Jewish Congress, but as soon as he landed, Goldmann, then living in Paris and critically ill, told him, "We've got to get fifty of the most distinguished Jews of the world to sign a statement to bring this war in Lebanon to an end." Klutznick responded, "But, first, let's see if we can write a statement."

Goldmann agreed and took up the subject at lunch the next day with Mendes-France, *Le Monde* correspondent Eric Rouleau, and Klutznick, agreeing to consider a draft statement the next day. That night Klutznick, with the help of his aide, Mark Bruzonsky, wrote a brief statement that became the basis for the next day's discussion. Klutznick recalls the scene, "Mendes-France is one of the best editors I've seen in my life. He would look at a word in typical French fashion in several languages, turning it around every which way. Four hours later, after sitting there fighting over every word, we had a statement."[31]

Its conclusion was forceful:

The real issue is not whether the Palestinians are entitled to their rights, but how to bring this about while ensuring Israel's security and regional stability. Ambiguous concepts such as "autonomy" are no longer sufficient, for they too often are used to confuse rather than to clarify. Needed now is the determination to reach a political accommodation between Israel and Palestinian nationalism.

The war in Lebanon must stop. Israel must lift its siege of Beirut in order to facilitate negotiations with the PLO, leading to a political settlement. Mutual recognition must be vigorously pursued. And there should be negotiations with the aim of achieving co-existence between the Israeli and Palestinian peoples based on self-determination.[32]

When it was finished, Klutznick asked, "What do we do with the damned thing?" Goldmann said, "We've got to get those other fellows. Branch out and find them." Klutznick protested that there was not enough time and suggested that Goldmann and Mendes-France issue it in their own names. The former prime minister said, "I've never done anything like that. I don't sign statements with other people." Goldmann and Rouleau added their encouragement, and, finally, Mendes-France said, "I'll sign provided you can get an immediate answer from Yasser Arafat."

Isam Sartawi, a close associate of Arafat, was in Paris at the time and arranged for a response by the PLO leader:

Coming at this precise moment from three Jewish personalities of great worth, worldwide reputation, and definite influence at all levels, both on the international scene and within their own community, that statement takes on a significant importance.

Klutznick took the podium at the meeting of the World Jewish Congress, then underway in Paris, to explain the declaration. The atmosphere, he recalled, was anything but cordial:

Heated is not the right word. If it had been heated it would have been better. It was sullen, solemn, and bitter. I tried to have the delegates understand why we spoke up as we did. I told them it was the first such statement Mendes-France had ever made. And I said they also should know that Nahum Goldmann does what he thinks is right. And he's not been condemned just once. He's been condemned many times in the past by those who later chose to follow him.[33]

The declaration brought headlines around the world, wide discussion, and some editorial praise. But it received little support among leading

Jews and was largely rejected by Jewish organizations as "unrepresentative and unhelpful." It was Goldmann's last public statement. He died within a month; a month later, Mendes-France also died.

A few Jews helped Klutznick defend the statement.[34] Newton N. Minow, a prominent Chicagoan who served in the Kennedy administration, praised Klutznick's "exemplary lifetime of leadership to Jewish causes and Israel" and "his independence and thoughtful criticism" in a column published in the *Chicago Sun-Times*. "As an American Jew pondering past mistakes, I believe that the American Jewish community has made some serious blunders in the past few years by choosing to remain silent when we disagreed with Israeli government policy."

Shortly after the Paris declaration, the world was horrified by the massacre of hundreds of civilians in the Sabra and Shatila Palestinian camps at Beirut. After four months of silence, Klutznick spoke at a luncheon in New York in February 1983. He launched a new crusade, pleading for the right of Jews to dissent:

> We cannot be one in our need for each other, and be separated in our ability to speak or write the truth as each of us sees it. The real strength of Jewish life has been its sense of commitment and willingness to fight for the right [to dissent] even among ourselves.[35]

In November Klutznick took his crusade to Jerusalem, attending, along with forty other Jews from the United States and fifteen other countries, a four-day meeting of the International Center for Peace in the Middle East. Klutznick drew applause when he told his audience, which included several Israelis: "If you listen to us when we speak good of Israel, then you must listen to us when we speak ill. Otherwise we will lose our credibility, and the American government will not listen to us at all."

By the time of his death in 1999—despite his proven commitment to Israel, his leadership in the Jewish community, and his unquestioned integrity—Philip Klutznick was rejected or scorned by many of his establishment contemporaries. Said one professional in the Jewish lobby community: "I admire Phil Klutznick, but he is virtually a nonperson in the Jewish community." Another was harsh and bitter, linking Klutznick with other critics of the Israeli government as "an enemy of the Jewish people."

Charles Fishbein, who for eleven years was a fundraiser and executive of the Jewish National Fund, provided a partial explanation for the treatment Klutznick received:

> When you speak up in the Jewish community without a proper forum, you are shunted aside. You are dismissed as one who has been "gotten to." It's nonsense, but it is effective. The Jewish leaders you hear about tend to be very, very wealthy givers. Some give to Jewish causes primarily as an investment, to establish a good business and social relationship. Such people will not speak up for a nonconformist like Klutznick for fear of jeopardizing their investment.[36]

These thoughts echo those of Klutznick himself in our last interview. "Try to understand. See it from their standpoint. Why should they go public? They don't want any trouble. They are a part of the community. They have neighbors. They help out. They contribute." He paused, pursed his lips a bit, then added, "They have standing. And they want to keep it."

Klutznick smiled. "They say to me, 'You are absolutely right in what you say and do, but I can't. I can't speak up as you do.'" Another pause. "Maybe I would be the same if I hadn't gotten all the honors the Jewish community can give me." Klutznick saw Washington policy as a major obstacle to reforming the lobby's tactics: "Let's not underestimate the damage that our own government does. Our government has been writing blank checks to Israel for a long time. As a result, Begin would come over here for a tour, then go back home and say, 'What are you complaining about? I go to the United States, where the government supports me and all the leaders of the Jewish community applaud and support me.'"

A Growing Gap in Our Liberal Tradition

"Jews never had it so good as they've had in the United States," mused I. F. Stone, one of America's most respected Jewish journalists who called himself a radical. Famous for his periodical, *I. F. Stone's Weekly*, which he issued for nineteen years, and for his independent views, he discontinued the weekly because, as he once said with typical self-mockery, he became "tired of solving the problems of the entire world every week."[37]

At seventy-six years old and with eyesight so weak he had difficulty reading even large type, Stone was anything but retired. He was still a hero on campuses across the country and in liberal circles for his views on non-Middle East topics. Indeed, even on those themes his following was always enthusiastic.

"Israel is on the wrong course," he said during an interview, just a few years before his death, while peering through the thick lenses of his eyeglasses. "This period is the blackest in the history of the Jewish people. Arabs need to be dealt with as human beings." "I am gloomy about the future," he said. He could name no one with the promise to lead Israel out of its disastrous policies.

Our conversation drifted to American Jews who dissent, and Stone recalled the day a publisher invited him to lunch and asked him to delete from a book he had written a passage recommending major changes in Israeli policy. The book, *Underground to Palestine,* deals mainly with Stone's experiences traveling with Jews from Nazi camps as they made their way through the British blockade to what is now Israel. The offending part was Stone's recommendation of a "binational solution, a state whose constitution would recognize the presence of two peoples, two nations, Arab and Jewish," to encompass all of Palestine. Stone refused to delete it, and as he wrote in the *New York Review of Books,* "that ended the luncheon, and in a way, the book. It was, in effect, proscribed."

According to Jewish journalist Carolyn Toll:

> From then on, Stone, who might have been a hero on the synagogue lecture circuit as the first American newsman to travel with Holocaust survivors, was banned in any Jewish arena by leaders determined to close the debate on binationalism and statehood.[38]
>
> In Israel, where Jews establish their identity by birth rather than membership in an organization, Stone would be a full-fledged dissident. But in the American climate of insecurity about non-Jewish majority views, such arbitrary loyalty tests have not been challenged by the same Jews who vehemently champion others' rights to speak freely.

Two years later, Stone's book was published in Hebrew—in Israel—with the offending passage intact. The book was widely read in the Middle East.

While he objected to the "excesses" of the lobby, Stone understood its motivations:

The Jewish people are apprehensive, fearful. They are afraid about the future. They feel they are at war, and many of them feel they have to fight and keep fighting.

He added, after a pause, "When people are at war it is normal for civil liberties to suffer."

Stone saw a dangerous gap growing in this liberal tradition:

I find myself—like many fellow American intellectuals, Jewish and non-Jewish—ostracized whenever I try to speak up on the Middle East, [while] dissidents, Jewish and non-Jewish, in the Soviet Union are, deservedly, heroes.[39]

But in the United States they are anything but heroes:

It is only rarely that we dissidents on the Middle East can enjoy a fleeting voice in the American press. Finding an American publishing house willing to publish a book that departs from the standard Israeli line is about as easy as selling a thoughtful exposition of atheism to the *Osservatore Romano* in Vatican City.[40]

Those who speak up pay a price, said Stone, noting that journalists with long records of championing Israeli causes are flooded with "Jewish hate mail, accusing them of anti-Semitism" if they dare express "one word of sympathy for Palestinian Arab refugees."[41]

In an essay in the *Washington Post* on August 19, 1977, Stone voiced his concern over "Bible diplomacy," particularly the effort to cite the Bible as the justification for Israel's continued control over the West Bank:

In the Middle Ages, as everyone knows, the Bible was under lock and key. The clergy kept it away from the masses, lest it confuse them and lead to schism and sedition. . . . Maybe it's time to lock the Holy Book up again, at least until the Israeli–Arab dispute is settled.

Stone died on July 17, 1989. Former presidential candidate Ralph Nader called him "the modern Tom Paine—as independent and incorruptible as they come. Notwithstanding poor eyesight and bad ears, he managed to see more and hear more than other journalists because he was curious and fresh with the capacity for both discovery and outrage every new day."[42]

Outrageous in the eyes of many American Jews, Stone went so far in his life as to criticize the Jewish nature of the State of Israel:

> Israel is creating a kind of moral schizophrenia in world Jewry. In the outside world, the welfare of Jewry depends on the maintenance of secular, nonracial, pluralistic societies. In Israel, Jewry finds itself defending a society in which mixed marriages cannot be legalized, in which the ideal is racist and exclusionist. . . . That is what necessitated a re-examination of Zionist ideology.[43]

"Anti-Zionist Jews"

Heading the reexamination were two American Jews, Elmer Berger and Alfred M. Lilienthal, Jr. From the very beginning, they warned against Zionism, forecasting grave danger to Judaism in the establishment of a Jewish state. With no apparent trepidation they separated themselves from what has become the mainstream of Jewish thinking and devoted their lives to a lonely, frustrating, and controversial crusade to alter the policies of the state of Israel. Long after Israel was established, broadly recognized, and supported by the world community, they continued to make a case against the Jewish state. Both were often scorned as "self-hating Jews."

Both Lilienthal and Berger persisted in their crusades despite attacks. The two constantly lectured, wrote extensively, and appeared at forums. Their work is as well known in the Arab world as in the United States, and more honored there than here.

In personality, the two had little in common. Lilienthal began as a lawyer, Berger as a rabbi. Lilienthal is a hard-hitting advocate in manner and speech. His mood shifts rapidly. Thoughtful and subdued one moment, he can be challenging the next. Berger, by contrast, was calm and unruffled, a patient listener. Even when his words thundered, his delivery was that of the soothing cleric.

Each had his audience, but neither had many outspoken disciples. The people who read Lilienthal's newsletter, *Middle East Perspective*, and followed his activities may not be numerous, but his books are found in public and personal libraries throughout the country and are frequently cited in speeches and articles.

Rabbi Elmer Berger's circle was perhaps smaller still—international audiences are hard to measure—but it appeared loyal. When he sponsored a two-day seminar in May 1983 at the Madison Hotel in Washington, D.C., the gathering attracted over two hundred people, principally journalists, scholars, clergy, public officials, and diplomats. All had at least two things in common: an interest in the Arab–Israeli dispute and affection for Elmer Berger, "the epitome of scholarship."[44] Berger died October 6, 1996.

Lilienthal began his crusade against Israel soon after the government came into being in 1948 and, at the age of seventy, had not let up when I interviewed him in 1984. His 1949 *Reader's Digest* article, "Israel's Flag Is Not Mine," warned of the consequences of Zionism. His first book, *What Price Israel?*, was published in 1953. It was followed by *There Goes the Middle East* in 1957 and *The Other Side of the Coin* eight years later.

In 1978 Lilienthal published his largest and most comprehensive work, *The Zionist Connection*, which focuses on the development and activities of the Zionist movement within the United States. An impressive 872-page volume that is studded with facts, quotations, anecdotes, and, here and there, colorful opinions and interpretations, it was described by *Foreign Affairs* as the "culminating masterwork" of Lilienthal's anti-Zionist career.

By 1984, his crusade had taken Lilienthal to the Middle East twenty-two times and across the United States twenty-six times.

For all his long-standing and vigorous endeavors for the peaceful reconciliation of Jews and Arabs, Lilienthal remains a lonely figure who is often shunned in the United States, even by those whose banner he carries the highest. Lilienthal says some people kid him as being the "Man from La Mancha." And true to the characterization, he frequently brings audiences to their feet by quoting from the song that had Quixote "reaching for the unreachable stars."

His greatest accomplishment, he says, is getting "some Christians to have the guts to speak up on this issue." Supposedly excommunicated from the Jewish faith by a group of rabbis in New York in 1982, Lilienthal scorns the action: "Only God can do that. I still feel very much a Jew."

"Affirm the Equal Value of All Beings"

In 1996, Rabbi Michael Lerner of San Francisco, founded Beyt Tikkun, a Jewish renewal movement that describes itself as the "progressive pro-Israel alternative to AIPAC [the American Israel Public Affairs Committee]." The organization insists on the right of the Palestinian people to self-determination, an end to the Israeli occupation, and the dismantling of the Israeli settlements.

In an article in the *Los Angeles Times* on April 28, 2002, Lerner wrote: "[We should] affirm the equal value of all beings. Reject all anti-Semitism, as well as all demeaning of Palestinians and Arabs. Let our elected officials and media know that you will no longer tolerate a political culture that prevents balanced and honest discussion of the Israeli–Palestinian conflict. But criticism of Israel must not slide into the denial of the validity of Israel's existence or anti-Semitic rhetoric. . . . Jews are affirming the highest values of their culture and religion when they conclude that being pro-Israel today requires pushing Israel to end the occupation. . . . All of us are outraged at the immoral acts of Palestinian terrorists. . . . But many of us also understand that Israeli treatment of Palestinians has been immoral and outrageous."

He dismissed as false the common assumption that PLO leader Yasser Arafat should have signed the agreement proposed by Ehud Barak, Ariel Sharon's predecessor as prime minister of Israel. Among other shortcomings in Barak's proposal, Lerner mentioned the plight of refugees: "Palestinian refugees and their families now number more than three million, and many live in horrifying conditions in refugee camps under Israeli military rule. Barak refused to provide anything at all in the way of reparations or compensation for the refugees." He could have added that the Barak proposal also left Israel in full control of all Palestinian borders and left most of the Israeli settlements intact. Lerner is the founder of a magazine named *Tikkun*.

Question Their Loyalty

While numerous Jewish academics, politicians, and rabbis have spoken out against Israel's brutal treatment of Palestinians and the active support that treatment receives from America's pro-Israel lobby, it should be noted that many "everyday" American Jews are equally brave in standing up to intense peer pressure and speaking their minds. From journalists to simply concerned citizens, the actions of these individuals defy the often-repeated conspiracy theories linking all Jews with Zionist aggression.

Haim "Harry" Katz—a New York Jew with a history of suing Jewish groups—is one such individual. In October 1992 he taped a telephone conversation with then-AIPAC president David Steiner in which the latter told Katz he had been "negotiating" with newly-elected President Bill Clinton over whom the president would appoint to the positions of secretary of state and national security advisor. Katz asked Steiner if AIPAC would actually participate in the selection of the new secretary of state. "We'll have access," Steiner replied. "We have a dozen people in [Clinton's] campaign, in the headquarters. . . . And they're all going to get big jobs."

Katz gave the tape to the *Washington Times*, citing a sense of fairness as his reason for doing so. "As someone Jewish, I am concerned when a small group has a disproportionate power. I think that hurts everyone, including Jews." The media maelstrom following the tape's release resulted in a full AIPAC denial of any truth to Steiner's comments, and in Steiner's resignation.[45]

In April 2002, after eighteen months of intense Israeli–Palestinian violence in a new *intifada*, *Philadelphia Weekly* managing editor Liz Spikol could no longer keep silent about the atrocities being committed by Israel in the occupied territories. After years of support, Spikol wrote, "Israel has crossed a line, and I—and many, many American Jews like me—will not be able to cross it with them." Despite explicit and implicit instructions never to publicly express disapproval of Israel's policies, Spikol felt a need to make her voice heard:

> I'm frankly embarrassed that Israel, in the name of preventing further oppression of the Jews, has now become the oppressor. The hypocrisy is enraging. And as an American Jew, I'm ashamed of my own government's lack of action.

Spikol notes an aspect of the conflict that is rarely discussed:

> Though people don't want to talk about it, this is also about race. Here in the United States, the rhetoric of racism was fashioned by slavery, by World

War II, by Ezra Pound—the list goes on. That's why it's shocking to hear Jews talk about Arabs using similar terminology, including lampooning physical characteristics and religious beliefs.

Unlike Berger and Lilienthal, many American Jews, including Spikol, do not reject out of hand Zionism as a whole, and they believe in a strong Israel. "I also fear for Israel itself," Spikol wrote. "More than anything, I want it to prosper. But for now—and for a change—I'm going to concern myself with justice, not sentimentality. I may be called a traitor, but I won't be silent anymore."[46] The reaction to Spikol's article was upsetting on several fronts. Initial responses from American Jews were overwhelmingly negative: in an interview for this book, Spikol read from the local Jewish *Exponent* newspaper, which published "a rather unflattering" editorial declaiming Spikol's "skewed thinking," then sent a copy to Spikol's office. "I definitely perceived it as a threat," she says, "You know, 'we're watching you.'"

In addition to being called "disgusting, repulsive, a self-hater" by numerous other Jewish Americans, Spikol was ostracized at community events. The day after attending a pro-Palestinian rally in Philadelphia, Spikol joined in a pro-Israel rally in order to report on the differences between the two. "As soon as people found out who I was, they didn't want to march next to me. With my own people, I'm *persona non grata*," Spikol said. Asked whether the harassment—including threatening calls to her mother's unlisted number—has affected her in any way, Spikol's reply was affirmative. "The whole experience—people misinterpreting my words, using them to attack me. . . . I just don't feel I should write on the subject again."[47]

While some speak out, others act. Jennifer Loewenstein, a Jewish human rights worker in the Gaza Strip, wrote a condemnation of those individuals who promote the false perception that Palestinians willingly offer up their children as part of a public relations campaign to gain sympathy. An e-mail full of expletives and abusive statements was quick to arrive.

Adam Shapiro, a nonobservant Jewish resident of Brooklyn, New York, received similar treatment. He joined an international solidarity movement on a trip to the besieged West Bank city of Ramallah in early 2002. While there, he met and shook hands with Palestinian leader Yasser Arafat. The response at home was terrifying. Shapiro's family received so many death threats they were forced to move to an undisclosed location. Thankfully, the threats did not affect Shapiro's belief in equality between Palestinians and Israelis. On May 26, 2002, he married fellow peace activist Huwaida Arraf—a Palestinian.

Another Jewish–Palestinian marriage sparked controversy a few months earlier in Kansas City. Livi Regenbaum, a writer for the *Kansas City Jewish Chronicle*, filed a discrimination complaint against the publication after being fired, she believes, because of her husband's ethnicity. According to the Jewish *Forward*, Regenbaum claimed that editor Rick Heller "initially expressed happiness" upon hearing of the marriage, "then asked her to spell her husband's name, after which he grew hostile and said 'I'm going to have to think about this.'" He didn't have to think very long: Heller fired Regenbaum the next day.

The *Forward* article did its best to portray Heller and the *Chronicle* in a good light, which is not surprising given the paper's record of support for Israeli settlements and denial of Palestinian rights. But actions speak louder than words, and this wasn't the first time a *Chronicle* employee had accused the publication of discrimination: managing editor Deborah Ducrocq was fired in November 2001 for publishing a letter that was "sympathetic to Palestinians."[48]

A letter of a completely different nature was published in *Forward* a week after the Regenbaum story. Benjamin Fogel of Delray Beach, Florida, criticized left-wing Jews who expressed sympathy for Palestinians. The letter falsely equated Judaism with Zionism, and called into question the loyalty of Jews who do not unflinchingly support Israel:

> I thought that Adolf Hitler and Stalin had taught them all that the only salvation for the Jews is a Jewish state that is viable and defendable. That was the case of all the leftists I knew. Most are now dead, but their conversion took place before they died. Unfortunately it seems not all were converted and not all died.[49]

11

Scattering the Seeds of Catastrophe

EFFORTS BY THE pro-Israel lobby to influence American opinion and policy most often focus on national institutions, particularly the federal government. Yet the lobby in its various forms branches out widely into American life beyond the seat of government. Local political leaders, businesses, organizations, and private individuals in many fields experience unfair criticism and intimidation for becoming involved in the debate over Middle East issues. Many have paid a price for speaking out. Particularly distressing are instances of discrimination against Americans of Arab ancestry.

The Stigma of Arab Ancestry

Pro-Israeli PACs contributed nearly a million dollars to Senate races in 1982 alone, and many members of Congress place a value on AIPAC support that is beyond accounting in dollars.[1] The political activism of such groups is accepted as a legitimate part of the American political system; yet when Arab Americans attempt to become involved in the electoral process, they find doors closed to them.

On October 14, 1983, W. Wilson Goode was in the midst of a hard fought campaign to become the first black mayor of Philadelphia.[2] The widely respected front-runner, popular with virtually every segment of the city's electorate, attended a fund-raising gathering one evening in the home of Naim Ayoub, a local businessman who had invited a number of friends—prominent academics, scientists, medical professionals, and business leaders—to meet Goode and contribute to his campaign.

After a short social interlude, during which he was told of the discrimination often suffered by people of Arab ancestry, Goode expressed concern and declared, with feeling, "I renew my pledge to be mayor of all the people."[3] Ayoub and his guests wrote checks to the Goode campaign. The candidate offered his thanks and departed. The total amount of the checks was $2,725, a small portion of the Goode campaign budget; yet it was enough to spark a heated controversy over Arab influence and the role of Israel in the campaign.

In the increasingly bitter final weeks of the campaign, Goode's main opponent tried to inflate the contribution into a scandal by disclosing that Naim Ayoub was regional coordinator for the American-Arab Anti-Discrimination Committee—a nationwide organization dedicated to opposing discrimination against people of Arab ancestry. Goode, who had been courting the large Jewish vote in the crucial northeast wards by constantly reaffirming his support for Israel, responded by announcing that the checks from Ayoub and his friends were being returned. He explained: "I want to make certain that no one is able to question my support for the state of Israel."

Jewish voters were apparently satisfied with Goode's explanation of his "mistake," as he went on to win the election with overwhelming Jewish support. Yet as one Jewish Philadelphian later observed: "One need not support the entire program of the Anti-Discrimination Committee to share the shock and pain of many of its members and friends over such a highly publicized affront to one of its leaders acting in his private capacity.⁴ Full participation in the political process should never be restricted to those who espouse only that which is currently popular."

The Goode episode was the precursor of similar incidents involving Senator Gary Hart and former Vice President Walter Mondale in their campaigns for the highest office in the land.

Arab Americans who have tried to maintain contact with their heritage have found unexpected difficulties. Anisa Mehdi, a New York–based TV producer and the daughter of the late Arab American activist and journalist Dr. M. T. Mehdi, observes that it can be "a frightening thing" to be an Arab in America: "I grew up in New York City with a very politically active father.⁵ If there would be a commemoration of the anniversary of the Deir Yassin massacre, usually that date would coincide with the Israeli anniversary parade. Jews would be on Fifth Avenue and we would be on Madison Avenue. There would be hundreds of thousands of people on Fifth Avenue and maybe ten of us on Madison Avenue. The point is there were at least 100,000 Arab Americans in New York City. Where were they? They were afraid to come out."

Arab ancestry can also be a liability outside politics, as Dr. George Faddoul, a specialist in veterinary medicine at the University of Massachusetts, could attest.⁶ Faddoul's origins are Lebanese, but he was born in Maine and has never had any interest in politics or international affairs. In 1974, Faddoul was working at the Suburban Experiment Station at Waltham, Massachusetts, a facility established by the university to service the farming community in the state. When the directorship became open, he decided to apply for it. After a distinguished career of more than twenty-five years, Faddoul felt that he deserved it and that such an administrative post would add an interesting new dimension to his work at the station.

Only one other applicant came forward, and a faculty committee voted 7–6 in Faddoul's favor. The rules of the university stipulate that only a simple majority was necessary, but the dean failed to appoint him. Faddoul's own investigation into the reasons for this revealed that there had been a number of slurs against him in the committee deliberations because of his Arab background. In the discussions, Arabs were described as "worthless." Faddoul's assistant, who possessed only a bachelor's degree, was named acting administrative director of the station. Only after pressing his case for seven years did Faddoul receive the position.

"80 to 85 Percent . . . Are Terrorists"

Arab Americans in the Detroit area have learned about discrimination firsthand.[7] In a June 1983 meeting in Detroit between U.S. custom officials and airline officials concerning the processing of luggage, a senior customs official declared that "80 to 85 percent of Arabs in the Detroit metropolitan area are terrorists and the rest are terrorist sympathizers."

This harsh accusation came after the arrest in 1983 of a twenty-nine-year-old Arab Canadian who tried to bring heroin hidden in a false-bottomed suitcase through the Detroit–Windsor tunnel, and a vendetta in which customs officials began to single out motorists who "looked Arab" for interrogation and automobile searches.[8] In one case, an eighteen-year-old girl was strip-searched.

Although the customs service later apologized for the remark charging Arabs with terrorism—the offending official received only a reprimand—a local publication joined in the racial stereotyping. After the arrest of a military officer from the Yemen Arab Republic (North Yemen) for attempting to smuggle guns out of the United States, *Monthly Detroit* magazine carried a story entitled "The Mideast Connection: How the Arab Wars Came to Detroit." Although it cited no examples of Arab Americans being arrested for gun or drug smuggling, the article portrayed the city's nearly 250,000 Arab Americans as a lawless and violent community.

"We Will Destroy You Economically"

Bias and intimidation assume many forms and know no geographical boundaries. Mediterranean House restaurant became an instant success after it opened in Skokie, a predominantly Jewish suburb of Chicago, in 1973.[9] With an Arab cuisine and a mainly Jewish clientele, owner Abdel-Hamid El-Barbarawi—a Palestinian-born naturalized American citizen—held his staff to a strict "no politics" policy. He fired two employees for becoming involved in political discussions with clients.

At the peak of its success, Mediterranean House was recommended in all major Chicago dining guides and was frequently praised in newspaper articles.[10] A growing business led Barbarawi to expand, opening several other restaurants under the same name in other areas.

On a summer night in 1975 a six-foot pipe bomb was thrown through the window of the restaurant in Morton Grove. The attack came late at night and no one was injured, but the restaurant was destroyed. Fire experts said the bomb was meant to "level the building."

Trouble returned a year later when Barbarawi and members of his staff emerged from his restaurant in Skokie at about 3:00 A.M. to discover that one side of the building had been covered with posters proclaiming that "Mediterranean House food in your stomach is like Jewish blood on your hands," and "Money spent here supports PLO terrorism." The graphic impact of the posters' message was enhanced by red paint and raw liver, which had been thrown on the walls. Although the vandals were nowhere in sight, Barbarawi discovered the editor of the *Chicago Jewish Post and Opinion* taking pictures of the display. The editor said he just happened to be passing by the place.

The next month, under the headline "Skokie Jews Unknowingly Funding Arab Propaganda," the periodical published an article that urged local Jews to boycott the restaurant, basing its recommendation on the fact that the Mediterranean House advertised on a weekly one-hour radio program called *The Voice of Palestine*.[11] Ted Cohen, author of the article, described the program as a source of "anti-Jewish propaganda."

Barbarawi points out that he advertised on six radio stations and also had commercials on several Jewish programs and an India-related program. "I was an advertiser, not a sponsor," he says. "I had never listened to *The Voice of Palestine* and was not interested in their editorial policy."

Publication of the Cohen article marked the beginning of the end for Barbarawi. A propaganda campaign was mounted against the restaurant. Leaflets urging local Jews to "Stop paying for Arab propaganda" were distributed door-to-door in Skokie. Large numbers of abusive calls and false orders forced Barbarawi to stop accepting orders by phone. One call threatened his life. In exasperation, Barbarawi interrupted one caller's invective with an anguished question: "Why don't you bomb the place like you did before?" The answer was chilling: "We wouldn't give you that satisfaction. We will destroy you economically. You will die while you are still living."

In a *Chicago Sun-Times* commentary, columnist Roger Simon conceded that *The Voice of Palestine* broadcasts were not anti-Semitic, as Cohen had charged, but concluded his column, oddly, by agreeing that Jews should hold Barbarawi "responsible for where his money goes" and backing the *Jewish Post and Opinion* in calling for a boycott.[12] Barbarawi feels that this commentary damaged business more than any other single factor.

Barbarawi appealed, to no avail, to local citizens of Arab ancestry, as well as to the local chapter of the Anti-Defamation League of B'nai B'rith to intercede with the Jewish community. He was told that the ADL had nothing against him. Director Abbot Rosen stated personal sympathy—"It's terrible; you should sue"—but did not counter the hate campaign mounted by the *Jewish Post and Opinion* and the unseen callers.

Meanwhile Barbarawi saw his revenues drop from $40,000 a month to less than $7,000. As regular Jewish customers stopped coming, a number of non-Jews told Barbarawi that their neighbors were refusing to speak to them because they patronized his restaurant. Facing financial ruin, Barbarawi in desperation turned to legal action, but high costs and repeated court delays finally forced him to abandon this last hope. In the end, the hate campaign of unseen enemies put him out of the restaurant business completely. After losing $3 million, Barbarawi had three dollars in his pocket when the local sheriff came to close down his restaurant.

Dick Kay, a reporter for Chicago television station WMAQ, summed up the fate of the Mediterranean House and its owner: "They really did a job on him, and it was the militant part of the Jewish community that did it."[13]

Such intolerance can also damage long-standing personal friendships. In mid-1983, author Stephen Green took the bound page proofs of his new book, *Taking Sides: America's Secret Relations with a Militant Israel*, to Edgar Bronfman, president of the World Jewish Congress and a close friend of the Green family for many years.[14] Together the two men had scattered the ashes of Green's father after his death five years before. The young writer wanted to explain his reasons for writing the book, which discloses intimate U.S.–Israeli military relationships. Bronfman declined to see Green. He directed his secretary, whom Green has also known for years, to respond. Green recalled her words: "Mr. Edgar does not want to discuss this book with you, Steve. You've written it. It's your affair, and he doesn't feel he needs to discuss it with you." Green was devastated that the man he had known and respected for so long would refuse even to speak with him. He recalled with irony that years earlier Edgar's father had frequently upbraided his son for "not doing enough" for Israel.

Vanessa Redgrave: An Activist Playing for Time

The Middle East conflict has affected the career of Vanessa Redgrave, a British actress who is widely hailed as one of the foremost stage and screen talents of her generation. Yet her success in the United States has been limited by her long history of political activism. While many performers shy away from controversial issues for fear of damaging their careers, Redgrave has structured her life largely around her political passions. Her career has suffered accordingly.

Redgrave's apprehension was apparent on Labor Day, 1983, when I interviewed her in a backyard studio in a residential area of Boston.[15] She had just cut a tape for a program directed to Arab Americans and was ill at ease. She spoke quietly of threats against her life, while glancing nervously through an open door. "I don't feel safe here," she said. "I've had so many threats."

Always controversial, Redgrave's opposition to the Vietnam War and sympathy for leftist causes led the U.S. government to refuse her a visa in 1971 when she wanted to come to the United States to discuss writing her autobiography and a possible motion picture. The refusal occurred despite the pleas of her publisher and the intervention of several public figures. Undeterred, she directed her activism increasingly toward support for the Palestinian people.

In 1978 the Jewish Defense League picketed the Academy Awards ceremony, in which Redgrave received an Oscar for her supporting role in the movie *Julia*.[16] The JDL was protesting her narration and financial backing of a documentary called *The Palestinians*, which included an interview with PLO chief Yasser Arafat. In her acceptance speech, Redgrave described the JDL picketers as "a small bunch of Zionist hoodlums whose behavior is an insult to Jews all over the world" and thanked the Academy for standing up to their intimidation. Many in the audience hissed and booed.

Another controversy arose in the summer of 1979, when it was announced that Redgrave would play the lead in a CBS television drama about Holocaust survivor Fania Fenelon, a member of the Auschwitz concentration camp orchestra who was spared death only to play music for other prisoners as well as camp officials.[17] Many Jews were outraged that Redgrave was chosen for the part. Fenelon herself declared, "Vanessa Redgrave playing me is like a member of the Ku Klux Klan playing Martin Luther King."[18] The network was criticized for keeping "an unusually tight lid on the names of sponsors" for the broadcast in an attempt to avoid expected pressures on them to withdraw.

The two people most responsible for what one columnist called "the Vanessa thing" were Bernie Sofronsky, the CBS executive in charge, and Linda Yellen, the show's producer. CBS explained that it could not bow to pressure. Yellen responded to the criticism more directly: "I had always adored her as an actress, and I turned to her as the best person for the part. Basically, I was unaware of her politically. I never considered firing her for her political beliefs. That would have been anathema to me, given what I know about blacklisting and the McCarthy era. I believe her performance is extraordinary and speaks for itself."[19]

The critics were nearly unanimous in acclaiming Redgrave's performance. One asserted that it "may be the finest ever seen on television."[20] But the excellence of the program did not quiet her detractors. The Simon Wiesenthal Center for Holocaust Studies in Los Angeles urged a nationwide boycott of the film, titled *Playing for Time,* and some Zionist groups went even further by urging a boycott of products sold by its sponsors.[21]

Obviously, Redgrave's talents as an actress were not the real issue. As the *Los Angeles Times* cogently observed: "Her dazzling portrayal of a Holocaust survivor has no bearing on the controversy. . . . The principle involved is the simple one of keeping separate things separate—in this instance, separating the artist on the screen from the eccentric and grating political activist off the screen."[22]

The difficulty in keeping this distinction clear was demonstrated again in 1982, when Redgrave was designated to narrate Stravinsky's

Oedipus Rex in a series of April concerts by the Boston Symphony Orchestra.[23] In the face of a vociferous outcry by the local Jewish community, the orchestra canceled the concerts without explanation. The announcement did not mention Redgrave by name, but as columnist Nat Hentoff pointed out, "There was no mystery. Wishing to offend as few people as possible—particularly during the spring fundraising season—BSO made its craven decision" not to do the performances with Redgrave.

Alan Dershowitz, a professor at Harvard Law School who has been noted both as a Zionist and as a defender of civil liberties, defended Redgrave's statement that, "No one should have the right to take away the work of an artist because of political views." Redgrave, who sued the orchestra and was awarded $100,000 in damages, represents a complicated case, in that her political views are disagreeable to more than just partisans of Israel. Nat Hentoff invoked the wisdom of Justice Oliver Wendell Holmes to suggest how Americans should react: "If there is any principle of the Constitution that more imperatively calls for attachment than any other, it is the principle of free thought—not free only for those who agree with us, but freedom for the thought we hate."

"A Consistent Pattern"

Efforts to stifle public debate on the Middle East focus to a great extent on the centerpiece of free speech in our country: the press. Over the years, support for Israel has almost become a requisite for respectability in journalism, just as it has in politics and other professions.

Edmund Ghareeb, a scholar who has written widely on the Middle East and the American media, observes that the media present "a rosy picture of Israel as the democracy in a sea of barbarians in the Middle East."[24] On the other hand, the Palestinians are often referred to as "Arab terrorists, the Arab is portrayed as a camel driver, somebody who is a murderer, or something of this sort." Journalist Lawrence Mosher agrees: "They have stereotyped the Arab as an unsavory character with dark tendencies, and they have ennobled the Israeli as a hero."[25]

Even *Time* magazine is guilty of perpetuating such stereotypes. In 1982 the magazine ran a four-color house advertisement with a photo of a sheik under a single-word headline: "Power."[26] Columnist Richard

Broderick described the sheik as "all you could want from an evil Arab—dyspeptic, garbed in traditional Saudi dress, he stares out at the camera with palpable malevolence."

Such stereotyping of Arabs is common in editorial cartoons. As Craig MacIntosh, editorial cartoonist for the *Minneapolis Star* pointed out, "The Arabs are always in robes, the Palestinians always in 'terrorist' garb, with an AK-47."[27] Robert Englehart, editorial cartoonist for Dayton, Ohio's *Journal Herald* agreed: "I could depict Arabs as murderers, liars, and thieves. No one would object. But I couldn't use Jewish stereotypes. I've always had the feeling that I'm treading on eggs when I try to do something on the Middle East."

The Israeli lobby works diligently to keep journalists from rowing against the tide of pro-Israel orthodoxy. This mission is accomplished in part through carefully arranged, "spontaneous" public outcries designed to intimidate. Columnist Rowland Evans wrote: "When we write what is perceived to be an anti-Israeli column, we get mail from all over the country with the same points and phrasing. There's a consistent pattern."[28]

The ubiquitous cry of "anti-Semitism" is brought to bear on short notice, and it is this charge that has been most responsible for compelling journalists to give Israel better-than-equal treatment in coverage of Middle East events. Even former Defense Department official Anthony Cordesman was not immune from this charge when he wrote a 1977 article, for *Armed Forces Journal International*, examining the Middle East military balance.[29] Observing, for example, that the number of medium tanks requested by Israel for the decade 1976–86 would approach the number to be deployed by the United States within the North Atlantic Treaty Organization, Cordesman questioned the need for ever-increasing U.S. military aid to Israel. For this straightforward assertion, the Anti-Defamation League of B'nai B'rith denounced the article as "anti-Israeli and anti-Jewish."[30]

"Too Controversial and Fanatical"

Journalist Harold R. Piety observed that "the ugly cry of anti-Semitism is the bludgeon used by the Zionists to bully non-Jews into accepting the

Scattering the Seeds of Catastrophe   323

Zionist view of world events, or to keep silent."[31] In late 1978 Piety, with-holding his identity in order not to irritate his employer, wrote an article titled "Zionism and the American Press" for *Middle East International,* in which he decried "the inaccuracies, distortions, and—perhaps worst—inexcusable omission of significant news and background material by the American media in its treatment of the Arab–Israeli conflict."[32]

Piety traced the deficiency of U.S. media in reporting on the Middle East to largely successful efforts by Israel and its pro-Israel lobby to "overwhelm the American media with a highly professional public relations campaign, to intimidate the media through various means and, finally, to impose censorship when the media are compliant and craven." He listed threats to editors and advertising departments, orchestrated boycotts, slanders, campaigns of character assassination, and personal vendettas among the weapons employed against balanced journalism.

Despite this impressive list of tools for media manipulation, Piety, drawing from his own experience, blamed the prevailing media bias more on editors and journalists who submit to the pressure than on the lobby that applies it. Pressure began to build against Piety's employer, the *Journal Herald,* in the late sixties as Piety's growing interest in the Middle East led him to write editorial pieces that were critical of Israeli policy. His editor received a long letter, hand-delivered by the president of the local Jewish Community Council along with a lecture on Middle East politics. A column asserting that American Jews "were being herded, and willingly so, into the Zionist camp" brought a lengthy response from the Zionist Organization of America and a delegation of six Jewish leaders to the newspaper's offices for a meeting with the editorial board.[33] A 1976 column on West Bank riots led Piety's editors to order him to write no more on the theme.

Upon writing another column in April 1977 on the anniversary of the Deir Yassin massacre, in which Jewish terrorists under Menachem Begin murdered more than 200 Palestinian villagers, he was sharply rebuked by his editors. Editor Dennis Shere informed Piety that he had received orders—presumably from corporate management—to "shut you up or fire you."[34] Piety was subsequently told that he was "too controversial and too fanatical" and that he would not receive a promised promotion to be editor of the *Journal Herald* editorial page. Under this pressure, Piety left his position.

"Mediawatch" Blinks Out

During the summer of 1982, Minneapolis columnist Richard Broderick devoted several installments of his "Mediawatch" column—a weekly feature on media coverage—to exposing inequities in American media coverage of the Israeli invasion. Among his findings: "Tapes, purportedly of [Yasser] Arafat's 'bunker' and 'PLO military headquarters' being bombed, aired over and over again, while tape of civilian casualties wound up on the edit room floor. . . . As Israeli ground forces swept through southern Lebanon, the American press continued to employ the euphemism 'incursion' to describe what was clearly an invasion."[35]

In local newspaper coverage, Broderick found: "While Palestinian and Lebanese civilians were being killed by the thousands, the *Minneapolis Star and Tribune* ran a front-page photo of an Israeli mother mourning her dead son. Later that same day, another photo showed a group of men bound and squatting in a barbed-wire enclosure guarded by Israeli soldiers. The caption described the scene as a group of 'suspected Palestinians' captured by Israeli forces. Simply being Palestinian, the caption implied, was sufficient cause to be rounded up."

Broderick also used his column to relate scenes of horror that were witnessed by the Reverend Don Wagner, who had been in Beirut inspecting Palestinian refugee camps when the Israeli bombing began. Wagner saw a wing of Gaza Hospital knocked down by the bombing, and he was in Akka Hospital while hundreds of civilian casualties were brought in. Wagner described his experiences to the Beirut network bureaus for NBC, ABC, and CBS, but their reports, which were beamed back to the United States, were never aired.

While such examples of bias are disturbing, still more so are the consequences suffered by the journalist who publicized them. Soon after the "Mediawatch" columns on Israel ran in the *Twin Cities Reader*, movie distributors of Minneapolis—who collectively represent the largest single source of advertising for the paper—began telephoning editor Deb Hopp with threats of permanently removing their advertising as a result of the Broderick column. Hopp mollified them by agreeing to print, unedited, their 1,000-word reply to the offending column.

Contrary to usual policy, Broderick was not allowed to respond to this rebuttal.

Later in the summer, Broderick reported an attempt, as he saw it, by Minnesota Senator Rudy Boschwitz to manipulate public opinion through the local media.[36] Boschwitz coordinated and appeared in a press conference with members of the American Lebanese League (ALL), an organization that endorsed the Israeli invasion. Boschwitz cited the testimony of league members in arguing that the people of Lebanon welcomed the Israelis. Broderick quoted in his column a report by the American-Arab Anti-Discrimination Committee that described the league as "the unregistered foreign agent of the Phalange Party and the Lebanese Front. They work in close consultation with AIPAC, which creates political openings for them. " Senator Boschwitz, upset at seeing this information made public, castigated Hopp and Broderick in a lengthy telephone call. Three weeks later, Broderick was informed that his services would no longer be needed at the *Twin Cities Reader*.

"Frau Geyer" Under Fire

Concern over appearances and external pressure also led the *Chicago Sun-Times* to drop the regular column of veteran foreign correspondent and syndicated columnist Georgie Anne Geyer for several months during the 1982 war in Lebanon.[37] The decision followed an outpouring of reader protest over Geyer's columns criticizing the war and Israeli policy. Letters assailed Geyer as "a well-known Jew hater," "an anti-Semite par excellence," and "an apologist for the PLO"—the sort of innuendoes to which Geyer had grown accustomed during many years of covering both sides of the Arab–Israel dispute. Frequently denounced in print, she has also been harassed with similar charges at lectures.[38]

Geyer, whose worldwide journalistic coups have made headlines for years, told me that receiving "this endless, vicious campaign of calumny and insults because you write what you know to be impeccably true" is the most distressing aspect of her life as a journalist.[39]

Editor Howard Kleinberg of the *Miami News* also suffered criticism for carrying Geyer's columns. He wrote in a 1982 editorial: "I cannot remember receiving more outside pressure on anything than I have about Georgie Anne Geyer's columns on Israel. . . . Geyer's antagonists have portrayed her not only as anti-Israel but anti-Semitic as well; 'Frau Geyer,' some of them call her."[40]

Aware of the violent response, Geyer suggested that Kleinberg not publish her column for a while, but he was adamant: "I steadfastly have refused to bow to the pressure." He added: "We carry syndicated columns of contrasting viewpoints because it is the role of newspapers to provide a vehicle for the exercise of free speech."

Although the *Chicago Sun-Times* later resumed publication of her column and the criticism abated, Geyer found that calling Middle East issues as she sees them exacts a personal price, and she noted sadly that her commentaries seem to have damaged permanently valued relationships with Jewish friends.

Ted Turner Caves In

In an ominous episode in June 2002, media giant Ted Turner, the billionaire founder of CNN, emerged from retirement to apologize for speaking his mind about Israeli terrorism. When he told a British newspaper that "both sides [Palestinians and Israelis] are engaged in terrorism," Israel's cable television company, YES, announced that it would cease broadcasting the popular CNN international feed to its viewers. CNN immediately broadcast a series of announcements in which it stated its disapproval of Turner's reference to Israeli terrorism. It also dispatched CNN executive Eason Jordan from Atlanta to Israel to extend personal regrets to YES executives and to try to make amends.

The upshot was that Turner caved under pressure and so did CNN. Turner apologized for making the remark and, as an added gesture of obedience to Israel's lobby, CNN promised that henceforth it would refuse to broadcast "without good cause" statements by the families of suicide bombers or people wanting to become suicide bombers. The "without good cause" reservation was, of course, a meaningless "fig leaf" gesture to the cause of free expression. YES resumed broadcasting CNN.[41]

On and Off the Enemies List

Branding critics and thoughtful analysts as "enemies" is another familiar tactic of the Israeli lobby. Those singled out for inclusion on enemies lists—particularly *The Campaign to Discredit Israel*, published by AIPAC, and the ADL's *Pro-Arab Propaganda in America: Vehicles and Voices*—rarely take issue with lobby criticism, perhaps in the belief that a direct response would only give undeserved credibility to their detractors. But in December 1983, a selective challenge to these enemies lists was offered by Anthony Lewis, a Jewish columnist who writes for the *New York Times*.

In two installments of his regular column, Lewis took issue with the inclusion on the 1983 lists of Professor Walid Khalidi, a professor who has taught at Oxford, the American University of Beirut, and Harvard.[42] Khalidi, who cofounded the well-known Institute for Palestine Studies, has long argued for a Palestinian state living in peace and mutual recognition with Israel. He outlined his position in a 1978 *Foreign Affairs* article, subsequently receiving sharp criticism from extremist groups in the Middle East and elsewhere. Hence Lewis was "astonished to find Professor Khalidi's name on lists of supposed anti-Israel activists."

Lewis exposed the techniques used to implicate Khalidi in a putative campaign to discredit Israel. First, AIPAC quoted him as saying in the 1978 article that Israel's existence is "both 'a violation of the principles of the unity and integrity of Arab soil and an affront to the dignity of the [Arab] nation.'" Khalidi had in fact referred to this as an old view that has been discarded. Second, the book identified Khalidi as a member of the Palestine National Council (PNC), a body that served as a PLO parliament, and claimed that on one occasion he "narrowly escaped expulsion" from the PNC for supporting George Habash's radical Popular Front. Khalidi responded that he has never attended a PNC meeting "because of [his] lifelong commitment to complete independence from all political organizations." Lewis added that Khalidi's views are the antithesis of George Habash's. Lewis concluded: "Some people see his very moderation as dangerous. He is a Palestinian nationalist, after all, and one must not allow that idea to have any legitimacy."

The *Times* published letters from both the ADL and AIPAC that protested the Lewis columns, and the ADL assigned a team of researchers to review previous Lewis columns in search of anti-Israeli bias.[43] Lewis was also sharply criticized in the January 1984 issue of *Near East Report*, the AIPAC newsletter.

The Perils of Non-Orthodoxy

A New York businessman almost made it onto "enemies list," thanks to media coverage of his views. Jack Sunderland, businessman and chairman of Americans for Middle East Understanding, a national organization that issues scholarly reviews, made statements supporting Palestinian self-rule and an end to Israeli West Bank settlement construction during a trip to the Middle East several years ago.[44]

His remarks were widely reported in the U.S. and foreign media, and shortly after returning to his New York home, Sunderland learned that a man had visited several of his neighbors and asked personal questions about his family, including his children's schedule and routes to and from school. Concerned for his family's safety, Sunderland engaged a private detective. Working with FBI cooperation, the detective soon located a graduate student who admitted to the obtrusive questioning and also to illegally gaining access to computer information about Sunderland's finances and credit record. The student said he was an employee of B'nai B'rith and that Sunderland was being investigated as a prospect for inclusion on the organization's "enemies list." Faced with the student's confession, B'nai B'rith officials refused to meet with Sunderland personally but agreed not to mention his name in future publications. When the "enemies list" appeared in 1983, under the sponsorship of B'nai B'rith's affiliate, the Anti-Defamation League, the organization Sunderland heads was listed as a "vehicle" of "Arab propaganda." Several officers were mentioned by name. Sunderland was not.

On a Saturday morning in 1977, producer Debbie Gage encountered peril of a different sort when she presented on a one-hour program of interviews with local people of Palestinian origin on Minneapolis Public Radio.[45] The station's switchboard was promptly swamped with calls demanding equal time for the Israeli viewpoint. Gage demurred, responding that she had decided to do her program because of the heavy coverage being given to the Israeli view in the local press. She saw her broadcast as "simply a small attempt to redress that imbalance."

The following Monday, news director Gary Eichten informed Gage that her job would be terminated in three weeks and that a program devoted to pro-Israeli views would be aired the following Saturday. Eichten denied that he was pressured into doing the follow-up program, but, as station intern Yvonne Pearson observed, "If dozens of angry phone calls aren't pressure, I don't know what is."

James Batal, a man of Lebanese ancestry, was interviewed on a Miami television program during the 1973 Arab–Israeli war.[46] He was seventy-two years old at the time, and he sought to explain the little-understood Arab view of the conflict. Following the broadcast of his interview, he received an abusive—and anonymous—phone call warning that his house would be burned down or bombed in retaliation for his remarks on television. Batal appealed to local police and the FBI, but was told that they were unable to provide protection. In desperation, he and his ailing wife closed their home and moved into a small apartment with her sister.

The late Grace Halsell, a noted writer on the Middle East, told of a similar incident that took place in late 1983.[47] While in Jerusalem, she visited Amal, a young Palestinian woman with whom she had become friends while living in Jerusalem some years before. An American television journalist had asked to interview Amal while she was employed as assistant to the United States vice consul in East Jerusalem, and her American boss had agreed to her being interviewed. When the interview was aired, however, she was fired. She explains, "I was thought to be too pro-Palestinian. I had merely said, in answer to a question, that my family lived in a house where Israelis now live."

Washington Reports

The consequences of publishing reports that do not convey such a congenial message can be even more drastic than loss of employment or public pressure from lobby groups. John Law, a veteran journalist who founded and edited the *Washington Report on Middle East Affairs,* a non-partisan newsletter published by the American Educational Trust, once described the aim of the publication in these words: "It would like to see Middle East issues approached in a way that will benefit the interests of the people of the United States, while being consistent with their standards of justice and fair play."[48]

On May 6, 1982, Law received a telephone call that threatened his physical safety and warned that he should "watch out." The following day John Duke Anthony, then an official of the American Educational Trust, was assaulted by two men near his home. One subdued Anthony by striking him on the head with a brick. The muggers took neither his money nor his credit cards—only his personal address book.

An editorial in the next issue of the *Washington Report* responded: "The man who threatened Mr. Law and the two men who assaulted [Mr. Anthony] were presumably hoping to deter them from doing their work. This is not going to happen."

And it didn't. In the spring of 2002, publisher Andrew L. Killgore and executive editor Richard H. Curtiss observed the twentieth anniversary of the *Washington Report*, which has grown to a circulation of more than 35,000. The publication is widely respected worldwide as the preeminent American source of balanced Middle East coverage.

Upon retirement from careers in the U.S. foreign service, Killgore and Curtiss decided to embark on a new nonpaid career of acquainting the American people with the reality of U.S.–Arab relations. It hasn't been easy. The two ran a series of ads in the late 1990s in several U.S. newspapers about politicians accepting funds from "stealth PACs"— those PACs whose names are ambiguous but whose goals are quite clear: to support Israel. The ads prompted journalists nationwide to investigate and report similar campaign contributions to elected officials in their regions—an uproar that was completely unacceptable to members of the pro-Israel lobby. Late one evening, Curtiss received a call from a man in California who warned, "You'll be dead by nine o'clock." Curtiss's response was quick and to the point: "Sorry, but it's past nine o'clock in D.C. already."

When asked if the daily threats and harassment the *Washington Report* receives made him fear for his safety, publisher Killgore—whose white Alabama family has fought for African American civil rights since the 1870s—replied with typical calm: "Zionists are a night flower— blooms in the dark, dies in the sunlight. I'm too well known, and the Zionist organizations are too afraid of negative publicity, for anything to happen to me."

While his physical safety seems assured, Killgore acknowledged that his views prevented him from advancing within the ranks of the foreign service as well he might have had he kept silent: "I know for a fact that I was chosen to be the first U.S. ambassador to Bahrain in 1974, but Kissinger vetoed me. When Carter came into office in 1976, several influential Zionists were no longer in power." Killgore became ambassador to Qatar the next year. He feels no bitterness for his former State Department colleagues who, despite privately agreeing with his fairminded approach to the Middle East, never spoke out. "Financially, it's suicide. At the time, most of us were poor kids working our way up. If you wanted to educate your kids, you kept quiet."

But Killgore never did remain quiet. "I don't know why," he says. "Maybe I wasn't smart enough to keep my mouth shut. But if I never got one pat on the back, it wouldn't matter. My dad would be proud of me if he knew what I've done. That's better than money."[49]

"Conviction Under False Pretenses"

Opinions that depart from the pro-Israeli line cost a New York journalist his job in early 1984. For ten years, Alexander Cockburn contributed the popular "Press Clips" feature to the *Village Voice* in New York. Although his topics and views were often controversial, his candor and originality were widely respected. One reader hailed him as "Guinness Stout in a world of 'Lite' journalism."[50]

In August 1982 Cockburn applied for and received a grant from the Institute of Arab Studies (IAS), located in Belmont, Massachusetts, to underwrite travel and research expenses for a book on the war in Lebanon.[51] The grant was not secret. It was recorded in the IAS public report, but in January 1984 the *Boston Phoenix* published a long article exposing Cockburn's "$10,000 Arab connection." The article provoked a storm in the editorial offices of the *Voice*. Editor David Schneiderman decided that Cockburn should receive an indefinite suspension without pay, but permitted him to reply to the decision in print. Cockburn defended the grant, contending that the IAS is a legitimate nonprofit organization, founded "to afford writers, scholars, artists, poets, and professionals an opportunity to pursue the full exploration of the Arab dimension of world history through their special field of interest."[52] He argued that the bottom line of the matter was that he "didn't properly evaluate the climate of anti-Arab racism." The book grant, he felt, constituted an ethnically dubious "connection" because it was "Arab money."

Readers were outraged by Schneiderman's treatment of Cockburn, and many wrote to protest his "conviction under false pretenses." It is sad that even in the United States, with its traditions of free speech, there are still people who, when it comes to Middle East issues, will use force and threats of force to try to prevent the dissemination of ideas they do not like.

Dow Jones Stands Firm

Major national media have not escaped these pressures. Organized letter campaigns are a favored tactic of pro-Israel groups. As Lawrence Mosher, a staff correspondent for the *National Journal,* observes: "[Such groups have] a seemingly indefatigable army of workers who will generate hundreds or thousands of letters to congressmen, to newspaper editors, etc., whenever the occasion seems to warrant it. . . . Editors are sometimes weighed down by it in advance and inhibited from doing things they would normally do if they didn't know that an onslaught of letters, cables, and telephone calls would follow if they write or show such and such."[53]

Mosher himself had experienced the pressures that speaking out brings. The *National Observer* of May 18, 1970, printed an article by Mosher on a little-noticed court case then pending in Washington, D.C. The case involved Saul E. Joftes, a former high official of B'nai B'rith, who was bringing suit against the organization and its officers. The charge: "Zionists have used B'nai B'rith—a charitable, religious, tax-exempt American membership organization—to pursue international political activities contrary to the B'nai B'rith constitution and in violation of federal foreign agent registration and tax laws."

Joftes had been disturbed by the "employment" by B'nai B'rith of a woman whose post was funded and controlled by the Israeli consulate in New York City. She was given the job of providing "saturation briefings" for Jews visiting the Soviet Union, but her main duty was to "channel information back to the Israeli government on who went to the Soviet Union and what Russians visited the United States." The woman, Mrs.

Avis Shulman, observed that "Jewish organizations, particularly B'nai B'rith, are especially useful" as a "base of operation." Joftes was obliged to meet her request that "a subcommittee" be "invented with her as 'secretary' to give her a handle that could be relatively inconspicuous but meaningful."

The one-year employment of Shulman was but one aspect of what Joftes saw as the Zionist takeover of B'nai B'rith's international operations. He resented being compelled to develop the organization to serve policy mandates of the Israeli government, with "the identity of B'nai B'rith itself taking a secondary role in fostering the interests of a foreign power."

Mosher's article went on to discuss the broader issue of national versus extra-national loyalties raised by Joftes's case, quoting the views of numerous national and international Jewish leaders.[54] He disclosed the mechanisms through which tax-free donations from U.S. Jews were sent to Israel for purposes other than the designated "relief," and he discussed the Senate Foreign Relations Committee hearings of seven years before, which had exposed and closed down an illegal Israeli propaganda operation in an organization called the American Zionist Council.

Shortly after the article appeared, the offices of Dow Jones, which owned the *National Observer,* were visited by Gustave Levy, senior partner in a New York investment firm, and a group of other Jewish leaders. The group did not dispute the accuracy of the article, but protested its publication as an embarrassment and an anti-Jewish act. They questioned the motives of Warren Phillips, then vice president of Dow Jones, in publishing the Mosher piece: "Why create public focus on this information?" Despite the pressure, Phillips stood behind his writer.

"Who Could Be Mad at Us?"

In its April 1974 issue, *National Geographic* published a major article entitled "Damascus, Syria's Uneasy Eden." The article discussed ancient and modern life in the Syrian capital, but a brief segment on the life of the city's small Jewish community caused a storm of protest.

Author Robert Azzi, a journalist with years of experience in the Middle East, found that "the city still tolerantly embraces significant numbers of Jews" and that Sephardic Jews enjoy "freedom of worship and freedom of opportunity," although they lived under a number of obtrusive restrictions, including strict limitations on travel and emigration. He had estimated that about 500 Jews had left Syria in the years following the 1967 war, and said that "reprisals against the families of those who leave are . . . rare."

A number of U.S. Jewish groups and many of the magazine's subscribers were outraged by Azzi's portrait of Jewish life in Syria. A torrent of angry letters poured into the offices of the National Geographic Society protesting the "whitewash" of Syria's treatment of its Jewish citizens and the refusal of the editors to correct Azzi's "shocking distortions." Society President Gilbert M. Grosvenor later recalled that his offices received more than 600 protest letters.[55] This correspondence was liberally seasoned with harsh charges, including "hideous lies," "disgraceful," "inhuman," "communistic propaganda," and "as bad as Hitler's hatred for the Jews."

One letter threatened Grosvenor's life. As the controversy grew, the Society even received a letter from Kansas Senator Robert Dole in which he expressed concern over the issue. He included a longer letter that he had received from the Jewish Community Relations Bureau of Kansas City. Unaccustomed to controversy, the *National Geographic* offices were shocked at the outcry raised over a small section of what had been seen as a standard article. Protestations by Grosvenor that the piece had been checked for accuracy by Western diplomats in Syria, the Syria desk officer at the U.S. State Department, and even several rabbis—none of whom had found any problems with the text—were unavailing.

The criticism culminated in a public demonstration by the American Jewish Congress (AJC) outside the Society's Washington offices in late June. Informed of the picketing outside the Society's opulent headquarters, a receptionist was incredulous: "Are you kidding? Who could be mad at us?"[56]

Phil Baum, associate executive director of the AJC, met with Grosvenor and declared that the picketing had become necessary due to the refusal of *National Geographic* to acknowledge its "errors" in print. This was the first instance of picketing against the National Geographic Society since its establishment in 1888. As the picketers prepared to depart after marching in near-100-degree heat, one told a *New York*

Times reporter, "The magazine doesn't print letters to the editor. This is our letter to the editor."

Grosvenor views the picketing basically as an AJC fund-raising event: "A simple matter of dollars out, dollars in.[57] You can hire pickets on short notice around this town." Although some of the picketers argued vehemently with *National Geographic* staffers who went out to speak with them, many were quite amiable. "We served coffee, doughnuts, and bagels to the picketers," Grosvenor recalls. "In fact, I think we picked up a few new members from the group."

At the same time, Grosvenor did not ignore the pressure generated by Baum and the AJC. The Society decided to print an editorial commenting on the episode—another "first" in the fifty-eight years of the organization. Personally signed by Grosvenor, it conceded, "We have received evidence from many of our Jewish readers since the article appeared that convinces us that we unwittingly failed to reflect the harsh conditions under which that small [Damascene Jewish] community has existed since 1948. . . . Our critics were right. We erred."[58]

"A Mimeograph Machine Run Rampant"

During the same period, CBS experienced a similar controversy over a *60 Minutes* segment dealing with the situation of Jews in Syria. The program, titled "Israel's Toughest Enemy," was broadcast February 16, 1975, and featured correspondent Mike Wallace.

As his point of departure Wallace said, "The Syrian Jewish community is kept under close surveillance." He noted that Jews could not emigrate, were required to carry special identification cards, and were also required to notify authorities when traveling inside Syria. Despite such restrictions, Wallace concluded, ". . . today, life for Syria's Jews is better than it was in years past." Wallace backed this claim with a number of interviews with Jews who were making their way comfortably in Syrian society. The most striking of these interviews was with a Jewish teacher. In it Wallace asked, "Where do all these stories come from about how badly the Jews are treated in Syria?" The teacher replied, "I think that it's Zionist propaganda." CBS was swamped with angry letters, and the American Jewish Congress branded the report "excessive, inaccurate, and distorted."[59] Protests were also sent to the Federal Communications

Commission (FCC) and the National News Council. As the complaints continued, Wallace realized that, for the first time, he had "come up against a conscientious campaign by the so-called Jewish lobby—against a mimeograph machine run rampant." He observed at the time: "The world Jewish community tends somehow to associate a fair report about Syria's Jews with an attack on Israel because Syria happens to be Israel's toughest enemy. But the fact is there is not one Syrian Jew in jail today as a political prisoner."

On June 7 of that same year, *60 Minutes* rebroadcast the segment on Syria, along with an account of the criticisms received and additional background on the film. The program also included a promise that Wallace would "go back and take another look" at the situation of Jews in Syria.

The second program, broadcast on March 21, 1976, disappointed critics who expected the second report to prove their charges: instead, it confirmed the findings of the first. A Syrian Jew who had fled Syria at age thirteen and lived in New York declared that Syrian Jews "in general are much more prosperous now than ever before."

Critics then turned to attacking Wallace personally. The February 1984 issue of *Near East Report*, the AIPAC newsletter, carried an anti-Wallace commentary by editor M. J. Rosenberg. He was disturbed by Wallace's observation in the January 8, 1984, edition of *60 Minutes* that "nothing affronts Syrian dignity and pride more than the fact that Israel has Syrian land, the Golan Heights—and Syria wants it back." Rosenberg responded that Wallace "mouths Syrian propaganda as if he were a member of the Ba'ath Party's young leadership group." Recalling the controversy of 1976–77, he wrote that "Wallace didn't learn much from that episode. After all, Mike Wallace is Jewish. Does he feel that he has to bend over backward to prove that he is no secret Zionist?"

A Double Standard Toward Terror and Murder

CBS radio also became a storm center at about the same time as the Wallace controversy. In March 1973, on its show *First Line Report*, White House correspondent Robert Pierpoint made a controversial statement regarding events in the Middle East.[60] Focusing on two recent incidents—a commando-style raid against Palestinian refugee camps 130 miles inside Lebanon's borders and the downing of a Libyan commercial airliner that had strayed over then Israeli-occupied territory in the Sinai Desert—Pierpoint compared the American response to acts of violence committed by Israelis to those committed by Arabs.

He observed that after the massacre of Israeli athletes at the 1972 Olympic Games in Munich, "the United States, from President Nixon on down, expressed outrage." Yet these two more recent acts by Israel had caused the death of more than a hundred innocent civilians, and there had been hardly a ripple of American response. Pierpoint's conclusion was blunt:

> What this seems to add up to is a double standard in this country toward terror and murder. For so long, Americans have become [so] used to thinking of Israelis as the good guys and Arabs as the bad guys that many react emotionally along the lines of previous prejudices. The fact is that both sides have committed unforgiveable acts of terror, both sides have killed innocents, both sides have legitimate grievances and illegitimate methods of expressing them.

Knowing that he had voiced an opinion rarely heard over network airways, Pierpoint was not surprised when CBS switchboards in Washington and New York were jammed for hours with protest calls after his broadcast.[61] The reaction grew so heated, in fact, that Pierpoint became concerned about the attitude of CBS management. Vice President Sandford Socolow told him ominously, "Bob, you're in real trouble," and Gordon Manning, another CBS executive added, "It doesn't look good for you!"—even though both men felt that the commentary had been professionally done and should be defended.

When they walked into the office of Richard Salant, CBS president, to discuss the matter, they quickly learned that Salant had already decided not to bow to the pressure. "Wasn't that a terrific broadcast Pierpoint did!" Salant declared, thus bringing the matter to a close within the CBS hierarchy.

For Pierpoint, however, the controversy lingered. He received more than 400 letters on his broadcast, some labeling him "a vicious anti-Semite" and describing his report as "like Goebbels's propaganda machine." He later remarked that his commentary had caused him to be perceived as a "public enemy" by some Jewish Americans.[62]

Soon after the *First Line Report* broadcast, news reporter Ted Koppel discussed the Pierpoint affair on ABC radio's *World Commentary*. Koppel cited the swift reaction of the pro-Israel lobby: "The Anti-Defamation League responded immediately. Regional offices of the ADL sent out letters the next day, enclosing copies of the Pierpoint report, and calling on friends of the ADL to send their protests to the local CBS affiliate station. That kind of carefully orchestrated 'spontaneous reaction' disturbs me just as much coming from the ADL as it would from a politically partisan group. It is a tactic of intimidation. I hope that the Anti-Defamation League wasn't trying to get Robert Pierpoint fired, because he's a decent and responsible reporter. But I suspect he will think long and hard before he does another commentary that might distress the ADL—which is why I did this one. American newsmen these days simply can't afford to be intimidated—by anyone."

Affordable or not, the intimidation tactic made its mark.[63] Under pressure, Pierpoint dropped a chapter relating the details of the broadcast uproar and its aftermath from his forthcoming book, *White House Assignment*. In the draft chapter, Pierpoint wrote that "a very powerful group of Jewish businessmen and representatives of national Jewish organizations had demanded to see CBS News president Richard Salant" and that "a delegation of Jewish businessmen" called for a retraction by CBS affiliate station WTOP in Washington, D.C.

In the excised chapter, Pierpoint candidly explained the impact of these events on his work as a newsman: "It was many months before I voluntarily discussed the Middle East on the air again." Recalling his decision, Pierpoint says that Elisabeth Jakab, a book editor for the publisher, G. P. Putnam's, predicted that the controversial chapter could affect sales of the book: "She told me that Jews are major book buyers and might boycott my book." Another Putnam staff member had similar advice: "Joel Swerdlow told me he didn't like the chapter, but he admitted he was emotional about the subject because he is Jewish. He suggested that I change the text or drop it." "Finally," concludes Pierpoint, "I gave in."

Indeed, in a March 1983 interview, Pierpoint admitted that the intimidating pressure found its mark beyond his self-censoring decision regarding the book chapter: "Ever since that strong reaction, I have been more aware of the possibility of getting into arguments with listeners and viewers, and therefore sometimes when I had a choice as to whether to do a broadcast on a topic like that or go in another direction, I probably went in another direction. You don't like to have constant arguments, particularly with people you may like and admire but don't agree with."[64]

"Set Right This Terrible Thing"

In 1981 Patsy Collins, chairman of the board of King Broadcasting in Seattle, was subjected to severe criticism for airing a series of reports on Israel and the West Bank.[65] Just before the Israeli invasion of Lebanon, she and a technical crew visited sites including Bir Zeit University in the West Bank, Hebrew University in Jerusalem, and the Israeli Knesset. They put together a series of eight four-minute segments, which were broadcast on the evening television news over eight consecutive days. The reports sought to portray the life of the Palestinians under Israeli occupation. A closing thirty-minute documentary was planned.

Although public reaction to the reports was mild, the local heads of the American Jewish Committee and the ADL visited the station to "set right this terrible thing." They demanded and received a private screening of the final documentary before it was broadcast. Unable to cite any inaccuracies in the piece, they criticized its "tone and flavor." Among telephoned complaints was one accusing Collins of being in the pay of the PLO.

The Israeli consul general in San Francisco, Mordecai Artzieli, telephoned with a stern demand that air time be provided to "refute the lies" in the program. The King stations in Portland and Seattle agreed to follow the closing summary with a 30-minute discussion between representatives of the Jewish and Arab communities, moderated by a member of the broadcast company staff. The planned discussion did not materialize, however, as no Jewish group would agree to send a representative to share air time with an Arab American. Collins believed that the refusal to take part in the discussion was urged by Consul Artzieli.

Reflecting on her experiences, Collins concluded: "I don't think there's any Israeli or Jewish *control* of the media at all. It's influence; and people can be influenced only if they allow themselves to be influenced." Criticism of Collins evaporated with the 1982 Israel invasion of Lebanon—during which Collins herself cited shortcomings in network coverage of the daily progress of the fighting. At the onset of the action, NBC was covering the attack on Lebanon not from Lebanon, but from Israel. Despite the courage of NBC crews in filming the progress and results the Israeli's advance to Beirut, film footage broadcast on the *NBC Nightly News* showed only Israeli forces on their way to Lebanon. Moreover, reports frequently described weapons used by Arabs as "Soviet-made," while the Israelis were never described as using "American-made" F-16s, or "U.S.-built" tanks.

Collins's comments paralleled those of Alexander Cockburn, who had noted in his *Village Voice* column how *New York Times* editors struck the word "indiscriminate" from foreign correspondent Thomas Friedman's August 3 report on the Israeli bombing of Beirut.[66] The action violated usual *Times* policy. Friedman sent a lengthy telex expressing his outrage: "I am an extremely cautious reporter. I do not exaggerate. . . . You knew I was correct and that the word was backed up by what I had reported. But you did not have the courage—guts—to print it in the *New York Times. You* were afraid to tell our readers and those who might complain to you that the Israelis are capable of indiscriminately shelling an entire city."

NBC Charged with Anti-Israel Bias

Despite the instances of NBC's pro-Israeli bias that were cited by Patsy Collins, Alexander Cockburn, Richard Broderick, and others, eight affiliates of the network in New York came under pressure in 1983 from partisans who alleged bias against Israel in *NBC Nightly News* coverage of the war in Lebanon.[67] Americans for a Safe Israel (AFSI), a New York–based lobbying organization, filed petitions with the Federal Communications Commission to prevent the eight affiliates in New York from renewing their broadcast licenses. AFSI director Peter Goldman described the NBC coverage as "deliberate distortion of the news," claiming that the network presented the war "in a manner favorable to the Arabs."

Goldman's campaign against NBC—presented in a film entitled *NBC in Lebanon: A Study of Media Misrepresentation*—had been backed by the Committee for Accuracy in Middle East Reporting in America (CAMERA), a Washington-based group that focuses its efforts primarily against anti-Israel bias it allegedly finds in the *Washington Post*.[68]

Lawrence K. Grossman, president of NBC News, called the AFSI charges "untrue and unfounded: The AFSI film distorted NBC News coverage and selectively ignored important aspects of NBC's reports."[69] He noted that the *Columbia Journalism Review* had praised the "overall balance" of NBC coverage, and that the *Washington Journalism Review* had criticized the AFSI film for "manipulation" of NBC's coverage of the war in Lebanon. Early in 1984 the FCC rejected similar AFSI petitions against seven NBC affiliate stations in New England, but the group did not relax its pressure. The petitions were revised and resubmitted.[70]

Such attempts to stifle media coverage deemed uncomplimentary to Israel were augmented with a $2 million media campaign by Israel designed to assure Americans that Israelis are nice, warm people and not bloodthirsty militarists.[71]

Lobbyist in the News Room

Like Thomas Friedman, William Branigin of the *Washington Post* covered the Israeli bombing in Beirut—but, unlike those of the *New York Times*, his editors did not delete "indiscriminate" from his front-page report. During the same period, however, *Post* editors experienced an intimidating presence in their newsrooms.

Fairness in reporting Middle East events has been a special concern of the *Washington Post* over the past several years. Complaints from pro-Israel groups about its coverage of Lebanon—especially the massacres at Sabra and Shatila—led to the unprecedented placement of a representative from a pro-Israel group as an observer in the *Post* newsroom.

The idea arose when Michael Berenbaum, executive director of the Jewish Community Council of Greater Washington; council president Nathan Lewin; and Hyman Bookbinder, area representative of the American Jewish Committee, met with *Washington Post* editors to inform them that the paper had "a Jewish problem."[72] The meeting followed substantial correspondence between the *Post* and Jewish community leaders. As an accommodation, executive editor Benjamin C. Bradlee agreed to have Berenbaum observe its news operations for one week, provided he not lobby or "interfere with the editorial process in any way."

Many members of the *Post* staff were unhappy about having to work under the surveillance of an outsider. News editor Karen DeYoung declared the idea "not the best in the world. . . . There's no question that someone following you around all day is an inconvenience." Columnist Nick Thimmesch found the experience "very intimidating."[73] He recalled a comment of one staffer that expressed the view of many: "Next thing you know, someone else will be in here."

Washington Post ombudsman Robert J. McCloskey termed the week a "worthwhile experiment": "Irregular, yes, but so is the shelling newspapers are taking."[74] Criticism from the Jewish community diminished somewhat as a result, but editors of other major newspapers were critical of the whole episode. *Boston Globe* editor Thomas Winship commented, "I understand the pressures the *Post* has been under from the Jewish Community Council, and I have sympathy for what the *Post* did, but I would hope personally that I would not do it."[75] Robert Gibson, foreign news editor of the *Los Angeles Times*, questioned the fairness of the *Post*'s decision: "I honestly don't know how one could do it for Jews and refuse to do it for Arabs."

When Moshe Arens arrived in Washington as Israeli ambassador to the United States in February 1982, he initiated monitoring and evaluation of the coverage given to Israel in American newspapers.[76] His scoring system showed that the *Washington Post* had distinguished itself as "by far the most negative" in reporting on Israel and the Middle East in 1982—the year of Israel's invasion of Lebanon. Arens noted with dismay that the massacre of hundreds of civilians in the Sabra and Shatila refugee camps in the fall of 1982 produced "a tremendous drop in the index, to the lowest point" since the beginning of the weekly survey.

Armed with a battery of graphs and charts, Arens presented his findings to Meg Greenfield, editor of the *Washington Post* editorial pages. Greenfield, who ranked among the most respected voices in U.S. journalism, disputed the very premise of the ratings.[77] She protested that the *Post* had fulfilled its "obligation of fairness" by having "as many of the important Arab and Israeli players as we could speak for themselves on our op-ed page." During the controversial Israeli invasion, pro-Israel commentaries by Israeli Foreign Minister Yitzhak Shamir, Abba Eban, Henry Kissinger, Alfred Friendly, Shimon Peres, and Arens himself had been printed. Two long editorials from respected Israeli newspapers had also appeared in the *Post*.

The *Boston Globe* was the only other paper contacted by Arens because of the low rating he gave its stories about Israel and the Middle East.[78] Former editor Thomas Winship recalled that Arens "started right off going after the American press on what he felt was very much a bias against Israel." Arens described the *Globe* as "one of the newspapers with the most negative attitude," and he made this view known to the local Jewish community.[79]

Like Greenfield, Winship rejected the idea of the ratings system: "My feeling is that having such a list smacks of the Nixon enemies list and strikes me as pretty close to harassment of the media."[80] Current *Globe* editor Ben Bradlee, Jr., describes the Arens study and his meetings with newspaper executives as "an unusually bold demonstration of Jerusalem's effort to put the American press on the defensive and make itself heard among opinion shapers."[81]

Pressure to "Stop the Ads"

Direct pressure to reject paid advertising that was viewed as being unsympathetic to Israeli interests was applied beginning in late 1982 against major media in Maryland, Pennsylvania, and the District of Columbia. The National Association of Arab Americans (NAAA), the oldest Arab American foreign policy lobbying organization in the country, purchased radio air time in these areas for commercials questioning the U.S. government's decision to increase aid to Israel.

Typical of the messages was this one, which was aired in Pennsylvania:

> While there are more than twelve million Americans unemployed, with over half a million from Pennsylvania alone, Congress decided to give Israel 2 billion, 485 million of your tax dollars. Senator Arlen Specter [D-PA] is on the Senate Appropriations Committee that wanted to give Israel even more. Is funding for Israel more important than funding for Pennsylvania? Call your senators and ask them if they voted to give your tax dollars to Israel.[82]

Thirteen Pennsylvania stations contracted to carry the NAAA message. Four of these canceled the ads after only three days of an agreed-upon five-day run. Mike Kirtner, an ad salesman representing two stations in Allentown, informed the NAAA that its ads were being taken off the air because "they were getting a lot of calls, hate calls, and a lot of pressure was coming down on the station to stop the ads." Station management refused to comment on who was pressuring the station to take the ads off the air.

Mike George, a salesman for an Erie station that canceled the ads, was more frank. He informed the NAAA that the station owner had been called by "a group of Jewish businessmen who told him that if he did not cancel the ads immediately, they were going to cause his radio and television stations to lose hundreds of thousands of dollars."

In Maryland, the NAAA sponsored similar messages citing the prominence of Congressman Clarence "Doc" Long (D-MD) in supporting aid to Israel.[83] Although the ads were aired on four stations in Washington, D.C., as well as four in the Baltimore area, a number of stations refused to carry them, calling them "anti-Semitic."

Later, in California, the NAAA found that stations in San Francisco, San Mateo, Berkeley, and Santa Clara were unwilling to carry the NAAA's paid message, despite editorial statements in some local newspapers supporting the NAAA's right to free speech. The stations offered no reason for their refusal.[84]

Ron Cathell, who served as communications director for the NAAA before its merger with the Arab-American Anti-Discrimination Committee, was not surprised by this apparent lack of accountability: "This has happened to us before. People have been threatened with financial losses to prevent them from having a talk show with us or running our ads. [But] it hasn't happened to this degree before. This week was really pretty stunning." Cathell added: "The only way to get [the Middle East conflict] resolved is to talk about it. And if we can't talk about it here in the United States, how do we expect them to talk about it in the Middle East?"[85]

"Someone Even Managed to Defecate into a Photocopier"

Israel's March 2002 incursion into the West Bank prompted unprecedented coverage of the Palestinian plight. Unfortunately, most of that coverage was presented outside of the United States. British *Independent* correspondent Robert Fisk, who has lived for years in Beirut, listed some of the disinformation tactics that accompanied the military assault, including "dishonest attempts to label any criticism of Israel as anti-Semitism, fraudulent assertions that the Israeli army behaves with restraint, mass rallies, and continued attempts to portray Palestinians as beast-like, suicidal animals."

"Europeans," Fisk continued, "are becoming weary of this cynical, ruthless conflict, tired of being called anti-Semites when they object to Israel's occupation. . . . And despite the roar of the old pro-Israeli pundits on the U.S. east coast and Israel's lobbying power over Congress, Americans are infuriated by the gutless, supine Middle East policies of their own government."[86]

One of these Americans is former CIA political analyst Kathleen Christison, who wrote an article questioning the "anti-Semitic" label so often used to silence critics of Israel. She cited an article by "honest, courageous" Israeli reporter Amira Hass, in which Hass described the devastation caused by Israeli forces during their month-long occupation of the Palestinian Ministry of Culture. In addition to damaging computers, books, and furniture, Hass offered the following, deeply disturbing images:

"There are two toilets on every floor, but the soldiers urinated and defecated everywhere else in the building, in several rooms in which they had lived for about a month. They did their business on the floors, in emptied flowerpots, even in drawers they had pulled out of desks. They defecated into plastic bags, and these were scattered in several places. Some of them had burst. Someone even managed to defecate into a photocopier. Relative to other places, the soldiers did not leave behind them many sayings scrawled on the walls. Here and there were the candelabrum symbols of Israel, Stars of David, praises for the Jerusalem Betar soccer team."

Reacting to the Hass report, Christison was "forced to ask some questions that the American majority will no doubt never hear." For example: "Can it, for instance, be called terrorism if an entire unit of the

Israeli army forsakes purity of arms and spends a month crapping on floors, on piles of children's artwork, in desk drawers, on photocopiers? Is this self-defense, or 'rooting out the terrorist infrastructure'? Is it anti-Semitic to wonder what happened to the moral compass of a society that spawns a group of young men who will intermingle their own religious and national symbols with feces and urine, as if the drawings and the excrement both constitute valued autographs?"[87]

Being labeled anti-Semitic is not, of course, the worst thing that can happen to a journalist. Quite a few, as noted earlier, receive death threats. Some are physically attacked. Fisk wrote: "Almost anyone who criticizes U.S. or Israeli policy in the Middle East is now in this free-fire zone. My own colleague in Jerusalem, Phil Reeves, is one of them. So are two of the BBC's reporters in Israel, along with Suzanne Goldenberg of *The Guardian*—all highly respected, eloquent reporters with a history of balance and objectivity in their reporting—and none of them American." Despite attempts at fairness, Fisk wrote, "the damage has been done. As journalists, our lives are now forfeit to the Internet haters. If we want a quiet life, we will just have to toe the line, stop criticizing Israel or America. Or just stop writing altogether."

Arabs and Muslims Organize

Thankfully, journalists like Fisk and Hass have not lowered their standards or ceased working altogether. And while their counterparts in the mainstream American media are difficult to locate, those reporters encounter great support from the burgeoning Arab American and Muslim American communities.

Muslim Americans have finally entered the mainstream of U.S. politics. In the spring of 1998, Muslim policy organizations, under the leadership of American Muslim Alliance (AMA) founder Dr. Agha Saeed, formed a coordinating council. It consists of the Council of American Islamic Relations (CAIR), the American Muslim Council (AMC), and the Muslim Public Affairs Council (MPAC), in addition to AMA. While the other groups follow broader agendas, the AMA focuses entirely on persuading Muslims to enter the political arena at all levels. In 2000, more than 700 Muslims were candidates for public office, and 152 were victorious.

Arab American organizations provide services parallel to those of the Muslim groups. Of these, the American-Arab Anti-Discrimination Committee (ADC), founded in 1980 by former U.S. Senator James Abourezk, has the largest membership. It is headed by Ziad Asali, M.D., a Palestinian Muslim who formerly operated a clinic in my Illinois constituency. His wife Naila, an Egyptian-born Christian, left her career to become the president of ADC and, later, a member of its board of directors. During our first meeting in Illinois in 1985, Mr. and Mrs. Asali mentioned their plan to retire from their professional careers and move to Washington, D.C., in order to devote their full time to challenges facing Arab Americans. The National Association of Arab Americans (NAAA) is now consolidated with the ADC, with former president Khalil Jahshan now serving as vice president. The Asali–Jahshan team brings commitment, skill in human relations, and broad experience to the cause.

Also notable is Ray Hanania, an award-winning Chicago journalist turned media consultant, who founded the *Arab American View* monthly newspaper in 1999. The same year, Hanania organized the National Arab-American Journalism Association, for which he serves as director. At the organization's second conference in Chicago in March 2002, 145 Arab American journalists from across the nation and several other countries participated. Hanania is author of the book *I Am Glad I Look Like a Terrorist: Growing Up Arab in America*. As a volunteer in Palestine, he recently trained local officials in media relations. A man of diverse talents, he moonlights as a stand-up comedian in Chicago nightclubs.

The Arab American Institute (AAI), whose agenda includes public policy issues as well as partisan activity through both major parties, is headed by its founder, Dr. James Zogby. The AAI helps carry out voter registration and partisan activities by Arab Americans. Zogby is a veteran campaigner for Palestinian rights, a columnist, and a frequent guest on television discussion programs.

Both ADC and AAI sponsor seminars, workshops, and activities on Capitol Hill and at the community level. Working closely with Muslim groups, they are established as a feature of the American political landscape. Will they become an effective counterbalance to Israel's lobby in time to avert the "filthy war," as Robert Fisk describes it, from engulfing America in a horrifying catastrophe?

12

What Price Israel?

IN THE AFTERMATH of 9/11, the people of the United States and their institutions struggled against disruptive forces. The nation was suddenly at war. Muslims and people of Arab ancestry found themselves constantly on the defensive as racial and ethnic profiling became facts of life. So did long lines at airports and anxiety about where terrorists may strike next. Spending for military purposes soared, plunging government surpluses into red ink. Funds for education and social services were cut.

Some people considered these disruptions to be byproducts of the U.S. government's decades-long blind support of Israel, but most Americans were not even aware of the nature and extent of this support. For many years, U.S. financial support for this small nation amounted to an annual minimum of $3 billion. During the Clinton administration the annual outlay exceeded $4 billion.

Money was only part of United States' support for Israel. The U.S. government often donated additional military weapons and material. In its diplomacy, it almost always sided with Israel, even when the American position was opposed by almost every other nation.

This deep attachment to Israel began as soon as the state came into being fifty-four years ago. Backed by a small but passionately committed minority of America's Jews, augmented later by growing groups of fundamentalist Christians, the lobby of the American Israel Public Affairs Committee (AIPAC) steadily strengthened its manipulation of U.S. political institutions into unconditional support of Israel's subjugation of the Palestinian people and the forcible takeover of Arab land. This transition occurred with little awareness by the American people, except those of Arab ancestry and Muslim affiliation.

Throughout the years, America's national leaders acted as if they were oblivious of the violations of international law perpetrated against the Palestinians by every Israeli government since the creation of the Jewish state. With only two brief exceptions years ago when the U.S. government sold military aircraft to Saudi Arabia, Israel's lobby always got what it wanted.[1]

After 9/11, lobby influence was nowhere more apparent than on Capitol Hill. Even as evidence of worldwide outrage against U.S. complicity with Israel's assault on the West Bank and Gaza mounted, a large majority of members of both the House of Representatives and the Senate remained beholden to AIPAC. They blocked any fair and open discussion of the U.S. national interest on Middle East policies, giving their allegiance on these issues to AIPAC, rather than to their home constituencies.

In the spring of 2002, when Israel's invasion of the West Bank was in full force, lobby influence remained so overwhelming that almost the entire membership of Congress approved what I believe to be the most biased resolutions on the Middle East in the institution's history. As discussed earlier, similar resolutions in both chambers heaped unstinting praise on the Israeli aggressors and harsh blame on Palestinian victims. In the House, only 21 of the 435 members voted no. Dr. James Zogby, president of the Arab American Institute, while deploring the spectacle, noted that several House members voted present and others did not vote. Still others announced their opposition, then, incredibly, voted yes. I found the voting record depressing, but Zogby cited a silver lining: "My estimate is that about 100 members displayed their opposition in one way or another. I interpret the vote as a sign of rising opposition to U.S.

Middle East policies."[2] In the 100-member Senate, Robert C. Byrd (D-WV) and Ernest Hollings (D-SC) provided the only negative votes.

No one in Washington was surprised by this legislative outrage, because every Congress since the administration of Dwight D. Eisenhower proceeded with a similar disregard of reality. It was simply the latest evidence that Capitol Hill is truly Israeli-occupied territory. Members of Congress are well informed about the true interests of the United States in the Middle East, but they are so intimidated they obey lobby direction. Based on my long, intimate experience in the Capitol Hill legislative process, I believe that most of those who cast affirmative votes on the resolutions privately resented being pressured by AIPAC and were embarrassed by having to vote against U.S. interests. Scores of times over the years, I have sat in committee and in the chamber of the House of Representatives as my colleagues behaved, as an undersecretary of state once described them, like "trained poodles" jumping through hoops held for them by AIPAC.

By voting affirmative on the biased resolutions in 2002, members of Congress ignored the centrality of the Palestinian plight in the hearts of many millions of people throughout the world, including Muslims and Arabs, who are closely linked across borders by religion and race. Also deeply distressed were millions of other people of conscience, many of them Christians and Jews. I estimate that at least 1.5 billion people rated the fate of the Palestinians and the religious shrines in Jerusalem as issues that towered in importance over all others, including Bush's war on terrorism. They blamed the catastrophe in the Middle East on the United States as well as on Israel. But only a tiny band among America's elected leaders seemed to care—or know.

"Israel-like Bombings Possible"

As the anniversary of 9/11 approached, neither the Congress nor the administration of President George W. Bush had awakened to these realities. Despite large protest marches in many countries, including the United States, and warnings of unprecedented severity from moderate leaders in the Middle East, the president and his chief advisers seemed unaware of grievances that prompted the protests. Instead of seeking out, identifying, and correcting errors and oversights in U.S. policy, they seemed totally focused on the possibility of further terrorism. Administration officials warned publicly—almost daily—of terrorist attacks against America that they deemed to be imminent. One morning, my hometown newspaper carried the headline "Israel like Bombings Probable," and *USA Today's* front page shouted: "Suicide bombs expected in USA. FBI chief calls such attacks 'inevitable.'" The news reports, like many others, contained not a word about the possibility that wrong policies of the U.S. government might be at the root of violence.

In late May, Bush summed up his worldview in an interview with Tom Brokaw, news anchor for NBC television: "This war is good versus evil, freedom versus tyranny." To Palestinians writhing under Israel's brutal occupation, his summation was outrageous and absurd. How could they be expected to believe that Bush stood for freedom and against tyranny when they knew from firsthand experience that the U.S. government consistently supported, year after year, the tyranny being inflicted on them?

To many of the victims of Israeli violence, Israel and the United States were the Middle East's "axis of evil." They knew that Israel, a nation of only six million people, could not have maintained its own brand of anti-Palestinian apartheid without the massive backing of Bush and every other president since John F. Kennedy.

Asked by Brokaw when the war on terrorism would end, the president replied: "When they don't want to hurt us any more." His words had a hollow ring to survivors of the military onslaught that had occurred a month earlier when Israeli forces, using bullets, bombs, tanks, and gunships donated by the U.S. government, brought death and destruction on a massive scale to the Palestinians in the Jenin refugee camp and the beleaguered cities of Ramallah, Bethlehem, and Nablus.

In this information age, it was a supreme irony to find the commander in chief of the world's remaining military superpower, as well as most U.S. citizens, out of touch with reality in the Middle East and worldwide anti–United States fervor. I cannot believe that Bush would have spoken as he did, making no reference whatsoever to grievances against U.S.–Israeli policies, had he comprehended the depth and breadth of worldwide resentment against the United States bias in Middle East policy.

Public opinion is not the only issue politicians must consider, but no politician can wisely ignore it. Bush should have known that the tide of world opinion was rising powerfully and fiercely against him and that, within the United States, the people supporting Israeli policies were actually a minority of the total population. A poll by Zogby International reported that 58 percent of Americans wanted the Israeli occupation of the West Bank and Gaza to end. Only 28 percent supported it. The same poll showed 71 percent supporting a Palestinian state.[3]

Clean Slate on Middle East Policy

When George W. Bush arrived at the Oval Office in January 2001, he had a reasonably clean slate on which to write Middle East policy. Although he catered to religious conservatives in his campaign, Bush had no apparent obligations to the pro-Israel lobby. In Colin Powell, he had a secretary of state who was experienced in United States and Middle East politics and respected worldwide. Bush could have wisely—and understandably—announced that the Middle East policies he'd inherited from previous administrations needed review and revision. He could have cleared his administration of complicity in Israeli misdeeds by announcing that he would establish policies to advance the security and well-being of Palestinians as well as Israelis.

Instead, twenty months into office, the Bush administration's only positive step toward evenhanded justice in the Middle East occurred when Powell announced the administration's support for an independent Palestinian state. The statement could have been presented as a major advance in policy, but instead it was cast only as a vague vision, a vision that would soon become more vague.

Aside from that announcement, the Bush response to Israeli–Palestinian turmoil consisted entirely of periodic demands that violence—especially Palestinian violence—must end so that political negotiations could resume. To Palestinians and their supporters, the call for negotiations was more of the same old delays. For years, Palestinian and Israeli officials engaged in protracted discussions that served only Israel's colonial interests, giving the Jewish state more time in which to continue the illegal expansion in number and size of Jewish settlements on Arab land. A major new usurpation occurred in the spring of 2002, when the Israeli government quietly began seizing Palestinian land to create "buffer zones" for the purported protection of Israelis living in the settlements.[4]

Jimmy Carter's Advice

In April 2002, Israeli Prime Minister Sharon buried the prospect of renewed negotiations by launching a war of death and destruction in Palestinian territory, in defiance of Bush's public demand that Israeli forces withdraw immediately. In a remarkable commentary, published the same month in the *New York Times,* former president Jimmy Carter cited the threat of cutting aid as a tactic that Bush could use to secure Israeli cooperation. Carter wrote:

> There are two existing factors that offer success to the United States. One is the [Arms Export Control Act] requirement that American weapons are to be used by Israel only for defensive purposes. It is certainly being violated by Israel in the recent destruction of Jenin and other cities and villages. Richard Nixon used this requirement to stop Israel's military advance, led by Ariel Sharon, into Egypt in the 1973 war. I used the same demand to deter Israeli attacks on Lebanon in 1979. [A full invasion was launched by Ariel Sharon after I left office.] The other persuasive factor is approximately $10 billion in American aid to Israel. President George Bush, Sr., threatened this assistance in 1992 in an effort to halt the building of Israeli settlements between Jerusalem and Bethlehem.

Carter noted that the steps he recommended did not encroach on the sovereign territory of Israel. They related only to lands that are recognized as Palestinian by international law.[5]

In the spring of 2002, despite the gathering worldwide storm of protest that followed the massacre at Jenin, Bush did not act on either of Carter's recommendations. Instead of issuing an ultimatum to Sharon, Bush ducked a showdown with both Sharon and Congress. On NBC's *Meet the Press,* Powell lamely acknowledged that the administration had no intention of cutting aid to Israel in any respect or degree.

As a side note, I mention my own experience with the Carter administration in its response to the Arms Export Control Act. In 1980, while still in Congress, I contended that Israel's use of U.S.-donated arms against the occupied territories and against Lebanon violated the Act, and I demanded that the administration halt aid to Israel. I noted that four years earlier, the United States, citing the same Act, had suspended aid when Turkey, a U.S. ally in NATO, invaded Cyprus. After weeks of prodding, Secretary of State Cyrus Vance sent me a letter of response, in which he admitted only that that Israel "may have violated" the Act.

A Missed Opportunity

As a Republican who worked vigorously for George W. Bush in the 2000 presidential campaign, I applauded him for publicly demanding in March 2002 that Sharon end his war on Palestinians, but I became distressed at his failure to back up the demand with responsible and effective action. With scores of lawyers on his staff, Bush was surely informed about his options under the Arms Export Control Act.

Imagine what might have transpired had Bush halted aid to Israel. Bush had full authority to act without consulting Congress; all he had to do was sign a document called a presidential determination. At that point at least, he had already made up his mind that Sharon's war should end, and any fair-minded observer would have agreed with former President Carter that Israeli forces were using U.S.-supplied weapons for purposes other than legitimate self-defense. If Bush suspended aid, pro-Israel members of Congress would likely protest, but given the president's authority to veto legislation and his high popularity, he could have marshaled sufficient public support, I believe, to head off a showdown with Congress or to prevail if one occurred.

Had Bush announced the suspension of aid, it would have been the most significant decision in U.S. Middle East policy in nearly a half-century. The U.S. government—and the American people—would suddenly be liberated from the burden of their subservience to Israel for the first time since 1967.

Consider the likely impact this would have had on world opinion. The spectacle of the world's military superpower being thoroughly manipulated by a small nation of six million people would have vanished like a bad dream. The many millions of people worldwide who have been dismayed and outraged at America's subservience to Israel would have rubbed their eyes in disbelief. Instead of hanging Bush in effigy and burning American flags, they would be proudly waving the flags and dancing in the streets. The most threatening foreign grievance against the U.S. government would subside.

Instead of engendering such welcome change, Bush again rolled out the White House red carpet for Ariel Sharon and called him a "man of peace." Shortly thereafter, in an act of exquisite acquiescence, the president signed an appropriation bill that gave Israel a bonus of $200 million in addition to its usual grant of $3 billion from the U.S. Treasury. Incredibly, the $200 million reimbursed Israel for the cost of the invasion that Bush had denounced.

"Dehumanization on a Vast Scale"

Why, in the wake of 9/11, did no one ponder the question "why?" Why did America and its leaders remain silent about Arab and Muslim grievances?

Perhaps it was partly, if not mostly, because Muslims are often considered "different," if not dangerous, by the general public—most of whom, I must add, have never knowingly met a Muslim or read a verse from the Qur'an. In research done for my book, *Silent No More*, I learned that Muslims were unfairly linked with terrorism long before 9/11. Misperceptions of Muslims as being less than human were nurtured by heavy television coverage of the suicide bombings in Israel that were carried out by individual Palestinian Muslims, while scenes of Palestinian suffering and death seldom reached American homes. Few Americans seemed aware that Palestinians had no weapons to defend themselves against heavily armed Israeli forces marauding through the West Bank and Gaza.

From its founding in 1948, Israel's government has treated Palestinians as inferior human beings that it was entitled to subjugate. Years ago, Israeli Prime Minister Golda Meir even denied that a Palestinian nationality existed. Her denial buttressed the fiction that Israel came into being in 1948 in "a land without people," a false notion that has been kept alive ever since in Israeli schoolbooks. Even the Palestinians, who can vote in Israeli elections, are set apart from Jewish citizens: Their cars display distinctive license plates. They are denied important social services. They have difficulty buying any real estate and, in effect, can live only in restricted residential areas. They are rarely able to secure construction and remodeling permits, while Jews receive them without delay.

This process of colonial domination and intellectual brutality advanced the destruction of the Palestinian national identity in the perception of the American people: Palestinians are not viewed as human beings struggling for freedom; they are portrayed as anti-Jewish terrorists who hate freedom. Columbia University professor Edward Said, born in Palestine, called Israel's treatment of Palestinians "dehumanization on a vast scale." He added, "The intellectual suppression of the Palestinians that has occurred because of Zionist education has produced an unreflecting, dangerously skewed sense of reality in which whatever Israel does it does as a victim. . . . This has nothing to do with reality, obviously enough, but rather with a kind of hallucinatory state that overrides history and facts with a supreme unthinking narcissism."[6] By helping Israel subjugate Palestinians, the U.S. government advanced this dehumanizing process. The president frequently expressed concern about security for Israelis but never about security for Palestinians. This bias reinforced the notion among Americans that, because Palestinians are ungovernable radicals, the Israeli government must impose harsh treatment in order to keep them under control. Uri Avnery, an Israeli peace activist and former member of the Israeli Knesset, concluded that the real aim of Sharon's March 2002 invasion of the West Bank was nothing less than "the destruction of organized Palestinian society itself."[7]

The U.S. media played a role in America's failure to explore and address Arab grievances. After 9/11, several television commentators rejected as "appeasement of terrorists" steps that would take Arab grievances into consideration. Their reasoning for this was the invariably uttered sound bite: "That is exactly what the terrorists want us to do." To the commentators, responding to legitimate grievances would be tantamount to caving in to the enemy. Except for a few dissenting voices, the misinformed American people seemed to agree.

The additional fear of being marked as anti-Jewish was another reason that Arab grievances were ignored. Any gesture of fairness to Arabs would be widely misconstrued as hostility toward Israel, and this, in turn, would lead to accusations of anti-Semitism. Speaking up for Arab rights could lead to all kinds of personal losses—businesses, friendships, even social standing. Almost everyone could find an excuse to stay quietly on the sidelines.

The Roots of Terrorism

U.S. complicity in Israel's illegal behavior began in earnest in 1967, when Israel, with the clandestine cooperation of President Lyndon B. Johnson, accelerated its takeover of Arab land. Following these conquests, Israel's U.S. lobby pressured the U.S. government into giving ever-increasing amounts of money and armaments, as well as unconditional political support, to the state of Israel. Little pressure was required. Conscious of the threat of being labeled anti-Semitic, members of Congress almost always cooperated.

So did the executive branch. Professor Noam Chomsky, who deserves recognition as the longest-standing Jewish American defender of Palestinian rights, believes the U.S. administration is guilty of "unilateral rejectionism," opposing any measures that could be viewed as anti-Israel. He believes the bureaucracy is a self-starter in this respect and needs no prodding. He contends that, in recent years, the U.S. government has acted on its own in providing decisive support to Israel's policies, under which "Palestinians have suffered terror, destruction of property, displacement and settlement, and takeover of basic resources, crucially water."[8]

Chomsky may be right in his assessment of the executive branch, but the intimidation factor is alive and well on Capitol Hill, where most members, while privately resenting the pressure, dutifully toe the Israeli line. If voting were kept secret, I am confident that aid to Israel would have long ago been heavily conditioned—if not terminated—in both chambers.

In the Oval Office, recent misleading influences on Middle East policy have come from several sources. The most influential group consisted of Republican members of Congress and other party members whose main concern was Bush's election to a second term as president. They welcomed support from all possible groups, especially the politically astute pro-Israel clique.

Another group consisted of staff members who felt constrained to defend the behavior of the state of Israel at all costs. This group included several Jews and fundamentalist Christians. The fundamentalists, often identified as right-wing Christians, were a major element in Bush's election to the presidency. Combined, the Jewish and fundamentalist Christian elements constituted less than 20 percent of the U.S. population, but they occupied positions of influence in Washington out of proportion to their numbers. Nevertheless, they still far outnumbered the ardently pro-Israel groups in the rest of the world.

Surprisingly, the White House staff, as well as the rest of the executive branch, was almost devoid of Muslims, a voting bloc that overwhelmingly supported Bush in his election to the presidency in 2000. In the balloting, Muslim voters gave Bush a national plurality estimated at two million. In Florida, the state that ultimately provided the electors that put Bush in the White House, an estimated 90 percent of Muslim voters cast their ballots for Bush. His plurality among Muslims was more than ninety thousand. Remarkably, twenty-six thousand of that plurality came from first-time voters.

Agha Saeed, who engineered the national bloc voting for Bush, summed it up: "U.S. Muslims crossed the political Rubicon. They formed a new coalition of voters." In the White House, Bush and his political lieutenants did not seem to notice.[9] As they planned Bush's re-election campaign in 2004, they could not count on bloc support from the Muslim community.

The third group consisted of gatekeepers, staff members whose duties included shielding the president from unpleasantness and limiting his appointments to people who would tell him what he wanted to hear.

These combined influences kept the president and top members of his team dangerously isolated from the real America—and the realities of the Middle East. Only a handful of major U.S. periodicals provided balanced coverage of the Israeli–Palestinian conflict. Knowledgeable viewers searched in vain for balanced reporting of Middle East events on television.

Arafat Gets Good Press—Briefly

The bias in reporting is intensified by public relations firms employed by pro-Israel groups. They closely monitor U.S. news coverage of Middle East events and react quickly and effectively when reports surface that are unfavorable to Israel.

News about the Middle East is informally but effectively censored before being broadcast or published in the United States. In contrast, some of the Hebrew press in Israel has been publishing unbiased, vibrant coverage of the Arab–Israeli conflict. For years before his death, in an effort to fill the void in America, Israeli peace activist Israel Shahak distributed a monthly English-language digest of news and commentary that was published in Israel's Hebrew newspapers.

Even the venerable Associated Press is not immune to pro-Israel intimidation. In late May 2002, a report written and dispatched by Associated Press veteran State Department reporter Barry Schweid was quickly modified after a flurry of telephone protests. The original version reported, accurately, that "the State Department recently informed Congress that there was no clear evidence that Yasser Arafat or other senior officials of the Palestine Liberation Organization ordered or knew in advance of terror attacks on Israel." Jewish groups angrily protested that the report wrongly portrayed Arafat as innocent and demanded that it be revised to drop the implication. Schweid told a caller that his office was "swamped" with protests. He said one of them, Representative Tom Lantos (D-CA), was "near hysterics" in demanding a "less innocent" portrayal of Arafat. Because of the protests, Schweid recalled the original dispatch and substituted a revised version. Evidently the revision did not satisfy Lantos and others, as two more versions followed, each portraying Arafat more guilty than those before.[10]

Partners in Awful Carnage

Due to this type of censorship, the American people hardly noticed the whirlwind of anti-American protests that swept much of the world in the spring of 2002. In many countries, government officials and common people alike expressed outrage when the United States did nothing to halt Israel's onslaught against Palestinians in the West Bank. The outrage prompted millions of people to join protest marches, many bearing posters lamenting the brutality of Israeli military forces, some burning Sharon and Bush in effigy, and others desecrating the flags of both nations.

The U.S. response consisted of little-noticed "advisories" urging Americans abroad to hunker down and be alert for anti-American violence. That was all. Not a hint that anyone in power in Washington recognized the possibility that U.S. policies were highly provocative.

Osama bin Laden's Motives

In his televised address to Congress after 9/11, President Bush dismissed the attacks as pure evil, planned by ex-Saudi Osama bin Laden, perpetrated by other Saudi dissidents, and motivated by their envy of the freedoms that the American people enjoy. He ignored two facts: First, that while people in countries more accessible to terrorists than the United States enjoy the same freedoms as Americans, only the United States suffered a major onslaught. Second, despite America's shortcomings, U.S. citizenship and the liberties it conveys remains a primary dream of millions of people worldwide, not a motive for terrorism. For example, hundreds of Saudis have happily gained U.S. citizenship, and many others are waiting in line.

Bin Laden's motives were plainly displayed on the Internet. In 1999, the PBS *Frontline* television series broadcast a documentary called *The Terrorist and the Superstar*. It was based on a lengthy filmed interview of bin Laden, in which he castigated the United States for supporting Israel's subjugation of the Palestinian people. The full text of the interview was placed on the Internet. The documentary brought to viewers samples of bin Laden's anti-American rhetoric, but not his impassioned statement of Arab grievances against the United States. The broadcast alleged that he played a major role in the 1998 bombing of U.S. embassies in Kenya and Tanzania, explosions that were fatal to U.S. personnel and many local citizens. It also examined the U.S. retaliatory bombing during the Clinton administration of Sudan and bin Laden's base of operations in Afghanistan.

In the documentary, bin Laden cast the peaceful religion of Islam in a false mold, calling on Muslims to make war on America and "kill Americans where they can and when they can." The documentary's producers made bin Laden seem all the more maniacal by omitting two important parts of his taped interview: In the first, bin Laden made his statement of grievances, condemning the U.S. government for its longstanding complicity in Israel's history of repression of the rights of Palestinians. In the second, bin Laden modified his call to kill all Americans, this time limiting his target to U.S. military personnel.

By omitting these statements from the broadcast, the producers left television viewers wondering what, if anything, triggered bin Laden's fiery verbal assault. Those who objectively examined the full text of the interview on the Internet after watching the televised broadcast could not escape the conclusion that the producers censored bin Laden's statements in a way that shielded U.S. aid to Israel—and Israel itself—from criticism.

I found other examples of censorship. In March 2002, CNN broadcast a taped commentary in which bin Laden strongly criticized the U.S. government, listing the same grievances he had stated in the PBS documentary interview. CNN rebroadcast the bin Laden commentary several times during the next few hours, but in each rebroadcast, bin Laden's complaint about U.S. aid to Israel was omitted. The omission may not have been an intentional act of censorship, but the effect was the same: U.S. aid to Israel was spared notoriety.[11]

"Unrelenting Israeli Terrorism"

A few days after 9/11, Secretary of State Colin Powell came close to linking the assault to the plight of Palestinians. When asked by a reporter why America is hated in the Arab and Muslim world, Colin Powell stated that it is "due to the Palestinian crisis." This comment, coming from America's senior foreign policy officer, should have triggered immediate congressional hearings to seek elaboration from Powell, as well as commentary by other experts in foreign policy.[12] The hearings might have led to an examination of U.S. responsibility for the Palestinian plight. There was no follow-up on Capitol Hill, in the media, or elsewhere.

Two weeks later, James J. David of Marietta, Georgia, a brigadier general in the Georgia National Guard who had extensive experience in the Middle East as a U.S. Army officer, was even more explicit than Powell. In an article, David declared that "the cause of this terrorism is our involvement in and support of the criminal behavior of the Israeli government. You can be certain that you will not hear this accusation from the controlled media, but nevertheless, let the truth be known. . . . The Palestinians and many of their Arab allies have been targets of a half-century of unrelenting Israeli terrorism. . . . Every Palestinian and Arab is aware that Israel's . . . terror could never have occurred without the active financial, military, and diplomatic support of the United States. That is why the Arabs hate us, and that is why they are trying to strike back at us. . . . Striking back at the terrorists is important, but getting to the source of terrorism is even more important."[13]

Three months later, in a letter to Powell, David wrote: "The United States' generous handouts to the Jewish state have done nothing but bring more turmoil and violence to the Middle East and to the soil of the United States. If America wants peace in the Middle East and is serious about fighting world terrorism, then it's time to get tough with Israel and end all military and economic aid to the Jewish state."[14]

International Herald Tribune columnist William Pfaff is among the few prominent commentators who promptly called for redress of Palestinian grievances. Two days after 9/11 he wrote: "The only real defense against external attack is a courageous effort to find political solutions for national and ideological conflicts that involve the United States. For more than thirty years, the United States has refused to make a genuinely impartial effort to find a resolution to the Mideast conflict. If current speculation about these attacks is true, and they do indeed have their genesis in the Israeli–Palestinian struggle, the United States has now been awarded its share in that Middle East tragedy."

Charley Reese, a syndicated columnist, expressed a similar theme: "I hope you don't believe the fairy tale that we were attacked because of our wealth or freedom or because someone sitting in a distant cave (with hundreds of millions of dollars in various banks, by the way) was jealous. That is disinformation. We were attacked and will be attacked as long as we support Israel's aggression and occupation of other people and their lands. Personally, I am deeply angered that people I love might die one day just because a bunch of politicians have their hands in the pockets of the Israeli lobby. That is a sordid, stupid, and useless reason for any American to die."[15]

These were lone voices of reason. The U.S. news media ignored the motivations cited by David, Pfaff, and Reese and focused almost exclusively on the Palestinian suicide attacks that were fatal to Israelis, citing them as fanatical terrorism. There were exceptions. In May 2002, the *Pittsburgh Post-Gazette* published Riad Z. Abdelkarim's explanation of why some Palestinians became bombers: "They have decided that as long as Palestinians suffer death, destruction, mayhem, displacement, humiliation, so will Israelis—wherever and whoever they may be."[16] The same month, Abdelkarim, a California physician, was jailed by Israeli authorities, delaying for ten days his scheduled return home after volunteering medical care to injured Palestinians in the West Bank.

Several years earlier, Israeli lecturer and former Knesset member Nurit Peled-Eichanan blamed the government of Israel when her daughter Smadar, thirteen, was killed by a Palestinian suicide bomber: "When you put people under border closure, when you humiliate, starve, and suppress them, when you raze their villages and demolish homes, when they grow up in garbage and in holding pens, that's what happens. Don't blame the extremist group Hamas. We are nurturing the Hamas by what we are doing."[17]

Encouraging Developments

Amid these mostly bleak clouds, bits of sunshine break through. In addition to the steadily rising political mobilization of Arab American and Muslim American organizations—with the Council of American Islamic Relations leading the way—groups without particular ethnic or national focus became increasingly active in Middle East policy at the national level.

Jerri Bird, the wife of a retired U.S. foreign service officer, divided her waking hours between two related causes: protesting the torture routinely inflicted by Israeli authorities on people detained or jailed; and sponsoring lecture tours across the United States by female trios from Jerusalem. After rearing a family and retiring from a career in educational administration, Bird is pursuing this dual unpaid career with vigor. Much of her energy is devoted to combating the indifference of the U.S. State Department to the torture of U.S. citizens.

She directs her activities from a small office that is headquarters for Partners for Peace, an organization of volunteers that she founded in 1991. The group shares office space with the Council for the National Interest (CNI), a separate activist organization on Middle East policy that I helped to found in 1989. CNI is headed by Jerri's husband, Gene Bird. Partners for Peace functions with only one paid staff member. About three hundred supporters meet the budget that averages $55,000 a year.

In June 2002, Bird was planning the fifth annual U.S. tour of what she calls "Jerusalem Women Speak: Three Women, Three Faiths, One Shared City." The tour group consists of three women who reside in Jerusalem—one a Christian Palestinian, another a Muslim Palestinian, and the third a Jewish Israeli. A different team is fielded each year. They put a human face on the conflict and offer their personal experiences and views of how a real peace can be achieved. Each tour is fast-paced, involving seventy public events within a ten-day period. The tour usually includes visits to ten cities and a minimum of five speaking events each day. The lectures draw large crowds and elicit good coverage by news media, sometimes nationally by CNN and C-SPAN.

Bird's other passion is protesting torture in Israeli jails and prisons. She and her colleagues have found evidence of the mistreatment of at least fourteen U.S. citizens, most of them of Palestinian origin. The efforts of the group may have led to shortened confinement for seven of them.

According to Bird, Israel's U.S. lobby maintains a grip on the U.S. State Department so absolute that Israel is able to torture U.S. citizens with virtual impunity. The June 2002 issue of the *Foreign Service Journal* featured a lengthy article in which Bird quoted several victims of torture and protested the indifference of U.S. officials. She wrote: "I regard [those who spoke out] as brave, because Shin Bet [Israel's security] officials told them as they left Israel, 'Don't cause us any trouble. Just remember we can get you, no matter where you are.'"

Bird wrote that she has compiled clear evidence that the U.S. government has known for at least twenty-four years that Israel uses torture during interrogations of Palestinians on a wide scale: "The United States had evidence that American children were also subjected to this abuse. Yet, over more than two decades, no effective action has been taken by the United States to halt this practice. Furthermore, the United States took great care to avoid any public admission that Americans had been tortured." Bird quoted Anwar Mohamed, one of the victims: "'I cannot believe that my government was powerless to take action on my behalf. Is it because I have an Arabic name?'"

According to Miftah, an Arab organization headed by prominent Palestinian educator Dr. Hanan Ashrawi, the Israelis have carried out more than 600,000 arrests or detentions. B'Tselem, an Israeli human rights organization, and Miftah agreed that 90 to 94 percent of those detained are tortured. Bird wrote: "Even when the lives of American citizens are at stake, the U.S. does not intervene effectively to safeguard them. How can this be justified?"[18]

"Matter-of-Fact References"

In May 2002, amid a threatening worldwide political storm complicated by the danger of war between India and Pakistan over Kashmir, President Bush offered a glimmer of hope on the Middle East front by speaking of Palestinian statehood as a clear objective of U.S. policy.

If he actually meant what he said, Bush became the first president to set a precise U.S. goal of any kind in Middle East peace negotiations. Except for Bill Clinton's commendable farewell message, in which he declared the inevitability of Palestinian statehood, Bush's predecessors never got beyond bland comments that the terms of peace must be left to negotiations between Palestinians and Israelis.

In early May 2002, *Mirror International* reported from Washington that "Bush has made Palestinian statehood central to U.S. policy in the Middle East. He is the first president to explicitly support a [Palestinian] state. Bush has envisioned two states, one Palestinian and the other Jewish, existing in peace side by side." The commentary added: "So ingrained has administration acceptance of Palestinian statehood become that Bush's assistant for national security, Condoleeza Rice, and Undersecretary of State Marc Grossman, made almost matter-of-fact references to Palestine in speeches last week to the American Jewish Committee." During a news conference, White House press secretary Ari Fleischer affirmed the president's support for statehood.[19]

A few days later, Powell mentioned the possibility of a "provisional state," a concept that Israeli Foreign Minister Shimon Peres promptly endorsed. Whether Palestinians will settle for anything less than full Israeli withdrawal from the occupied territories remains to be seen. A provisional state might mean nothing more than maintaining the "status quo," with Israel remaining fully in charge of Palestinian destiny. At the least the Powell–Peres discussion suggested that U.S. commitment to Palestinian statehood was still, one might say, provisional.[20]

A month later, it became even more provisional when Bush, in an unpresidential public outburst of personal animus, demanded that Yasser Arafat step down from Palestinian leadership before progress toward statehood occurred.

What Price Censorship?

When I wrote the first edition of this book, my main concern was the destructive effect of Israel's lobby on free political speech in the United States. I predicted that the lobby's success in eliminating any semblance of debate about Middle East policies would lead America into serious difficulty.

At no point did I anticipate that the lobby's success in stifling free speech could set in motion a chain reaction that would lead to calamitous events at home and abroad. Consider these developments:

- U.S. complicity in a campaign to destroy an entire nationality
- A horrific attack on the U.S. mainland
- A war in Afghanistan and the likelihood of more wars to come
- Worldwide anti-American protest marches
- Serious damage to America's worldwide reputation as champion of human rights and the rule of law

As you ponder this recitation, the following questions deserve attention:

If the United States had refused partnership in Israel's crimes against the Palestinians and other Arabs, would Israel have been able to maintain its subjugation of the Palestinian people decade after decade? Any fair analysis would yield an answer in the negative. In the absence of unconditional U.S. support, Israel would have discarded its ambitions for "Greater Israel" and negotiated the terms of peaceful coexistence with its neighbors years ago.

Would America have suffered 9/11? My answer is no. All evidence that is available today points to 9/11 as being the crime of disaffected Arabs, mainly Saudis, led by Osama bin Laden. According to bin Laden, they were outraged by what he described as the corrupting influence of the

United States on the Middle East, particularly its support of Israel's subjugation of Palestinian human rights. If these "corrupting influences" did not exist, and if the U.S. government had dealt with Israel in a normal, traditional way by demanding specific standards of conduct in exchange for U.S. aid, America, in effect, would have blocked Israel's illegal campaign of territorial aggrandizement and retained its great Arab reservoir of goodwill. Barring the absence of some anti-Arab blunder in U.S. policy, Arab terrorists would have no reason to attack the United States.

Of course, the United States government has not refused partnership with Israel. On the contrary, every president and every Congress over the years have reiterated loyal, unconditional support of Israel. These statements are usually cast as assurances of undying support for that nation's security, with no reference to the need of Palestinians for security. Those serving in Congress often publicly declare Israel's right to exist within secure borders, and they probably do so more frequently than they repeat the pledge of allegiance to the flag of the United States.

I have yet to hear any member of Congress declare the right of Palestine to exist within secure borders. Nor have I heard any member, while applauding Israel's right to exist, take note of the fact Israel lacks defined borders—the only nation in the world with that dubious distinction. The United States' partnership with Israel has, moreover, never been fully defined. In public discourse it remains as murky as Israel's borders: no treaty between the two states exists.

No U.S. president, I am certain, ever called his cabinet together to announce that henceforth his administration would proceed as a coconspirator with Israel in criminal activity against the Palestinians. Nor has any Congress been that explicit. Nor, I dare say, did any lawmaker anticipate, at any point, that the effectiveness of Israel's lobby in stifling free speech about the Arab–Israeli conflict would be a major factor in leading the American people into their present difficulty.

America's descent into intimate involvement in Israel's unlawful activities advanced step by step, beginning in 1967. The most basic, fundamental cause of this dreadful decline is the lobby's greatest success: the elimination of free, open, unfettered discussion in the United States about what U.S. policy in the Middle East should be. Israelis enjoy free, rigorous debate of Middle East policy in their parliament, media, and private life, but Israel's U.S. lobby has stifled all such debate in America for nearly forty years.

As a member of Congress I was a close observer of this descent. To my alarm, at no point in Israel's oppressive occupation of Palestinian lands did any prominent officials in Washington lament the violation of Arab rights, criticize Israeli behavior, or attempt to establish conditions on U.S. aid to Israel. Only a few small voices of individuals and private organizations petitioned Congress for full debate.

During Israel's brutal assault on the West Bank and Gaza in 2002, few complaints were heard on Capitol Hill. No one introduced resolutions of rebuke or offered legislative remedies. And if there were cries of complaint from American clergy, they were too soft to hear. Only mosques echoed with words of sorrow, lament, and anger. Elsewhere, America seemed to have run out of moral outrage.

Why the silence? Why the unwillingness of people and institutions to speak out? Why the absence of debate over America's complicity in Israel's scofflaw record?

The answer is found in the earlier pages of this book. With few exceptions, members of Congress, presidents, the nation's editorial writers, the clergy, and the nation's vast array of nongovernmental advocacy organizations have been afraid to speak out. I cannot recall any of the major political players in Washington even noting the absence of unfettered debate. They were afraid to challenge Israel or its U.S. lobby at any level for fear of being called anti-Semitic. The operative word was fear.

I understand, perhaps better than most people. In my years in Congress, I can recall moments when I yielded to the intimidating influence of the lobby. I could have been more resolute in words and deed. In protest against U.S. complicity in Israel's misdeeds, I should have opposed in speech and vote every dollar of aid to Israel. Instead, I always voted in the affirmative. I told some of my colleagues that I did not want to be viewed as anti-Israel, because my opposition was to the behavior of the state, not to the state itself. In retrospect, I see it was a distinction without a difference.

A Fateful Chain of Occurrences

In Washington, the absence of rational discussion led directly to a gross pro-Israeli bias of enormous unintended consequences which, in turn, made the U.S. government a partner with Israel in the humiliation and destruction of Palestinian society. During the past twenty years, the lobby for Israel got exactly what it wanted from Capitol Hill and the executive branch. In the preceding thirty years, it got almost everything it wanted.

Through the years, the U.S. government provided support—military, political, and financial—without which Israel could not have carried out its devastation of Palestinian society. Well known worldwide, except in America, this complicity led to deep-seated and widespread hatred of the governments of both Israel and the United States—the major factor, I believe, in triggering 9/11.

This fateful chain of occurrences reminds me of an old fable: For want of a nail, a shoe was lost; for want of the shoe, a horse was lost; for want of the horse, a rider was lost; for want of the rider, the war was lost; for want of victory, a kingdom was lost. In the present crisis, the absence of rational debate was the lost nail. The present-day plight of a great nation called America is the ultimate loss.

When I informed a senior State Department official that I believed 9/11 was substantially rooted in U.S. complicity in Israel's crimes, he replied "I agree with you, and I believe a majority of the State Department officials I deal with would also agree." My estimate is that millions of people in this country and abroad have reached the same conclusion.

The United States was not an innocent bystander in Israel's assaults on Arabs. American fingers did not pull triggers, but they wrote checks to the Internal Revenue Service that paid for the weapons the Israelis used, and they cast ballots that elected officials who gave a steady green light to Israel's illegal activities.

By supporting Israel unconditionally, America turned its back on long-cherished ideals and principles. As expressed in the Declaration of Independence and the U.S. Constitution, all Americans are pledged to stand against bigotry and intolerance and for the rule of law, equal justice for all, and due process even for the most despicable people among us. Instead, year after year, our government has helped Israel violate each of these principles.

For Want of a Nail

Some aspects of 9/11 may remain a puzzle forever, but one thing is clear: it was a monstrous crime, and everyone with any responsibility for it should be brought to justice.

The ongoing crimes against Palestinians are also monstrous. The victims deserve the dignity of citizenship in a state of their own, and they deserve it now. They should not be asked to settle for an interim experiment, a limited, transitional, quasi-state of some form. After all the suffering they have endured, and no matter what provisional steps may be considered, many thousands of Palestinians will insist on unadulterated justice. They will not give up whatever means of violent resistance are possible until Israeli forces withdraw completely, Israel relinquishes control of all settlements, and a truly independent, viable Palestine comes into being.

Now and in the foreseeable future, only the president of the United States can apply enough leverage to force Israel to meet these requirements. Can the presidential will be generated?

In early 2002, Saudi Crown Prince Abdullah set the stage. He secured the unanimous approval of Arab states for a plan for peace with Israel. Under it, all of these states, most of which remain technically at war with Israel, agreed to establish normal, peaceful, diplomatic relations if Israel would withdraw from the Arab territory it seized in the June 1967 war. The plan was also approved by the Palestinian leadership, and, surprisingly, Hamas, an organization often identified with Palestinian suicide bombings in Israel. Opinion polls showed approval by the majority of Palestinians, Israelis, and Americans. On learning of Abdullah's proposal, President Bush telephoned his congratulations.

As I write, the essential link—Israeli governmental approval—is still missing. It is clear that Ariel Sharon, who holds power by a thin margin and is faced with strong opposition from the ultraorthodox Jews and other right-wing parties, will not cooperate in the absence of strong outside pressure. The only possible source of adequate leverage is the president of the United States.

A former foreign minister of France pointed the way. On June 17, 2002, Hubert Vedrine made a powerful public appeal: "President Bush . . . should impose a peace settlement. He must do it. He should do it. He can do it. Nobody else is in a position to do so. Only the president of the United States has the necessary means and authority. If he takes the lead, the whole world will support him—except, perhaps, American conservatives and the Israeli right wing, as well as the most radical Palestinian movements and terrorist networks. But all these opponents can be overcome."[21]

Vedrine packed a lot of wisdom into a few words. The president of the United States must act. He alone has the resources for success. To be effective, the president must disenthrall himself from past decisions and utterances and issue an unequivocal ultimatum to the Israeli prime minister of the type suggested by former President Carter. Like similar threats issued effectively to Israel in past years by both Carter and Nixon, it should be conveyed privately but firmly. Israel must understand that no further U.S. aid will be provided until it ends its occupation of the Arab land it seized in the June 1967 war.

The president should do more than threaten. He should hold the carrot as well as the stick. Bush must offer help during the adjustment period as Israelis and Palestinians become accustomed to their new relationship. The bitter layers of blood, agony, hatred, and passions for vengeance on both sides will not be easily or quickly put aside. If the new border is devoid of armed monitors, violence may erupt despite the best efforts of local leaders.

To maintain peace as citizens on both sides settle down to the first promise of a stress-free existence in years, the United States should offer troops as part of a multinational force charged with providing security along the entire border. In making the offer, the president can usefully cite the success of the multinational monitoring force, consisting mainly of U.S. troops, that has kept the peace along the Israeli–Egyptian border for many years.

Confronted with the ultimatum, the Israeli prime minister would have to decide between two main alternatives.

The first: He could simply ignore the ultimatum, as Sharon did when confronted with Bush's demand that he "immediately" stop Israel's invasion of Palestinian land in the spring of 2002. In that circumstance, if Bush stands firm in demanding full compliance, Israeli citizens, appalled at the cutoff of U.S. aid, would force the prime minister's resignation or remove him from office in the next election.

The second: Faced with that prospect, the prime minister, Sharon or his successor, would agree to the presidential demand.

I would expect the prime minister to follow the rule that guided Charles deGaulle of France during his long public career: "When something is inevitable, turn it to your advantage." By complying with the ultimatum, the prime minister would turn the U.S. demand to his personal advantage: he would assure his place as the preeminent peacemaker in Israeli history.

The president could readily explain his decision to the American people, stating that U.S. support of Palestinian statehood was legally and morally the right thing to do, and that military necessity required that U.S. support be stated quickly. He could cite a historic precedent: during a deep national crisis 140 years ago, President Abraham Lincoln announced that he acted out of military necessity in freeing all slaves in states of the Union that were then in rebellion. Bush could correctly say that in today's national crisis, the decision to help free the Palestinian people from Israeli occupation had to be prompt and decisive because of military necessity. This decision could not be implemented overnight, but even the early stages of implementation would ease anti-American passions and help rally worldwide support of the president's anti-terrorism campaign.

Would Congress, spurred by Israel's lobby, be able to block the president's initiative? It is my belief that Vedrine was correct in forecasting that the president would receive immediate, near-unanimous support. The immediate high level of U.S. endorsement would, I am sure, convince AIPAC of the futility of resisting. As a veteran of Capitol Hill, I am confident that the president would prevail if a showdown surfaced with either the lobby or Congress.

Grim Reality, New Hope

Israelis and Palestinians alike yearn desperately for an end to strife, death, destruction, and hate. All would welcome an end to the miserable, frightful existence that now afflicts both communities, and they would surely rejoice if the president of the United States accepts this great, urgent challenge.

The president—and all of us—must face a grim prospect. A terrible, violent eruption is almost certain to follow if the Palestinians' long-held dream of viable statehood is thwarted. Some of the violence—perhaps much of it—can be expected to strike America.

The world knows that the president of the United States holds the power and bears the responsibility to bring peace to the Middle East. He alone controls the resources that can quickly bring realistic promise of a safe, dignified life to both Israelis and Palestinians. In the words of Vedrine: "No one else is in a position to do so."

By accepting this responsibility, the president would bring special dividends to the people of the United States. He would calm the raging winds of fury that now threaten America. He would bring new luster to the name America as the U.S. government once more becomes the champion of human rights and the rule of law for all people in all lands everywhere.

Acknowledgments

ALFRED M. LILIENTHAL, a Jewish lawyer and author, warned a half-century ago in his prophetic book, *What Price Israel?*, that the establishment of Israel would lead to deep trouble for the United States and Judaism. Together with his other valiant literary endeavors, *What Price Israel?* inspired much of the information in the closing chapter of this volume. I first met this great man on November 24, 1978, when he called at my office in the U.S. House of Representatives to give me a copy of his latest and greatest book, *The Zionist Connection.*

If policy-makers in Washington had heeded Lilienthal's warning, Jews and Arabs would have lived happily together all these years, and many thousands of people in the Middle East would have been spared violent deaths. Moreover, I believe that 9/11 would never have occurred. I welcome this opportunity to thank Lilienthal for the inspiration and understanding that he provides me and thousands of other people.

The most recent contributor to my ongoing education about the Middle East is Nizar Wattad, a 2002 *summa cum laude* graduate of George Washington University and a member of the editorial staff of the *Washington Report on Middle East Affairs,* a magazine published nine times a year by retired U.S. Foreign Service officers Andrew L. Killgore and Richard H. Curtiss. They granted Wattad a part-time leave of absence so that he could apply his skills in bringing coherence and grammatical order to my text. Noor Naciri, a Nashville friend of many years, and Wolf Fuhrig, a retired professor and neighbor, also provided valuable editorial criticism. Our grandson, graduate student Andy Findley, provided critical research.

This book had its genesis in early December 1982, when I was called to the Republican cloakroom, an area just off the floor of the House of Representatives where congressmen receive telephone calls, have a light lunch, or await legislative developments. The House was engaged in a post-election "lame duck" session, finishing business that had been put off by campaign pressures. Waiting on the phone was a nationally prominent citizen I had known and admired for years. He expressed his regret at my defeat at the polls the previous month, then suggested that I write a book about Israel's lobby, even proposing the title. He insisted that I not mention his name in the text.

That telephone call was one of the most momentous of my life. It started me down a fascinating trail of discovery that has absorbed most of my time and energies ever since. It led me to write this book and its subsequent editions, two other books—*Deliberate Deceptions: Facing the Facts About the U.S.–Israeli Relationship,* published in 1993 by Lawrence Hill Books, an imprint of Chicago Review Press, and more recently by the American Educational Trust; and *Silent No More: Confronting America's False Images of Islam,* published in 2001 by Amana Publications in Beltsville, Maryland—and more than two hundred articles that have been published in magazines and newspapers.

In preparing the text, I had the support of many people. To my amazement, no one declined to be interviewed, but I was not surprised when several of them insisted on anonymity. Much of the information in the text was volunteered by career government officials who want the public to be aware of how the lobby functions, but who insisted that their own names be withheld. Four of the five people who contributed the most to the actual editing of my manuscript made the same request. Recognizing the lobby's capacity for retribution, they said such mention would harm their careers. One said bluntly, "In helping you, I'm taking a big chance. If this gets out, I will be fired from my job." Robert W. Wichser, a good friend and for fourteen years the director of my congressional staff in Washington, is the only member of this group that I feel free to identify. He perished in flood waters in December 1985.

Fortunately, I can publicly recognize several other people who also provided yeoman service: Donald Neff, the former Middle East correspondent for *Time* magazine who has written five books on the Arab–Israeli conflict; the late George W. Weller, author and former foreign correspondent for the *Chicago Daily News*; and former Senator James Abourezk, who founded the American-Arab Anti-Discrimination Committee in 1980.

For eighteen months my attachment to a word processor was so constant that my wife, Lucille, occasionally described herself—without really complaining—as a Wang widow, taking the name of the equipment I used in writing the first edition. In fact, when she first learned that I was considering writing this book, she offered to live on beans and water if need be to see the project to completion. The Spartan diet was unnecessary, thanks to a grant provided by Sangamon State University, since renamed the University of Illinois in Springfield. The grant was funded by the American Middle East Peace Research Institute.

My quest for a publisher began in March 1983 and was predictably long and frustrating. In declining to represent me, New York literary agent Alexander Wylie forecast with prophetic vision that no major U.S. publisher would accept my book. He wrote, "It's a sad state of affairs." Bruce Lee of William Morrow and Company called my manuscript "outstanding," but said his company concluded that publishing it "would cause trouble in the house and outside." Robert Loomis of Random House called it an "important book," but his employer decided the theme was "too sensitive." Twenty other publishers also said no.

In July 1984, veteran publisher Lawrence Hill agreed to take the gamble. When he died in March 1988, I lost a friend, and the cause of human rights lost an able advocate. He would rejoice, I am sure, to know that *They Dare to Speak Out* now appears in an expanded, updated edition, as well as in Arabic, Indonesian, Malaysian, Urdu, and German.

Since publication of the first edition in June 1985, response to this book has been remarkable. The work has elicited more than 50 reviews in periodicals, more than 100 appearances on television and radio programs, and lectures on 30 campuses. Despite lobby attempts to curtail sales in the early months of its publication, the total sold soon topped 300,000. I received more than 900 letters and telephone calls from readers. All but a handful were cordial, and most of them asked what they could do to help curb the influence of Israel's lobby.

Many of these readers became supporters of the Council for the National Interest (CNI) and its affiliate, the CNI Foundation, both Washington-based organizations that I helped found. Gene Bird, a former U.S.

Foreign Service officer, is president of CNI. Former Representative Paul N. "Pete" McCloskey is chairman of the board of directors. Former Ambassador Edward L. Peck heads the CNI Foundation. If you wish to help—and I hope you will—write to CNI, 1250 4th Street SW, WG-1, Washington, D.C. 20024, or call (202) 863-2951. To keep informed on important issues and developments, read the *Washington Report on Middle East Affairs*. To subscribe to the publication, write to P.O. Box 53062, Washington, DC 20009, or call (800) 368-5788.

Notes

Preface

[1] *Washington Post*, April 17, 2002.
[2] John Abrams, "Wolfwitz Booed at Pro-Israel Rally," Associated Press, April 15, 2002.
[3] E-Mail form Bahrain, May 14, 2002.
[4] Findley, Paul, *Deliberate Deceptions: Facing the Facts About the U.S.-Israel Relationship* (Washington, DC: American Educational Trust, 1995).
[5] Lynfield and Macmillan, "Are the Israelis Guilty of Mass Murder?", *The Scotsman*, April 19, 2002.
[6] "Palestinians in Jenin Camp Turn Down U.S. Relief Aid," Reuters, April 25, 2002.
[7] Andrew Clark, "House Panel Clears Aid to Israel, Palestinians," Reuters, May 10, 2002.
[8] *Time*-CNN poll, April 12, 2002.
[9] Martha Ezzard, "Few Question Congress' Blind Support for Sharon," *Atlanta Journal-Constitution*, May 12, 2002.
[10] "Profiles in Courage: U.S. Lawmakers Stand Up for Moral Justice in Middle East," *Arab News*, May 5, 2002.
[11] Ezzard.
[12] *CAIR Bulletin*, May 3, 2002.

Chapter 2: King of the Hill

[1] Paul N. McCloskey, address before Conference on "U.S. Economic and Policy Challenges in the Arab World," sponsored by American Arab Affairs Council, Birmingham, Alabama, March 4, 1983.
[2] A number of professionals in pro-Israel lobbying groups provided information for this chapter, but fearing an adverse impact on their future careers, preferred to remain anonymous.
[3] James G. Abourezk, interview, July 27, 1984.
[4] *New York Times*, September 7, 1982. M. J. Rosenberg, editor of *Near East Report*, stated in an interview on September 5, 1983 that his publication does not publish criticism of Israeli policies lest this be construed as a schism within the pro-Israel Jewish community.
[5] Letter to the author from Don Bergus, July 10, 1984.
[6] Stephen Rosenfeld, *Present Tense*, spring 1983.
[7] *Washington Post*, September 27, 1983.
[8] Interview with confidential source.
[9] *Richmond Times-Dispatch*, October 2, 1983.
[10] White House Press Release, October 18, 1983.
[11] John Wilhelm, statement to the Board for International Food and Agricultural Development, January 5, 1984.
[12] Interview with confidential source.
[13] *New York Times*, March 15, 1984.

[14]*Washington Post*, April 10, 1984.

[15]Interview with confidential source.

[16]The United States had engaged in indirect talks with the PLO during the Israeli invasion of Lebanon in 1982 and earlier during the Carter and Nixon administrations.

[17]*National Journal*, May 13, 1978.

[18]*Congressional Record*, October 3, 1984 page H10961, hearings, Trade Sub-committee, Ways and Means Committee, May 22, 1984.

[19]*Mideast Observer*, November 15, 1984.

[20]Ibid., November 1, 1983.

[21]Janine Zacharia, "Israel's Stake in Congress," *Jerusalem Post*, December 18, 2000.

[22]*Jewish Exponent*, November 11, 1983.

[23]Federal Election Committee Summary Report, 1999–2000 election cycle.

[24]Eli Kintisch, "Campaign Finance Bill May BE Boost for Jewish Grassroots Donors," *Forward*, March 22, 2002.

[25]"Pro-Israel and Arab-and Muslim-American PAC Contributions," *Washington Report on Middle East Affairs*, May/June 2001.

[26]*Wall Street Journal*, August 3, 1983.

[27]*Village Voice*, June 14, 1983.

[28]Thomas Dine, address before Jewish community leaders, Austin, Texas, November 1982.

[29]*Yedi'ot Aharonot* (Jerusalem), November 27, 1984.

[30]George Sunderland, "Counterpunch Special Report: Our Vichy Congress," www.counterpunch.org, May 9, 2002.

Chapter 3: Stilling the Still, Small Voices.

[1]*Congressional Record*, June 5, 1980.

[2]McCloskey, interview, May 10, 1983.

[3]*Congressional Record*, June 5, 1980.

[4]*New York Times Magazine*, April 18, 1971.

[5]McCloskey, address to Kenna Club, Santa Clara, California, August 13, 1982.

[6]McCloskey, *Truth and Untruth, Political Deceit in America.*

[7]Ibid.

[8]*HaKol* (Stanford University), March 1981.

[9]*New York Times Magazine*, April 18, 1971.

[10]McCloskey, interview, May 10, 1983.

[11]*New York Magazine*, June 14, 1971.

[12]Ibid.

[13]*San Jose Mercury*, October 23, 1978.

[14]McCloskey, interview, May 10, 1983.

[15]Letter from McCloskey to Earl Raab, August 11, 1981.

[16]*Los Angeles Times*, August 2, 1981.

[17]Ibid.

[18]*Redlands Daily Facts*, April 11, 1981.

[19]*San Francisco Examiner*, August 17, 1981.

[20]*San Francisco Examiner*, August 26, 1981.

[21]*B'nai B'rith Messenger*, August 7, 1981.

[22]Letter from McCloskey to B'nai B'rith Messenger, October 21, 1983.

[23]*B'nai B'rith Messenger*, October 2, 1981.

[24]Douglas Blomfield, interview, October 8, 1983.

[25]*B'nai B'rith Messenger*, August 7, 1981.

[26]McCloskey, interview, May 10, 1983; also see *Palo Alto Times Tribune*, August 17, 1982.

[27]*Heritage and Southwest Jewish Press*, August 7, 1981.

[28]*San Francisco Examiner*, August 15, 1982.

[29]McCloskey, interview, May 10 1983.

[30]*Sacramento Bee*, December 17, 1982.

[31]*Los Angeles Times*, August 2, 1981.

[32]*Congressional Record*, September 22, 1982.
[33]*Congressional Record*, December 21, 1982.
[34]McCloskey, interview, May 10, 1983.
[35]Ibid.
[36]Ibid.
[37]The memorandum, dated March 1, 1983, was headed: "To ADL regional directors from Justin J. Finger."
[38]Letter to McCloskey to David Marks of the guest Professorship Board of ASSP; see also *Stanford Daily*, November 9, 1982.
[39]*Stanford Daily*, February 8, 1983.
[40]*Stanford Review*, May 25, 1983.
[41]*Washington Post*, July 28, 1983.
[42]*San Jose Mercury News*, May 27, 1983.
[43]*Stanford Daily*, April 29, 1983.
[44]Letter to Jeffrey Au from Prof. Hubert Marshall, April 19, 1983.
[45]*Washington Post*, August 19, 1979.
[46]*Washington Star*, August 21, 1979.
[47]*Washington Post*, August 21, 1979.
[48]Ibid.
[49]Ibid.
[50]Ibid.
[51]*Washington Post*, August 22, 1979.
[52]Ibid.
[53]*Washington Star*, August 23, 1979.
[54]*Washington Post*, August 23, 1979.
[55]Walter Fauntry, interview, July 26, 1983.
[56]*Washington Post*, September 17, 1979.
[57]*Washington Post*, September 21, 1979.
[58]*Washington Post*, September 23, 1979.
[59]*Jews Speak Out: Views form the Diaspora*, a pamphlet published by International Center for Peace in the Middle East (Tel Aviv).
[60]Michael Nieditch, interview, September 24, 1983.
[61]Charles Whalen, letter to the author, February 17, 1984.
[62]Richard Nolan, interview, February 17, 1984.
[63]*Chicago Sun-Times*, October 17, 1981.
[64]*Washington Post*, October 25, 1981.
[65]*Mideast Observer*, November 1, 1983.
[66]*Washington Post*, May 12, 1983.
[67]Public meeting, room 2200, Rayburn Building, Washington, September 26, 1984.
[68]Ibid.
[69]Regard for the influence of pro-Israeli lobbying interests compelled the Congressman to request anonymity.
[70]Sheldon Richman, "AIPAC President Resigns," *Washington Report on Middle East Affairs*, December/January 1992/1993.
[71]Mervyn Dymally, interview, March 8, 1984.
[72]Ibid.
[73]Ibid.
[74]Letter from Dymally to Barry Binder, February 29, 1984.
[75]Dymally, interview, March 8, 1984.
[76]Ibid.
[77]*Wall Street Journal*, August 3, 1983.
[78]Hearings of the Subcommittee on Europe and Middle East, February 28, 1983.
[79]*New York Times*, November 11, 1983.
[80]*Congressional Record*, November 8, 1983.
[81]Anonymous Capitol Hill source.

[82] *Congressional Record*, November 10, 1983.

[83] Ibid.

[84] Ibid.

[85] Ibid.

[86] Ibid.

[87] Near East Report, May 11, 1984; *Washington Report on Middle East Affairs*, May 28, 1984

[88] Nick Rahall II, letter to the author, June 8, 1984.

[89] Ibid.

[90] Rahall, interview, June 8, 1984.

[91] *Congressional Record*, September 28, 1983.

[92] Interview with a confidential Administration source present at the discussion.

[93] Zacharia, "Israel's Stake in Congress," *Jerusalem Post*, December 18, 2000

[94] Barbara Ferguson, "Profiles in Courage: U.S. Lawmakers Stand Up for Moral Justice in Middle East," *Arab News*, May 5, 2002.

[95] Speech of honorable Mark Green of Wisconsin in the House of Representatives, May 2, 2002.

[96] CAIR press release, May 2, 2002.

Chapter 4: The Deliberative Body Fails to Deliberate

[1] Hassan, Crown Prince of Jordan, interview, May 11, 1983.

[2] *Time*, September 20, 1982.

[3] *Jewish Chicago*, October 1982; *Chicago Sun-Times*, September 14 and 16, 1983.

[4] *Illinois Issues*, November 1977; *Nation*, December 11, 1976; March 3, 1979, March 5, 1979; *Foreign Affairs*, October, 1974.

[5] *Chicago Magazine*, June 1979.

[6] *Chicago*, June 1979.

[7] *Chicago Daily News*, November 1, 1974.

[8] *New York Times Magazine*, February 22, 1970; *Washington Post*, November 24, 1970.

[9] *New Republic*, February 24, 1979; *Nation*, March 3,1979.

[10] *Washington Post*, February 9, 1979; *Christian Science Monitor*, February 5, 1979.

[11] Adlai E. Stevenson III, interview, June 9, 1983.

[12] Ibid.

[13] The Israel Bond "Man of the Year" designation was awarded to Stevenson on December 15, 1974, and recorded in the Congressional Record, January 10, 1975. The AJC in 1977 awarded Stevenson a commendation and a plaque for his work opposing the trade boycott against Israel. The Weizman Institute established the Adlai E. Stevenson III Chair in endocrinology and reproductive biology in recognition of the Senator's steadfast support of the Institute and its work.

[14] *Jacksonville Journal Courier* (Jacksonville, Illinois), August 31, 1982. Though the Washington office of AIPAC had produced the defamatory document, an AIPAC spokesman at the time expressed displeasure at seeing AIPAC material thus used in a political campaign. Such political smear tactics have become less common for AIPAC under the more sophisticated leadership of director Thomas Dine.

[15] Adlai Stevenson, *The Middle East: 1976*, report to the Committee on Banking, Housing and Urban Affairs, U.S. Senate, on his study mission to the Middle East conducted between February 10 and 25, 1976.

[16] *Congressional Record*, June 17, 1980.

[17] Ibid.

[18] Stevenson, interview, June 9, 1980

[19] Rennan Lee Teslik, *Congress, the Executive Branch and Special Interests: The American Response to the Arab Boycott of Israel.*

[20] Stevenson, interview, June 9, 1983.

[21] Letter from Theodore R. Mann to Adlai Stevenson III, July 28, 1977.

[22] *Jewish Chicago*, October, 1982.

[23] *Jacksonville Journal Courier*, August 31, 1981.

[24] *Sentinel*, September 30, 1982; *Waukegan News Sun*, November 9, 1982.

[25] *Chicago Sun-Times*, June 27, 1982.

[26]*Chicago Sun-Times*, September 14, 1982.
[27]Stevenson, interview, June 9, 1983.
[28]Bettylu Saltzman, interview, June 16, 1983.
[29]Grace Mary Stern, interview, October 18, 1983.
[30]Stevenson, interview, June 9, 1983.
[31]*Time*, November 15, 1983.
[32]*Chicago Tribune*, September 10, 1982.
[33]*Chicago Sun-Times*, September 16, 1982.
[34]Stevenson, interview, June 9, 1983.
[35]*Time*, November 15, 1982.
[36]Illinois Supreme Court Docket No. 57637, Agenda 52, November 1982.
[37]*Waukegan News Sun*, November 9, 1982.
[38]*Chicago Sun-Times*, September 14, 1982.
[39]Rick Jasculca, interview, October 18, 1983.
[40]*Present Tense*, spring 1983.
[41]Stevenson, interview, June 9, 1983.
[42]*New York Times Magazine*, November 24, 1984.
[43]Haynes Johnson and Bernard N. Gwertzman, "Fulbright, the Dissenter."
[44]Ibid.
[45]*New York Times*, June 2, 1974.
[46]*Foreign Affairs*, Spring 1979.
[47]*Time*, June 10, 1974.
[48]J.W. Fulbright, "The Arrogance of Power."
[49]*Congressional Record*, August 1, 1963.
[50]Walter Pincus, interview, November 14, 1983.
[51]Ibid.
[52]*National Journal*, May 18, 1970.
[53]*New York Times*, August 23, 1970; *National Observer*, August 31, 1980; *New Republic*, October 10, 1970.
[54]*New York Times*, April 5, 1971; Fulbright, "The Crippled Giant."
[55]"Face the Nation" (on CBS), April 15, 1073; *Washington Post*, May 31, 1973.
[56]*Washington Post*, May 31, 1973.
[57]*Christian Science Monitor*, January 24, 1974; *New Republic*, April 27, 1974; *Newsweek*, June 10, 1974.
[58]Fulbright, interview, June 3, 1983.
[59]Pincus, interview, November 14, 1983.
[60]*New York Times Magazine*, May, 1974.
[61]Fulbright, interview, June 3, 1983.
[62]Memorandum from the Washington office of B'nai B'rith, May 7, 1974.
[63]*National Observer*, November 16, 1974.
[64]*Washington Post*, November 5, 1974; Fulbright, address at Westminster College, Fulton, Missouri, November 2, 1974.
[65]Fulbright, interview, June 3, 1983.
[66]*National Observer*, November 16, 1974.
[67]Abourezk, interview, August 1, 1984.
[68]*Near East Report*, February 13, 1974.
[69]I.L. Kennen, letter to Ms. Carol V. Bernstein, February 25, 1974.
[70]AIPAC later sent a memorandum to its Connecticut membership, as well as, state leaders, denouncing Ribicoff for his attendance at the luncheon.
[71]Abourezk, *On Democracy and Dissent* (Middle East Affairs Council, 1977).
[72]*Boston Globe Magazine*, April 29, 1984.
[73]Interview with confidential source.
[74]Ibid.
[75]Ibid.
[76]The letter was sent to President Ford on May 21, 1975.

[77] *Washington Post*, March 8, 1978.
[78] Ibid.
[79] *Washington Post*, May 7, 1978.
[80] Ibid.
[81] *Washington Post*, April 22, 1978.
[82] Ibid.
[83] Interview with confidential source.
[84] *Wall Street Journal*, March 13, 1978.
[85] Interview with confidential source.
[86] Ibid.
[87] *Washington Star*, April 16, 1981.
[88] AP Wire Service, September 21, 1981.
[89] *Washington Post*, September 28, 1981.
[90] Ibid.
[91] AP Wire Service, September 21, 1981.
[92] *Washington Post*, November 25, 1981.
[93] *Boston Globe Magazine*, April 29, 1984.
[94] *Washington Post*, July 9, 1973.
[95] *Washington Post*, December 5, 1971.
[96] *Nation*, December 8, 1975; *Washington Post*, November 26, 1975.
[97] Biography of Senator Charles Mathias, Jr., prepared by the office of Senator Mathias, June 1, 1978.
[98] *Baltimore Sun*, December 3, 1980.
[99] *Washington Post*, June 2, 1974.
[100] *Washington Post*, June 28, 1981.
[101] *Baltimore Sun*, December 8, 1980.
[102] Ibid.
[103] Biography of Senator Mathias.
[104] *Foreign Affairs*, spring 1981.
[105] *Jewish Times* (Baltimore), July 3, 1981.
[106] *Evening Sun* (Baltimore), July 13, 1981.
[107] *Jewish Times*, July 3, 1981.
[108] *Baltimore Sun*, November 5, 1981.
[109] Discussion of difficult issues involving the Middle East, Israel and American Jews, such as the AWACS sale to Saudi Arabia, always raises the issue of anti-Semitism on Capitol Hill; *Washington Post*, November 29, 1981; *New York Times*, October 28, 1981.
[110] *Jewish Times*, July 3, 1981; Baltimore Sun, July 6, 1981.
[111] *Jewish Times*, July 3, 1981.
[112] Senator Mathias, interview, August 3, 1983.
[113] *Baltimore Jewish Times*, October 29, 1982.
[114] *Washington Post*, June 28, 1975.
[115] *Jewish Times*, October 29, 1982.
[116] *Chicago Tribune*, July 21, 1983.
[117] Interview with a confidential source.
[118] *New York Times*, August 16, 1984.
[119] *Journal-Register* (Springfield, Illinois), December 8, 1984.
[120] Paul Simon, interview, December 7, 1984; *Journal-Register*, December 8, 1984.
[121] Interviews, Percy, November 13, 1984, and Simon, December 7, 1984.
[122] *Yedi'ot Aharonot* (Jerusalem), November 27, 1984.
[123] Arab News, *Bahrain Daily*, April 5, 2001.

Chapter 5: The Lobby and the Oval Office

[1] Charles Barnett, interview, November 1, 1983.
[2] Myer Feldman, interview, October 30, 1983.
[3] Confidential interview.
[4] John Snetsinger, "Truman, the Jewish Vote, and the Creation of Israel"; Robert Donovan, "Conflict

and Crisis: the Presidency of Harry S Truman, 1945-1948"; Roberta Feuerlicht, "The Fate of the Jews."

[5]Snetsinger, op. cit.

[6]Feuerlicht, op. cit.

[7]Evan M. Wilson, "Decision on Palestine"; *Christian Science Monitor*, June 16, 1981.

[8]Confidential interview.

[9]Wilson.

[10]Quoted by Tillman, op. cit.

[11]Stephen Green, "Taking Sides: America's Secret Relations with a Militant Israel"; Wilbur Crane Eveland, "Ropes of Sand: America's Failure in the Middle East."

[12]Green, op. cit.

[13]Ibid.

[14]Ibid.

[15]Stephen D. Isaacs, "Jews and American Politics."

[16]Green, op. cit.

[17]Ibid.

[18]Ibid.

[19]Ibid.

[20]Ibid.

[21]Ibid.

[22]Isaacs, op. cit.

[23]Eveland, op. cit.

[24]Green, op. cit.

[25]Ibid.

[26]So close was Johnson's friendship with the Krims that they were the first beyond the Johnson family to learn of the president's decision not to seek re-election in 1968.

[27]Neff, interview, May 23, 1984.

[28]Green, op. cit.

[29]Isaacs.

[30]Henry A. Kissenger, "Years of Upheaval."

[31]Richard M. Nixon, interview, July 26, 1984.

[32]*Manchester Guardian*, October 10, 1976.

[33]George W. Ball, "The Past Has Another Pattern."

[34]Ibid.

[35]*Foreign Affairs*, Winter, 1975/76; *New York Times*, August 25, 1982.

[36]*Washington Post*, July 11, 1982.

[37]Ball, interview, June 10, 1983.

[38]Confidential interview.

[39]*Economist* (London), October 20, 1979.

[40]*New York Times*, October 12, 1979.

[41]*New York Times*, October 22, 1979.

[42]*Washington Star*, October 13, 1979.

[43]*Christian Science Monitor*, October 16, 1979.

[44]*The Nation*, November 3, 1979.

[45]*Washington Post*, October 15, 1979.

[46]*Los Angeles Times*, December 29, 1974.

[47]*Washington Post*, November 6, 1979.

[48]Ibid.

[49]*New York Times*, October 15, 1979.

[50]*Washington Post*, December 27, 1983.

[51]Ibid.

[52]Ibid.

[53]*Chicago Tribune*, December 5, 1983.

[54]$300 million was to be spent in the U.S. for development of the Israeli Lavi fighter plane, while an additional $250 million was authorized to be spent in Israel. This $250 million, an unprecedented U.S. subsidy to a foreign industry, was the issue behind the Rahall amendment.

[55]*Near East Report*, December 23, 1983.
[56]*Washington Post*, March 16, 1984.
[57]*New York Times*, March 15, 1984.
[58]*New York Times*, March 22, 1984.
[59]Ibid.
[60]*Washington Post*, March 2, 1980.
[61]*Washington Post*, March 5, 1980.
[62]*Wall Street Journal*, March 5 and 7, 1980; *Washington Post*, March 6 and 12, 1980.
[63]Ibid.
[64]Feuerlicht.
[65]*Washington Post*, November 6 and 9, 1980.
[66]Albert Joseph, interview, August 15, 1984.
[67]*Wall Street Journal*, March 23, 1984.
[68]*Los Angeles Times*, July 14, 1984.
[69]"United States Senator Gary Hart on the Issues: Israel and the Middle East (two page summary prepared by the Hart presidential campaign, undated)"; *Near East Report*, January 13, 1984.
[70]*New York Times*, September 15, 1983; *Near East Report*, January 6 and 13, 1984.
[71]*Boston Globe*, February 15 and 20, 1983.
[72]Ibid.
[73]*New York Times*, September 14, 1983.
[74]Confidential interview.
[75]Lucius Battle, interview, May 21, 1983.
[76]*New York Times*, February 4, 1979.
[77]Ibid.
[78]*Washington Post*, March 14, 1984.
[79]*Washington Post*, October 6, 1979.
[80]*Washington Post*, October 12, 1984.
[81]*Newsweek*, January 16, 1984.
[82]Ibid.
[83]*Washington Post*, March 29, 1984.
[84]*Chicago Sun-Times*, February 27, 1984.
[85]*Washington Post*, April 7, 8, and 14, 1984.
[86]Confidential interview.
[87]Scott McConnell, "Bush vs. Sharon: The Sequel," www.antiwar.com, April 9, 2002.
[88]Ibid.
[89]Lawrence McQuillan, "Bush Exerts Careful Pressure on Israel," *USA Today*, April 10, 2002.
[90]George Szamuely, "Israel's Powerful Friends," *New York Press*, June 6, 2000.
[91]McQuillan.

Chapter 6: Penetrating the Defenses at Defense and State.

[1]This chapter is based upon interviews with 17 present and former officials from the Department of Defense the Department of State, and the White House. Where considerations of career security permit, these sources have been identified.
[2]Thomas Pianka, interview, November 17, 1983.
[3]Neff, "Warriors for Jerusalem."
[4]Les Janka, interview, August 16, 1983.
[5]Zbigniew Brzezinski, interview, October 31, 1983.
[6]Israel is the only country where the United States permits such limitations.
[7]Andrew Young, interview, May 10, 1983.
[8]See Chapter Two.
[9]*Newsweek*, September 3, 1979.
[10]*Washington Post*, March 2, 1977.
[11]*Washington Post*, February 18, 1977.
[12]Abourezk, interview, August 1, 1984.
[13]Legislation was introduced in 1984 to provide Israel with open U.S. financing for its foreign aid activities. See Chapter Two.

[14]Ambassador John C. West, interview, April 18, 1983; *New York Times*, April 20, 1980.

[15]*New York Times*, April 20, 1980.

[16]In the wake of the AWACS vote, the United States agreed to boost the level of aid to Israel by $300 million per year for a period of four years.

[17]*Washington Post*, January 24, 1981.

[18]L. Dean Brown, interview, January, 1984.

[19]Harold Saunders, interview, May 19, 1983.

[20]Talcott Seelye, interview, May 14, 1983.

[21]*Defense Week*, July 27, 1981; *Focus*, February 15, 1982; *New Statesman*, May 6, 1983.

[22]*Washington Post*, April 6, 1978.

[23]*Jewish Week* (Washington, D.C.), July 17-23, 1983.

[24]Memorandum from John H. Davitt, Chief of Internal Security Section, Criminal Division, to Philip B. Heymann, Asian Attorney General, Criminal Division.

[25]"Stephen Bryen," www.auroraamerica.com.

[26]"In These Times," April 17-May 3, 1983; *Atlantic Monthly*, May 1982.

[27]Admiral Thomas Moorer, interview, August 24, 1982.

[28]*Deland Sun News* (Deland, Florida), August 11, 1983; *USA Today*, August 12, 1983.

[29]*Washington Post*, August 10, 1983.

[30]Janka.

[31]Ella Bancroft, "Meet Anne at 'Pollard's Place' in Tel Aviv," *Washington Report on Middle East Affairs*, July/August, 1995.

[32]Shawn L. Twing, "American Engineer Who Admitted Giving Classified Information to Israel is Back at Work," *Washington Report on Middle East Affairs*, July/August, 1986.

[33]Richard Curtiss, "On the Pollard Affair," *Washington Report on Middle East Affairs*, July/August, 1986.

[34]Twing.

Chapter 7: The Assault on Assault

[1]Moorer.

[2]James M. Ennes, Jr., *Assault on the* Liberty.

[3]*New York Times*, June 8, 1967.

[4]U.S. Naval Institute Proceedings, June 1978.

[5]Admiral Donald Engen, interview, August 29, 1983.

[6]Ennes, op. cit.

[7]*New York Times*, June 10, 1967.

[8]*Washington Star*, June 16, 1967.

[9]*U.S. News and World Report*, June 26, 1967; *Defense Electronics*, October 1981.

[10]*New York Times*, June 18, 1967.

[11]Admiral Isaac Kidd, interview, October 7, 1963.

[12]Office of Assistant Secretary of Defense (Public Affairs), news release, June 28, 1967.

[13]Ennes.

[14]*New York Times*, June 29, 1967; *Washington Post*, June 30, 1967.

[15]*New York Times*, July 1, 1967.

[16]*Washington Star*, June 30, 1967.

[17]*New York Times*, July 7, 1967.

[18]Ennes, interview, April 30, 1983.

[19]Ennes, *Assault on the* Liberty.

[20]Ibid.

[21]Ibid.

[22]*National Review*, September 5, 1967.

[23]Ennes, interview, April 30, 1983.

[24]Defense Electronics, October 1981.

[25]Commander Lloyd N. Bucher, interview, April 10, 1983.

[26]Ibid.

[27]Moorer.

[28]Ennes, *Assault on the* Liberty; *Pacific Northwest*, September 1982.

[29] *Christian Science Monitor*, June 22, 1982.

[30] *USS* Liberty *Newsletter*, December 1982.

[31] White House memorandum from James U. Cross to Harry McPherson, June 20, 1967.

[32] White House memorandum from Harry McPherson to James U. Cross.

[33] Engen, August 29, 1983.

[34] Yitzak Rabin, *Rabin Memoirs*.

[35] President Lyndon Johnson, *Vantage Point*.

[36] These understated numbers reflect estimates that appeared in some newspapers before the full casualty count was known; *New York Times*, June 9, 1967.

[37] Moshe Dayan, *Story of My Life*.

[38] *Washington Post*, July 18, 1982; Ennes, interview, August 10, 1982.

[39] Ennes, *Assault on the* Liberty.

[40] Letter from Seymour Hersh to Robert Loomis of Random House, 1979.

[41] Ennes, interview, April 30, 1983.

[42] *Middle East Perspective*, June 1981.

[43] Ennes.

[44] Ibid.

[45] Ibid.

[46] Bucher.

[47] *Jewish Veterans*, April/May/June 1983.

[48] Moorer.

[49] Ennes, "The USS *Liberty*: Still Covered Up After 35 Years," *Washington Report on Middle East Affairs*, June/July 2002.

[50] Ibid.

[51] John E. Borne, "The USS *Liberty*: Dissenting History vs. Official History (Reconsideration Press, 1996).

[52] Neff, "Warriors for Jerusalem."

[53] James Bamford, *Body of Secrets: Anatomy of the Ultra-Secret National Security Agency* (New York: Doubleday Press, 2001).

[54] Suzy Hansen, "The Assault on the USS *Liberty*," www.salon.com.

[55] Bryant Jordan, "Key Investigators Express Belief That Israel Deliberately Attacked U.S. Ship," *Navy Times*, June 26, 2002.

[56] E-mail from James Ennes, July 2, 2002.

Chapter 8: Subverting Academic Freedom

[1] Information on this and subsequent pages about AIPAC's Political Leadership Development Program is largely drawn from public remarks by Jonathon Kessler made at an AIPAC workshop in Washington, June 12, 1983, and literature distributed at the workshop.

[2] www.aipac.org/documents/welcomecampus.html.

[3] Edward Said, interview, July 20, 1983.

[4] George Bisharat, interview, June 21, 1983.

[5] *Harvard Law Record*, May 7, 1982.

[6] *Harvard Law Record*, April 30, 1982.

[7] *Harvard Law Record*, May 6, 1983.

[8] Noam Chomsky, letter to the author, July 10, 1983.

[9] James Scamus, interview, January 25, 1984.

[10] *Daily Californian* (University of California at Berkeley), April 15, 1982.

[11] *Daily Californian*, April 14, 1982.

[12] *Daily Californian*, April 15, 1982.

[13] Schamus, letter to the author, January 29, 1984.

[14] *San Francisco Examiner*, October 25, 1982.

[15] *Daily Californian*, October 20, 1982.

[16] John D'Anna, interview, July 8, 1983.

[17] *Arizona Daily Wildcat* (University of Arizona, Tucson), March 2, 1983.

[18] *Arizona Daily Star*, March 4, 1983.

[19]Letter form Zionist Institutions to "Business Concerns Advertising in the Arizona Daily Wildcat and All Ad Agencies in Tucson," dated March 15, 1983.

[20]Willem A. Bijlfeld, letter to the author.

[21]Eqbal Ahmad, interview, September 24, 1983.

[22]S. C. Whittaker, interview, January 30, 1984.

[23]*Bryn Mawr-Haverford College News*, November 4, 1977.

[24]Kendall Landis, interview, June 17, 1983.

[25]*Evening Bulletin* (Philadelphia), November 5, 1977.

[26]*Bryn Mawr-Haverford College News*.

[27]Willis Armstrong, interview, June 22, 1983.

[28]Stephen Cary, interview, July 12, 1983.

[29]*Phoenix* (Swarthmore College), November 2, 1977.

[30]James Platt, interview, July 27, 1983.

[31]*Jewish Exponent* (Philadelphia), November 11, 1977.

[32]Copy of Ira Silverman's confidential AJC memorandum dated November 28, 1977.

[33]Harrison Wright, interview, July 25, 1983.

[34]*Phoenix*, February 8, 1978.

[35]*Phoenix*, November 9, 1977.

[36]*Bryn Mawr-Haverford College News*, November 11, 1977.

[37]*Philadelphia Enquirer*, November 9, 1977.

[38]Copy of letter from Armstrong to Friend dated April 11, 1979.

[39]Thomas D'Andrea, interview, July 29, 1983.

[40]Peter F. Krogh, interview, September 27, 1983.

[41]John Ruedy, interview June 21, 1983.

[42]*Georgetown Voice*, November 1, 1977.

[43]*Washington Star*, May 4, 1977.

[44]Ibid.

[45]*Chronicle of Higher Education*, September 25, 1978.

[46]Ibid.

[47]*Washington Star*, July 27, 1978.

[48]*Chronicle of Higher Education*.

[49]*Washington Post*, September 9, 1980.

[50]*Washington Post*, February 24, 1981.

[51]John Ruedy, interview, June 21, 1983.

[52]*Washington Post*, February 25, 1981.

[53]*Washington Post*, February 14, 1981.

[54]*Washingtonian*, October, 1981.

[55]Peter F. Krogh, interview, September 27, 1983.

[56]Father Kail Ellis, interview, January 11, 1984.

[57]"CSIS in Brief," from inside cover of Center for Strategic and International Studies, Georgetown University, Publications, 1983.

[58]Ibid.

[59]Letter from Akins to Hameed, August 22, 1983.

[60]Copy of letter of appointment, November 11, 1980.

[61]Copy of CSIS memorandum, October 8, 1980.

[62]Copy of telax form Jordan to Pat Denny, August 30, 1981.

[63]Jean Newsom, interview, July 26, 1983.

[64]Trish Wilson, interview, August 2, 1983.

[65]Paul Sutphin, interview, August 1, 1983.

[66]George Smally, interview, June 26, 1984.

[67]This account, from Hameed, was confirmed in substance by Amos Jordan in an interview, April 5, 1984. Jordan specified that while Hameed's work was mentioned, it was "not central to the discussion" with Emerson.

[68]Hameed's account. Jordan says he was interviewed "once" by Emerson and makes no mention of a draft.

[69]*New Republic*, February 17, 1982.

[70]*Platt's Oilgram News*, February 18, 1982.

[71]Onnik Maraschian, interview, August 11, 1983.

[72]Copy of CSIS memorandum "RE: Attached Platt's Oilgram Article," February 22, 1982.

[73]Draft of a Proposed Report: U.S. Assistance to the State of Israel, prepared by the staff of the U.S. General Accounting Office (1983).

[74]Amos Jordan, letter to the author, April 12, 1984. In the letter, Jordan states that this incident occurred in October 1981, not February 1982.

[75]Jordan denies this, saying the new charge replaced the old. He also denies that the charge was made retroactive and says it was applied "to all project directors at the Center."

[76]Hameed acknowledged a temporary deficit of about $12, 000, which he had expected to cover through CSIS sales of his report.

[77]The date and other details of the burglary are confirmed in the report of the Metropolitan Police Department, Washington, D.C., complaint number 109-933.

[78]Hameed's account.

[79]Jerri Bird, "Blaming the Victim," *Chronicle of Higher Education*, February 8, 2002.

[80]Anthony Lewis, "It Can Happen Here," *New York Times*, December 1, 1981.

[81]John S. Sugg, "Muslim-American Activism," *Washington Report on Middle East Affairs*, January/February 2001.

[82]Francis A. Boyle, " Law and Disorder in the Middle East," *Americans for Middle East Understanding*, Vol. 35, Issue 1, January/March 2002.

Chapter 9: Paving the Way for the Messiah

[1]Lee Hamilton, interview, August 2, 1983.

[2]Thomas Wiley, *American Christianity, the Jewish State and the Arab-Irsraeli Conflict* (Occasional Papers Series, CCAS, Georgetown University, 1983).

[3]Speech reprinted in Near East Report, June 5, 1981.

[4]*New York Times*, October 28, 1981.

[5]*Economist* (London), 3-9 March, 1984.

[6]Letter to Mike Evans Ministries supporters, January 23, 1984.

[7]George Otis, letter to High Adventure Holyland Ministry supporters.

[8]World Lebanese Association, www.wlo-usa.org, July 21, 1999.

[9]*Near East Report*, November 20, 1981.

[10]Grace Halsell, *Prophecy and Politics* (Chicago: Lawrence Hill Books, 1986).

[11]Wiley, op. cit.

[12]Dewey Beagle, interview, January 12, 1984.

[13]White House press release, October 18, 1983.

[14]Feuerlicht, "The Fate of the Jews."

[15]*New York Times*, January 15, 1984.

[16]*Near East Report*, December 16, 1984.

[17]*New York Times*, January 15, 1984.

[18]The Friends of Israel Gospel Ministry, Inc., centered in Collingwood, New Jersey, is one of a number of American evangelistic organizations that take Jewish conversion as a primary goal. Its 1983 Mission Update report referred to more than 2, 000 meetings on "Jewish evangelism, missions, prophecy, and deeper life" conducted during the year, in addition to the distribution of nearly one million copies of its various publications.

[19]*New York Times*, December 1, 1981.

[20]*New York Jewish Weekly*, October 19, 1980.

[21]*New York Times*, December 1, 1981.

[22]*Atlanta Constitution-Journal*, February 20, 1981.

[23]*New York Times*, January 15, 1984.

[24]Ernest Volkmann, "A Legacy of Hate."

[25]The Middle East policy statements of eight of the leading U.S. Christian churches were collected in "Where We Stand," a pamphlet published in 1972 by the Middle East Peace Project.

[26]Wiley, op. cit.

[27]Volkmann, op. cit.

[28]Ibid.

[29]National Council of Churches of Christ Statement, April 2002.

[30]Peggy Briggs, interview, October 7, 1983.

[31]Feeley, interview, October 6, 1983.

[32]Greg Degiere, interview, January 16, 1984.

[33]*Nuclear Times*, February 1984, cited in *Palestinian/Israel Bulletin*, March 1984.

[34]*Life*, April 2, 1965.

[35]*Washington Post*, June 17, 1977.

[36]The 1972 Palm Sunday sermon and a number of statements reacting to it were collected in "The Jerusalem Debate," a pamphlet published in 1972 by the Middle East Affairs Council (A.R. Taylor and J.P. Richardson, eds.).

[37]Ibid.

[38]Ibid.

[39]*Washington Post*, April 4, 1972.

[40]Volkmann op. cit.

[41]*Washington Post*, April 8, 1972.

[42]Dean Francis Sayre, interview, July 23, 1983; *Washington Star*, April 6, 1972.

[43]Taylor and Richardson, op. cit.

[44]*Washington Post*, April 4, 1972.

[45]*Christianity Today*, April 28, 1972.

[46]Reverend Joseph L. Ryan, press conference, April 6, 1972.

[47]Sayre.

[48]Ibid.

[49]*Washington Evening Star and Daily News*, September 11, 1972.

[50]Ibid.

[51]Ibid.

[52]Ayoub Talhami, interview, February 6, 1984.

[53]Sr. Miriam Ward, interview, February 6, 1984; Wagner, interview, February 3, 1984.

[54]*Jewish Week-American Examiner*, January 14, 1982.

[55]Ward.

[56]*Jewish Week-American Examiner*.

[57]Ward.

[58]Jeffrey G. MacDonald, "Christians Hit Theological Rift on Mideast Policy," *Christian Science Monitor*, May 14, 2002.

[59]Sharon Samber, "With Israel Isolated, Support Strong From Christian Right," *Washington Jewish Week*, May 30, 2002.

[60]Richard Penaskovic, "Islam and the Conflict in the Middle East," April 8, 2002.

[61]*The Tennessean*, May 29, 2002.

[6]Samber.

Chapter 10: Not All Jews Toe the Line

[1]Vincent James Abramo, "Orthodox Judaism and the Oslo Peace Process," *Thesis*, August 2001.

[2]Liz Spikol, "I May Be Called a Traitor, but I Won't Be Silent Anymore," *Arab News*, April 14, 2002.

[3]*Progressive*, August 1979.

[4]Ibid.

[5]Ibid.

[6]Ibid.

[7]Irving Howe, *New Perspectives: The Diaspora and Israel*.

[8]Feuerlicht.

[9]Ibid.

[10]*Washington Post*, June 4, 1983.

[11]Ibid.

[12]*Progressive*, August 1979.

[13]Ibid.

[14]*Washington Report on Middle East Affairs*, April2, 1984.

[15]Feurlicht, interview, October 19, 1983.

[16]Gail Pressberg, interview, November 4, 1983.

[17]*Washington Post*, December 14, 1982.

[18]Richard Cohen, "Who's Anti-Semitic?" *Washington Post*, April 30, 2002

[19]John Wallach, interview, April 15, 1983.

[20]*Washington Post*, December 14, 1982.

[21]Wallach.

[22]*Village Voice*, June 29, 1982.

[23]Charles Fishbein, interview, October 11, 1983.

[24]*The Autobiography of Nahum Goldman*, trans. By Helen Sebba.

[25]Nahum Goldman, "The Jewish Paradox."

[26]*Jewish Week* (Washington, D.C.), September 2-8, 1982.

[27]*Chicago Tribune*, December 3, 1981.

[28]*Chicago Sun-Times*, December 8, 1981; Klutznick, interview, September 19, 1983.

[29]*Chicago Sun-Times*, December 3, 1981.

[30]*Near East Report*, November 20, 1981.

[31]Klutznick.

[32]*Christian Science Monitor*, July 14, 1982.

[33]Klutznick.

[34]*Chicago Sun-Times*, October 20, 1982.

[35]*Jewish Post and Opinion* (USA), February 23, 1983.

[36]Fishbein.

[37]I.F. Stone, interview, April 24, 1983.

[38]*The Progressive*, August 1979.

[39]*New York Review of Books*, March 1978.

[40]Ibid.

[41]*Lincoln Review*, autumn 1979.

[42]Ralph Nader, "I.F. Stone," 1989.

[43]Naseer Aruri, "A Tribute to Rabbi Elmer Berger," *Washington Report on Middle East Affairs*, January/February 1997.

[44]Ibid.

[45]Sheldon L. Richman, " AIPAC President Resigns," *Washington Report on Middle Eastern Affairs*, January/February 1997.

[46]Spikol.

[47]Nizar Wattad, interview with Liz Spikol, June 14, 2002.

[48]Nacha Cattan, "Jewish Reporter Says Marriage to Arab Cost Her Job," *Forward*, April 19, 2002.

[49]*Foreword*, letters page, April 26, 2002.

Chapter 11: Scattering the Seeds of Catastrophe

[1]*Wall Street Journal*, August 3, 1983; Mideast Observer, November 1, 1983.

[2]*Philadelphia Enquirer*, October 16, 1983.

[3]*Philadelphia Enquirer*, October 19, 1983.

[4]*Jewish Exponent* (Philadelphia), November 11, 1983.

[5]Anisa Mehdi, interview, September 4, 1983.

[6]Elaine Hagopian, interview, April 16, 1984; *Chicago Tribune*, July 13, 1975.

[7]*ADC Bi-Weekly Reports*, April 1-15, 1984.

[8]*Monthly Detroit*, February 1984.

[9]Abdel Hamid El-Barbarawi, interview, September 7, 1983.

[10]*Bilalian News*, October 7, 1977.

[11]*Chicago Jewish Post and Opinion*, July 2, 1976.

[12]*Chicago Sun-Times*, November 11, 1977.

[13]Dick Kay, interview, September 15, 1983.

[14]Stephen Green, interview, March 5, 1983.

[15]Vanessa Redgrave, interview, September 4, 1983.

[16]*Los Angeles Times*, April 5, 1978.

[17]*Midstream*, January 1980.

[18]*New York Times*, September 25, 1980.

[19]Ibid.

[20]*Los Angeles Times*, September 28, 1980.

[21]Ibid.

[22]Ibid.

[23]*Village Voice*, June 8, 1982.

[24]*Split Vision*.

[25]Ibid.

[26]*Twin Cities Reader*, July 1, 1982.

[27]Harold R. Piety, *Split Vision*.

[28]*National Journal*, January 8, 1972.

[29]*Armed Forces Journal International*, October 1977.

[30]*Washington Post*, October 27, 1977.

[31]*Journal Herald* (Dayton, Ohio), November 13, 1975.

[32]*Middle East International*, December 1978.

[33]*Journal Herald*.

[34]Harold R. Piety, letter to the author, July 27, 1983.

[35]*Twin Cities Reader*, June 17, 1982.

[36]*Twin Cities Reader*, August 19, 1982.

[37]Georgia Ann Geyer, interview, May 16, 1983.

[38]Georgia Ann Geyer, "Buying the Night Flight."

[39]Geyer, interview.

[40]*Miami News*, April 4, 1983.

[41]"Israel Will Keep CNN on Air," *USA Today*, June 24, 2002.

[42]*New York Times*, December 22, 1983, January 16, 1984; *Foreign Affairs*, July 1978.

[43]*Boston Globe Magazine*, April 29, 1984.

[44]Jack Sunderland, interview, June 3, 1983.

[45]*Twin Cities Reader*, July 1, 1982.

[46]Wafiya El-Hossaini, interview, April 17, 1983.

[47]*Middle East International*, January 27, 1984.

[48]*Washington Report on Middle East Affairs*, May 17, 1982.

[49]Wattad interview with Andrew L. Killgore, June 6, 2002.

[50]*Village Voice*, February 7, 1984.

[51]*Village Voice*, January 24, 1984.

[52]Ibid.

[53]*Split Vision*.

[54]Lawrence Mosher, interview, November 16, 1983.

[55]Gilbert M. Grosvenor, interview, March 31, 1983.

[56]*New York Times*, June 21, 1974.

[57]Grosvenor.

[58]*National Geographic*, November 1974.

[59]Russell W. Howe and Sarah H. Trott, *The Power Peddlars: How Lobbyists Mold America's Foreign Policy*.

[60]"First Line Report," March 7, 1973.

[61]Robert Pierpoint, interview, March 8, 1983.

[62]Pierpoint, unpublished manuscript.

[63]Pierpoint, interview.

[64]Ibid.

[65]Patsy Collins, interview, April 30, 1983.

[66]*Village Voice*, October 7, 1982.

[67]*Washington Report on Middle East Affairs*, May 28, 1974.

[68]Goldman was featured as a panelist at the first national CAMERA Conference, held November 20, 1983 in Washington, D.C.

[69]NBC News press release, May 3, 1984; *Columbia Journalism Review*, November/December 1982.

[70] *Washington Report on Middle East Affairs*, May 28, 1984.
[71] *Minneapolis Star and Tribune*, April 3, 1983.
[72] *Washington Journalism Review*, March 1983.
[73] Nick Themmesch, interview, April 11, 1983.
[74] *Washington Post*, November 10, 1982.
[75] *Washington Journalism Review*.
[76] *Washington Post*, November 10, 1982.
[77] *Washington Post*, November 12, 1982.
[78] *Washington Post*, November 10, 1982.
[79] *Jewish Week* (Washington, D.C.), November 4-10, 1982.
[80] *Washington Post*, November 10, 1982.
[81] *Boston Globe Magazine*, April 29, 1984.
[82] *Sunday Call-Chronicle* (Allentown, Pennsylvania), January 16, 1983.
[83] *Evening Sun* (Baltimore, Maryland), November 4, 1983; *Washington Post*, November 7, 1982.
[84] *Times* (San Mateo, California), November 1 and 9, 1982.
[85] *Sunday Call-Chronicle*.
[86] Robert Fisk, "The Solution to This Filthy War," *The Independent*, May 8, 2002.
[87] Kathleen Christison, "Israel, a Light Unto Nations?" www.counterpunch.org, May 11, 2002.

Chapter 12: What Price Israel?

[1] A notable exception was Moshe Caret's brief term as prime minister.
[2] *Interview*, June 1, 2002.
[3] Poll from Mirror International, May 8, 2002.
[4] Dafna Linzer, Associated Press, June 3, 2002.
[5] Jimmy Carter, *New York Times* op-ed, April 21, 2002.
[6] *Al Ahram Weekly*, April 22, 2002.
[7] Uri Averny, Mirror International, April 8, 2002.
[8] Noam Chomsky, *The Guardian*, May 11, 2002.
[9] Paul Findley, *Silent No More: Confronting America's False Images of Islam*, (Amana Publications, 2002).
[10] E-mail from James J. David, June 2, 2002.
[11] Findley.
[12] *AMEU Public Affairs Series*, #33, March 2002.
[13] James J. David, "The Source of Terrorism," *Media Monitors Network*, October 1, 2001.
[14] David, letter to Colin Powell, January 12, 2002.
[15] Charley Reese, King Features Syndicate, May 2, 2002.
[16] *Pittsburgh Post-Gazette*, April 3, 2002.
[17] "Report on Ha'aretz, Jerusalem," *USA Today*, January 30, 1995.
[18] *Foreign Service Journal*, June 2002.
[19] Mirror International, May 15, 2002.
[20] Ted Anthony, "Report on Jerusalem," Associated Press, June 13, 2002.
[21] Hubert Vedrine, *Washington Post*, May 17, 2002.

Index